D0403941

This volume is sponsored by
the Center for Chinese Studies
University of California, Berkeley

The Chinese Enlightenment

The Chinese Enlightenment

Intellectuals and the Legacy of
the May Fourth Movement of 1919

Vera Schwarcz

UNIVERSITY OF CALIFORNIA PRESS
Berkeley · Los Angeles · London

University of California Press
Berkeley and Los Angeles, California

University of California Press, Ltd.
London, England

© 1986 by Vera Schwarcz

Printed in the United States of America

2 3 4 5 6 7 8 9

Library of Congress Cataloging in Publication Data

Schwarcz, Vera, 1947–
    The Chinese enlightenment.

    Bibliography: p.
    Includes index.
    1. China—Intellectual life—20th century.
2. China—History—May Fourth Movement, 1919.
3. Intellectuals—China.   I. Title.
DS775.2.S38   1985   951.04   85–1078
ISBN 0-520-05027-4 (cloth : alk. paper)
ISBN 0-520-06837-8 (pbk. : alk. paper)

The paper used in this publication meets the minimum
requirements of American National Standard for Information Sciences—Permanence of Paper for Printed
Library Materials, ANSI Z39.48-1984. ∞

To those in China and closer to home who share Montesquieu's conviction: "It is not a matter of indifference that the minds of the people be enlightened."

Contents

Illustrations

Preface

History and historians, Benedetto Croce warned, cannot escape the stamp of present concerns. This book takes Croce's warning as positive injunction. Its themes mirror an ongoing debate about the significance of the event of 1919 in China and abroad. In 1969, when I first began research for this study, the May Fourth movement was already a subject of controversy in the scholarly literature published in Taiwan, Japan, Europe, and the United States. From the writings available to me at that time, it appeared that the significance of the May Fourth movement was to be found either in the political patriotism or in the literary inventiveness of its participants. To augment these views of May Fourth, I focused my own analysis on the theme of cultural revolution—a revolution that began in the late 1910s and that I thought, then, had culminated in the Great Proletarian Cultural Revolution of 1966–69.

The concern with the problem of enlightenment emerged later. It was the result of an intensified dialogue with contemporary history. As I came to see Mao Zedong's Cultural Revolution in a new light, I began to ask new questions about the significance of earlier events as well. By the sixtieth anniversary of the May Fourth movement, in 1979, it became clear to me that the later Cultural Revolution was one of the most complex tragedies of the twentieth century. To reckon with the sources and implications of that tragedy required nothing less than a thorough revision of my previous interpretation of the May Fourth movement of 1919.

The opportunity to revise my views of May Fourth came in 1979–80, while I was living and studying at Beijing University. To be so close in time and place to the event that had been the subject of my research for a decade was at once inspiring and disconcerting. Before I could take advantage of the voluminous new information available about the event of 1919, I had to discard some of the old assumptions that I had brought with me. Foremost among those was the assumption that the thought emancipation of the late 1910s had reached its fruition, first in the political liberation of 1949 and then in the cultural iconoclasm of 1966–69. The longer I lived in China, the more I understood the ways in which the May Fourth legacy served as a troublesome reminder of China's incomplete emancipation from its feudal past. Chinese intellectuals, survivors and admirers of May Fourth alike, have been the concrete embodiment of that reminder. Their insistence that the May Fourth goals of science and democracy have yet to be achieved in the People's Republic has made them subject to repeated waves of persecution. Now, with a new policy toward intellectuals inaugurated in the post-Mao era, the problem of enlightenment can be broached in public once again.

Among those who have raised this thorny issue most consistently have been the octogenarian survivors of the May Fourth movement. In the course of my sixteen months in China, 1979–80, and two subsequent visits in 1981 and 1983, I was particularly fortunate in being able to meet and interview eight intellectuals who had been a part of the "new youth" generation of 1919. Xu Deheng, Yu Pingbo, Ye Shengtao, Zhu Guanqian, Feng Youlan, Jin Yuelin, Zhang Shenfu, and Liang Shuming represent a broad spectrum of commitment from political patriotism to cultural iconoclasm. These by now thoroughly Confucian gentlemen took pains to explain to me the reasons for their youthful revolt against tradition. They also spoke about the many bitter campaigns against intellectuals, some directed against them individually. Remarkably free of rancor, they described the recent political events that had robbed them of their peace of mind and that forced them repeatedly to change their views about their own work. In our conversations, they did not seek to justify themselves but rather to tell their story in their own terms.

In spite of all their difficulties, these octogenarians continue to bear witness to the aspirations of May Fourth. They continue to be deeply interested in, and surprisingly well informed about, Western culture. At the same time, they remain thoroughly committed to a critical evaluation of the Chinese past. Six decades after the event that shaped their disparate views, they all share the conviction that China has yet to achieve a vision of modernity that is truly consonant with its distinctive cultural heritage.

Throughout these conversations with May Fourth veterans, subjects that we did not talk about, questions that lingered unanswered, silences that followed the retelling of a particularly painful episode were integral

to the history that did emerge. That view of history was further augmented by conversations with those who were students of the May
Fourth generation: intellectuals who are now in their sixties, and with
younger scholars now doing research on May Fourth. Their generosity
with time and historical sources, and their candor about their own experiences in the 1940s, 1950s, and 1960s, enabled me to realize that the
May Fourth movement is far from over, that intellectuals remain the
vulnerable spokesmen for the ideals of science and democracy.

The distance between those ideals and the realities in China was
brought home to me by my own observations of the latest enlightenment
movement: the Democracy Wall movement of 1978–79. Arriving in Beijing in February 1979, at the height of official and non-official concern
with the emancipation of thought, and departing a year and a half later,
when Democracy Wall was, once again, just a barrier for a parking lot
full of buses, I glimpsed something about the significance of May Fourth
that had eluded me a decade earlier. Halting and costly, the quest for
enlightenment must go on in China as long as autocracy, bureaucracy,
and dogmatism retain their hold on the minds of political leaders and of
the masses.

May 1, 1984
Middletown, Connecticut

Acknowledgments

During the decade and a half that this book was being conceived, written, and repeatedly revised, a large number of colleagues and friends offered invaluable support. Teachers who became friends along the way were the first to encourage my pursuit of this topic in graduate school. Foremost among them were Mary Wright, Don Price, Jonathan Spence, Lyman Van Slyke, and Harold Kahn. Without their patient encouragement in the first stage of research, from 1969 to 1977, I might have given up the effort to probe deeper into a topic as vast and as complex as the May Fourth movement. After my graduate school years, professional colleagues in the China field have consistently expressed interest in and offered helpful criticism of the argument presented here. Among the many to whom I owe a debt of gratitude are the participants of the New England China Faculty Seminar, especially Benjamin Schwartz, John K. Fairbank, Merle Goldman, and Paul Cohen. The final version of this manuscript has also benefited immensely from the thorough and insightful criticism of Frederic Wakeman and Jerome Grieder. Without their commitment of time and energy to this project—a commitment that far exceeded any expectations of collegial support—this would have been a narrower, more pedestrian monograph.

In China, too, there have been a large number of friends and colleagues who nurtured this project and enabled me to undertake a thorough revision of its themes. Among the many who shared their resources and insights with me were professors Li Shu and Li Xin of the Modern History Institute, Li Zehou of the Philosophy Institute, and Wu Xiaoling of the Literature Institute. At Beijing University, in addition to support from the staff of the Foreign Students' Office and of the Chinese Literature Department, I benefited greatly from conversations with Professors Wang Yao, Yue Daiyun, Yuan Liangjun, Zhang Zhuhong, Lin Geng, Zhang Zhilian, and others. Beyond Beijing University, a large number of other intellectuals, both cultural and political leaders, took time to discuss the significance of the May Fourth movement with me. Foremost among them was Mr. Zhou Yang, who in a personal interview in May 1983 strongly encouraged this comparative approach to the problem of enlightenment. My deepest gratitude, of course, is reserved for the octogenarian veterans of the May Fourth era whom I was privileged to meet and interview in Beijing. Xu Deheng, Yu Pingbo, Ye Shengtao, Zhu Guanqian, Feng Youlan, Jin Yuelin, Liang Shuming, and Zhang Shenfu taught me more than I could ever hope to learn from books.

At Wesleyan, my colleagues and students have been an eager, critical audience for views about China developed in this book. It is also here that I met and benefited so much from the editorial talents of Jeannette Hopkins, Director of the Wesleyan University Press. My student research assistants—Ma Shaozhong, Norman Kutcher, Deborah Wang, Naogan, Mao Tong, and Chun Chan—provided the ongoing, practical support that enabled me to work on the manuscript and teach at the same time. In the actual production of this work, my manuscript editor Sally Serafim provided the kind of careful questioning that only a dedicated professional can. In this, our second collaboration, I am more indebted to her than ever.

Research for this project was funded by the American Council for Learned Societies, the Committee for Scholarly Communications with the People's Republic of China, the American Philosophical Society, and Wesleyan University.

Finally, I wish to thank the inner circle of my family and friends who helped me to endure and to enjoy those hectic times in which I nearly lost sight of the final goal. It was their confidence in me and in my work that enabled me to bring this project to fruition.

A Note on Romanization

This book employs the *pinyin* system for the transliteration of Chinese names. Developed on the mainland, this system is currently becoming standard around the world. Thus familiar names such as Chou En-lai, Mao Tse-tung, Peking, and Nanking appear in the text in the slightly more novel forms of Zhou Enlai, Mao Zedong, Beijing, and Nanjing. Futhermore, in keeping with Chinese language source references, Sun Yatsen and Chiang Kaishek are referred to as Sun Zhongshan and Jiang Jieshi. In citing Western language sources that use the older Wade-Giles romanization system, however, references to persons and places were left unchanged. Finally, unless otherwise indicated, all translations are the author's own renditions.

Introduction: The Particularity of Enlightenment in Modern China

> Enlightenment is man's emergence from his self-inflicted immaturity. Immaturity is the incapacity to use one's own understanding without the guidance of another. This immaturity is self-inflicted if its cause is not a lack of understanding but a lack of courage to use understanding without the guidance of another. *Sapere aude!* Dare to know! Be guided by your own understanding! This is the watchword of enlightenment!
>
> *Immanuel Kant, "What Is Enlightenment?"*[1]

Modern China's answer to Kant's question "what is Enlightenment?" reflects the exigencies of its own history. This is a history marked by the rise of modern nationalism, by the unfolding of a rural-based revolution, and by the quest for emancipation from a feudal worldview. The significance of these simultaneous processes has long been recognized by those who view China as a paradigm for the third world. It remains to be fully understood by social theorists concerned with the universal tension between modernization and social change.[2] One dimension of that tension, most apparent in the lives and work of critical intellectuals, is the conflict between nationalism and cultural critique—or, in Chinese terms, between the external imperatives of *jiuguo* (national salvation) and the internal prerequisites of *qimeng* (enlightenment). The Chinese intellectuals who wrestled with this disparity most consciously were themselves beneficiaries of modern education at home and abroad. They shared their compatriots' commitment to a strong and independent China and proved that commitment by active participation in the twentieth-century Chinese revolution.

Unlike purely patriotic revolutionaries, advocates of enlightenment have refused to place the blame for China's backwardness—for its prolonged "self-inflicted immaturity"—on outside aggressors. They have resisted the temptation to glorify the native past even in times when China's survival as a nation was endangered by European, Japanese, or American imperialism. Instead, they have persisted in drawing attention to the burden of China's feudal tradition; more specifically, to the ethic of subservience to patriarchal authority, be it that of the family or of the state bureaucracy. The enduring hold of this ethic on the minds of the Chinese leaders and masses alike makes the challenge of enlightenment an explosive and important issue even today.

In eighteenth-century Europe, to ask "what is enlightenment?" was another way to pose the age-old question "what is truth?"[3] Kant's answer summarized the thoughts of an entire generation of philosophers; he defined enlightenment as self-emancipation from religious dogma. It was an answer that built upon a long tradition of rational doubt. Twentieth-century Chinese intellectuals, by contrast, were unable to draw upon the assumptions of such a tradition. They had to ask and answer Kant's question in their own terms. Their reflections on the problem of "what is enlightenment?" and its corollary "what is truth?" are markedly less abstract than those of their European predecessors. They convey an urgent, almost inchoate desire for emancipation from the ethic of self-submission.

The urgency of their thought movement sets Chinese advocates of enlightenment apart from their European colleagues. This distinctive tone may be glimpsed in a manifesto published by a group of Beijing University students who, in their own way, and in keeping with the exigencies of their own times, tried to follow up Kant's watchword for enlightenment in the spring of 1919. Unlike the eighteenth-century philosophers who had assumed that it was their right to "dare to know," these youthful founders of the *New Tide* Society could only hope that they would be allowed to discover their own understanding. Therefore, their publication reads as a strident and rather naive echo of the measured ruminations of the sage of Königsberg:

Most people in China today do not live what may be called a truly human life. They are fettered by destructive customs and rules of propriety that destroy individual integrity. We cannot help but be anguished and try to redress this injustice. Therefore, we call on all students in China to forsake the old examination system mentality and to adopt modern scientific thought! We must rid ourselves of arbitrary credulity and adopt the spirit of objective doubt. We must stand on the side of the future rather than the present [social system]. We must forge a temperament that might overcome society rather than be overcome by it.[4]

In spite of this hasty tone, the twentieth century Chinese enlighten ment represents a critical elaboration of its European precedent. Its champions—those intellectuals who took it upon themselves to forsake, or at least to expose, "the examination system mentality," "arbitrary credulity," and a national temperament all too accustomed to being "overcome by society"—faced a challenge that was quite different from that of eighteenth-century philosophers who sought to free themselves from the "guidance" of religion. The Chinese intellectuals were battling entrenched habits of self-repression which were upheld by familial au thority rather than theological dictate. Thus, enlightenment in the Chinese context had to mean something other than what it did in Europe during Kant's lifetime: a program of *disenchantment* that would replace religious superstitions with truths derived from the realm of nature.[5] In twentieth-century China, enlightenment requires a prolonged, still ongoing *disengagement* from the bonds of duty and loyalty that have kept sons obedient to fathers, wives obedient to husbands, and ministers obe dient to rulers for centuries.

During the European enlightenment the source of "self-inflicted im maturity" was identified as Christian dogmatism enforced through the corrupt and arbitrary authority of the Church. In modern China, on the other hand, the origins of spiritual lethargy were traced back to Con fucianism, or more precisely to those elements of the Confucian tradition that comprised the *lijiao*, the cult of ritualized subordination.[6] This cult had been perpetuated through the institution of the examination system and represented an adaptation of the ethic of filial piety to the needs of the imperial bureaucratic state. Using the most intimate emotions that prevail within the family, the cult of subordination was comprised of "three ropes and five bonds" (*sangang wuchang*)—all of which required that inferiors submit themselves to their superiors with a glad and open heart. Thus, the "three ropes" prescribed the duties of the prince, the father, and the husband in guiding their inferiors, whereas the "five bonds" elaborated further the sentiments that ought to prevail between prince and minister, father and son, older brother and younger brother, husband and wife, friend and friend. Although all these "ropes" and "bonds" were predicated on some degree of mutuality, all but the last precluded the kind of autonomy and equality that became the goal of self-emancipation during the twentieth-century enlightenment move ment.

The vengeance with which modern Chinese iconoclasts attacked psychological conformity and social inertia mirrored the intensity of eighteenth-century assaults on what Voltaire called "the delirium of religion."[7] Unlike their European predecessors, however, Chinese advocates of enlightenment could not console themselves with the imminent triumph of scientific truth over blind belief. Since the object of their concern was not the unquestioned faith in a transcendent God, but rather the unquestioning obedience to patriarchal authority—be it that of emperor, father, or party chief—they had to prepare for a more protracted struggle against the social and political impulses of their compatriots. Over time, these impulses had become identified with essential Confucian values that, in turn, were seen as the source of the spiritual superiority of Chinese civilization. Iconoclastic intellectuals who would challenge this presumed superiority were deemed every bit as dangerous as European philosophers who quarreled with the concept of a supernatural God.

"Destructive" and "dangerous" were accusations quite familiar to Chinese admirers of the European enlightenment. In the context of a nationalist revolution, however, they also faced an added charge: that of being "un-Chinese." Therefore, it was more difficult for them to persevere in the project of cultural criticism than it had been for European philosophers, who did not worry about being seen as "un-French," "un-English" or "un-German." Eighteenth-century iconoclasts had been confident members of a cosmopolitan community of *Aufklärer* (enlightened ones). They had developed and maintained their intellectual kinship regardless of political and national boundaries. Their spiritual heirs in twentieth-century China, on the other hand, came of age at a time when the question of national identity was paramount. As citizens of an embattled, defensive China, they were and remain vulnerable spokesmen for enlightenment. Even today, their attempts to discover and use critical reason still face the "guidance" of nationalistic loyalties.

ENLIGHTENMENT AND THE QUEST FOR MODERNITY

In twentieth-century China, as in Europe a hundred and fifty years earlier, the discovery of critical reason has been heralded as a sign of transition from tradition to modernity. In both contexts, this transition turned out to be neither as clear-cut nor as easily consummated as first envisaged by advocates of enlightenment.[8] The lingering hold of outworn values, Christian as well as Confucian, on supposedly modern men and women, continues to shock those who had hoped to replace superstition and prejudice with objective doubt. For Chinese intellectuals, this shock has added reverberations. Having witnessed, participated in, and survived several political revolutions, they have more reason than European philosophers to fear the re-emergence of old habits of mind.

Efforts to launch China onto the path of genuine modernity have, from the beginning, been marked by the intellectuals' awareness of the protean nature of traditional culture. These critics of native habits of mind needed an alternative place to stand from which they might continue to call into question the values that so many of their contemporaries considered to be natural and immutable. So, they turned to the West (or, more frequently, to Japanese interpretations of Western texts and ideas). The more Chinese radicals relied on the perspective of cultural relativism, the more they risked being accused of imposing a Western concept of modernity upon a unique Chinese civilization. Those who took that risk did so because events in Chinese history itself confirmed, and continue to reconfirm, the tenacity of feudalism at the heart of a supposedly modernized, even revolutionary society.

The question of how to become a modern nation antedates the problem of enlightenment in Chinese history. From the mid-nineteenth century onward, Confucian officials have tried to find the best way to increase the power and prestige of the state so as to enable it to withstand foreign aggression. The formula worked out in the 1880s by the reform-minded scholar Zhang Zhidong still appeals to patriotic revolutionaries determined to ensure China's survival in a world of rapacious nation-states. Zhang's suggestion was simple enough: "Chinese learning as the goal, Western learning as the means" (*zhongxue wei ti, xixue wei yong*). This *ti-yong* formula became more complicated in practice, however. Political reformers discovered that embedded in Western "means"— that is to say, in technological expertise—were distinctive goals that were inimical to the fundamental values of Chinese, or more precisely Confucian, civilization.[9] The inseparability of means and ends in both Western and Chinese learning posed an awkward and lasting dilemma for cultural conservatives. It also provided the key opportunity for cultural radicals who sought to revive and to strengthen China by re-evaluating native traditions with the tools of critical reason learned from abroad.

The first generation to take issue with Zhang Zhidong's *ti-yong* formula emerged during the first decade of the twentieth century. Having traveled to Japan and Europe, these still-Confucian scholars began to voice publicly their doubts about the superiority of Chinese learning, especially those elements of it that were codified in and rewarded by the imperial examination system. Their criticism of the native cultural legacy became sidetracked, as we shall see in the first chapter, by the passions of China's first nationalist revolution—the anti-dynastic revolution of 1911. Bent upon reforming Confucian education, most of these intellectuals ended up fighting against the "foreign" Manchu rulers whom they envisaged as the chief obstacle to national salvation and renewal. Thus, it fell upon subsequent generations to follow through with the implications of an early twentieth-century insight: that *jiuguo*, national salvation, depends first and foremost on a commitment to *jiuren*, the salvation of mankind, or more precisely, to a critical-minded humanism.[10]

This insight about the primacy of culture may be traced to the failure of political revolution in 1911. Once the optimism of anti-dynastic mobilization wore off, the tenacity of outworn cultural values became all the more apparent. A group of erstwhile revolutionaries now embarked upon the quest for a new worldview. This quest was more thorough than any of the quests previously undertaken by the Confucian reformers. Founders of *Youth* magazine (later renamed *New Youth*), these intellectuals tried to make sense of the re-emergence of old habits of mind, in particular of the emperor-worship mentality, even after there was no longer an actual Son of Heaven on the throne in Beijing. Their conclusion, documented in chapters 2 and 3, was that China needed a radical transvaluation of values. The object of their New Culture movement was to dig up the common tendencies toward self-submission and expose them. Such tendencies, in their view, had prevented their compatriots from taking advantage of the possibility of national and individual autonomy opened up by the revolution of 1911. Rallying around the slogans "Science" and "Democracy," this first generation of enlightenment intellectuals looked to their descendants to actualize the hope of emancipation from the ethic of subservience. They wanted this "new youth" to prove that a truly modern nation-state could not come into existence in China unless it first sanctioned the human rights of critically minded citizens.

Thus, the stage was set for the historic action of a new generation—called here the May Fourth generation. Comprised of students who had congregated in and around National Beijing University (Beida) in 1919, this group of younger intellectuals took it upon themselves to carry through the vague hopes of their iconoclastic mentors. Their age and their educational experiences before entering Beijing University made them more distant from the Confucian tradition and therefore less angry at it. In contrast to their teachers, who had been obsessed with the tenacity of feudal habits of mind ever since the failure of the revolution of 1911, these students were more rational in their cultural criticism. Also, they were less pessimistic about political action and thus were able to respond more promptly to the political crisis occasioned by the end of World War I.

This generation's rallying point was the event of May 4, 1919. What began as a demonstration to protest China's treatment at the Paris Peace Conference developed during the following year into a national movement for cultural and political awakening. This broader movement included literary and family reforms as well as an increasing commitment by the educated elite to gain a mass hearing for their radical views. Spreading their ideas through street lectures, this younger group of intellectuals was able to put their mentors' ideas to the test of practical social action. They emerged from this first encounter with the unawakened masses full of confidence both in themselves and in critical reason—the tool with which they aimed to rouse their less enlightened contemporaries. Luo Jialun, one of the leaders of the student demonstration and also a founder of the New Tide Society, wrote one year after the event of 1919 that the glory of May Fourth lay in shaking China out of its prolonged backwardness:

Before, we Chinese students had claimed to be able to smash heaven with our words and aimed to overturn the earth with our pens.... Only this time [during the May Fourth movement] did we begin to struggle with the forces of darkness with our bare fists... China before the May Fourth movement was a nation gasping for breath. After the May Fourth movement, it is a more vital, lively nation. The glory of the May Fourth movement lies precisely in getting China to move.[11]

This rather dramatic claim to having gotten China to *move* was and remains the core of the myth of May Fourth. It suggests the appealing possibility of an irrevocable and total break with the past. Beneath this myth, as this book argues, lies the more prosaic but more enduring significance of May Fourth. Far from having set China on the irreversible, glorious path of enlightenment, the event of 1919 marked the first of a series of incomplete efforts to uproot feudalism while pursuing the cause of a nationalist revolution. Intellectuals were at the forefront of this effort then, as they are now. Relatively immune to "the forces of darkness" by virtue of their modern scientific education, this minority has been able to infuse new vigor in a "nation gasping for breath." They were, as we shall see, in a particularly good position to shake off the burden of the *ti-yong* formula. This meant that they were no longer compelled to subordinate Western scientific rationality to the claims of China's spiritual civilization. Their capacity for and interest in cultural relativism set them apart from most of their compatriots—the less educated masses as well as the Confucian guardians of "national essence." Thus, when they claimed to have "moved" China, or at least to have gotten it moving, they were reaffirming the need for something more than a national salvation effort based on "Chinese ends" and "Western means."

Bombastic in their tone, arrogant in their image of themselves as bare-fisted warriors against the forces of darkness, simplistic in their condemnation of tradition, May Fourth intellectuals appeared to Westerners visiting China at the end of World War I as familiar types: latter-day philosophers of the European enlightenment. Teilhard de Chardin, John Dewey, and Bertrand Russell all noted in their writing about China that the search for a new culture seemed to be a frantic version of the European movement of a century and a half earlier. Bertrand Russell and Teilhard de Chardin responded with ambivalence to what they found in China in the 1920s: a rush toward the same modernity that they hoped to leave behind in Europe.[12] Dewey, on the other hand, although suspicious of the hasty tone of the May Fourth movement, was, on the whole, more positive in his response. Less eager to find relief from the pressures of Western modernity in an idealized image of an harmonious, traditional China, he was able to note, even if critically, the promises of the incipient Chinese enlightenment. In his capacity as contributor to *Asia* magazine, Dewey wrote in 1921:

The movement is still for the most part a feeling rather than an idea. It is also accompanied by the extravagances and confusions, the undigested medley of wisdom and nonsense that inevitably mark so ambitious a movement in its early stages.... One could easily hold up the whole movement to ridicule, as less than half-baked, as an uncritical, more or less hysterical mixture of unrelated ideas and miscellaneous pieces of Western science and thought.... And yet, the new culture movement provides one of the firmest bases of hope for the future of China.[13]

An accurate enough description of the mood, if not exactly the content, of the May Fourth movement, Dewey's characterization might be equally appropriate for the early stages of the European enlightenment. The difference, however, is that in Europe, proponents of enlightenment had benefited from a relatively peaceful century before the French Revolution of 1789. During that period, several generations of philosophers were able to build upon each other's ideas and to criticize each other's views in the context of undisturbed philosophical debate. The May

Fourth movement, by contrast, was a much shorter event, a thought interval really, amidst a series of political and social revolutions. This condensation of enlightenment history led May Fourth intellectuals, cosmopolitan by temperament and nationalist revolutionaries by vocation, to become more conscious of their own social mission than their European predecessors.

INTELLECTUALS AS AGENTS OF ENLIGHTENMENT

During the decades that followed the May Fourth movement of 1919, Chinese advocates of enlightenment were forced to reconsider and to refashion, at times even to abandon, their vision of intellectual emancipation. The twin phenomena of political violence and anti-imperialist mobilization created a climate of urgency that challenged the intellectuals' commitment to a slow-paced revolution of ideas. It also called into question their image of themselves as forerunners of cultural awakening. Having set out to reform the mental habits of their countrymen, May Fourth intellectuals ended up changing their own outlook on the relationship between already-enlightened thinkers and the still-to-be-awakened populace. As chapter 4 shows, they had to revise their image of themselves as leaders of new culture, ahead of and above the common people (*pingmin*), and learn to accept a more circumscribed role as fellow travelers among the ranks of the revolutionary masses (*dazhong*).

At the beginning of the May Fourth movement, self-styled "new youths" still saw themselves in terms of a traditional model, that of *xianzhi xian juewu zhe*—those first to know and first to become enlightened.[14] Although they rebelled against much of the Confucian content of this model, modern intellectuals retained the conviction that they had a unique cultural mission. This sense of a special calling was no longer dependent on status derived from the examination system but rather on their own efforts to become disinterested scholars, *xuezhe*. Because they refused to seek bureaucratic positions in the corrupt warlord governments of their day, these scholars portrayed themselves as ideally suited to bring enlightenment to their more oppressed, more timid countrymen. In the wake of the social revolution of the 1920s, however, they discovered that both their knowledge and their courage were more limited than what they had imagined at the height of May Fourth. Those who could no longer hold on to their previous self-image as pioneer-prophets of enlightenment, yet wanted to keep up with the historical changes at hand, transformed themselves into *zhishi fenzi*—members of a politicized intelligentsia, or, more literally, knowledgeable elements of a larger, class-conscious body politic.

As mere fragments of a politicized society, May Fourth veterans still retained their distinctive cultural mission: the mission of enlightenment. During the dispirited 1930s, when the domestic White Terror inaugurated by the Guomindang became aggravated by Japanese aggression in North China, they managed to bring about a revival of May Fourth concerns. They pressed on with the call for emancipation from feudal values even when such values were attacked as inimical to the goal of mobilization against foreign enemies. The more strident the voice of cultural conservatives in this period, the more cogent the argument of those who believed that there could be no *jiuguo*, national salvation, without *qimeng*, enlightenment.

In fact, as chapter 5 illustrates, the New Enlightenment movement of 1937–39 was able to combine in a novel way the political imperatives of resistance to Japan with an anti-feudal culture movement. This effort, however, was short-lived. As so often before, critically minded intellectuals were accused of eroding national self-confidence, or more simply, of not being Chinese enough. They and their enlightenment movement became subject to "sinification"—a code word for enforced abandonment of cosmopolitan commitments and of dispassionate criticism of national shortcomings. Once enlightenment and enlighteners became "sinified," they became less effective in reminding China of its incomplete emancipation from feudal culture.

And yet, throughout all these political upheavals, May Fourth veterans never quite forgot the original aspirations of enlightenment. Whenever the pressures for patriotic mobilization relaxed somewhat, they turned to recollections of the event of 1919 as the most concrete way to bring the unfinished project of cultural awakening to the attention of their compatriots. In the faction-ridden 1940s, 1950s, and 1960s, they shaped their personal memories into didactic allegories. Within the limits of official commemorations, they told and retold the story of May Fourth in ways that left no doubt that China had yet to acquire the basic prerequisites of genuine modernity: science and democracy. The allegory of May Fourth, as documented in the last chapter, continues to inspire each new generation of culture critics that comes of age on the Chinese mainland as well as on Taiwan.

The vulnerable yet tenacious bond between intellectuals and the legacy of May Fourth is, thus, the most encompassing theme of this book. Its origins and variations are analyzed thematically rather than chronologically. Therefore, the reader is asked to follow a web of ideas instead of a thread of events.[15] Throughout, the emphasis is upon the intellectuals' own vision of what China needs to emerge from its prolonged "self-inflicted immaturity." Western ideas, Western mentors, and Western models of autonomy provide the background for this inquiry into a distinctively Chinese commitment to enlightenment. Far from being a mere imitation of the European precedent, this commitment will be shown to be a complex and creative response to dilemmas that still confront us as Western intellectuals. The century and a half separating the Chinese from the European enlightenment has made Chinese intellectuals more aware of the risks involved in challenging the deep-seated assumptions of their contemporaries. They have embraced the calling of the "combative thinker"—which in eighteenth-century Europe had connoted a refusal to abide by Christian dogma and to search for truth through reason and experience[16]—knowing critical reason to be a frail weapon against the lure of prejudice. And yet, they have persevered in their "negative," "destructive" mission precisely because they have witnessed the reemergence of blind belief in the wake of each major political upheaval from the Republican Revolution of 1911 through the Cultural Revolution of 1966–69.

Differences between China and the West do not diminish the pathos of the Chinese enlightenment. Its advocates have paid dearly for their dedication to ideas that transcend the exigencies of a particular tradition. They accepted those exigencies while seeking to alter the foundations of national identity. In the context of a nationalist revolution, they persevered in the arduous yet necessary revolution of values.[17] They continued the quest for a new worldview when all that seemed to matter was a new world order. I hope that their quest will be of interest to all those concerned with the cultural issues frequently overlooked in the course of political revolution. To precipitate that interest, there is no better starting point than Zarathustra's rebuttal to Hellishnoise, the fierce guardian of political history:

Believe me, friend Hellishnoise: the great events—they are not our loudest but our stillest hours. Not around the inventors of new noises, but around the inventors of new values does the world revolve; it revolves inaudibly.[18]

ONE

May 4, 1919: The Making of a New Generation

We are not speaking here of similarities among men but of the world in which men live ... of problems arising from their world and their relationship to them.... Common problems do not arouse a common reaction; they affect the young, the mature, and the old quite differently.

Julian Marias, *Generations: A Historical Method*[1]

The world looked bleak on the eve of the May Fourth incident in 1919. In the eyes of older Chinese intellectuals, it appeared as if a long night of barbarism was about to engulf both China and Europe. Confucian gentlemen lingered on in a post-Confucian world, bemoaning the beastly mores of their younger contemporaries. Unwilling to "stain" their own hands "to kill the beasts,"[2] they appealed to the ruling warlords to stem the tide of liberal reform. The warlords, however, had other, more pressing business to attend to. The war in Europe, which they had joined on the side of the Allies, was about to end. For China, this brought a disappointing victory. Hopes of winning back Chinese territories held by Germany since the 1890s were about to be dashed at the Paris Peace Conference.

Along will political hopes, the Great War called into question Chinese admiration for Western civilization. The capacity for self-inflicted devastation that the war revealed had shocked Western and Chinese observers alike. In 1919, the same year in which Spengler's *The Decline of the West* was a best-seller in Europe, Liang Qichao, a Chinese observer at the Paris Peace Conference, would write home that Europeans "are like travelers in the desert and have lost their direction.... They are in utter despair.... They once had a great dream about the omnipotence of science. Now their talk is filled with its bankruptcy."[3]

Back in Beijing, middle-aged cultural radicals in their thirties and forties dismissed the warnings and worries of more traditional scholars like Liang Qichao. They retained their faith in science and Western civilization even as they sank deeper and deeper into their own despair about cultural change in China. Despite the political revolution that had taken place in 1911, nothing seemed to have changed in the eyes of this generation bent upon a more profound soul-transformation. They had wanted to save China by changing it from within. Now they noted grimly that the masses of Chinese people continued to submit themselves to would-be emperors and crude warlords. The prospect of awakening the minds of their countrymen—a goal since 1915—was rapidly fading.

In this despondent mood, Lu Xun, the man who would become China's foremost modern writer, buried himself in the study of ancient stone rubbings. He was thirty-six years old in 1917—a young man weighed down by middle-aged weariness—when an old friend and fellow cultural radical came to ask him to contribute to a journal called *New Youth*. Filled with despair, Lu Xun argued: What's the point? China is too mired in its past. Those who seek to bring it into the present are too few, too lonely, and too weak. He likened Chinese tradition to an impregnable prison:

Imagine an iron house having not a single window, and virtually indestructible, with all its inmates sound asleep and about to die of suffocation. Dying in their sleep, they won't feel the pain of death. Now if you raise a shout to awake a few of the light sleepers, making these unfortunate few suffer the agony of irrevocable death, do you really think you are doing them a good turn?[4]

Lu Xun's friend, the historian Qian Xuantong, would not accept this thoroughly bleak metaphor. He argued back: What if a few inmates were to awaken after all? Would there not have to be some hope, therefore, of destroying the iron house? Lu Xun, still doubtful, agreed to leave the rubbings and pick up his pen. His first vernacular short story, "Diary of a Madman," appeared in the May 1918 issue of *New Youth*. It described the bitter fate of one of the "light sleepers," a young man who woke up briefly only to discover that the loftiest values of his family and his village amount to nothing more than cannibalism. Who but a madman, Lu Xun taunted his readers, would dare to read between the lines of the Confucian classics? Who but a madman would dare to discover the awful truth on each page where in between the words "virtue and benevolence" is the hidden message: "Eat people!" The last lines of the story hint at the only hope that Lu Xun's generation could fathom in such murderous circumstances:

1.   Post-cultural revolution oil painting of the May Fourth demonstration. Intellectuals are once again in the center of the demonstration, with the "surging masses" all around.

"Perhaps there are still children who haven't eaten men? Save the children."[5]

On May 4, 1919, the "children" Lu Xun had hoped to save entered history on their own terms. It was a typical early May Sunday in Beijing: a cool, windy day, only somewhat less cloudy than most spring days in North China. By one thirty in the afternoon, over three thousand students had gathered in Tiananmen Square. Most of them wore the uniform of their literati predecessors: long silk gown with short padded jacket. Some had donned Western bowler hats. Of the thirteen colleges and universities that were represented, the last group to arrive were the leaders from Beida (National Beijing University). They had been delayed by police officers and representatives from the Ministry of Education who had been sent to persuade them not to disturb the peace of the capital.

Undeterred, the Beida contingent marched to the square and opened the mass meeting. Its delegates restated for their fellow students the purpose of the demonstration: to protest China's treatment at Paris. The news from Europe, which had spread rapidly in the days previous to this gathering, was that Qingdao, the major port of Shandong province and a German naval base since 1897, was in danger of being handed over to Japan. Secret agreements between France, Great Britain, and Japan had come to light that shocked young Chinese defenders of the Allies' cause. To make things worse, the Chinese government turned out to have exchanged its own secret notes with Japan, agreeing, in principle, to Japanese sovereignty over the Shandong peninsula. Faced with these two *faits accomplis*, students took to the streets in a desperate effort to take history into their own hands.[6]

At two o'clock, student demonstrators set out toward the Foreign Legation quarter, carrying placards that read "Give Us Back Qingdao!" "Refuse to Sign the Peace Treaty!" "Oppose Power Politics!" and "China Belongs to the Chinese!" Along the route of the march they passed out a handbill entitled "Manifesto of All Beijing Students." It was addressed at once to the distant Allies, asking them to rectify the injustice perpetrated in their name in Paris, and to the Chinese people closer by, asking them to rise up against those who would betray the national interest. Through this manifesto, the students proclaimed their rage and declared their actions to be righteous and, therefore, of common concern to all Chinese people. In the impassioned language of Lu Xun's madman, but with an edge of confidence that the solitary rebel could have never imagined, the manifesto declared:

This is the last chance for China in her life and death struggle. Today we swear two solemn oaths with all our countrymen: 1) China's territory may be conquered, but it cannot be given away; 2) the Chinese people may be massacred, but they will not surrender.

Our country is about to be annihilated! Up, brethren.[7]

Whether the majority of their countrymen were ready to subscribe to these oaths was a question the students did not stop to ask themselves. They acted in the conviction that they must do something. This conviction set Lu Xun's children decisively apart from their "mad" predecessors. Their manifesto and their demonstration signaled the emergence of a new generation, young men who were more political and more optimistic than their mentors. They proceeded to make a unique contribution to the Chinese revolution that had begun before their time.

SOME OF THE MAY FOURTH YOUTHS

The author of the manifesto of May 4, 1919, was Luo Jialun, a twenty-two-year-old Beida junior. This native of Jiangxi province would later become president of Qinghua University (1928–30) and then of the Guomindang-controlled Central University (1932–41). Before his death in Taiwan in 1969, he held the prominent post of director of the National History Museum with special responsibility for the Nationalist Party Archives. An intense young man at the time of the May Fourth incident, Luo stood out among his contemporaries by reason of his fiery temper and his unscholarly looks. Among the other self-consciously refined young men, he was notorious for his "uncouth looks," his "bear paws," and his supposed weakness for the "glitter of gold."[8] Yet those who followd his lead in the Beida delegation shared the sentiments of the manifesto he had drafted in haste that very morning. After all, Luo was quite well known to them as one of the founders and editors of *New Tide*—the Beida student magazine dedicated to spreading new knowledge and a spirit of criticism among China's fledgling new youth. The frenzied message that "this is the last chance for China in her life and death struggle" which demonstrators distributed to passersby that Sunday afternoon echoed the call for cultural awakening proclaimed over the past five months by Luo Jialun and fellow *New Tide* editor Fu Sinian.

These two young men had met in the summer of 1917, the same year in which Lu Xun decided to abandon ancient stone rubbings, when they both sat for the entrance examinations at Beijing University. Fu Sinian, one year older than his friend, had arrived as Beida with advanced training in classical Chinese studies. After graduation, he went on to gain scholarly renown as a researcher in historical linguistics and as director of the Institute of History and Philology of the Academia Sinica, a position he held for twenty-two years. He died in Taiwan in 1950 after having served for a year as chancellor of the newly established National Taiwan University. More erudite by training and less political by temperament than Luo Jialun, Fu Sinian managed to find common ground with his friend through their shared interest in foreign languages, especially English and German, and in contemporary Western philosophy. Together, Luo and Fu were able to mobilize a small but dedicated group of Beida students to join them in a thorough, informed criticism of Chinese culture and the Confucian mentality. That effort, begun in January 1919 with the first issue of *New Tide*, accelerated beyond the editors' wildest hopes four months later.

Fu Sinian was not exactly unprepared for the political activism of May Fourth. A native of Shandong province, he took the threat of Japan quite personally. In February 1919 he had already rephrased Blake to assert that "great things are done by jostling in the streets. Nothing is done when men and mountains meet."[9] And yet, once he found himself in the streets, he tried to calm the frenzied jostling of his fellow students. One of the twenty-two Beida representatives elected at an emotional meeting on the night of May 3, Fu arrived at the city-wide meeting the next morning quite unprepared to be named chairman of the planning committee. It was he who told the other delegates to meet at Tiananmen Square at one o'clock and to be prepared to march, peacefully, to the Foreign Legation quarter.

Later in the afternoon, as one of the marshals of the demonstration, Fu continued to argue for moderate action. When fellow students frustrated by the long, fruitless wait outside the legation quarter shouted

"On to the Foreign Ministry!" "On to the Homes of Chinese Traitors!" he urged them to turn back. Unable to control the situation, he took up the flag and led the demonstrators to the house of Cao Rulin, minister of communication and chief spokesman for Japanese interests inside the Chinese government. There, while his brother Fu Siyan led the break-in, Fu Sinian continued to counsel restraint.[10]

Again his words fell on deaf ears, as the angered students smashed furniture and set the house on fire. Shortly before six o'clock, the police, who had been benevolent observers through most of the afternoon, suddenly charged the demonstrators. While most of the students managed to scatter into side alleys—Fu Sinian and Luo Jialun among them— thirty-two were caught and arrested. Among those who fell into the net of the police were fellow Beida activists Yang Zhensheng and Xu Deheng.

Yang, Fu Sinian's co-provincial from Shandong, also took the Japanese threat as a personal insult. His attachment to his native soil was to deepen in the years after he graduated from Beida as he became a widely known patriotic professor of literature and eventually president of Qingdao University (1930–37). He died in China in 1956, having served as chairman of the literature department of the Northeast People's University as well as a member of the Changchun city Political Consultative Conference.[11]

Twenty-nine years old at the time of the May Fourth incident—one of the older youths who nonetheless shared his generation's enthusiasm for rebellion—Yang was known as one of the "hot-headed radicals" of the Beida literature department. A member of the *New Tide* Society since its founding in October 1918, he had been drawing upon himself, quite consciously, the ire of more conservative professors. Yang Zhensheng and fellow *New Tide* member Yu Pingbo became preferred targets of attack by Gu Hongming, the Confucian gentleman who taught the history of European literature. They in turn took delight in retaliating. While Gu would lecture, holding on proudly to his long braid—a symbol of his devotion to the deposed Manchu dynasty—Yang Zhensheng would sit in the back of the class and make up lines such as "His emperor along with his queue / Should have been cut down at the root long ago! / His emperor along with his queue / Should have been sent to the antique shop long ago!"[12]

The young man who took such delight in mocking the remnants of old culture at Beida rushed forward to take part in the birth of the new. The night of May 3, at the same meeting at which Fu Sinian was elected one of the Beida representatives, Yang Zhensheng had made a fervent speech about the humiliation of his native province. The next day he joined the demonstration and eagerly followed the crowd to Cao Rulin's house. Inside, less timid by temperament than Fu Sinian, he joined in smashing the furniture and was also there when angry students happened upon the sitting room where Cao's concubine and Zhang Zengxiang, China's minister to Japan, had been hiding. He took part in the beating that left Zhang feigning death until the police arrived.

In jail, over the next three days, Yang Zhensheng had time to reconsider his actions. Though he did not regret any of them, he remained haunted by political nightmares. Late at night, he saw images of gun-wielding Japanese marines, of the frightened ghost of Cao's young concubine, of police officers plunging their clubs into his brain. As he awoke, he struggled to regain confidence, to recapture a sense of righteousness about the "crimes" he and the others were being accused of in court.[13] One way to lighten the burden of transgression against the conventions of social order was to join in the written statement submitted to the court by fellow Beida activist Xu Deheng. This statement, echoing Luo Jialun's manifesto, restated the students' right to speak as the conscience of China:

> We, the thirty-two students, Xu Deheng and others, declare that Cao Rulin and Zhang Zengxiang who have committed treason should be punished. They are hated by everybody who has courage. The May Fourth incident was simply an outbreak of indignation based upon the consciences of the several thousand students and tens of thousand of citizens in Beijing. Because it cannot be considered a crime so far as the intention is concerned, why should we be suspended and prosecuted?[14]

Xu Deheng, more than Yang Zhensheng, had reason to believe himself innocent. Yang was a critic of Chinese culture; Xu viewed himself, purely and simply, as a patriot. A founder of the *Citizen* magazine in 1918, this native of Jiangxi (the home province also of Luo Jialun) had arrived at Beida determined to save China, to stem the tide of humiliation instigated by foreign aggressors. This passion evolved into an enduring commitment in Xu's mature years as he continued to pursue a prominent activist role in the national salvation movement of the 1930s. Having gained public prominence as a patriot during the anti-Japanese war, Xu continued to use his prestige to speak out against the Guomindang in the late 1940s. At ninety-four the oldest survivor of the May Fourth generation in China, he is currently one of the country's top political leaders in his capacity as vice chairman of the Standing Committee of the People's Political Consultative Conference.[15]

On the eve of the May Fourth incident, Xu Deheng was a twenty-

nine-year-old fellow student of Yang Zhengsheng's in the literature department. Although he felt a strong antipathy for cultural radicals like
Yang who would blame China's weakness on its own Confucian habits of
mind, Xu managed to make common cause with them in a moment of
patriotic emergency. Along with Deng Zhongxia, co-founder of the
Citizen and later an organizer of the Communist Party, Xu worked hard
to spread the news of China's humiliation at the Paris Peace Conference.
He helped plan the meeting held the night of May 3 and was one of the
chief spokesmen there, rousing the emotions of his fellow students with
an oratory that matched the intensity of the banner written by a native of
Shandong in his own blood.[16]

The next day, Xu Deheng was in the front line of the demonstration
with Luo Jialun and others. At Cao Rulin's house, Xu was among the
most irate of Zhang Zongxiang's attackers. He was also among those
who made their way into Cao's bedroom, where an angry student "set
fire with a cigarette match to the green gauze covering the traitor's
bed."[17] That night in jail, angered further by poor treatment from his
jailers and untroubled by remorse, Xu Deheng, the ardent patriot,
composed the following lines:

> To purge clean the shame from Chinese hearts and minds
> We stand today as prisoners.
> Among the thirty-two arrested,
> There is none who fears death.
> We thrashed the traitors thoroughly and burned the
>   Cao mansion to the ground.
> In ferreting out traitors we've spared no cost,
>   including death.
> We'd do anything to save China.[18]

Xu Deheng, the hero of his own story, was not the only one to celebrate in verse the dawn of a new era. May 4, 1919, was a turning point
even in the lives of Beida youths who could not be in the square that
Sunday, who had no share in the burning of the Cao mansion, who did
not live to retell the tale of their days in jail for years to come. They, too,
had a claim to being part of the generation of "children" in whom Lu
Xun had placed his hopes. They, too, imagined themselves uncontaminated by the cannibalistic old society and lived their youth, for a while at
least, as if they were spiritually free.

One of those unable to be at the demonstration was Yu Pingbo, the
youngest member of the *New Tide* group, who would become, in time,
one of China's foremost literary critics, especially of the great classical
novel *Dream of the Red Chamber*. Barely twenty in 1919, and the son of a

renowned family of Confucian scholars, Yu did attend the meeting on the night of May 3, but he was forbidden by his parents to leave the house the next day. This did not prevent him from taking an active role in propaganda activities after the incident itself, however, or from writing bitter essays condemning China's traditional ethics. At eighty a victim-survivor of the Cultural Revolution, Yu Pingbo still considers himself a member of the May Fourth youth. He continues to celebrate, through commemorative poems, that formative event:

> We handed out white money on the streets
>   (During the student strike at Beida, because of a
>   shortage of paper, we wrote out slogans on
>   "white paper money"—which was used for
>   funeral ceremonies. How childish we were
>   then!)
> Winds were rising and blowing all kinds of opinions,
>   criticisms,
> We did not worry if our words were sweet or bitter.
> We just wrote in the newly born vernacular.
> We were so young, so active then.[19]

Idealism

Another young man absent from Tiananmen Square on the day of May 4th was Gu Jiegang, Fu Sinian's roommate at Beida and co-founder with Fu of the *New Tide*. Gu, who went on to become one of China's most renowned critical historians, contented himself with working on a series of articles attacking the old family system. Afraid of his father's wrath, not unlike Yu Pingbo, Gu published this work in the *New Tide* under the pseudonym Chengyu. Zhu Ziqing, friend of *Citizen* founder Deng Zhongxia but by conviction a member of the cultural radicals' circle at *New Tide*, was also absent from the demonstration on May 4. Zhu was too gentle, too even-handed by temperament, to be swept up in the violent passions of the student activists. And yet this young man "who hardly seemed a youth to those who knew him,"[20] went on to write some of the most thoughtful essays and stories about his own generation of May Fourth intellectuals. Shortly before his death in 1948, he reaffirmed his sense of belonging to that epoch-making event as he wrote: "The May Fourth movement marks the beginning of a totally new era. Liberalism became firmly established upon the foundation of autonomous employment for intellectuals. Those of us in the world of education were pursuing independent careers, not serving as officials or waiting to become officials. As students, we were able to choose among many different careers, and were thus freed from having to take the one path of becoming a bureaucrat. Thus we became emancipated from the

2. Three young writers in 1919, from left to right: Ye Shengtao, Zhu Ziqing, and Yu Pingbo.

ruling elites. No longer acting as the effete nobles and bookworms of earlier times we became members of a new intelligentsia.... We began to be more concerned with courage than with propriety."[21]

Their own ability to forsake the caution and self-doubt of their scholar-official predecessors surprised the May Fourth students themselves as much as it did the society around them. Once out in the streets, however, they remained determined to open a new chapter in China's history. Ranging from the ardently patriotic Xu Deheng to the mild-mannered Zhu Ziqing, they were united by a pledge to save their nation from the destruction it seemed to be bringing upon itself. They believed, in keeping with Lu Xun's vision of new youths, that they were uncontaminated by the lethargy of the old society. They claimed that they were the repository of a unique spirit, which they intended to spread to the rest of their countrymen. On May 26, Luo Jialun, using a new pen name, "Resolute," published the first article that referred to the incident of May 4 as a "movement." Emphasizing the qualities of mind and heart that set students apart from the society at large, he stated:

> This movement shows the spirit of sacrifice of the students. Chinese students used to be eloquent in speech and extravagant in writing, but whenever they had to act, they would be overly cautious.... This time, and only this time, they struggled barehanded with the forces of reaction.... The students' defiant spirit overcame the lethargy of society. Their spirit of autonomy (*zijue*) can never be wiped out again. This is the spirit which will be needed for China to be reborn.[22]

The spirit of sacrifice, defiance, and autonomy that Luo Jialun claimed as the unique attribute of students was precisely what Lu Xun and his colleagues had hoped for when they pledged themselves to "save the children." And yet, once "the children" emerged as historical actors in their own right, the older generation of cultural rebels was taken aback. They were surprised by the speed with which the student movement spread throughout China in the weeks following the May Fourth incident. They worried about the uncontrollable waves of patriotic passion that were unleashed among the uneducated masses. In the end, they chose to cheer the students on while at the same time warning them against settling for temporary, hasty, incomplete victories.

Chen Duxiu (1879–1942), Dean of Humanities at Beida and one of the teachers most sympathetic to the student movement, was also one of the first to admonish it. Though unprepared for the burst of student activism, he joined in it wholeheartedly. Forty years old at the outbreak of the student movement, Chen risked public ridicule by standing on the street handing out patriotic pamphlets. And yet, this enthusiastic supporter of youth turned out to be its most insightful critic as well. On June 8,

1919, three days before his arrest and imprisonment for participation in the student movement, Chen Duxiu wrote an article that underscored his generation's difference with the students. Entitled "Should We Be Patriotic After All?" his essay posed a question unthinkable for younger activists. It went on to restate the teachers' priority, which was not so much to *save* China as to *change* it. Unconvinced that patriotism—an affirmation of devotion to the nation and its people in their present condition—would serve this goal, Chen urged the students to hold on to rational skepticism. Juxtaposing emotional fervor with clear thought, he wrote:

> Since the outbreak of the Shandong crisis, patriotic chanting is heard everywhere. It is therefore all the more important to raise the question: should we be patriotic or not? To ask this rational question in the midst of an emotional upheaval is particularly important, since reason is frequently in conflict with mass psychology.... Nationalism is chiefly an emotional response. It can drive people to extreme, irrational behavior—take the example of the German and Japanese military.... [N]ationalism is just another excuse for harming people, making them blind, mad enough to sacrifice themselves. We uneducated, ignorant, disorganized Chinese people aren't fit for patriotism yet, much the less for long-range reflection about what kind of country we want. But this need not always be so.[23]

REFORMERS, DOUBTERS, AND BUILDERS: THE GENERATIONAL BACKGROUND OF MAY FOURTH

Less than two weeks had passed between Luo Jialun's claim that students had overcome political lethargy once and for all and Chen Duxiu's warning that China was not yet fit for patriotism. How could the world appear in such different light to teachers and students who were participant-observers of the same historical event? Part of the answer may be found in the disparate ways in which history intersected with biography in the lives of the young and the middle-aged. Although contemporaries in time, they were the products of what the sociologist Karl Mannheim has termed disparate "generational locations."[24] Each had been shaped by a set of familial circumstances, educational opportunities, and historical events that linked them to some of their coevals more than to others.

Each generation experienced the year 1919 from its own perspective. This generational location, in turn, delineated—limited, really—the range of feelings, thoughts, and actions evoked by that year's events. As Mannheim wrote: "Any given location restricts the range of self expression open to the individual to certain circumscribed possibilities. This negative delineation, however, does not exhaust the matter. Inherent is a positive sense in which location is a tendency pointing toward certain modes of behavior, feeling and thought."[25] Luo Jialun's inclination to view May Fourth in epoch-making terms is thus a hallmark of his generation, setting it apart form the generation of skeptics like Chen Duxiu. Being in their late twenties, the students experienced and assimilated the incident of 1919 differently from their contemporaries who were in their thirties or in the forties. The youths who believed that they had shattered China's despondency single-handedly were, in fact, the beneficiaries of a prolonged assault on traditional politics and culture begun in the late nineteenth century. Two generations before them had already challenged the assumptions of the Confucian imperial system: first through the reform movement of 1898 and, in more recent memory, through the anti-dynastic revolution of 1919. Whereas May 4, 1919, was the pivotal event in the lives of the student generation, their predecessors had been shaped with equal decisiveness by the hopes invested, and then lost, in the events of 1898 and 1911.

Born in the 1890s, the May Fourth students experienced the world quite differently from the other reformers born in the 1860s and early 1870s like Liang Qichao or the revolutionaries born a decade later like Chen Duxiu. The students could, and did, embrace the politics of patriotism precisely because they were free of the weight of disappointment that still burdened their older contemporaries in the spring of 1919. Unlike the generation of 1898, which had tried and failed to save China from above by relying on a reform-minded emperor, the May Fourth students were convinced that they could save China from below, by awakening the social consciousness of their countrymen. Unlike the generation of 1911, they were not filled with suspicion about the slavish character of ordinary people—a trait which participants in the anti-dynastic revolution discovered after they had deposed the emperor, when they found their countrymen all too eager to submit to the ceremonial authority of new pretenders to the status of Son of Heaven. Building upon the experiences of previous generations, the students were able to take full advantage of the historical opportunity of 1919. They were both participants in, and shaped by, the demonstration on May 4. Thus, they may be properly called the generation of 1919.[26]

Pen names reveal generational differences perhaps more starkly than was intended. Luo Jialun, as we have seen, less than two weeks after the May Fourth incident chose to sign himself as Yi, the Determined, the Resolute. This pen name captures the self-image of an impassioned, arrogant generation convinced of its ability to alter the course of history. It stands in marked contrast to the name adopted by Qian Xuantong, one of the teachers at Beida most active in the *New Youth* circle of Chen Duxiu and Lu Xun. In 1925, in an act that culminated his career as a rebel against the classics, he decided to rename himself Yigu, Doubter of Antiquity. Qian, in turn, was a more emotional iconoclast than his own hero-mentor, Liang Qichao. Liang, a rationalist reformer all his life, had announced his own self-image in 1903, when he published his first collection of essays in Tokyo under the title *Yinbing shi zhuanji*—Collected Works from the Ice Drinker's Studio.

Despite their posturing, such pen names do hint at the disparate history that shaped these three generations: that of the scholarly Ice Drinker, the ardent Doubter of Antiquity, and the activist Resolute. They suggest a deepening self-confidence among Chinese intellectuals, who have always assumed themselves to be responsible for the fate of their country. They also trace a line of descent from those who tried to save China by reviving its cultural traditons, to those who sought to overthrow the old culture to make room for modernity, and, finally, to those who were able to design the outlines of a new culture that was at once modern and Chinese.

Liang Qichao, the Ice Drinker, had been part of the first generation to probe the sources of China's lethargy and to articulate a coherent proposal for the reform of the Chinese worldview. Qian Xuantong, the Doubter of Antiquity, was a member of the generation that dared to carry the quarrel with tradition to the point of divorce. Their iconoclastic stance toward inherited language and values had been hard to achieve. For many, it remained a lifelong compulsion. Luo Jialun, the Resolute, on the other hand, was part of a generation that was able to interpret and to reinterpret much of what Liang's generation felt compelled to defend and Qian's generation felt compelled to reject.

Free of the burden of both loyalty and treason to the Confucian tradition, the May Fourth generation went on to make, in the words of the historian philosopher Li Zehou, "the most significant contribution" to the development of modern Chinese history. In a recent overview of the six generations of modern Chinese intellectuals from the reformers of 1898 to the post-Cultural Revolution generation of the 1970s, Li has argued:

The third generation was the most creative and the most important generation.... This may be termed the *chuangzao moshi* generation: the pattern-making, model-building, paradigm-articulating generation.... They defined parameters of thought and action in a decisive, innovative fashion.... They were builders and believers who followed previous generations of doubters and destroyed and benefited from them.[27]

The debt of the builders' generation to the reformers and the destroyers who preceded them is great indeed. Without the painful transitions and uncertainties of Liang Qichao's and Qian Xuantong's generations, the May Fourth students might never have discovered their own vocation as political activists. Before they could go out into the streets to protest and hand out manifestos declaring their right to speak for the conscience of the nation, they had to learn to talk back more brazenly to those in power. Simply put, the May Fourth movement of 1919 would have been inconceivable without the emergence of a type of new intellectual in the first decade of the twentieth century. Only thinkers who were more autonomous in their social position and more independent-minded in their social outlook than the scholar-officials who had served the last dynasty could lay the foundations of a genuinely new culture in China.[28]

The spirit of autonomy, of *zijue*, which Luo Jialun celebrated in his 1919 article on the May Fourth movement, is the cumulative achievement of the first three generations of modern Chinese intellectuals. Far from belonging to the students only, it was passed down to them by those who had inaugurated the struggle for emancipation from the imperial bureaucratic state. The generation of 1919 was the last—and thus the decisive—generation to break the bonds that had tied generations of their predecessors to the hierarchy of emperor and minister. As sociologist Alvin Gouldner has suggested, the call for autonomy is a distinct historical event that marks a shift in the relationship between intellectuals and political authority. It signals their demand for more power over their own lives:

The emphasis on "autonomy" is not simply to be understood as a spiritual value important to intellectuals, or as desired because without it they are unable to work properly. Autonomy is not only a work requisite or an ethical aspiration, but it is also an expression of the social interest of the New Class (modern intellectuals) as a distinct group. The stress on autonomy is the ideology of a stratum that is still subordinated to other groups whose limits it is striving to remove.... This quest for autonomy expresses a *political* impulse toward self-management.[29]

In China, the key to the emergence of the new intellectuals was their liberation from the imperially sponsored examination system. That liberation began slowly and haltingly during the life of Liang Qichao. Born in 1873, Liang had been steeped in classical studies—a "normal childhood" that heralded nothing more than a promising career as a Confucian official. In fact, by the age of sixteen, this son of a farming family had become one of the youngest successful candidates for the *juren* degree in the provincial examination at Canton. Although he failed repeatedly to pass the examination for a metropolitan degree, Liang turned this bad luck into a message for his contemporaries. He began to write about China's problems with the full awarencess that he himself stood on the edge between the moribund Confucian literati and a new generation of cultural revolutionaries.

After he had met and apprenticed himself to the most famous Confucian reformer of his day, Kang Youwei, Liang Qichao embarked upon a lifelong quest for alternative ways of serving and saving his native land. That search included a strong interest in Western learning, encouraged by Kang and inspired further by Liang's reading of historical sources and his stay in Japan in the early 1900s. For a brief moment in 1898, he got close enough to the center of power to try to implement his vision of reform through the edicts of a sympathetic emperor. Then, disappointed by this unsuccessful involvement in institutional change, Liang forced himself to ask what was wrong with Chinese culture more generally and what was wrong with the Chinese mentality.

These questions set Liang Qichao apart from his literati predecessors and marked the beginning of the Chinese enlightenment movement. Such questions could not have been asked if intellectuals before Liang had not already become interested in Western learning and in what Western philosophy, not just Western technology, could do to change the Chinese world.[30] But earlier advocates of Western learning, most notably Wang Tao (1829–98) and Yan Fu (1854–1921), had championed their cause from outside the world of scholar-officials. Liang Qichao and his colleagues brought the challenge of Western learning into the heart of the Confucian bureaucracy. That challenge, in turn, set off ripples of innovation and doubt which eventually led to the abolition of the examination system in 1905. The abolition of the examination system, in turn, opened up new educational opportunities and new educational careers for the next generation of cultural radicals.

The rift between intellectuals and the state that had begun in the late nineteenth century developed into a decisive break during the life of Qian Xuantong. Born in 1887 into a renowned family of scholar-officials, Qian seemed even more suited for a bureaucratic career than Liang Qichao. Being born a decade later, however, meant that he was able to chart for himself a career even more independent of the government than Liang Qichao could imagine possible, or than was considered respectable for a Chinese intellectual. Although his own father was secretary of the Board of Rites, one of the most conservative agencies of the imperial

government, Qian was able to defy the ruling dynasty early and dramatically. In 1904, influenced by his reading of Liang's essays from the Ice
Drinker's Studio he cut off his queue in defiance against the Manchu
rulers. By 1906 he was in Japan, studying anarchism and Esperanto on
the one hand and joining in the revolutionary organization of Sun Yatsen on the other.

The search for educational experiences abroad became the hallmark
of the Qian Xuantong generation of cultural radicals.[31] They were at
once pushed out of China and pulled toward foreign countries. By the
turn of the twentieth century, the Chinese educational environment had
thwarted these intellectuals' political expectations. At the same time,
they were keenly aware of their lack of politically relevant knowledge.
They were also pulled abroad by the possibility of fulfilling themselves in
ways that were forbidden at home. Arranged marriages and the strictures of filial piety weighed heavily on them. Foreign study was thus a
search both for more effective means to save the nation and for new
identities that might be discovered more freely in a distant environment.

This generation, like that of Liang Qichao, was transitional, and
knew itself to be so. Its members felt themselves caught between new
and old China, and they wrote about the problem endlessly. Trying to
serve the cause of the future, they argued that

New and Old are absolutely incompatible; the words of the compromisers prove
that they don't understand either the New or the Old. They are the criminals of
the New World and the petty thieves of the Old. All problems of the present stem
from the fact that the banners of New and Old are unclear. The reason for this is
that definitions of New and Old are unclear.[32]

Unwilling to compromise, yet faced with a world in which choices
were unclear, the members of Qian Xuantong's generation became more
bitter than that of Liang Qichao. That bitterness was often turned
against themselves as they searched their individual and their collective
consciences for any trace of compromise with the Old. The aspect of
their lives that was most open to this scrutiny was their professional
careers. Not becoming an official was, in their eyes, the most concrete
sign of virtue. Contempt for bureaucratic careers, in turn, led most of
them to turn toward academic scholarship. Some became professionally
committed to literature; most prepared themselves to be full-time educators. These professional educators opened the way for and nurtured the
student generation of May Fourth.

Luo Jialun, born in 1896, was the son of a lower-rank scholar-official.
Unlike Qian Xuantong, who had to break with his eminent father in
order to become something other than an official, Luo was encouraged to

pursue a modern education. His father was a district magistrate—the lowest official position in the imperial bureaucracy—a man conservative by training but progressive by inclination. Witnessing the demise of the last dynasty, he decided that his son would be better prepared for the new world in a Western-style school, the Fudan Secondary School in Shanghai. Thus, long before he enrolled at Beijing University in 1917, Luo Jialun had the benefit of the modern schooling that earlier generations had searched for, often haphazardly, abroad. Like other prominent members of the generation of 1919, Luo Jialun went abroad only after the May Fourth movement. In the fall of 1920, he went to the United States to study history and philosophy at Princeton and Columbia universities. By that time, his own and his generation's identity and social mission were firmly established.

The students, thus, built on the foundation laid by the reformers and the doubters who preceded them. These builders bore upon their shoulders the hopes of those who had rebelled and failed before them. In 1919, when they took it upon themselves to awaken their countrymen, they were able to act swiftly and effectively precisely because they were re-enacting gestures made on a smaller scale by earlier generations. In the words of Erik Erikson, "they knew who they were and clung to that awareness" more confidently than their predecessors.[33]

The students' posture of confidence was based on the assumption that they had achieved something unprecedented. For a while it seemed as if the May Fourth youth had forgotten that the spirit of autonomy, which Luo Jialun claimed to be the attribute of his generation solely, had been something longed for and fought for by earlier generations. In fact, it was Liang Qichao who first introduced the ideal of autonomy to Chinese intellectuals. Through his writings on enlightenment thought in general and his admiration of the Japanese enlightenment more specifically, Liang gave the next two generations their first glimpse of what would become the May Fourth enlightenment movement.

JAPANESE ORIGINS OF THE CHINESE ENLIGHTENMENT MOVEMENT

Liang Qichao was twenty-two years old when China suffered its worst humiliation of the nineteenth century—the defeat of 1895. More than the series of losing battles with Western powers that began with the Opium War of 1840–42, the 1895 war with Japan brought home for Liang's generation the inadequacies of the traditional Chinese world-view. Some Confucian literati, especially the older reformers known as the *yangwu pai* (barbarian affairs experts), were already intensely aware of China's material backwardness. They had tried to save China by selective borrowing of Western technology. After the 1890s, however, their strategy appeared bankrupt in the eyes of younger patriots like Liang Qichao, who now began to grapple with the problem of China's cultural backwardness. By turning simultaneously to Western political theory and classical Chinese scholarship, these intellectuals hoped to salvage the true essence of Chinese culture. Their efforts and their failures constitute the prologue to the twentieth-century enlightenment movement.

The military defeat of 1895 had an added edge of shame for Confucian literati used to thinking of Japan as the "land of the Eastern dwarfs," a condescending allusion to Japan's extensive borrowing from China as far back as the Tang dynasty (618–907). Shame, however, became translated into an intense curiosity about Japan, especially about the Meiji Restoration of 1868. This event captured the imagination of intellectuals like Liang Qichao who became convinced that it held the key to Japan's ability to modernize more swiftly and more effectively than China. Their curiosity was not confined to the political event that had brought into power in Japan a reform-minded emperor and a fiercely patriotic samurai elite. This curiosity developed into an enduring fascination with the cultural phenomenon known as the Japanese enlightenment,[34] the intellectual thought movement which guaranteed reformers that institutional innovations in Japan would be matched by a new worldview among leaders and followers of the Meiji Restoration. Chinese intellectuals were so taken by this phenomenon, in fact, that they borrowed the word for enlightenment, *qimeng*, from the nineteenth-century Japanese intellectuals, who had called themselves "enlightenment scholars," *keimō gakusha*, which in Chinese is *qimeng xuezhe*.

In Japan the group that called itself "enlightenment scholars" was made up of a small, select number of ex-samurai who congregated around a new magazine, *Meiroku zasshi*, founded in 1874. It included men like Fukuzawa Yukichi, Katō Hiroyuki, and Nakamura Masanao, whose ideas Liang Qichao was to popularize in China after the failure of the reform movement of 1898.[35] Dedicated to deepening Japan's quest for modernity, these scholars argued that civilization (*bunmei*, in Chinese, *wenming*) was inseparable from intellectual awakening (*kaika*, in Chinese, *kaihua*). In the first article of the first issue of *Meiroku zasshi*, one of the editors, Nishi Amane, described the goals of the Japanese enlightenment in terms that came very close to describing the dilemmas of late Qing intellectuals:

My colleagues and I have often drawn comparisons with the various countries in Europe.... Envying their civilization and our own unenlightenment, we have suffered unbearable sorrow, having finally concluded that our people seem indeed to be incorrigibly ignorant.... The government's fine policies not withstanding, the people remain unenlightened as before..... [I]t is naturally the responsibility of those in authority in good time to guide the people tenderly by the hand from ignorance to the level of enlightenment, just as one gently removes all weeds without pulling up the seedling.[36]

For a brief interval, history was kind. It appeared as if the Japanese advocates of enlightenment would indeed be able to remove the weeds without pulling up the seedling. Through their essays and semi-public lectures, the *keimō gakusha* proceeded to raise many of the same issues that Chinese intellectuals grappled with later, including the problem of a vernacular language, the relationship between men and women, the shortcomings of national character, and the dangers of the traditional spirit of subservience.[37] The tone in which these issues were addressed during the Japanese enlightenment was, however, far more cautious than that of the later Chinese enlightenment. The *keimō gakusha* confronted a government unwilling to tolerate even guarded talk of representative politics. Reneging on its initially liberal policy toward freedom of the press, the Meiji government presented these high-level intellectuals with an impossible choice: "either lay down their brushes or revise their thoughts to conform to the government's dictates."[38] Unwilling to compromise their purpose, the enlightenment intellectuals ceased publication of their journal in February 1876, only two years after they had begun.

Although their publication was short-lived, the *keimō gakusha* bequeathed a thirst for enlightenment to subsequent generations of Japanese—and Chinese—intellectuals. In 1919, when enlightenment-oriented students at Beijing University were searching for a name for their journal, Luo Jialun suggested *Xinchao* (New Tide), a name taken from the Japanese enlightenment periodical *Shinchō*, which had been founded in 1904 to recover and to further the spirit of the nineteenth-century enlightenment scholars.[39]

The possibility for an enlightenment movement in nineteenth-century Japan, much as in eighteenth-century Europe and in twentieth-century China, was predicated upon the emergence of independent intellectuals. Autonomy, the goal of all three enlightenment movements, was defined in Japan as an obligation of intellectuals toward society. Unable to claim autonomy as a right, Fukuzawa Yukichi compellingly argued for the benefits that autonomy would bestow on all of the society in his famous

1874 essay, "The Duty of Scholars." This widely read and much debated work claimed that Japan would have no hope of advancing toward
genuine modernity unless it encouraged the development of "private
scholars." Especially critical of intellectuals who had a smattering of
Western learning and a vast longing for official position, Fukuzawa
argued:

> Japanese civilization will advance only after we sweep away the old spirit that
> permeates the minds of the people.... The scholars of Western learning must fill
> this role. But ... I have more than a few doubts about their actual behavior,
> because such scholars and gentlemen are aware of the existence of official posts
> but unaware of the existence of their private selves.... [T]heir minds are solely
> directed to the state, while remaining attached to their ingrained education.
> They think that they cannot accomplish anything except through govern-
> ment.... No one has the sincerity of mind to be independent.[40]

Fukuzawa's all-encompassing lament presages that of Liang Qichao,
who was caught in a similar predicament at the end of the nineteenth
century. Liang, too, tried unsuccessfully to foster independence of mind
among intellectuals bent upon obeying the dictates of officials higher up.
In September 1898, Liang became a "private scholar" by necessity. A
fugitive from law after the failure of the Hundred Days of Reform, he
remained on the empress dowager's "most wanted" list long after he fled
to Japan in secret. Cast away from the center of power that he and his
mentor Kang Youwei had enjoyed briefly, Liang began to contemplate
more deeply the spiritual lethargy of his countrymen. He, like Fukuzawa
Yukichi in Japan, identified lack of awareness as the source of China's
malady. In contrast to Fukuzawa, however, Liang diagnosed this sickness as having spread far beyond the intellectuals, who were traditional-
ly subservient to the state. Writing to Kang Youwei in 1900, Liang
argued that the Chinese people as a whole were diseased and enlightenment thought might be the sole last-minute remedy:

> Today we see a catastrophic culmination of the corruption and degeneration
> that have afflicted China in the past few thousand years. The prime source of this
> corruption and decay must be traced to the slavish character [of the Chinese
> people].... [W]hat is needed [is] to make people conscious of their character,
> and thus enable them to shake free from control by others. The illness [of slavish-
> ness] cannot possibly be cured without taking the medicine of liberty.[41]

Liang's prescription for China's problems, while echoing the concerns
of Fukuzawa Yukichi and inspired by European *philosophes* like Rousseau, set him apart from the spokesmen for both the Japanese and the
European enlightenments. In China, the goal of the enlightenment
movement became not only liberty for intellectuals but the transforma-

tion of national character. To achieve this goal, Liang Qichao, like the next two generations of doctors of the soul, began with the reform of Chinese fiction. The belief that changes in literary practice constitue the most direct challenge to the ethic of subservience became the underlying and distinctive motif of the Chinese enlightenment movement.

Unlike European or Japanese advocates of enlightenment, Chinese intellectuals had to cope repeatedly with the phenomenon of political failure. In China, cultural change evolved as a domain of special concern, more so than it had in either Europe or Japan. Thus it was not surprising that in 1902, while still in exile in Japan, Liang Qichao simultaneously launched two journals. One was called *Xinmin* (New People) and the other *Xin xiaoshuo* (New Fiction). The connection that Liang made between a new national character and a new fiction set the stage for the literary revolution to be enacted during the May Fourth movement:

To renovate the people of a nation, the fictional literature of that nation must first be renovated ... to renovate morality, we must renovate fiction, to renovate manners we must first renovate fiction ... to renew the people's hearts and minds and remold their character, we must first renovate fiction.[42]

In the end, Liang's efforts to remold hearts and minds through fiction failed. He did, however, leave the Chinese world of letters irrevocably altered by his own graceful style and his patient exposition of enlightenment thought. The one area in which he proved truly successful was his astute critique of Confucian reformers. Having been one of them himself before his exile in Japan, he knew their passions and prejudices intimately. He confronted them armed with a new notion, that truth was the product of open debate. He also held fiercely to the conviction that no point of view may be considered valid until it has been stripped of the biases of its exponent. Liang was thus particularly effective in unmasking the fallacies of nineteenth-century literati who had tried to preserve the essence of Chinese culture through the means of Western technology. Reluctant to accept any new ideas that did not coincide with Confucianism, they had raised Confucius above truth—Liang's highest value after his encounter with enlightenment thought. For himself, Liang confessed: "I love Confucius, but I love the truth more."[43]

The next generation did not love Confucius as Liang had. It went on to use truth against Confucianism more bitterly and more pointedly than he had imagined possible. Yet despite the gulf of feeling that separated Liang Qichao the Ice Drinker from Qian Xuantong's generation of doubters and destroyers, he was their intellectual progenitor. When they

launched their own enlightenment movement, they were drawing extensively on Liang's admiration for the Japanese enlightenment and on his
critique of the Chinese national character.

FAILURE OF REVOLUTION:
PROLOGUE TO ENLIGHTENMENT

The failure of the reform movement of 1898 had precipitated Liang
Qichao's assault on the slavish character of the Chinese people. The
failure of the 1911 revolution, in turn, awakened the next generation to
the ingrained habit of submissiveness even after submissiveness had
ceased to be a virtue enforced by the state. Whereas the young Liang
Qichao had invested all his hopes in institutional reform from above,
these iconoclastic doubters spent their youth tearing down institutions
from below. Like Liang, they rediscovered the importance of culture in
the aftermath of bungled politics.

In the years immediately following the failure of the 1911 revolution,
this generation became suspicious of patriotic politics—as we saw from
Chen Duxiu's warnings of June 8, 1919. Their early, intense involvement
with the national salvation movement of the first decade of the twentieth
century set Chen's generation apart from the next generation of student
activists, who had been spared the disillusionment of 1911 and were thus
able to endow patriotism with a new meaning in their demonstration on
May 4, 1919.

Soon after the revolution of 1911, the teachers-to-be of the May
Fourth generation began to realize that the republic they had longed
for and fought for had been stillborn. The ideal of a genuine *minguo*—
a people's nation—receded further and further as leaders and followers
alike proved to be not only ignorant but contemptuous of *minzhu* (democracy). The mentors of the May Fourth youth stood helplessly by as the
vast majority of the Chinese people continued to submit themselves to
Confucian rituals as if a revolution had never taken place. In 1912, the
new president of the Chinese republic, Yuan Shikai, founded the so-called
Confucian Religion Society to promote the values of filial piety that
he deemed necessary for loyal citizenship. The next year, he crushed an
attempted "second revolution" by assassinating its democratically
minded leader. In 1914, the national worship of Confucius was re-
instated by law because Yuan believed "the masses of people were unenlightened and the revival of old ceremonies was a practical measure to
check the moral decline since the revolution."[44]

In early 1915, the president himself conducted the imperial rites of worshiping Confucius and ordered the reintroduction of Confucian classics into primary schools. By December 1915, after a carefully orchestrated campaign, Yuan Shikai agreed "reluctantly" to become emperor. He planned to found the "Glorious Constitution Dynasty." His dreams of becoming emperor were ended by gentry opposition and by his own death in 1916.

Less than a year later, the military governor of Anhui province, Zhang Xun, tried to restore the Manchu emperor, Pu Yi, by marching into Beijing with twenty thousand long-queued soldiers. Chased out by northern warlords, Zhang was the last politician until the 1930s to scheme for monarchical restoration. Future iconoclasts like Chen Duxiu, Qian Xuantong, and Lu Xun, who had been witnesses to these events, were so traumatized by them that they resolved to expose all unenlightened tendencies among their countrymen. In the wake of the failure of republican politics, they dedicated themselves to tearing up submissiveness by its cultural roots.

This dedication led them to sever their ties with the reformers and the revolutionaries who had preceded them. It left these iconoclastic doubters more alone and more lonely than even their most idiosyncratic predecessors had been in their time. Before 1911, these intellectuals had been close to older leaders of the nationalist revolution, especially to Zhang Taiyan (1864–1936), founder of the influential Patriotic Study Society. Following Zhang's example they had hoped to transform politics in light of the pure essence of classical Chinese culture. After 1911, they grew disillusioned with essences altogether.

Zhang Taiyan had fired their imagination, at first, through a notorious act of defiance against the "foreign" Manchu rulers. He had cut off his queue at a public meeting in 1900. Two years later, in Japan, he became involved with Sun Yatsen and emerged as one of the most articulate spokesmen for nationalist revolution. Although there were many other heroic activists in the decade leading up to 1911, few could match Zhang's ability to articulate the ethical imperatives of revolution. In 1906, at the end of a three-year imprisonment for his role in editing an anti-Manchu newspaper, Zhang published his manifesto, *The Morality of Revolution*. Through this essay he reached out to those long held to be unimportant and even immoral by scholar-officials: peasants, workers, peddlers, and physicians. He was, in effect, ringing the death-knell of the old bureaucratic theory and practice of politics.[45]

Zhang Taiyan was much more than a skilled propagandist for the anti-Manchu cause, however. He also helped to broaden the context of the anti-Confucian thought movement of the next generation. By drawing upon Buddhist philosophy, especially the Vijnanamatra School, he sanctioned rebellion against the Confucian malady of craving riches and honor, wealth and rank. Buddhism enabled Zhang himself to approach philosophy from a new perspective. But through Buddhism he also raised questions about epistemology, the nature of consciousness, and the nature of ideological deceit. These questions would later become quite explosive in the hands of May Fourth intellectuals. Their usage of the term *qimeng* (enlightenment) retained Buddhist connotations, even as they went on to take part in a social and cultural revolution that Zhang Taiyan found unfathomable. Enlightenment, in their writings, developed beyond the meaning it had had for Zhang—a cognitive goal—and became an act of will through which an individual's awakening would transform all of society.[46]

Finally, Zhang Taiyan was an important model for the critical scholarship of later iconoclastic intellectuals. Through his meticulous approach to problems of verification in historical texts, he opened the way for the next generation's broader assault on the ideological assumptions of tradition. Zhang himself had tried to preserve the purity of "national essence" (*guocui*) in his philological investigations of ancient forgeries. His followers debunked the idea of national essence with the very tools given them by their mentor. Later iconoclastic intellectuals like Qian Xuantong were aware of their indebtedness to Zhang even as they promoted doubt rather than faith in antiquity. They also paid homage to him as a disinterested scholar—an autonomous intellectual finally emancipated from the subservience and utilitarianism that had characterized the life and work of earlier scholar-officials.[47]

Members of the first generation of modern Chinese intellectuals, Liang Qichao and Zhang Taiyan led the way to the threshold of enlightenment. They were, however, unable and unwilling to cross it into the strange, lonely, doubt-filled world beyond. In the aftermath of the Republican Revolution of 1911, they parted ways with the next generation of iconoclasts. Precursors of the May Fourth enlightenment, in spite of the political differences among them, had all been motivated by a single-minded commitment to *jiuguo*, national salvation. Their intellectual and emotional energies had been focused on making China strong, and enabling it to survive foreign aggression. The iconoclasts, less concerned with China's political weakness, went on to probe the indigenous sources of their nation's spiritual and intellectual backwardness.

One of those who turned away from the politics of national salvation most dramatically was Chen Duxiu—the participant-critic of the stu-

dent movement in 1919. As a young man in Japan in the 1900s, Chen
had been deeply influenced by the ideals of Zhang Taiyan and his
Patriotic Study Association. Chen, also, cut off his queue with revolutionary flair. He then organized a volunteer student army, and returned
to his native province of Anhui to start a youth corps modeled on the
Patriotic Study Association. In the years before 1911, Chen, like other
young men of gentry background, had been consumed with the problem
of national salvation. He wrote bitter articles about the lack of patriotism
in China and the importance of foreign technology, about the importance of studying military science and mining technology.[48] The republican revolution, appropriately enough, found him as a teacher at the
Zhejiang Infantry School, and distributing revolutionary propaganda
to a newly formed student army.

Five years later, in the midst of Yuan Shikai's restoration attempt,
Chen confessed his total disillusionment with the politics of national
salvation. In an article entitled "My Own Final Awakening," Chen
abjured his past interest in "political awakening," the term he now
used, almost contemptuously, for political revolution. Turning away
from "superficial politics," he declared himself committed to a more
fundamental issue: ethical emancipation. "Ethical awakening," he
claimed, is "the most thorough awakening, it is my own deepest, truly
final awakening."[49] With a touch of self-mockery, this otherwise somber
man urged his fellow countrymen to undertake this "finally final
awakening." To spur them on, he decided to renounce in public the
many causes that had seduced his generation, especially the politics of
patriotism, which they had embraced only to discover how unworthy of
devotion the new republic really was. Reflecting on Yuan Shikai's efforts
to enthrone himself as emperor, Chen Duxiu asked his fellow revolutionaries to realize how quickly political reaction could, and did, clothe
itself in the mantle of republicanism. "In the guise of republican politics,"
he concluded, "we are now subjected to the sufferings of autocracy."[50]

It was in the context of post-revolutionary China, then, that the problem of enlightenment arose most sharply in the minds of Chen Duxiu's
generation. As the promise of parliamentary government eroded year by
year under the pressure of monarchical schemes, the issue of democracy,
or more precisely, of a democratic outlook, came to dominate the concern
of some of the young men earlier consumed by anti-Manchu patriotism.
It was they who now wrote tirelessly about the need for autonomy, for
zijue, literally self-consciousness.

To have *zijue*, to be *zijue* was to act in terms similar to what Kant toward the end of the eighteenth-century European enlightenment had defined as autonomy: "the courage to be guided by one's own understanding."[51] In twentieth-century China, it was easier to muster one's own courage than to achieve one's own understanding. Unable to draw upon the Protestant culture that had nurtured Kant's vision, Chinese intellectuals inherited instead a tradition that made individualism not merely sinful, but nearly inconceivable. Many had been drawn to the cause of national salvation precisely because it utilized anti-individualistic traditions to accomplish new ends. Old loyalties had been easily transferred to new institutions like the modern nation-state. The case for autonomy in twentieth-century China thus had to be argued again and again against remorseless pressures to subsume the self in a nationalist fervor.

Chen Duxiu was the first to make the argument for autonomy, in the 1915 article "Patriotism and Autonomy." In response to the manifest failure of parliamentary institutions, Chen argued that "patriotism," the cardinal virtue of the *jiuguo* cause, was nothing but blind loyalty to the state. His anguished presupposition was that China had not been able to become a nation at all, precisely because it lacked a consciousness of the importance of autonomy. In Chen's view, what China urgently needed, instead of emotionally ardent patriots, were people who were capable of thinking clearly about specific problems. This essay was a warning addressed to Chen's fellow intellectuals against sinking into the quagmire of contemporary politics. It was also a call to acquire socially useful knowledge. In his conclusion, Chen pleaded with his fellow intellectuals to withdraw from political life and devote themselves to educational activities and moral reform.[52]

A year later, in 1916, educational work would become synonymous with moral reform at the newly invigorated National Beijing University. It was at this unique institution that the two generations of students and teachers met each other, and it was here, too, that they laid the foundation for an unprecedented cultural renaissance. Three years before the Beida delegation assumed the lead in the May Fourth demonstration, the seeds had been sown for a new relationship of intellectuals to society. Once one generation had become more daring, more independent in the uses of its own knowledge, the next generation was able to carry both the daring and the knowledge onto the streets of Beijing. There, the intellectuals' hopes for a new culture developed into a widespread enlightenment movement, whose scope and pace Chen Duxiu could not have imagined possible when he wrote his confessional essay on his own final, personal awakening.

3.   Aerial view of Beijing University, 1915.

BEIJING UNIVERSITY BEFORE 1916: SEEDS
OF AN INTELLECTUAL AWAKENING

The educational institution that was to attract and protect the May Fourth generation had had a complex history long before their arrival. For the previous two decades, it had been the battleground between advocates of Chinese and Western learning, and between loyalists to the examination system and pioneers of modern education. From the university's inception, the forces of the new had the leading edge. Confucian scholars, who had been just as radical in their day as teachers and students of May Fourth would be in theirs, had cleared the way for a series of extraordinarily imperial edicts in the summer of 1898. During the short-lived Hundred Days of Reform, they persuaded the Guang Xu Emperor to authorize funds for the establishment of the Imperial University, or *Jingshi Daxue*, as it was called at that time. The decree of 1898 had been couched in the cautious language of radicals who sensed themselves ahead of their time. Behind that caution, however, lay their unyielding determination to create a new institution to train men of talent to assimilate the knowledge of East and West. The goal of this educational reform was to foster among Confucian scholars the old but forgotten spirit of "searching truth from practical life."[53]

The imperial decrees of June and July, 1898, culminated a prolonged effort by reformers like Kang Youwei and Liang Qichao to persuade the

4.   One of the main entrances to Beijing University, 1915.

emperor that only men of talent could and would save China from her imminent annihiliation. On the face of it, there was nothing new or unorthodox about their suggestion that the nurturing of human talent would be the decisive undertaking in China's struggle for political survival and cultural renewal. This was, after all, a long-standing Confucian article of faith, imbedded in the pedagogical theory that sustained the examination system itself. What made Kang and Liang's advocacy novel, however, was its call for the creation of a new kind of an educational institution. Instead of the existing system of *shuyuan*, traditional local academies, where candidates for the examination system learned to memorize the classics, Kang and Liang envisioned a new network of professionally managed *xuetang*, where students would be required to study foreign languages and modern sciences along with the more traditional subjects.[54]

With the meaning of "talent" thus redefined to connote expertise in Western learning, "men of talent" became potential enemies of the vested interests of the traditional bureaucratic state. It is surprising, in this context, that when the empress dowager crushed the reform movement in September 1898, she annulled all of the reform edicts save the one that provided funds for the establishment of the Imperial University. To be sure, she tried to minimize its novelty by appointing as its first superintendent the well-known conservative scholar Sun Jianai. But still, a new vision of learning—an approach which bore the imprint of the modern, Western education—had become institutionalized in the Chinese world of letters.

Under Sun Jianai, a foreign expert was appointed to take charge of the Western faculty. He was W. A. P. Martin, an American Presbyterian missionary who had served as the head of the Tongwenguan. Established in 1862, the Tongwenguan had been a language school meant to prepare officials who were expected to handle foreign affairs in a manner more in keeping with foreign law and foreign diplomatic practice. Martin thus brought to the newly established Imperial University his long experience in translating Western textbooks and in devising a modern curriculum that suited the needs and interests of Chinese officials.[55] Jointly, Sun Jianai and W. A. P. Martin developed a program of study that included the study of foreign languages such as English, French, Russian, German, and Japanese as well as selected courses in applied mathematics and astronomy. Although the new aspects of the curriculum were quite limited in comparison to the old, they did provide an opportunity for the exploration of foreign ideas previously deemed extraneous to genuine Confucian studies.

Most of the students enrolled at the Imperial University before 1912 were, however, not interested in such opportunities. They, and their teachers, still had the mental orientation of office-seekers. Required by law to be holders of a *juren* degree upon their entrance to the university, they were first and foremost concerned with advancing themselves in the imperial bureaucratic system. Taking time off from school to study for and take the imperial examinations was just one sign of their old-fashioned priorities. While in school, they continued to behave as officials-in-waiting: gambling, whoring, and, in general, expecting society to reward them for the mere fact of being students of the Imperial University.[56]

The first thorough challenge to the old-fashioned ways of doing things at the Imperial University came less than half a year after the October revolution of 1911. In February 1912, the noted translator and promoter of Western learning Yan Fu (1854–1921) was appointed its superintendent by newly elected president Yuan Shikai. During his brief tenure, from February through November, 1912, Yan Fu tried to transform this Qing remnant into a genuinely modern educational institution. He spoke for the interests and values of professional educators and insisted that competence in foreign languages and contemporary sciences was the hallmark of a genuine university graduate.

For two decades before his appointment to the Imperial University,

Yan Fu had been introducing to his contemporaries the works of Herbert Spencer, Adam Smith, John Stuart Mill, and Montesquieu. Before him, Western ideas had been introduced to China primarily by Westerners, and often for some ulterior reason, such as Christian proselytizing. Yan Fu, on the other hand, was one of the first Chinese intellectuals to read the literature of Western political economy in English and to select from it what would serve the interests of his own culture. Educated in England at the Greenwich Naval College, he had returned to China in 1879 to begin a career in which he was often frustrated in office-seeking, but successful in promoting his own new-found worldview: Social Darwinism.[57] Like so many of the reform-minded literati of his generation, Yan had been seeking the sources of the prowess of the West. He declared that he had found them in the newly emerging doctrine of competition and survival of the fittest. Although he went on to translate a range of political and social literature whose implications were far broader than the ideas of Social Darwinism, all of Yan Fu's later work bore the imprint of his concern for China's survival as a nation in a world of rapacious nation-states. Yan Fu valued the wealth and power of the state above individual liberty and autonomy.[58]

Later advocates of enlightenment were to reverse Yan Fu's priorities. In their view, a willingness to compromise individual autonomy for the sake of state power had characterized literati for centuries—and this habit of subservience would have to be overcome from within. And yet, even as they themselves tried to become new, independent-minded scholars, the May Fourth intellectuals drew upon the work of Yan Fu. His translations of Mill's *Logic* and Jevons's *Logic*, especially, were key weapons in the May Fourth attack on the intuitive, unscientific reasoning characteristic of traditional Chinese philosophy, as we shall see later. When May Fourth students discovered that they needed a notion of systematic reasoning before they could undertake a systematic criticism of tradition, they turned to Yan Fu with an eagerness that surprised the aged translator. Yan Fu had meant only to augment Chinese ways of thinking. By 1919, however, he had become an unwitting ally of those who wanted to change them altogether.[59]

In February 1912, when he was appointed head of the Imperial University, Yan was already a tired and despondent man. Not quite sixty years old, he had been used, and almost wrung out, by a procession of warlords who asked him, alternatively, to examine students returning from abroad, to compile dictionaries of technical terms, to advise them on how to draw up regulations for a constitutional government. The events of 1911 had found him reservedly optimistic about this revolution. His optimism, however, was to wear thin as his own career became entangled with the aspirations of Yuan Shikai. In the years betwen 1912 and 1916, in fact, he emerged as one of the chief supporters of Yuan's restoration attempts. But even as he moved toward political conservatism, Yan Fu remained a radical in educational thought. During the eight months he was in charge of Beijing University, he made his first and last attempt to change the institutional structure of Chinese education. Although he left a disappointed man, the institution he had tried to change was, in fact, irrevocably altered by his presence and his vision.

At first, Yan Fu contented himself with revitalizing the foreign languages aspect of the curriculum at the Imperial University. He hired more foreign teachers and insisted that students attend lectures and hold meetings using foreign languages, especially English. For a while, in the eyes of conservatives, the Imperial University seemed to be turning into a sanctuary for "the blind worship of Western civilization."[60] Then, in May 1912, it became apparent that Yan Fu's challenge to the ethos of the Imperial University was to be more profound. In a letter to the Ministry of Education he asked to change the name of the institution to *Beijing Daxue*, Beijing University. It would, in his view, make more explicit that his was a modern institution of higher learning rather than a haven for old-fashioned office-seekers in the new republican era.[61]

While promoting the cause of professional, modern education, Yan Fu also became embroiled in a fight over faculty salaries. Arguing against a suggestion that salaries should not exceed sixty *yuan* a month, Yan pointed out the unfortunate treatment of university professors in comparison to other officials of the Chinese government. Why, he asked, should teachers be different from well-paid, secure, and largely idle bureaucrats in various government offices?

The teachers who work at our school at the present are treated like temporary, expendable employees. There is no way to measure their talents and no hope that they can be promoted and rewarded according to their accomplishment. Officials in the central and local governments, by contrast, are paid according to their administrative rank regardless of the amount of work they do or whether it is satisfactory work or not.... Recruiting high quality teachers in our current circumstances is becoming more and more difficult. Should the new policy [of limiting salaries be passed] many teachers will ask to leave. The school, in effect, will be shut down.... Thus, the only reasonable thing to do is pay faculty full-time, in keeping with their full-time work. I myself, as president of the university, am willing to accept a 60 *yuan* salary as a sign of my willingness to obey the dictates of the government.[62]

The response to Yan Fu's complaints was a further threat to shut down the university. Although he won the tactical battle, Yan Fu lost the strategic war. The Imperial University was renamed Beijing University, and he had the honor, briefly, of using for the first time, the title University President (*xiao zhang*). But by November 1912, Yan's opponents in the Education and the Finance ministries had won the upper hand, partly by spreading rumors. They used rumors about his opium addiction (a habit that he never denied) to secure his dismissal from the university. Before he left, however, Yan Fu wrote a final plea to those who treated modern higher education as an expendable nuisance. Arguing against those who had suggested that Beida be closed down once and for all because of its poor management, he wrote:

Beijing University was founded more than ten years ago. To close it now would be to throw away the efforts of a whole nation made over these years, as well as to waste the millions of *yuan* invested in it.... In today's world, every civilized country has many universities ranging in number from tens to many hundreds. If we cannot preserve even one, especially one already in existence, it is unfortunate indeed.... Our nation now has countless enterprises in need of countless funds. The financial need of one university is but a drop in the sea.... To be sure, Beijing University is not yet as good as the best universities in the United States or Europe.... But its quality can be improved day by day. But if we don't do anything, it will never be improved.... As far as poor management is concerned, as long as the school is not closed down the hope of improvement remains.[63]

As this letter suggests, Yan Fu was a moderate in thought and speech. Moderation, however, was not a quality of vision appreciated in his day. The conservatives whose voices were stronger than his own both in the government and at Beijing University won the first round of the battle over educational reform, but not before the seeds of radical change had been planted at Beida.

In the spring of 1912, while Yan Fu was pleading with the Education and the Finance ministries not to decrease faculty salaries and not to shut down the university for poor management, a new group of teachers began arriving at Beida. Disciples of Zhang Taiyan, they launched a direct assault on the power and prestige of a faction known as the "Dongcheng School." The Dongcheng faction was comprised of ardent advocates of old literature in the School of Letters. They were led by Lin Shu, a well-known translator of Western fiction who, in contrast to Yan Fu, lacked both first-hand knowledge of Western languages and an intellectual openness to Western culture. The reign of Lin

Shu's faction, which had been almost totally secure during the first decade of the twentieth century, began to loosen as a new group of Chinese educators with foreign training began to congregate at Yan Fu's Beida.

Among those who arrived at this time was Shen Yinmo (1887–1964), a linguist and calligrapher who later became active in the May Fourth Enlightenment movement. A graduate of Kyoto University, Shen was one of the first modern, professional educators on the Beida staff. In 1914, two years after Shen's arrival, a friend from his studies in Japan, Qian Xuantong, was also hired. In 1916, Shen Yinmo and Qian Xuantong jointly recommended the hiring of their co-revolutionist from Japan, Chen Duxiu.[64] After Chen Duxiu was hired as Dean of Humanities, the door was further opened to the core group of professional educators who would become the mentors of the May Fourth generation. In early 1917, Chen himself suggested that Hu Shi—another professionally trained scholar, who had just completed his Ph.D. under John Dewey at Columbia—join the Beida faculty. At the end of that year, he also insisted on the need for a full-time, knowledgeable librarian. Li Dazhao, who a few years later would join Chen in founding the Chinese Communist Party, was hired for the post.

This network of faculty sponsorship and support, which began during Yan Fu's brief tenure as president of Beijing University, continued and developed under the leadership of Cai Yuanpei, the visionary educator who took over the presidency of Beida at the end of 1916. Working together, independent-minded teachers and tolerant administrators were able to create the unique intellectual climate that came to be known as the "*Beida xuefeng*." Meaning literally the "Beida winds of learning," this term began to gain currency in the wake of the May Fourth movement. It was only when the rest of Chinese society woke up to the fact that a new, rebellious spirit was brewing at the old Imperial University that the architects of enlightenment became fully cognizant of what they had done. In 1923, on the occasion of the twenty-fifth anniversary of the founding of Beida, Zhu Wushan, a student who had participated in the May Fourth movement and the founding of the Chinese Communist Party, summed up the *Beida xuefeng* as the "spirit of daring to do."[65] This was at once an elaboration of the vaguer ideal of "daring to know" that had motivated older advocates of enlightenment, and a departure from it. It also summarized what had been achieved at Beijing University over the years, in spite of what might have seemed the failure of reformers like Yan Fu.

5. Cai Yuanpei, official photograph taken in 1917, during his first year as president of Beijing University.

BEIDA UNDER THE LEADERSHIP OF CAI YUANPEI: 1917–1919

On December 26, 1916, Cai Yuanpei (1876–1940), one of the most widely admired educators of the early republican period, accepted appointment as president of Beijing University. With Yuan Shikai recently deceased, Li Yuanhong, his successor as president of the republic, decided to court some of the famous intellectuals who had previously been regarded with suspicion or held in disrepute. Initially, Li offered Cai Yuanpei the governorship of Zhejiang province, only to be turned down by telegram from France, where Cai was busy promoting education for Chinese workers and work-study programs for Chinese students.[66] When an offer to take over the national university in Beijing came, however, Cai Yuanpei found his passion for educational reform too strong to resist. Having glimpsed the possibilities of thought revolution through educational change during his work at the Patriotic Academy (*Aiguo Xueshe*, founded in 1901) and during his brief tenure as minister of Education in Sun Yatsen's cabinet in 1911, Cai was eager for another chance to promote his vision. Furthermore, after prolonged study in Germany (first from 1907 to 1911 in Leipzig and then from 1912 to 1913 in Berlin) he felt himself equipped with the practical knowledge of what a genuinely modern institution of higher learning should be like.[67] His confidence and optimism were nearly boundless when, on the eve of the May Fourth movement, he asserted: "After twenty years our university is finally like Berlin University."[68]

For his admirers and detractors alike, Cai Yuanpei seemed to be the most visible source of inspiration of the New Culture movement at Beida though few in China knew or cared as much as he about the world of Berlin University. All that was both good and bad about Beida on the eve of the May Fourth movement was credited to or blamed on Cai Yuanpei. A most striking example of this tendency to make Cai the exclusive focus of the story of the new Beida may be seen in a retrospective appraisal by Jiang Menglin, the man who took over the presidency of Beijing University during the May Fourth movement itself (when Cai Yuanpei resigned for a brief interval):

If you throw a stone into a body of still water, rings of waves begin to rise and travel further and further, ever widening and extending away from the center. In Peking, capital of China throughout five dynasties and more than ten centuries, ... the brief tide of the reform [of 1898] had ebbed and vanished into history; only a few shells remained witnesses to the vicissitudes of fortune in that placid ancient capital. But the university, in which were clustered the living shells that contained pearls, was destined to make a valuable contribution to culture and thought within the short span of one generation. The man who threw the stone of intellectual revolt into that placid water was Dr. Tsai Yuan-pei, who in 1916 became chancellor of the university.[69]

Those who would condense the history of Beijing University to the era of Cai Yuanpei tend to forget that many of the reforms he institutionalized had in fact, been championed by earlier presidents of Beida, most notably Yan Fu. But Cai succeeded dramatically and publicly while Yan Fu failed—and failed miserably—accused of personal frailties such as opium addiction. As a result, it was Cai who became the emblem of academic freedom, the guiding philosophy of professional higher education in China for generations to come. To this day, whenever Chinese educators want to argue for a more tolerant policy toward intellectuals and toward the knowledge they represent, they appeal to the name and the aura of Cai Yuanpei.[70]

In 1916, however, the "waters" of the Chinese intellectual world were by no means as placid as Jiang Menglin had claimed. Nor were teachers such as Shen Yinmo and Qian Xuantong, already at Beida, mere "living shells." In fact, many of the reforms that Cai Yuanpei implemented had been designed and recommended by these teachers before his arrival in 1916. They, too, like Yan Fu, had tried to place the institution in the hands of professional, modern-minded educators who would have some measure of institutional autonomy from the warlord government. Financial guarantees for the university, a greater role for faculty participation in university affairs, and a regular program to send students and faculty abroad were all elements of a plan developed before 1916 and implemented after 1917.[71]

Rather than the man who cast a stone into placid waters, Cai Yuanpei was the stone itself, which changed the pattern and the range of waves radiating outward from Beida. He had a catalytic effect upon the mood of learning. Before his arrival, the Beida faculty had been horrified, it seems, when Shen Yinmo lent reference books to students. Teachers had always seen themselves as guardians of the secrets of learning; books were their private key to power. For teachers like Shen, therefore, one of the memorable changes of the Cai Yuanpei administration was something as simple as sharing books with students. The students, on the other hand, were not greatly impressed by the faculty's willingness to lend books. Beneficiaries of their teachers' reforms, they wanted more. They wanted not only to borrow and use books—they wanted new books. Feng Youlan, one of the students who experienced the transition from the pre– to the post–Cai Yuanpei Beida, recalled how the "boring" and "feudal" books circulated at Beida before 1916 remained in use for a long time thereafter.[72]

Be that as it may, Cai Yuanpei's presidency transformed Beida in deeper, more enduring ways than that of any other educator before or since. He brought to Beida a vision of the *purpose* of education that overcame the deep despair among intellectuals disillusioned by the failure of the revolution of 1911. At a time when the public domain was filled with Confucian gentry willing to adjust their principles to the practical needs of the ruling warlords, Cai put forward the call for learning that would serve educational needs alone. He argued that education should benefit the quest for learning first and foremost. Into an institutional setting structured so that the only answer to the question "What is education for?" would be "Politics," Cai injected a note of idealism close to naiveté. His answer was "education for a worldview" (*shijieguan jiaoyu*). Taking up the quest for a more resilient, more enduring worldview that had preoccupied Chinese intellectuals since Liang Qichao, Cai suggested something new: esthetics as a cure for the superstitious, slavish mentality of old China.

Education for a world view is not something to chatter about every day. Moreover, its relation to the phenomenal world cannot be described in dry, simple words. Then, in what way we attain it? The answer is through esthetic education (or education for artistic appreciation, *mei-kan chih chiao-yü*). *Mei-kan* is a conception combining beauty and solemnity and is a bridge between the phenomenal world and the world of reality. This concept was originated by Kant.... When you feel related to actual phenomena neither by craving nor loathing but are purely absorbed in artistic appreciation, then you will become a friend of the Creator and will be close to the conception of the world of reality. Therefore if an educator wishes to lead people from the phenomenal world to the conception of the world of reality, he must adopt esthetic education.[73]

The Beida students who took to the streets on May 4, 1919, and the teachers who remained their enthusiastic but critical supporters had, obviously, taken the quest for a new worldview far more literally than Cai Yuanpei had intended. Not content with a contemplative appreciation of reality, they sought to change the views and the attitudes of their countrymen more directly. Still, even as they acted with the kind of forceful intention that was antithetical to Cai's vision of esthetics, even though they "chattered" about the problem of "world view" endlessly in periodicals like *New Youth* and *New Tide*, they were deeply indebted to Cai Yuanpei's vision of education. He had been, after all, the first among them to dismantle the institutional structure that had tied generations of their predecessors to the old worldview. It was Cai's own rejection of "practical education"—education meant to prepare students to maneuver for positions as bureaucratic officials—that opened the way for the new social activism of the May Fourth generation.

A year and a half after his arrival at Beida, after he had restructured the curriculum and departmental organization in keeping with his vision of a Berlin-like national university, Cai Yuanpei turned his attention to the non-academic component of student and faculty life. It was then that he discovered to his dismay how deeply entrenched the old bureaucratic mentality still was among these members of a supposedly modern intellectual community. To counter their spiritual slothfulness, Cai organized the Society for the Promotion of Virtue (*Jinde hui*). Founded in June 1918, this organization required its members to conform to "eight abstentions" (*ba bu*—a word play on *ba gu*, the eight-legged examination system it was meant to replace). Among these eight abstentions, there was a distinct hierarchy: First and foremost, members of the society were expected to abstain from visiting brothels, gambling, and taking concubines. Next, they were to pledge themselves to reject any position in the government bureaucracy and to refuse to run for parliament. Finally, those members who were able to thus prove themselves publicly virtuous were also expected to train themselves to give up smoking, drinking, and eating meat.[74]

6. Li Dazhao, *New Youth* editor and chief
librarian of Beijing University.

Cai Yuanpei's intention in founding the Society for the Promotion of
Virtue was to supplement the learners' academic skills with a moral
perspective of life. This was, in effect, a return to one of the oldest, most
venerated Confucian principles. Formulated first in a text known as
"The Great Learning," it stated that all social reform must begin with
the "clarification of one's own virtue" (*daxue zhi dao zai ming, ming de*).[75]
That Cai himself would recall this old Confucian principle in his battle
with corrupt "practical education" was quite understandable. He was,
after all, not just a modern educator but also one of the foremost Confucian literati of his age. After having passed the highest degree, that of
jinshi, in 1892, he had been a fervent reformer-critic of the examination
system for more than two decades before his arrival at Beida.

The students and faculty who joined his Society for the Promotion of
Virtue, on the other hand, had had quite a different philosophical background and quite disparate expectations about how to shape their social
and political futures. Among the seventy teachers and some three hundred students who joined Cai's organization were to be found some of
the key figures of the May Fourth movement. Li Dazhao, the new librarian, led the roll of *New Youth* members in the society, while Luo Jialun,
Fu Sinian, Kang Baiqing, Zhang Shenfu, and Pan Jiaxun represented
the *New Tide* members who joined the group.[76]

How, we might ask, did the old Confucian notion of "promotion of

7. Chen Duxiu, *New Youth* founder and dean of humanities.

virtue" accord with the iconoclastic goals of these May Fourth intellectuals? Part of the explanation for this seeming contradiction may be found in the new intellectuals' image of themselves as independent, critical scholars, thoroughly emancipated from the pressures and temptations of their office-seeking predecessors. To join Cai's organization was, in effect, to confirm for themselves, and for society around them, that they were free from political ambitions. Membership in the society also enabled them to gain experience in organizational life without becoming tainted by the "practical politics" of the warlord regimes. Armed with the righteousness and the skills that Cai's society provided, the younger generation was able to go out into the streets on May 4, 1919, and redefine the meaning of politics in a way that Cai Yuanpei could not have earlier imagined possible or desirable.

Abstention from old-fashioned politics and sensual indulgence was not the only principle that Cai Yuanpei bequeathed to the May Fourth generation. He also provided it with a concrete appreciation of academic freedom that would be useful in the exploration of issues that ranged far beyond the intellectual life of the university. The source of Cai's own commitment to academic freedom may be found in the hiring policy developed shortly after his arrival at Beida. "Moral gentlemen"—even if they frequented prostitutes somewhat less often, and even if they studied the classics for the sake of the classics—still fell short of Cai's goal of

8. Hu Shi, *New Youth* editor and chairman of the English department.

hiring educators for a new worldview. Their own knowledge was insufficient to endow students with a persuasive perspective on moral issues. When Cai came face to face with the inherent limitations of the Confucian "amateur ideal" he began to hire professionals like Chen Duxiu and Hu Shi.

To justify to himself and to conservative elements within the university why such "professionalism" in academic life was not inimical to Confucian scholarship, Cai developed the formula *jianrong bingbao*: broadminded and encompassing tolerance of diverse points of view. In the name of Confucian tolerance Cai began to promote academic freedom. The intellectual liberties he safeguarded through the *jianrong bingbao* formula were (and remain today) unprecedented in Chinese education. It was the formula, for example, that Cai used to justify financial support for *New Youth* magazine, which Chen Duxiu brought with him from Shanghai to Beida. After all, Cai reasoned, the journal represented the "private" nonacademic occupation of the would-be dean of Humanities.[77]

"Private" soon enough developed into "purely scholarly"—Cai's own elaboration of the protective doctrine of *jianrong bingbao*. As faculty and students began to use their journals to promote rebellion against conventional learning and conventional social mores, the president of the university justified their actions by claiming that they were engaged

in "pure research." Thus, the vague Confucian ideal of tolerance became a cover for the anti-Confucian thought and activities of the May
Fourth generation. Protected by Cai Yuanpei, the New Culture movement developed more rapidly and spilled out of Beida more dramatically
than it might have otherwise.   *Beida → Outside World*

Cai himself, all through the spring of 1919, refused to believe that
anything more than critical scholarship was going on at Beida. He was,
therefore, somewhat taken aback by a March 26 letter from Fu Zengxiang, minister of education, asking him to curb the activities and
influence of the *New Tide* Society and its magazine. Fu saw the social
danger inherent in the *jianrong bingbao* principle more clearly than Cai
himself. He warned the president that in the guise of academic freedom, a group of young intellectuals was about to reach out of the university and stir up the masses. This, Fu argued, was not in keeping with
the traditional notion of scholars as the moderating mentors of society.
Jianrong bingbao, he argued, risked bringing upon Beida the vengeance of
more conservative elements:

> Even since the publication of *New Tide* the capital has been filled with critical
> views toward those involved in this matter.... Recently, I have been concerned
> that criticisms and disputes [at Beida] might escalate into combat and spill out
> from the sphere of scholarly concern. Our nation's ethical and social codes are
> deeply engraved in the hearts of the people.... If one wants to change or correct
> these, one must take care to understand them well, to find ways that are smooth,
> acceptable, proper. All that is done rashly or that flies in the face of the ancient
> ways will necessarily fail.... The teachers and students in your school are men of
> broad learning—but their self-cultivation must become more complete before
> they can be in accord with the flow of current views, and affect the population in
> a truly effective fashion. If they impose their rash opinions on the masses arbi-
> trarily, nothing good can ever come of it.... [T]he transmission of learning is like
> a great river.... [Y]ou ought to guide it, to channel its flow. You must not let it
> overflow widely and flood the surrounding area.[78]

Cai Yuanpei's reply, written one month before the May 4 demonstration, defended the *New Tide* magazine as a "purely scholarly" student
endeavor, concerned only with "beneficial Western learning" and very
secondarily interested in a criticism of tradition. The president pointed to
the students' interest in scientific theories as a sign of their reliability as
scholars—as men of letters, in the traditional sense of the word. To justify and defend his own principle of *jianrong bingbao* Cai also cited the
existence at Beida of more conservative student societies and journals.
Restating his faith in the Confucian philosophy of broad-minded tolerance, he concluded:

If the *New Tide*'s views turn out to be troublesome and shocking [beyond the sphere of scholarly discussion] I will certainly persuade the students to be more careful.... I also hope that virtuous, prominent persons such as yourself will be able to dispel unreasonable views [complaints] outside the university. For myself, I will persuade [*New tide* members] to be diligent in their studies and not to engage in activities that transgress the parameters of the social order.[79]

Cai Yuanpei's defense, however, came too late. The spillover from scholarship to action was already under way. Because the intellectual world surrounding Beida was ready for the ideas of the students, they were able to set in motion a powerful current that carried along both the tolerant president of Beida and the moderately sympathetic minister of education.

On May 4, 1919, it was Fu Zengxiang's unhappy duty to write the official proclamation taking account of the "flood" which had emanated from Beida:

Today, at 1 P.M., two thousand students held a meeting to demonstrate against the government's diplomatic policies. This is a troublesome, unfortunate occurrence. To maintain public order and student discipline, we call upon all schools to assume prompt responsibility for the disorderly behavior of their students.[80]

Three days later, on May 8, under pressure to restore order, to tame a river he had had no intention of releasing quite so dramatically, Cai Yuanpei submitted his resignation to the minister of Education. On May 11, under fire himself for not doing enough to stem student strikes and public speeches in defense of the May Fourth activists, Fu Zengxiang resigned as well.

A new generation now claimed center stage unprotected by the rationalizations of its mentors. Yet, without the fragile faith in academic freedom championed by Cai Yuanpei, they would have never been able to muster the courage to take to the streets on May 4, 1919. Without the dedicated support of mentors in the *New Youth* group they would have not had the confidence to articulate their own vision for awakening China. In spite of their reputation as destroyers, May Fourth youths were, in fact, builders, who carried out into society, out among the common people, the hope of enlightenment which their predecessors had kept to themselves.

TWO

The Emergence of New Intellectuals: Generational Collaboration and Debate

The problem of creating new intellectuals consists in the critical elaboration of the intellectual activity that exists in everyone.... To be a new intellectual means to no longer rely on eloquence, which is an exterior and momentary mover of passions, but to be an active participant in practical life, as constructor, organizer, permanent persuader.

Antonio Gramsci, "On Intellectuals"[1]

Beijing University students who viewed themselves as China's new intellectuals received their first taste of practical life during the demonstration of May 4, 1919. During the following months, in the course of drafting manifestos, organizing other students in the capital, going to jail, facing prosecution, and finally mobilizing nationwide support from students, workers, and merchants, they discovered their mission as permanent persuaders. When these youths first set out to arouse their countrymen with the news of China's humiliation at Versailles, however, they had not yet come to terms with the limitations of eloquence. In fact, most of them acted as righteously indignant literati had in centuries past. Self-styled mentors of the ignorant commoners, they were convinced of their right to bring political abuse to the attention of power-hungry rulers.[2]

Among those who took to the streets on May 4, 1919, however, there were some students who had already begun to question the right of educated men to speak for and about the speechless masses. This minority was comprised of those who had been advocating a New Culture movement for several months before the outbreak of the patriotic demonstration. They were, as we have seen, the beneficiaries of a thought trend inaugurated by older cultural radicals who had congregated at Beida in the period from 1912 to 1918. With the aid of mentors such as Chen Duxiu, the dean of humanities, and his colleagues Li Dazhao, Hu Shi, Lu Xun, Shen Yinmo, Qian Xuantong, and others (who had already founded the *New Youth* magazine), the students were able to conceive and carry out their own distinctive mission. They founded their own journal and society, the *New Tide*, to propagate a new, more activist vision of enlightenment. Alone, neither students nor teachers would have been able to fathom, much less carry out, a nationwide cultural awakening. Together, they were able to convince first themselves, and slowly the rest of their countrymen, that a critique of China's feudal habits of mind was a prerequisite for long-range, effective national salvation.

Before they could convince others of the priority of cultural awakening, however, these new intellectuals had to come to terms with the fact that they themselves were the progeny of China's old thought. To change China thus meant, first and foremost, to change themselves, the carriers of its cultural legacy. The self-transformation of men of letters thus emerged as the goal of the New Culture movement, even before the demonstration of May 4, 1919. The means toward that goal, adopted as early as 1917, was language reform. By choosing to write in the vernacular—in the spoken language called *baihua*, as distinguished from the classical idiom known as *guwen* or *guanhua* (officials' talk)—iconoclastic intellectuals signaled their determination to break with the traditions of their literati predecessors.

That determination, however, would have had little social consequence without the intellectuals' engagement in practical social mobilization. It is only when they decided to speak about their concerns to a constituency previously shut off from the ideas and ideals of educated men that Beida students really began to explore their role as permanent persuaders. The Beijing University Commoners' Education Lecture Society, as we shall see, was the organization which facilitated the spillover of the New Culture movement from Beida into society at large. A student association founded in March 1919, this lecture society provided the first setting in which advocates of enlightenment and patriotic conservatives collaborated to mobilize their countrymen. Through street-corner speeches, which evolved into village and factory talks in the half-year after the May 4 demonstration of 1919, students gained a first-hand knowledge of the actual state of Chinese society.

Setting out to teach, students ended up hearing far more than they

9. Chen Hengzhe, *New Youth* contributor and the first woman on the Beijing University faculty, a professor of history.

10. Zhu Xizu, *New Youth* contributor and professor of history, 1919.

had anticipated. The frustrations they encountered in spreading the message of new culture forced them to further relinquish their lingering attachment to literati eloquence. Gradually, they became conscious of just how deeply they themselves were imbued with old ways of thinking, talking, and writing. The new intellectuals thus emerged when, and only when, they could see how they themselves fell short of the message of enlightenment.

DISILLUSIONED EDUCATORS AND THE QUEST FOR A NEW YOUTH

The teachers' generation that prepared the way for the May Fourth enlightenment was thoroughly steeped in Confucian learning. Although most of its members refused to take part in the examination system sponsored by the imperial government up until 1905, they all had a firm foundation in classical texts. Furthermore, their familiarity with the worldview they sought to overthrow went beyond book knowledge. In their everyday lives, these iconoclastic intellectuals had been forced to marry, produce sons, mourn parents, obey elders—all in keeping with the strictures of China's native ethical tradition. Even though they had studied abroad before 1919 and had thereby tasted some of the freedom of thought and action still forbidden to men of letters at home, radical intellectuals had returned to China with meager hopes for their own personal emancipation. Once back, they focused first on political revolution against the Manchu rulers, and then, disheartened further, on the cultural awakening of the still untainted youth.

Their own predicament as a transitional generation between old culture and new was keenly felt by these professional educators. While they still carried in mind memories of modern technology and enlightenment thought from their travels in Japan and the West, they could not shut their eyes to the backwardness of China. They thus held up the banner of the new, only to realize more clearly the inertia of the old. All around them, both inside Beida and outside of it, the more numerous, more vocal, more powerful defenders of Confucian culture were to be found. Li Dazhao, the librarian brought to the university on the recommendation of Chen Duxiu, expressed this feeling of inescapable closeness between old and new in an essay written one year before May Fourth. His conclusion evoked the claustrophobia felt by fellow radicals:

Contradictions in the life of present-day China are due to the fact that people who differ greatly in their awareness of the New and the Old have to live their lives as close neighbors. In other words, the distance between New and Old is vertically too far and horizontally too close. In terms of time, they are separated too much. In terms of space, they are too close.[3]

An unwelcome intimacy between the advocates of old and new culture was just one aspect of the predicament of Li Dazhao's generation. The other was loneliness. Having broken with the conventions and expectations of their contemporaries, the iconoclastic teachers were left in a generational wilderness, as it were. Once in a while, a voice came from far away—such as that of the older rebel Wu Yu. Born in 1872, educated as a lawyer in Japan, he had been waging his own solitary battle against filial piety, by appealing to Daoism and Legalism, native alternatives to the monopoly of the Confucian worldview. In 1916, from his home province of Sichuan, he joined forces with the radical teachers at Beida. Some years later, one of them, Hu Shi, recalled the lonely struggle of Wu Yu in terms that mirror the admiration of an entire generation:

He was "the street cleaner of the Chinese world of thought"—who tries to lay the dust of Confucian refuse with the water of enlightenment. For this unrewarding task he was berated by the people of the Old school because he failed to appreciate the delectable fragrance of Confucian refuse. Tired and discouraged, Wu Yu wanted to give up his work as hopeless when he came upon another group of street cleaners (Chen Duxiu and others) performing the same task and he gained fresh courage to continue his work.[4]

The effort to drench Confucian refuse with the waters of enlightenment was exhausting for Wu Yu and his compatriots among the teachers' generation. As a result, their sense of commonality was often anxious and tenuous. They searched for kindred spirits, only to happen upon each other by chance. Each iconoclast had struggled alone before coming upon street cleaners performing the same task. Each had lost faith in Confucian solutions to China's modern problems on his own. Even when these rebels appealed to each other for support, they never quite lost their sense of isolation.

This mood of loneliness may be glimpsed early, even before like-minded teachers had gathered in sufficient numbers to challenge the conservative atmosphere of Beijing University. Chen Duxiu, for example, who sounded so confident in the printed pages of *New Youth*, expressed himself rather differently in a 1917 letter to Hu Shi. Hu, who was still in the United States, had just submitted an article to *New Youth* that was to launch the literary revolution. After praising Hu's efforts abroad and informing him of the precarious financial situation of his own journal in China, Chen Duxiu concluded his letter with an urgent plea: "You must come back with urgent haste. So much needs to be done. There are too few of us in this pathetic society who are willing to carry on this work. So few people are suited for the tasks we have in mind."[5]

Finding so few comrades among their contemporaries, the teachers' generation, not surprisingly, turned to youth as a constituency more capable of the tasks they had in mind and perhaps more open to them. This conscious quest for allies among the younger generation provided the basis for a common program among older rebels who otherwise held very disparate views about China's problems and its solutions. The quest for youthful allies, in time, developed into a veritable cult of youth which held that children were at all times, and in all ways, superior to their elders. In the Chinese context, where age had been assumed to be *inverting tradition* the source of all wisdom, to single out youth as the most precious repository of social creativity was, in effect, to turn tradition on its head.

The teachers' cult of youth may be glimpsed as early as September 1915. In this month, Chen Duxiu launched the journal that would become the rallying point of his generation, by an appeal to youth—the one group in society he believed had escaped contamination by the Confucian worldview. On the first page of the first issue of *Youth Magazine* (later renamed *New Youth*) the editor passionately acclaimed:

I, with tears, place my plea before the fresh and vital youth, in the hope that they will achieve self-awareness and begin to struggle. What is this self-awareness? It is to be conscious of the value and possibility of one's young life.[6]

Chen Duxiu's tear-filled plea in the fall of 1915 contained the seeds of what would become his generation's common faith. Yet, at the time, it was also a sign of his own loneliness and despair as a rebel against tradition.

In the next several years, other middle-aged iconoclasts who had declared themselves to be on the side of youth began to forge a shared identity. Despite their underlying (and still largely unarticulated) differences, this motley group of disenchanted educators found common cause in admiring the natural potential of those younger than themselves. Marginal and few in number, these rebels against Confucianism saw that they could be easily defeated in their efforts to create a new culture. They feared not only the opposition of warlord governments but also their own inner complicity with the Confucian tradition. Hence, they made a concerted appeal to students who were only slightly younger than themselves. From its inception, then, the teachers' mission of enlightenment was dependent on another constituency rather than on their own circle of lonely iconoclasts.

These teachers wrote about youth with a depth of feeling that went beyond the depiction of a new agent in history. Their impassioned appeal drew upon centuries of unexpressed appreciation of sons by their fathers. In revolt against a tradition that made veneration of the aged into a state-enforced ethic, these teachers inaugurated one of the most profound emotional transformations in twentieth-century China. That transformation may be glimpsed also in Gao Yihan's 1916 essay "The Enemy of Youth," which attests further to the complex hopes and fears that comprised the older iconoclasts' cult of youth:

Oh! How I love youth! How I respect youth! These beloved and treasured young people are fortunate to be born into this unprecedented, glorious, awe-inspiring world of the twentieth century!... I also sigh for the youth whom I love and respect. How unfortunate for them to be born at this time of competitive living, in this world of the twentieth century, where all is strife. These beloved and treasured young people are also damned by being born in a country whose people are weak and often humiliated. China is in increasingly grave danger! I fear so for our youth![7]

Gao Yihan's essay, like Chen Duxiu's plea one year earlier, goes one step beyond the Social Darwinist faith embraced by his generation before 1911. In the wake of failed political revolution, we find that intellectuals no longer glorified strife and competitive living. They were now less interested in the wealth and power of the state—goals deemed most urgent by predecessors such as Yan Fu. The cult of youth, thus, inaugurated a new concern with individual development and with self-fulfillment. It was to become the hallmark of the Chinese enlightenment. No longer as optimistic as he had been a year earlier, Chen Duxiu himself began to write about China's need for "new youth."

By 1916, the cult of youth was undergoing changes that would estrange it further still from Social Darwinism. One year after the first issue of *Qingnian zazhi* (*Youth Magazine*), Chen renamed the journal *Xin qingnian* (*New Youth*). He announced the change in an essay that made it clear that from now on age alone could not be considered a reliable criterion of "youth consciousness."

In this essay, Chen forced himself and his readers to confront the fact that the majority of Chinese youth were sliding into old patterns of thought and action. The bitterness that characterized Chen's earlier writings about the decadent tradition surfaced here in descriptions of a decrepit Chinese youth. Physically feeble and spiritually self-indulgent, Chinese students were deemed unworthy of the challenges of twentieth-century living. Such young people were, according to Chen, living fossils.

Precious and beloved youth, if you consider yourselves twentieth-century people, you must get rid of old attitudes. Rid yourselves of the reactionary and corrupt old thinking about officialdom and wealth and develop a new faith.... Precious and beloved youth, forsake this narrow, selfish mentality and develop the characteristics of a *new youth*. Bury the old youth whose narrow-mindedness led to conservatism and corruption. Be different![8]

Burdened by ingrained tendencies, this new youth was thus asked to conquer its own tradition-bound mentality before it could become a viable force for enlightenment in China.

SELF-AWARE NEW YOUTHS: BENEFICIARIES OF TRADITION

The cult of youth provided a common mission for the older, disillusioned generation of intellectuals. It also helped shape the common consciousness of students on the eve of the May Fourth movement. Fully aware that the hopes and fears of their mentors were invested in them, the younger generation congregating at Beida between 1917 and 1920 readily assumed the role of saviors of China. They had a sense of cohesion and of shared purpose that their teachers lacked. At Beida, they were able to develop their disparate cultural and political commitments under the protective mantle of Cai Yuanpei's *jianrong bingbao*—broadminded and encompassing tolerance policy. Within one class, for example—the one entering Beida in 1917—Cai was able to tolerate, even encourage, the emergence of three different student societies and journals: the culturally conservative *Guogu* (*National Heritage*), the politically activist *Guomin* (*Citizen*) and the enlightenment-oriented *Xinchao* (*New Tide*).[9] Although not all of these students would meet Chen Duxiu's

criteria of "new youth," they all believed themselves to be different from
their predecessors and were determined to make an unprecedented impact on Chinese society and thought.

It was thus a combination of biographical circumstance and generational self-consciousness that enabled Beida students to assume the
leadership of the May Fourth movement. Admired for their natural
potentialities, called upon to consummate the break with the crippling
traditions of their scholar-official predecessors, the younger generation
acted their part more convincingly than older iconoclasts. As early as
January 1918, we glimpse this sense of confidence in Luo Jialun's article
"Young Students," published in the teachers' journal *New Youth*.[10] Luo
was part of that small, vocal minority of Beijing University students who
chose to model themselves on Chen Duxiu's 1916 vision of a genuinely
new youth: not feeble, not self-indulgent, not conservative. But to go
beyond these negative images, students discovered that they had to leave
behind the teachers' ideal of broad-mindedness and to develop their own
program for new culture. What they brought to the movement, sparked
by the older generation, was fidelity, a quality of mind and heart that
Western psychologist Erik Erikson has identified as a capacity for commitment peculiar to youth: "the strength of disciplined devotion ...
gained in the involvement of youth in such experiences as reveal the
essence of the era they are to join—as beneficiaries of tradition ... as
renewers of its ethical strength, as rebels bent on the destruction of the
outlived."[11]

The students, as we have seen, were indeed "beneficiaries of tradition." They had been too young to be traumatized, as older literati-
critics had been, by China's humiliating defeat in 1895 and by the failure
of the reform movement of 1898. Their individual careers had not been
thrown in disarray by the abolition of the examination system in 1905.
They were even too young for their hopes for revolution to be dashed
by the events of 1911–13 and by the monarchical restoration attempt
of 1915. Spared these disillusionments, these new youths joined the
teachers' cause with fresh vigor. Less burdened by anger against tradition, they became, in time, its more rational critics.

The student's perspective on the "problem of New versus the Old"
was, thus, rather different than that of their older mentors. For earlier
generations the New had been a vague entity, a hope of emancipation
from old culture. For the students, on the other hand, the New was a
nearly certain possibility. Building on the promise held out by their
elders, they asked not if a new culture could be actualized but rather *how*
and at what *cost*. Teachers like Li Dazhao wrote about the confusion
occasioned by the tenacity of the old customs and values. The students

described the ambiguous blessings of a new worldview: "What is most fortunate is the New. What is saddest is the New."[12] The older generation never tired of pointing out instances of Confucian hypocrisy and corrupt politics. The students, typically, chose the terminology of modern logic to describe the "problem of the New and Old": "The Old is plural, the New is singular.... the Old is relative, the New is absolute.... the Old is matter, the New is force."[13]

The students, too, became iconoclasts. Their iconoclasm, however, was milder in tone and content than that of their teachers. They knew the Confucian texts nearly as well as their teachers. They were, in fact, part of the last generation of Chinese intellectuals who were at once familiar with the Confucian inheritance and well-versed in Western scholarship. These youths were linked to tradition by emotional ties. Unlike their teachers, they had not been expected to become scholar-officials. Nurtured by grandfathers who were quite sanguine about the pointlessness of an official career in the twentieth century, these students developed a deep appreciation of the native past.

This appreciation, however, had developed apart from the pressures of the imperial examinations. Whereas their fathers had struggled to advance through the examination system and their teachers had struggled to reject it, the students were freed structurally from it. They enrolled in modern secondary schools, while at the same time continuing to learn from their Confucian grandfathers. Either retired from office or, not infrequently, contemptuous of office-holding altogether, these mentors could instruct and inspire their grandsons without the burden of emulation. Fu Sinian, for example, when recalling the people whom he most admired and respected, placed his grandfather, Fu Liquan, at the head of the list.[14] Fu Liquan, after gaining a low-level degree, had refused to take further examinations, rejected all offers of government positions, and devoted his life to varied interests ranging from medicine and the martial arts to calligraphy. It was this man, scornful of the stuffiness of the scholar-official's life, who began to teach the classics to Fu Sinian at the age of five. He showed him how to savor, not merely to memorize, Confucian texts. Especially fond of the book of *Mencius*, he was responsible for his grandson's life-long interest in the concept of *ren*— benevolence. This concept of *ren* was of great interest to other self-aware new youths as well. It was to figure prominently in the later work of philosophers Feng Youlan and Zhang Shenfu—fellow students of Fu Sinian at Beida. This interest in *ren* stands in marked contrast to the teachers' contempt for it, as expressed, for example, in Lu Xun's bitter denunciation of it in "Diary of a Madman."

Grandfathers were, thus, a living conduit of Confucian tradition for the "children" Lu Xun had sought to save. As companions and virtual playmates, these men tutored their grandsons in a setting that defied the rigid conventions of subservience that were enforced with a vengeance in the lives of older iconoclasts. Intellectuals of the teachers' generation often went through life with a bitter familiarity with classical learning as a pedagogical regimen. The students, by contrast, acquired an esthetic appreciation for it as a cultural inheritance. This enabled them to gain and maintain an intellectual distance from the anti-Confucianism that consumed their teachers. With an esthetic perspective, grandsons were able to see through and around the things grandfathers taught them. This playful skill emerges sharply in a passage from the autobiography of historian Gu Jiegang, Fu Sinian's roommate at Beida:

It was a habit of my grandfather's, whenever he and I were strolling along in the street or going out to the country to sweep the ancestral tombs, to explain to me the significance of inscriptions over doorways, memorial arches, or bridges that we happened upon. He insisted on telling me the history of each of these and on our return home he would write out a list of things we had seen, each in its proper sequence. In this way I developed a taste for the most fundamental of historical notions, namely that things before our eyes have not been there since the beginning of time but represent the slow accumulations of the ages—a concept that has been of lifelong benefit to me.[15]

This sense of relative comfort with tradition was, however, greatly shaken by the teachers' urgent call to critical thought. Gu Jiegang's rather serene predisposition toward the material evidence of the past was to be jolted at Beijing University by none other than Qian Xuantong, the Doubter of Antiquity. Qian—a student of Zhang Taiyan (who was in turn a pupil of *New Tide* member Yu Pingbo's famous great-grandfather)—instructed Gu Jiegang how to be suspicious about the evidence of "the accumulation of the ages." Together, Qian and Gu went on to found modern, critical Chinese historiography.

Surprisingly perhaps, poised between Confucian grandfathers and anti-Confucian teachers, the student generation did not lose its intellectual footing. The students joined the cause of enlightenment eager to do their share but aware of the distinctive nature of their own tasks. In no small measure, the credit for the students' confidence in their identity must be given to their radical-minded teachers. Strident in their public stance, frequently despairing in private, the older iconoclasts tried nonetheless to shield their students from these extremes. They were endlessly patient with the personal dilemmas of the "new youth," and they assumed responsibility for their careers long after they had been graduated from Beijing University.

11. Qian Xuantong, *New Youth* editor and professor of Chinese literature.

Among themselves, teachers often squabbled about the best strategy to defy conservative literati. In their interactions with students, however, they were open to appeals for harmony and moderation. This capacity for public militance and private consolation comes through, for example, in a 1918 letter written by *New Tide* member Zhang Shenfu to Hu Shi. In this letter Zhang sounds rather different from Chen Duxiu, who had written a year earlier to ask for reinforcement of "troops" on the radicals' front:

I came to visit you but you were, unfortunately, not in. In *New Youth* recently, Chen Duxiu and Qian Xuantong mocked the idea of teaching Chinese classics on the basis of Western learning. I am not brave enough to speak up on this subject.... So, I can only hope that you will moderate this condemnation of Chinese classics and ill-informed praise of Western learning.[16]

Zhang Shenfu's 1918 appeal to Hu Shi to moderate debates within the ranks of new culture advocates was not a solitary gesture of hope. It reflected a deepening trust and collaboration between teachers and students that were to ripen in the founding of *New Tide*. By the spring of 1918, the teachers themselves had gathered at Beida in large enough numbers to be able to actively sponsor the coming together of the new youth they had been looking for and longing for for years. Their most concrete means of support was to provide the younger generation with a public forum through which to express its own views and opinions. Under the guidance of a new editorial committee comprised of Li Dazhao, Chen Duxiu, Shen Yinmo, Qian Xuantong, Hu Shi, Lu Xun, Zhou Zuoren, and Liu Bannong, *New Youth* magazine began to solicit student contributions. Thus we find that in April 1918, Fu Sinian published his first article, "Fundamental Errors in Contemporary Chinese

12.   Beijing University students and teachers on an outing, 1919. From left to right: Lei Guoneng, Li Dazhao, Liang Shuming, and Zhang Shenfu.

Scholarship," in *New Youth*. In May, Yu Pingbo published his first vernacular poem, "Spring Stream," in the same journal, while in June, Luo Jialun's translation of Ibsen's *Doll's House* appeared in the special *New Youth* issue dedicated to the Norwegian playwright.

By the fall of 1918, yet another intergenerational collaboration was under way. Chen Duxiu, Li Dazhao, and Zhang Shenfu jointly founded the new magazine, *Weekly Critic* (*Meizhou pinglun*). Inspired by the defeat of Germany in the First World War (at a time when many other Chinese intellectuals pointed to Europe's devastation as a general sign of the moral bankruptcy of modern Western civilization), these three tried to develop a forum through which they might express admiration for the West while remaining vigilant against the *qiangquan*, the "arbitrary authority," they identified with Germany.[17] In the first issue, Chen, Li, and Zhang reaffirmed the ideal of *gongli*—public truth—and proclaimed their determination to make it manifest through their political news magazine, which would be quite different from the more culture-oriented *New Youth*. Two years later, in the fall of 1920, the three founders of the *Weekly Critic* organized the first cell of what would become the Chinese Communist Party.

Beida students who went on to make their own distinctive contribution to the New Culture movement were thus the beneficiaries of considerable aid and comfort from enlightenment-oriented teachers. Without the harsh, strident voices of their mentors, they might never have discovered the more reasonable timbre that became their own. The anger of their predecessors enabled students to declare themselves pioneers of a new age. Thus, the manifesto of *New Tide*, published in January 1919 in the first issue of the journal, asserted without any hesitation that Beida students were thoroughly unlike any other generation of educated Chinese youths. Having paid due credit to the institution that had nurtured their spirit of confident independence, they went on to claim that as students, they were finally in a position to spread the ethos of Beijing University to the rest of Chinese society:

New Tide is a journal that is the outcome of collaboration among Beijing University students. Although our university has been in existence for twenty-one years, there has been, unfortunately, no precedent for a student-initiated publication.... In the past, this university claimed to be engaged in academic training, but in fact all it ever did was to turn out civil servants.... In the past, there was nothing to distinguish the atmosphere of the university from the rest of society. Those who were trained within it could not but be made to fit the present social order. Now, however, our university is fortunate to be part of a world-wide trend, and therefore it can aspire to lead the path toward the Chinese society of the future. With this kind of spirit ... the intellectual purpose of the university might yet spread all over China, might yet have great influence indeed.[18]

THE FOUNDING OF *NEW TIDE*: A SHARED AWAKENING

On October 13, 1919, two months after the editorial reorganization of *New Youth* and shortly after the first appearance of *Weekly Critic*, twenty-

13. Some student members of the *New Tide* Society in 1919: far left, Fu Sinian; second from right, Yu Pingbo; center, Li Xiaofeng.

two Beida students held the first organizational meeting of what was to become the *New Tide* Society. The youngest among them was the twenty-year-old literature major Yu Pingbo (who later gained both fame and notoriety as chief interpreter of the classical novel *Dream of the Red Chamber*). The oldest was a thirty-two-year-old Cantonese philosophy major, Tan Mingqian (later known as Tan Pingshan, founder, organizer, and martyr of the Chinese Communist Party). Having been singled out by their teachers as the embodiment of China's hopes, these students had grown tired of "doing nothing practical."[19] They also shared their teachers' conviction that youth was not in itself enough to merit the title of "new intellectual." Young people had to show society more concretely just what they were capable of by shaking off the burden of traditional expectations. Merely to refuse to become an official—a commitment most of these students had already made by joining Cai Yuanpei's Society for the Promotion of Virtue—was not enough.

The idea of a new, student-organized study society thus emerged in the context of the students' growing awareness that they could and should do something different from their teachers. The particular goal they set for themselves was to find a new audience for the growing enlightenment movement. Whereas the teachers' journal *New Youth* was addressed to older, more sophisticated culture critics, the students decided to address their journal *New Tide* to middle-school graduates—the constituency they believed to be most endangered by old habits of mind. Declaring that the challenge which university students faced (despite

their more modern, open-minded academic community) was the same as
that of their younger compatriots throughout China, the founding members of *New Tide* wrote:

> Through this magazine we desire to cooperate with students of all middle schools
> in the country to fight for spiritual emancipation.... Our hope is that all students
> will discard the examination-system mentality and embrace modern scientific
> thought,... that they will consider themselves pioneers of the future.[20]

The young men at Beida, who, in writing, were so certain that they
were pioneers of the future, were considerably more ambivalent about
that possibility in conversations among themselves. In fact, it was shared
despondency about being able to become truly emancipated from society
that brought together the initial group in October 1918. In his recollection of the mood that led to the founding of *New Tide*, Fu Sinian describes
how individual discontent led to a sense of common mission among his
fellow students at Beida:

> We came together as a result of a shared awakening; each person felt that his
> previous life and thinking had been aimless.... This can be called a similar
> mind-set.... I believe that the purest, deepest, most durable feelings are those
> based on a shared mind-set. These far surpass religious or familial alliances.
> Those of us who came together did not have previous contact.[21]

Fu Sinian's October 1919 evocation of the "shared awakening" of
fellow *New Tide* members a year earlier at once described and distorted
the origins of the students' society—a tendency to remember history
selectively that persists even today. Because *New Tide* members went on
to become leaders in all aspects of China's intellectual and political life,
their youth has been the subject of curiosity and distortion. Insofar as
they became symbols for opposing sides of the Communist versus
Nationalist conflict in the 1930s, 1940s, and 1950s, the details of their
early commonality have been glossed over in the partisan scholarship
about the May Fourth movement published both in China and on
Taiwan. Fortunately, recent recollections of surviving participants have
augmented prevailing interpretations of the origins of the *New Tide* Society. Now octogenarians, these intellectuals are less afraid of political
pressure and more concerned with the judgment of history. Thus, with
the aid of *New Tide* memoirs by Li Xiaofeng, Feng Youlan, Yu Pingbo,
Ye Shengtao, and others,[22] we are finally in a position to get a fuller
glimpse of the sources of the students' "shared awakening" at Beida.

Contrary to Fu Sinian's claim, we are now able to reconstruct the
existence of a broad range of contacts between Beida students on the eve
of the May Fourth movement. These contacts and associations suggest a

14.   Some student members of the *New Tide* Society in 1920: second from right, Zhu
Ziqing; center right, Luo Jialun; first from left, Gu Jiegang.

far more traditional commonality among *New Tide* members than the
spontaneous, emotional resonance Fu described in his recollections. On
December 3, 1919, for example, the *Beijing University Daily* published the
names of the founders of the *New Tide* Society (see appendix A). This list
suggests that one of the most important sources of solidarity within the
student generation was provincial origin. Four out of the six officers of
the society were from Shandong province: Luo Jialun, Fu Sinian, Yang
Zhensheng, and Xu Yanzhi. In an institutional context in which one of
the most prevalent forms of association was "Societies of Fellow Provin-
cials," the gathering of like-minded students from Shandong was rather
typical. Equally natural were departmental affinities, especially among
students who entered Beida in the same year. Thus, it is not surprising
that *New Tide* members Kang Baiqing, Yu Pingbo, and Fu Sinian were
all students in the Literature department who had entered the university
in 1916. Furthermore, they had been brought together by their interest
in a new course entitled "The History of European Literature" taught
by Zhou Zuoren, an important mentor and later the editor of *New Tide*.
Finally, most of these students studied—and became close friends—
with Hu Shi, the first Beida professor with a Ph.D. in philosophy from
the United States.

   Yet another, again predictable source of student affinity was dormitory living. Gu Jiegang was thus drawn into the society because he was
Fu Sinian's roommate. Gu later on introduced into the society his friend
from secondary school, Ye Shengtao, a *New Tide* member too poor to

afford the 300 *yuan* tuition at Beijing University. Ye nonetheless had kept abreast of thought trends in the New Culture movement through a network of friendship that preceded the May Fourth movement itself. Finally, older brothers, like Sun Fuyuan, brought younger siblings, like Sun Fuxi, into *New Tide* as well.[23]

Co-provincials, roommates, classmates, *New Tide* members gravitated toward each other quite naturally. Their mutual self-discovery was less anxious, less embattled than that of the teachers who formalized their association around the *New Youth* editorial board in the spring of 1918. These students looked to each other for support in furthering intellectual interests not necessarily antithetical to the education offered at Beida, and yet clearly beyond its scope. They were enthusiastic participants in their mentors' causes, whether they be the reorganization of the national heritage (*zhengli guogu*) or language reform. At the same time, however, they developed questions, issues, and concerns that were reflections of their own generational setting. Most striking among the intellectual interests that set this generation apart from its predecessors were an informed curiosity about formal, analytical logic and a prolonged inquiry into modern psychology. Their teachers, as we shall see in the next chapter, had neither the time nor the inclination to pursue topics that were so far removed from the urgent social problems of the day.

The students' journal, more than the journal of the teachers, was filled with English words, expressions for novel concepts that the students sought first and foremost to elucidate for themselves. The April 1919 issue of *New Tide*, for example, on the eve of May Fourth, contained Wang Jingxi's explanation of the meanings of "behavioralism," "the unconscious," "perception," and "desires," all in light of Pillsbury's *Psychology of Reasoning* and Dewey's *How We Think*. It also included Zhang Shenfu's discussion of mathematical logic, in particular the meaning of "function" and "principle of variability"; Xu Yanzhi's translation of Russell's "The Problems of Philosophy"; and the ruminations of Kang Baiqing on ancient Daoist theories of "phallicism" and "sympathetic magic."[24]

Obsessed with how much they did not know, with how much there was yet to read, to translate, and to digest, *New Tide* members made their own self-awakening the focus of both their society and their journal. Ordinary middle-school students throughout China were unlikely to understand the dense pages of a magazine so stuffed with foreign words and alien concepts. And yet, the Beida students' desire to overcome their own ignorance of Western scholarship did convince others. Eventually some urban youths would also view the spirit of criticism as indistinguishable from an informed appreciation of both Chinese and foreign cultures. Unlike their teachers, who were consumed with the need to overthrow tradition in one generation, the *New Tide* students knew that they stood in a continuum of destroyers and builders. As the manifesto of the *New Tide* Society made clear, they saw themselves as performing the functions of both:

> Members of our society are shallow in their learning. In this time of transition we cannot claim to shoulder the awesome task of awakening our countrymen in its entirety. Nonetheless, we will devote all our strength to show all the people of China the true spirit of our school.[25]

The twenty students who signed this manifesto in January 1919 knew that they represented only a small fraction of a student body of more than two thousand. Nonetheless, they were convinced that they, and they alone, embodied the true spirit of Beida. This conviction spread to others beyond the university in the months before the demonstration of May 4, 1919. As one of the early letters to the editors of *New Tide* put it: "Only Beijing University could have produced persons like the *New Tide* members. Credit for this, of course, must be given to Mr. Cai Yuanpei and other brave professors ... who inspire students to take up the difficult questions of 'What is a life perspective all about?' 'How should we scientifically investigate our national heritage?'"[26]

The teachers, who were assumed to inspire students in their quest for a new life perspective and a scientific assessment of tradition, saw their mission quite differently. They had looked to the student generation as an ally in the battle of New against Old. The very hopes for rebellion that they had placed upon this new youth made them impatient with the students' concern with scholarly ignorance and book learning. Within their own circle, these older intellectuals had deemed it quite appropriate to expose and to share self-doubt. In public, however, they tried to maintain a posture of confident militance. The *New Tide*'s willingness to talk openly about the shortcomings of the students' own command of new knowledge—and its pages filled with halting explorations of Western and Chinese scholarship—evoked, not surprisingly, the ire of older mentors.

THE OWL AND THE SNAKE:
A GENERATIONAL DISPUTE ABOUT
NEW TIDE

From its inception, the *New Tide* aroused both the interest and the suspicion of older enlightenment intellectuals. When Fu Sinian approached Chen Duxiu for funds for the new journal in the fall of 1918, he was at first rebuffed. The dean of humanities, an outspoken advocate of the New Culture movement, did not trust this student of literature who was known for his closeness to Professor Huang Jigang, an enemy of enlightenment. Over the next couple of months, Chen Duxiu was persuaded of Fu's sincerity, overcame his reservations, and gave full financial and moral support to the *New Tide* project. Chen's economic backing was as important as the spiritual support students received from the *New Youth* group. It enabled students to become publishers—an unprecedented opportunity for young intellectuals of their generation. Later, this financial support became a source of vulnerability. As Beida became subject to pressures by conservative opponents to stop subsidizing the *New Tide*, student publishers began to panic. Although some university funds continued through 1923, the students were compelled to learn how to raise money on their own. The experience of soliciting support outside the university, in turn, enabled some *New Tide* pioneers, such as Li Xiaofeng, to become leading figures in Chinese publishing in the late 1920s.[27]

In the months before the May 4 demonstration, the older generation remained concerned about the "softness" of youth in the battle between New and Old. The teachers had become hard—fierce in their iconoclasm against a tradition they knew intimately. Strident in their public advocacy of enlightenment, they were less willing to acknowledge the limitations of their own knowledge and vision. The students, by contrast, endlessly bemoaned both their own inadequacies with respect to modern learning and society's hostility to their self-awakening.

The teachers worried for the students and also worried about the students. Determined to save and to nurture youth, they were not prepared to see young people flounder intellectually or emotionally. The suicide of a Beida student, Lin Deyang, on November 17, 1919, brought the older generation's worries out into the open. *New Youth* teachers viewed Lin's suicide as a confession of weakness, a sign of youth's inability to understand and fight society directly. *New Tide* members, on the other hand, came out loudly in support of Lin's action. They saw in it a justification of their suspicion that youth was the most endangered element of Chinese society. Luo Jialun expressed the *New Tide* view most succinctly when he wrote:

We, the youth of this generation, must struggle to change the environment, to transform this despicable present into a more bearable one. But, if our fighting energies are exhausted and our intelligence is drained, we must commit suicide.... I feel that Mr. Lin had struggled for a long time and was frustrated in his struggle.... He did not kill himself; society killed him! If society will not change quickly, I fear that many other enthusiastic, brave youths will commit suicide one by one. Society stands by, so unfeeling. Educators! I beg you to open your eyes and see.[28]

Educators at Beida, ranging from John Dewey, who was a visiting lecturer there at the time, to Li Dazhao and Jiang Menglin, took Luo's plea to heart. Their response was to warn students, to plead with them to become at once more patient and more tough-minded. Chen Duxiu responded to Luo Jialun most directly and insightfully when he wrote in January 1920:

Thought [not only society] can kill.... Those who advocate new thought must be careful to use the movement of new thought to wash off the darkness of society. But, they must not allow the new thought tide to kill, or to aggravate the harshness experienced by the individual.... Has recent thought been this morbid, and killed people? Yes, yes ...[29]

Here was a remarkable and painful admission by one who had meant to nurture the young that his own generation's thoughtful intentions had, in fact, been thoughtless.

This public discussion between Chen Duxiu and Luo Jialun on the issue of student suicide parallels another one between Fu Sinian and Lu Xun. Again, the issue was how strong youth had to be in order to resist society, to overcome it rather than be overcome by it. It was sparked by a request from Fu in May 1919 for suggestions about ways to improve *New Tide*. Lu Xun's answer came in the form of a letter questioning the students' emphasis on Western knowledge at the expense of a concerted attack upon the native tradition. In his letter, the older writer noted the plethora of translations of the latest scientific theories from abroad and wondered out loud whether the students were not providing, inadvertently to be sure, solace for conservative, old-style gentlemen.

Lu Xun's purpose in writing this letter was to warn *New Tide* members that new knowledge, by itself, was no threat to established Confucian conventions. He argued that students had to be better prepared to attack and to be attacked in the war between new and old culture. He asked them to function as conscious "snakes" against the old order, to dare to bite and to poison their own patrons in society. A realistic militant, Lu Xun also acknowledged that *New Tide* members might have good reason to wish (but unrealistically, in his view) not to be too noticeable in the eyes of their enemies. He thus concluded: "The snake, naturally, does not want to cause its own death. The way of the viper, however, is the only way and it is important to carry it through to the bitter end."[30]

Fu Sinian's letter of response conceded that students had been a bit overzealous in their curiosity about Western scientific theories. At the same time, however, he reaffirmed his generation's belief that they bore the burden of overcoming their ignorance of world thought. Fu's letter to Lu Xun, thus, revealed that *New Tide* members were ambivalent rather than reluctant to assume the role assigned to them by older intellectuals:

We are in that period of our lives in which we seek to learn. Our knowledge and abilities are inadequate. Not to pursue our studies and to shout [proselytize for the New Culture movement] would be unfair toward our own selves. But today's China is a sad and lonely place; there is no one else who dares to shout. So we have to go ahead and shout, and shout until we wake up everybody.... Some people say that we are mere night owls [not snakes]. But to be a night owl isn't so bad at all: at night all other sounds have been stilled, so only the owl's cry is heard. Although lonesome, the night owl can wake up the night-prowling tomcat, the tomcat can wake up the cock, and the cock can wake up the dawn. With the dawn, things might yet become better.[31]

The teachers, thus, saw themselves as snakes, poisoning long-held beliefs of their contemporaries with the venom of rational doubt. The students, on the other hand, imagined themselves as owls—disturbing the sleep of their countrymen with the clamor of knowledge from abroad.

In spite of their disparate self-conceptions, both snakes and owls were deemed equally dangerous and immoral by conservative intellectuals inside and outside of Beida. The venom of rational doubt when combined with the clamor of Western learning threatened the old gentlemen more acutely than either might have alone. What made iconoclastic teachers and students so hateful in the eyes of their opponents was the premonition that both their doubts and their knowledge diminished the intellectuals' privileged position in society. The threat to the literati's monopoly over culture was, at first, only implicit in the advocacy of the New Culture movement. When the snakes and the owls joined forces to promote a literary revolution, it became explicit.

As the focus of the May Fourth enlightenment shifted from culture in general to language change more specifically, it provoked the ire of the old gentlemen more directly. To have doubts, to think for oneself, even to proselytize those doubts and thoughts among other intellectuals was one thing. To claim that these doubts and thoughts could be shared by everyone and should be made available to the common people was another. By August 1919, when the Lu Xun–Fu Sinian exchange already seemed like ancient history, one of the most articulate spokesmen of the conservative faction lashed out against owls and snakes alike. Gu Hongmin, the Confucian gentleman with the proud queue who taught Western literature at Beida before the arrival of the new group of professional educators, used English, the language admired by the iconoclasts, to indict them. Writing for *Millard's Review*, he dared them:

Just fancy what the result would be, if ninety percent of [China's] four hundred million people were to become literate. Imagine only what a fine state of things we would have if here in Peking, the coolies, mafoos, chauffeurs, barbers, shopboys, hawkers, hunters, loafers, vagabonds, *hoc genus omne*, all became literate and wanted to take part in politics as well as the University students.... we would then not be able to say, like the French King, as we do now in our friendship bureaus, meetings, and conferences and in our telegrams to Paris, "L'état cest [*sic*] moi"—*we* are China.[32]

INTELLECTUALS AND LANGUAGE: THE HISTORICAL BOND

When Gu Hongmin taunted May Fourth intellectuals to own up to the fact of their own arrogance, he was not that far off the mark. Some of the "snakes," like Lu Xun, Chen Duxiu, and Hu Shi, and some of the "owls," like Fu Sinian, Luo Jialun, and Yu Pingbo, men who were in the forefront of the literary reform movement, did in fact believe that "we are China." The activism of the May Fourth movement by itself, the telegrams, demonstrations, and street corner talks, had not challenged this aspect of the intellectuals' conceit. Even as they tried to reach out to coolies, shopboys, hawkers, and loafers, they still held on to the old Confucian notion that "those who know are the first to become awakened. Those first awakened enlighten those less awake."[33] This ancient formulation, as Gu suspected, lay beneath the modern intellectual desire to bring enlightenment and literacy to the masses. It was their determination to make literature the instrument of enlightenment, however, that he saw as new and worrisome. This determination threatened to undo the special bond between intellectuals and language that had been forged over two thousand years of Chinese history.

Although correct in his guess that intellectuals still saw themselves as if they were China, Gu Hongmin was wrong in portraying this vision as monarchical. In fact, for centuries Chinese intellectuals had made language their own special domain of cultural activity, as a defense mechanism against rulers who, like Louis XIV, believed "l'état c'est moi!" In the face of political absolutism, educated men in China had carved out a special role for textual knowledge, and by extension for themselves. It was the lofty position to which the classical language had been elevated in the course of Chinese history that guaranteed some semblance of autonomy to intellectuals, who otherwise were thoroughly subordinated to nobles, and, later, emperors.

This effort to win autonomy through language may be glimpsed even before the founding of the first imperial bureaucratic state in 221 B.C. The forerunners of modern intellectuals, the ancient *shi*, were a special class of servant-advisers who rose to power due to their possession of the literary skills needed by a warlike but illiterate nobility. Sought after by various kings and princes, they were able to develop nearly "contractual relationships"[34] with masters who would have never acknowledged a need for mutuality otherwise. In the climate of intensified political struggle that marked the Warring States period, 403–211 B.C., the *shi* had adopted a martial spirit of their own, manifested in vigorous intellectual controversy over problems of statecraft and philosophy. They became further and further removed from their ancestors, the earliest literati, who were called *ru*. For centuries before Confucius' birth, the *ru* had been in charge of burial ceremonies, astrological calendars, and the rituals of ancestor worship.[35]

After the establishment of the imperial state in 221 B.C. and its ideological consolidation during the Han dynasty (202 B.C.–A.D. 202), intellectuals lost some of the autonomy and vigor they had developed during the Warring States period. Once the emperor became elevated to a supreme position in the earthly as well as the cosmic hierarchy, the erstwhile *shi* were unable to demand, or even hope for, contractual mutuality. Instead, they wrapped themselves up in special scarves, hats, feathers—symbols that signaled their unique relationship to language and to books, which contained an ethical code still deemed useful by the supreme ruler. From the second century A.D. onward, scholars were known as *rujia*, Confucian literati waiting to be used by the all-powerful Son of Heaven. Their sphere of autonomy became even more circumscribed after the Song dynasty (960–1127), when the examination system became the only formal means of recruiting intellectuals talent into the service of the state.[36]

Bookish, inward, servile, the latter-day scholar-officials bore little resemblance to the vigorous *shi* of old admired by the May Fourth intellectuals.[37] And yet, even as they were losing some political autonomy in relationship to the emperor, traditional intellectuals were consolidating their privileged relation to language and culture. Calling themselves *wenren*, literally, men-of-the-word (*hommes de lettres*), they proclaimed that it was mastery of the classical language and of the Confucian classics that accounted for their social eminence, not simply their willingness to submit to the emperor.

Indeed, these *wenren* took very seriously their unique responsibility toward *wenhua*, culture. With their monopoly over the written language nearly complete, they set themselves above and apart from the *xiaoren*—the mean folk, who were characterized by vulgar ignorance of matters close to the heart of educated gentlemen. Knowledge of classical Chinese, the language of the texts that were the subject of the examination system, thus became a dividing line between literati and peasants, in addition to disparity in wealth. As a result, a wide gulf developed between the language, social customs, and religious beliefs of the common people and of the intellectuals.[38] It became one of the goals of the Chinese enlightenment movement to bridge that gulf, or at least to expose the pretensions of elite culture as well as the shortcomings of folk traditions.

The means adopted during the May Fourth movement to bridge that gulf was literary reform. From our point of view today, we can see that although their goal was novel, the intellectuals' approach was indebted to tradition. Bent upon nothing short of a revolution in their countrymen's ways of feeling and thinking, the new intellectuals turned to literature, as their predecessors had done for centuries. Inheritors of China's elite culture, they were keenly attuned to the centrality of language in their own tradition. They knew well the power of language to balance the power between absolute monarchs and increasingly subservient scholar-officials. As critical intellectuals before them had done for centuries, May Fourth radicals also turned to the *wenren*'s privileged connection with language to bring their concerns into the public domain. A preference for literary reform as a way to put forth ideas of social change that were otherwise intolerable to political authorities thus preceded the May Fourth intellectuals' concern with literature.

In fact, from Han Yu, in the late eighth century, through Liang Qichao in the early twentieth century, there stretched a long tradition of using a "new literature" to "save the nation." Repeatedly throughout Chinese history, intellectuals had resorted to literary reform in order to awaken their countrymen. That reform included innovations in both style and content meant to alert Chinese readers to the abuses of power from above. May Fourth intellectuals thus were hardly the first to commit "word crimes" in Chinese history. They were, however, unprecedented in turning language into a weapon against the intellectuals' privileged relationship to culture.

The immediate predecessors of the May Fourth student generation had advocated literary reform, specifically, the use of plainer language in the writing of fiction, to address new social constituencies such as the small merchant class that had grown up in China's coastal cities. May Fourth intellectuals, by contrast, did not use language reform merely to save the nation or to inform those further down on the social scale. Rather, they used a new language to communicate among themselves and to write about themselves for the public outside of Beijing University. Through their intergenerational collaboration, teachers and students were able to accelerate the pace of language reform. They pressed beyond a concern with how one writes to the question of how one thinks, and finally, to how one speaks out on social issues.

An awareness that the written language of the elite had become severed from the spoken language of the common people preceded the May Fourth movement itself. Earlier reformers who had attempted to enliven *wenren* literature by incorporating into it words, sayings, dialects from below, however, had not questioned the right of intellectuals to speak to and for the masses. The May Fourth literary revolution, by contrast, challenged the value system which had supported the social prominence of classical language for nearly two thousand years. By championing a new vernacular literature, *baihua*—literally, literature of plain talk—new intellectuals brought about a vernacularization of values[39] that was broader and more radical in scope than any other previous language reform movement. By bringing ideas, not only words, from popular folk culture into the literature of the elites, they began to shake the foundation of the authority of intellectuals not over language alone, but in society as well. By tampering with language as thoroughly as they did, May Fourth enlighteners began to dismantle the single most important barrier between the *wenren*, the men-of-the-word, and the *pingmin*, the wordless common folk. As these men of the word began to write for wordless commoners and talk about their concerns to them, they also learned to hear and to see themselves anew.

The critical implications of *baihua* literature were not apparent, even to its proponents, in the beginning of the New Culture movement. In fact, when they first spread the call for a new language beyond their small circle at Beijing University, the new intellectuals couched their message in the more familiar, more acceptable metaphors of Social Darwinism. As an April 1919 article by a journalist using the pen name "Posthumous Life" argued, the new literature was nothing more than a cultural form best suited to China's need for survival in the modern world:

If something new survives and flourishes, it is not because the old does not have the wherewithal to survive. Anything new can succeed only if it can prove it is irresistible. The new literature we are proposing today is in keeping with the tide of the times and hence is irresistible.... Anyone who swims against this current is bound to appear ridiculous,... actually harmful to the nation.... Adherents of the old school, last-ditch defenders of classical language, are being impaled on this dilemma without even being aware of it.[40]

This talk of "irresistible tides" tends to conceal how radical the May Fourth literary challenge really was. Conservative opponents like Gu Hongming, however, were prompt to realize just how deeply the new intellectuals were questioning the social preeminence of *wenren* over *ping-min*. They accused *New Youth* and *New Tide* editors of the old charge of "word crimes," and thus forced them to defend themselves publicly. In the course of their defense, teachers and students reaffirmed their shared commitment to enlightenment and spread its message far beyond their own circles at Beida. Thus, language change accelerated the impact of May Fourth politics and brought about the very specter so feared by Gu Hongming: Intellectuals after 1919 could no longer claim so readily or so confidently that "we are China."

LITERARY REVOLUTION: THE PRODUCT OF GENERATIONAL COLLABORATION

Two years before members of the *New Tide* group encountered each other and launched their student journal, their teachers were already united by a shared concern with literary reform. Their unity in this venture, as in so many others, bore the impact of their disparate educational experiences and intellectual interests. Qian Xuantong, for example, arrived at his commitment to a new literature through prolonged curiosity about classical philology and Esperanto, which he explored during his pre-1911 years in Japan. Hu Shi, on the other hand, began to show active interest in the Chinese tradition of vernacular literature while pursuing his study of philosophy in the United States. In contrast, Chen Duxiu began to work for literary reform only after his keen disappointment with the 1911 revolution, when he needed a new means to implement his "finally, finally awakening" from the bondage of the Confucian worldview.

It was Hu Shi who provided both Qian Xuantong and Chen Duxiu with a concrete strategy for literary reform. In the course of his studies at Cornell and Columbia universities, he had already set time aside for critical examination of the *Dream of the Red Chamber* and *Water Margin*— both semi-vernacular works representative of traditional Chinese realistic fiction. At the same time, he tried his hand at new vernacular poetry. Most of the other Chinese students studying in the States scorned or mocked Hu's attempts to interest them in either the traditional vernacular or new poetry. In 1915, Hu wrote a poem in response to these Confucian gentlemen so at ease with life in America and yet so stubborn about giving up their attachment to what Hu viewed as the "dead language" of classical poetry:

> How soon can a revolution in poetry begin?
> As soon as we write poems like anything else.
> What is ornate, bedecked, has lost its vigor,
> What seems to be genuine poetry, might not be so at all.
> As I start out bravely to write my humble works,
> I come upon you, who are all accomplished writers.
> Let's join our forces, rather than mock one another,
> Let's not go on being corrupt Confucian scholars.[41]

When it was actually launched, the language movement opened with a rather mild salvo: Hu Shi's January 1917 article in *New Youth*, "Tentative Suggestions about Literary Reform." This was an address from one *wenren* to other *wenren*. It focused simply on ways to write more clearly, more pithily, more realistically. All Hu Shi's suggestions, in fact, might have been put forth equally well by any traditional reformer who sought to revive the nation by cleansing its ways of literary expression.

In the very next issue of the magazine, however, Chen Duxiu escalated the tentative tone of Hu Shi's proposals with his own essay, "Literary Revolution." Here, Chen indicted not only the stagnant literature of recent times but also the "painted, powdered, obsequious, over-mannered, pedantic, obscurantist" literati who were its authors. He pointed his finger directly at the social constituency that used the classical literature as the basis of its social and political supremacy.

In March 1918, Qian Xuantong, in a letter to Chen Duxiu, went so far as to single out language as the essence of China's social problem. He spelled out the logical—though drastic—implications of what it meant to change Chinese society through literary reform:

You, sir, have exerted yourself in the cause of overthrowing Confucianism, of reforming ethics. You believe that, if the problem of ethics is not dealt with in a fundamental way, this country of ours doesn't have much hope at all.... I, personally, have this to add: If you want to get rid of Confucianism, you cannot but get rid of the Chinese language. If you want to get rid of the naive, crude, rigid mentality of ordinary people, you cannot but first get rid of the Chinese language.[42]

Within the community of *New Youth*, the call for literary reform began to spill over into a concern with the relationship of language to consciousness. *Now Tide* members expanded that concern by further exploring how vernacular language could be used for more realistic fiction. They became pioneers and sponsors of new literature. In 1923, when the

New Tide magazine stopped publication, a *New Tide* literature series was launched by Beida graduates Li Xiaofeng and Sun Fuyuan (with the help and advice of their teachers Lu Xun and Zhou Zuoren). The *New Tide* series was responsible for bringing to the Chinese reading public the first reasonably priced edition of Lu Xun's collection of short stories, *Call to Arms*, as well as works by Zhu Ziqing, Bing Xin, Guo Moruo, and others.[43]

For several years before 1923, *New Tide* students had already been keenly aware that the most significant contribution of *New Youth* was in the realm of language reform. Therefore, they made a conscious effort to go beyond their teachers' proposals by focusing upon the psychological aspects of literary reform. In conversations and letters among themselves, they continued to debate Qian Xuantong's assertion that to change Chinese mentality, one must first undertake a thorough repudiation of the Chinese language. In fact, whenever one of their members (Gu Jiegang, for example) tried to suggest that literary reform was secondary to thought change, Fu Sinian, in his editorial capacity, would defend the inseparability of the two causes. In a public letter to his roommate Gu Jiegang, Fu wrote in April 1919:

You propose that we stress reform of ways of thinking and put less emphasis on literature. But this is wrong. The mind is not a void. It cannot be changed at will. Literature is the practical tool to change it. In the next issue I plan to write a piece on "Vernacular Literature and the Psychological Revolution" to deal with this problem. I hope you will respond to it critically.[44]

When Fu Sinian wrote about the "revolution of feeling" that had to go along with literary form, he was consciously drawing attention to an inward (*neixin*) aspect of vernacular literature overlooked by teachers caught up in public polemics against classical language. To raise questions about the limited range of emotions that could be expressed in classical fiction was, in effect, to render more contingent the chain of causality between literature, language, and thought change. Fu Sinian's conclusion reflects the point of view of his generation. They believed that to change thought, one had not only to get rid of language but also to dig out and dig up "the inert emotional passivity, the dreamlike trance" that underlay classical language and literature.[45]

The psychological approach of *New Tide* intellectuals was most apparent in their experiments with new poetry. More than any other literary form, poetry had been the domain in which the prowess of traditional language and of traditional literati had been displayed most effectively. Members of the teachers' generation like Hu Shi had invaded and assaulted this domain, trying their own hand at modern free verse without ever taking the time to reckon with the strong emotional attachments that underlay resistance to changing the language of poetry. The students, however, were more conscious of themselves as trespassers in this, the most sacred area of traditional culture.

The pains the students took to polish and to justify their experiments with vernacular poetry testify to this self-consciousness. Some, like Kang Baiqing, found the endeavor too burdensome to sustain and abandoned the project of new poetry, returning into the fold of the classicists after 1923. Others, like Zhu Ziqing, continued to write classical poetry in secret—afraid to let the public know that he had "betrayed the cause in his heart."[46]

During the May Fourth enlightenment itself, *New Tide* member Yu Pingbo broached the question of society's psychological reaction to new poetry quite explicitly. In October 1919, he catalogued the reasons for widespread opposition to vernacular poetry. Acknowledging that the classical language was an extraordinarily succinct instrument of poetic expression, Yu conceded that new poetry was clumsy and coarse by comparison. Nonetheless, he went on to argue that opposition to new poetry, in the end, was not linguistic but social and psychological:

If you want to understand why Chinese society refuses to accept new poetry, you must first understand the unseen side of Chinese social life.... It is miserable, dark.... So those who guide elite culture would prefer poetry to be cosmetic. They sanction love poems, vague descriptions of natural beauty.... They would prefer not to make public our society's many-layered domestic shame.... Because we [new language poets] insist on writing about all of that, they naturally hate us.[47]

Yu Pingbo's generation went on to air its "domestic shame" publicly in short stories. Less anxious about the use of words in stories than in poetry, members of the *New Tide* turned to this literary form eagerly. Nearly every one of them wrote short stories. Those by Wang Jingxi, Luo Jialun, and Ye Shaojun were singled out by Lu Xun as early as May 1919 as important contributions to the development of new fiction in China.[48] In their stories students exposed their own families' ways of maintaining decorum through arranged marriages and described the repression of affection between spouses, and even between siblings. Their stories aired not only domestic shame but also other less familiar but no less "shameful" social issues such as prostitution, drug addiction, and unemployment. Students thus used new literature to stretch their own sensibilities, as well as to question the worldview of their less rebellious contemporaries.

Unlike their teachers, they were keenly aware of the clumsiness of their efforts in this new enterprise. They also spoke about its limitations and self-serving purpose in public. Wang Jingxi, for example, in the preface to a collection of his *New Tide* stories entitled *Snowy Night*, expressed his generation's sense of limited achievement as follows:

I have tried to depict faithfully some life experiences I have witnessed. I aimed for precise detail ... but found my judgmental attitude interfering all the time. I have tried to be objective and truthful within the limitations of my own world-view (*rensheng guan*).... Yet I feel that I fell far too short of standards I have set for myself.... [M]y powers of perception (*guanchali*) are narrow and shallow ... not unlike so many others trying their hand at a new function, writing on whim.... Because of these limitations, I'm convinced I'll never be a good writer. Furthermore, I'm going abroad soon to find a new way to make my living [as a professional psychologist].... I can only hope that these poor experiments will inspire other potential writers who might have more talent of observation and imagination....[49]

Wang Jingxi's ruminations and self-doubt were not unique. Other students who tried to put into practice the theories of literary reform advocated by older *New Youth* intellectuals also had to reason out for themselves the implications of the vernacular language movement. One of those was Luo Jialun, who undertook the task of explaining the teachers' ideas for his own generation in a question-and-answer article published in the May 1919 issue of *New Tide*. Frankly doubting the motivation and skills of some of the students who had jumped on the bandwagon of new literature, he spelled out some of the more complex implications of the teachers' program for literary reform. His explanation, in turn, went beyond the teachers' views of the connection between language and social change.

To write "realistic literature," Luo Jialun argued, one should seek to "make it real to real people." The new literature should not only deal with topics from "real life," but also address itself to the audience's literacy level and class circumstances. Only then would vernacular literature be truly different from the old literature, which was for and by literati. Furthermore, Luo pointed out, advocates of *baihua* had to think out what "*bai*" really meant. In his own view, Luo explained, "*bai*" meant not only clear language (*qinqbai*), unadorned language (*libai*), and spoken language (*shuobai*), but also *pingbai*, the common language of (working) people.[50]

This connection between plain language and the common people was to be the distinguishing insight of the student generation. They then went on to put this insight into practice in society. In March 1919, when

New Tide members, in collaboration with activist but culturally conservative fellow students such as Xu Deheng and Deng Zhongxia, decided to found the Beijing University Commoners' Education Lecture
Society, the stage for the May Fourth movement was fully set. The concrete organizational framework of this lecture society was what enabled
the students to take their vision of the new culture and its language out
into society at large. Their teachers, Hu Shi and Chen Duxiu among
them, had limited their suggestions for a new literature to something
livelier and more humanistically inclined than the moribund, outworn
guwen (classical) literature over-burdened with the language of officialdom (*guanhua*).[51] The younger generation, on the other hand, by challenging directly society's fear of the vernacular language, *baihua*, uncovered a deeper, more explosive fear of *pingmin*, the common people.

These students tried to do more than simply enliven the reading matter of educated elites. They tried to hand over the language and thoughts
of new intellectuals to the "coolies, mafoos, chauffeurs, shopboys, etc."
who had been assumed to be uneducable, thoughtless, and wordless by
literati such as Gu Hongming. Yet even as they did so, they did not
foresee how this passing on of the Beida literary revolution into the
streets and the villages around the university would, in time, challenge
their own privileged status in society. Without any premonition of class
consciousness, they were willing to rail against the privileges of the
scholar-officials who came before them. As Xu Deheng's October 1919
speech to his fellow students in the Commoners' Education Lecture Society made clear, those who would teach, awaken, and mobilize the common people had to reckon with the wordlessness to which the *pingmin*
had been condemned for so long:

In our bureaucratized society, common people can only work as oxen and horses
for lords and gentlemen. There have been countless servants, coolies, rickshaw
pullers ... but they have not been heard from thus far.... [T]he backwardness of
our society is due to the backwardness of education for the common people....
[T]he few educated people have never been ready to give their knowledge to the
people, lest the system of their class become more difficult to maintain.[52]

The Beida students who decided to "give knowledge to the people" did
so literally, through the medium of language transmission. In the process, they became what Antonio Gramsci termed, in a different historical
context, "permanent persuaders." Before they could persuade others,
however, they had to convince themselves that it was indeed possible,
even necessary, to speak to, about, and for those "who have not been
heard from thus far."

THE BEIJING UNIVERSITY COMMONERS' EDUCATION LECTURE SOCIETY

Two months before the demonstration of May 4, 1919, a group of Beida students took on the mission of speaking to the common people. Until that point, the controversies surrounding the literary revolution and the battle of New against Old had been restricted to periodicals within the university and to some curious or outraged intellectuals outside. With the founding of the students' lecture society, these debates were taken outside the circle of educated *wenren*, and their content altered by encounters with the *pingmin*. Without the teachers' support and initiative, the younger generation might not have had a message to spread beyond the university at all; but without the students' willingness to preach on street corners, in turn, their mentors' visions would have likely faded, drowned out by the noisier constituency of conservative intellectuals.

The students who participated in the organization of the lecture society had mistrusted each other at first. Culturally radical members of *New Tide* did not see their purpose to be the same as that of the activist group that had founded the *Citizen* (*Guomin*) Society and *Citizen* magazine in the winter of 1918–19. They focused their efforts on their own and their countrymen's spiritual awakening from feudalism. *Citizen* students, on the other hand, viewed cultural iconoclasm as an obstacle in the way of national salvation, because it drew attention to China's spiritual shortcomings in her hour of political need. *Citizen* members were proud veterans of the anti-Japanese protests of May 1918 in which students from several universities in the Beijing-Tianjin area had tried to present a petition to the president of the Chinese republic. The protest failed, but the Beijing University contingent decided to pursue these activities with an organization decided to keeping the country alert to the ongoing danger of national humiliation.

Dedicated to the cause of national salvation, *Citizen* activists were from the beginning impatient with, and hostile to, the enlightenment movement advocated by both *New Youth* and *New Tide*. In the words of one of the founders of the *Citizen*, Zhang Guotao, the members of the society believed that

the whole student body should take part in a Save-the-Country Movement. Saving the country is more important than anything else. From the deepest conservatives to the anarchists, everyone should rise up and unite to save the country. Save the country first![53]

The "whole" student body did not take up this cause in the winter of 1918–19. Teachers like Li Dazhao, who was less suspicious of patriotic emotions than Chen Duxiu and less obsessed with the shortcomings of the national character than Lu Xun, took more than a passing interest in the activities of the *Citizen*. A young instructor of esthetics, Xu Beihong, designed the first cover of the *Citizen*. It depicted a thoughtful young man who, filled with worry for the fate of the nation, cups his chin in his hand and looks with determination toward the future. Finally, university president Cai Yuanpei wrote the introduction to the new student publication, expressing his hope that it would take on the responsibility for propagating "broad and profound learning" in the country as a whole.[54]

On the basis of Cai Yuanpei's hopes, Li Dazhao's support, and Xu Beihong's painting, one might conclude that in self-image and purpose there was little difference between the *New Tide* and the *Citizen*. Both societies sponsored publications that reflected the self-consciousness of educated young men bent upon awakening China. In fact, however, the *Citizen* founders were, at first, active opponents of the goals of *New Tide* radicals. Deng Zhongxia typified their interests. One year behind Fu Sinian in the literature department, Deng had arrived at Beida in 1917 armed with the *Records of the Grand Historian* and *Mirror to Government*— texts that legitimated public concern in a traditional Confucian framework. Sticking to his calligraphy practice and to his antipathy for the enlightenment movement, he became involved in the anti-Japanese boycott of 1918. Shortly after this, he became one of the moving spirits of the *Citizen* Society.

Those who joined the *Citizen*, thus, believed that to "save the country" was not only the first priority but the exclusive course of action. As Xu Deheng, another founder of the *Citizen*, recalled, opposition to the New Culture movement was an explicit corollary to their emphasis on national salvation.

The *Citizen* ... was the product of the (May 1918) petition movement. All our funds were collected from student dues. This was not so for the *New Tide* ... sponsored by the Beida school authorities. The *New Tide* influence was greater [than that of our journal].... Its moving spirit was Fu Sinian. We were against Fu Sinian and Chen Duxiu.... [B]ut after the May Fourth demonstration we began to get along with them because they began to support us in organizing the rapidly growing student movement.[55]

Xu Deheng's recollection, like Zhang Guotao's, is only partially accurate. Both emphasize the social significance of May Fourth in light of later ideological commitments. Their memoirs are striking for the

15. Deng Zhongxia as Beijing University student.

absence of any reference whatsoever to collaboration with *New Tide* members before May Fourth, especially in the context of the Commoners' Education Lecture Society.

In fact, by March 1919, members of *New Tide* and the *Citizen* were actively working together to set up this student organization. The existence of this association suggests a continuum between knowledge and action in the May Fourth era, or more precisely, a common ground between knowers and doers that has been neglected by participants and scholars alike. Overlapping membership between *New Tide* and *Citizen* societies and the lecture society (see appendix) indicates a shared commitment among China's new intellectuals. This commitment has been ignored or distorted by those who would argue May Fourth "knowers" did not do much, or that "doers" were so bent upon action that they were careless and condescending toward knowledge. To be a permanent persuader, in Gramsci's terms, one had to both know and do, and this is precisely what *Citizen* and *New Tide* members set out to accomplish in March 1919.

Two months before the actual demonstration of May 4, leaders of the *Citizen* Society like Deng Zhongxia, Liao Sucang, Zhang Guotao, and Xu Deheng had already realized, on the basis of their own frustrations in patriotic activities, that China could not defend itself against national humiliation without a broader national-awakening movement. That realization was followed by a more open-minded attitude toward the literary revolution advocated by enlightenment intellectuals. At the same time, leaders of the *New Tide* Society such as Luo Jialun and Kang Baiqing grew disenchanted with the narrow audience of the New Culture movement. They became eager to carry the advocacy of enlightenment beyond their own small circle of fellow doubters into Chinese society at large.

New Tide founder Gao Yuan, who went on to become one of the founders of the lecture society as well, most clearly voiced the disenchantment of these intellectuals. In an article called "Anti-secretism," published in *New Tide* on the eve of collaboration with the *Citizen*, he traced Chinese social, political, and cultural evils to the proclivity toward secretism between men and women, between officials and subjects of the state, and among nations. He concluded with an impassioned plea that suggests some of the reasons why champions of enlightenment, though suspicious of mass society and of crowd opinion, joined the effort to speak out:

Secrets arise from stealthy pursuit of self-interest [either by groups or by individuals].... Humanity should develop in keeping with the principles of mutual aid, not mutual extortion. Secretive actions are incorrect; mutual aid can be carried out if only we collaborate with each other to think of ways of doing so. If all of us were to start talking together, secretism could not help but be abolished.[56]

"Talking together" is precisely what Beida students decided to do in the spring of 1919. A shared desire to expose the "stealthy pursuit of self-interest" so prevalent in Chinese society enabled leading figures of the *Citizen* and the *New Tide* to form the new lecture society. Both sides became convinced that speaking out would further the goals of their respective associations more effectively.

The Beijing University Commoners' Education Lecture Society announced its formation in the March 26 issue of the *Beijing University Daily*. In keeping with the spirit of the *New Tide* manifesto, this announcement claimed that the students were merely spreading the "spirit of Beida." Like *New Tide* members before them, founders of the lecture society also arrogated to themselves the right to define, in unprecedented terms, the spirit of Beida that they were about to propagate in the society at large.

This, too, was a far cry from the "pure research" Cai Yuanpei had hoped for in his introduction to the *Citizen* or the "spirit of objective doubt" to which the *New Tide* manifesto had dedicated itself only three months earlier.

There are two kinds of education: academic education and education that reaches out to the people. The latter happens through open-air speeches and through publications issued for this purpose. The foundation of a republic must be the education of the common people.... If, however, only the offspring of the rich are able to enjoy academic education, while poor children have no chance to go to school at all—the foundation of our republic will be shaken. What is the remedy, then? Open-air speeches.... Beijing University is an egalitarian university. An egalitarian university must emphasize implementation of social equality. Therefore common-people's education can and will prevail.[57]

Although the lecture society's presumption that Beida as an institution was committed to egalitarianism was novel (and untrue), the form and content of the society's activities were quite conventional. For centuries before Beijing University students decided to stand on street corners on Sunday afternoons, Confucian gentry had been engaged in *xiang yue*, periodic village lectures ordered by the state to exhort the common people to obey family authority and to lead virtuous, peaceful lives. Formalized in the seventeenth century as a means of ideological control over the vast illiterate population, the *xiang yue* system appealed to and perpetuated a view of intellectuals as mentors of the common people.

Although they looked like gentlemen of earlier times in their long silk

16. Some members of the Beijing University Commoners' Education Society giving a lecture and handing out leaflets in the wake of the May Fourth demonstration of 1919.

gowns, and although they sounded as incomprehensible as literati must have sounded to the villagers centuries before, the Beijing University students who took to the streets in the month before May 4, 1919, had in mind something altogether different. They were not sanctioned by the state, and thus they managed to subvert a traditional form of state-sponsored loyalty. Whereas Confucian scholars had counseled the virtues of submission, of unquestioned acceptance of the ways of the ancient sages, members of the *New Tide* and the *Citizen* societies advocated the opposite.

Having overcome their differences concerning the need for a new culture in China, the speech makers, in effect, took to the street corners with many of the same issues that had been discussed in the pages of enlightenment magazines. Thus we find on April 3, 1919, Luo Jialun, who had already written a great deal about the "problem of men and women" and about the family system as the source of China's problems, lecturing on the streets of Beijing on the topic "Family Reform." The next day, Deng Zhongxia, who had previously opposed the New Culture movement, lectured on a very similar topic, "The Family System." On April 5, Deng carried his support of enlightenment ideas further by attacking the emperor-worship mentality prevalent among the masses in a talk entitled "Modern Emperors Are Finally Doomed."[58]

From the pages of their journals and from within the walls of Beida, these students brought onto the streets such non-Confucian concerns as "Labor and Intelligence," the topic of Xu Deheng's talk on April 3. These questions had been quite alien to traditional gentlemen, and raising them signaled the emergence of China's new intellectuals. Before them, educated men had assumed that those who labored with their mind, that is, who were educated, were necessarily better than and above those who labored with their physical strength. Now that student lecturers took to the streets to advocate the benefits of critical intelligence, they could not but assume that it was not a quality of mind reserved for their own kind. When they argued that all people were capable of thinking for themselves, of re-evaluating the values handed down through tradition, they were, in effect, appealing to the critical capacities of the common people, those who had for so long been deemed either gullible or dangerous. To appeal to the masses' critical intelligence entailed, at the same time, a questioning of the masses' previously held beliefs. Imperceptibly, perhaps even unwittingly, student lecturers bent upon awakening the common people began to atack the common people's own habits of mind. When *New Tide* members like Kang Baiqing and Yu Pingbo took to the streets under the auspices of the lecture society to speak on topics such as "Superstition" and "Down with Illusions,"[59] the enlightenment movement, in all its complexity, was poised to spill into the May Fourth movement.

New intellectuals (to use Gramsci's term) thus emerged in China out of a complex process of generational collaboration and debate. In the period 1917–19, their relationship to each other and conflicts with each other defined the identity of teachers and students far more than anything they said or did in society at large. But precisely because they were the inheritors of China's cultural tradition and because they had identified themselves so closely with its language and literature, their attempt to change conventions of speaking and writing proved to be a catalyst for a broader social change. By becoming conscious of who they were, they aroused the self-consciousness of hitherto dormant elements of Chinese society. By revealing publicly the limitations of their own learning, they eroded the unquestioned authority of learned men in Confucian society. Finally, by acknowledging the privileges of their own education, they were prompted to spread its benefits to those who had been denied them.

But with all their good will and organizational skill, Beida students would have amounted to nothing more than traditional reformers had their message not been as unique as it was. In the end, it was a commitment to enlightenment generated for and within the community of new intellectuals that ensured their success beyond it. If they had been less willing to cut open the sores of their own cultural inheritance, they might not have been able to diagnose, much less help cure, their compatriots' political diseases.

The May Fourth Enlightenment

We agree fully with French positivist philosopher [Auguste] Comte,
who said: If you want to reform politics, you must first change habits of
mind. His words are particularly apt for the sorry situation of contemporary Chinese politics and society, which is caused by an obstinate
mentality.... Chinese mentality today had three characteristics: it is
slavish, autocratic, and chaotic. Our thought revolution aims to change
slavish mentality into independent thinking, to change autocratic mentality into egalitarian thinking, to change chaotic mentality into logical
thinking.

Luo Jialun, "Reply to Mr. Zhang Puquan"[1]

In December 1919, *New Tide* founder Luo Jialun chose the form of a
public letter to sum up his generation's vision of enlightenment. He was
responding to open praise addressed to *New Tide* editors by the older
anarchist philosopher Zhang Zhi (referred to above as Zhang Puquan).
Luo's choice reflects the need for a safe yet meaningful context in which
to articulate the goals of a thought revolution barely one year old. Zhang
Zhi's initial letter was sparked by despondency over the monarchical
schemes of Yuan Shikai and Zhang Xun. The seasoned but despairing
anarchist pointed to the short history of *New Tide* as the only source of
hope in the gloomy world of Chinese letters. In a society where the vast
majority of the population remained beholden to the aura of ceremonial
politics and to the subservience it required, Zhang looked to the Beida
youths for a sign that Chinese ways of thinking might be able to be
challenged after all.

While he praised the accomplishments of the *New Tide* group, Zhang
Zhi had also warned the students not to get sidetracked by the fervor
of patriotic politics. To underscore his point—that there is no other way
to save China but to change the mental outlook of its masses—he reminded the students of a political motto of his favorite French thinker,

Auguste Comte. By quoting Comte, Zhang was consciously appealing to the students' admiration for the scientific thought of a philosopher they already were familiar with from their quest for positive knowledge about social phenomena.[2]

Luo Jialun's "Reply to Mr. Zhang Puquan" took up the challenge of the older revolutionary. Reaffirming his generation's appreciation for positivist thought, Luo went on to spell out its implications for their present concerns. First, he argued, "we must realize that the crimes of Yuan Shikai and Zhang Xun are not individual crimes but harmful phenomena emanating out of the very nature of Chinese mentality."[3] Once the burden of guilt had been shifted from a set of corrupt, foolish individuals to a gullible, superstitious national community, the goals of the Chinese enlightenment movement became clearer. As in Europe two centuries earlier, self-styled intellectuals (such as Luo Jialun) took it upon themselves to alter the habits of mind of their contemporaries. They aimed to spread disbelief and uneasiness—what another French philosopher, Condillac, termed *inquiétude*—in a society where blind faith in tradition and subservience to autocracy had long prevailed.

Older intellectuals such as Zhang Zhi had become interested in French thought and the new Chinese culture movement because they needed new ideas to justify their revolt against authority, tradition, and the family. The students, on the other hand, wanted more than a change of ideas about the world. Their "thought revolution" aimed to transform their own mental habits as well as their contemporaries' customary responses to the world. The teachers, especially Chen Duxiu, had admired Comte for his utilitarianism, and used him to attack their compatriots' ceremonious attachment to tradition. The students made use of Comte's methodology to analyze more concretely the origins of their own worldview. With the aid of Comte and other Western philosophers, they discovered the power and rigor of critical reason. *New Tide* intellectuals, in spite of their grand ambitions, exhibited a marked humility as they considered the potential and the limitations of modern thought. Their special object of concern was individual and social psychology. Their older mentors, consumed by the war between New and Old and determined to be heard above the din of conservatives who labeled them "radical, perverse, and destructive," had been forced to demand enlightenment.[4] They had had no time to make a reasonable argument for it. The students, by contrast, were beneficiaries of others' hoarse voices and so could try to rise above the shouting. They sought to advance the cause of enlightenment by expanding the sphere of criticism.

These youths, however, who in December 1919 defined thought

revolution in terms of "independent, egalitarian, and logical thinking,"
quickly realized that they faced tougher obstacles than those that had
confronted their French and Chinese predecessors. With the May
Fourth experience fresh in mind, they became aware of how readily social
activism could become a substitute for the prolonged, difficult challenge
of mental transformation. In keeping with Zhang Zhi's warning, they
tried to prevent themselves and their contemporaries from drifting off the
course of enlightenment. So, shortly after the event of 1919 they restated
the importance of the quest for *zijue*, or genuine autonomy, even in the
midst of patriotic mobilization. This restatement was made under the
pressure of rapidly unfolding political developments and was, therefore,
not as convincing as they had hoped. Unlike the French philosophers of
the eighteenth century, *New Tide* youths did not have the leisure of several decades of philosophical criticism before having to put their thoughts
into action. As a result, their thought revolution, as well as their efforts at
social mobilization, were often hasty and ill-informed. Furthermore,
their frequent appeals to Western ideas made them acutely vulnerable in
a context of patriotic fervor. Although most of their contemporaries were
ready to embrace the cause of national renewal, few were willing to trace
the causes of China's weakness to her own native traditions. May Fourth
intellectuals who did so were frequently accused of being "un-Chinese."
Nonetheless, they persevered in the dual challenge of mental change and
political reform long after their dispersal from the protective community
offered to them at Beida.

A commitment to the simultaneous transformation of self and world
thus became the distinguishing characteristic of the May Fourth generation. In the short half decade from the launching of the *New Tide* in 1919
to the next outburst of patriotic politics (during the May Thirtieth movement of 1925), they forged intellectual and personal solidarities that
marked them for the rest of their turbulent public lives. These solidarities are even more striking precisely because of the disparate experiences of May Fourth youths after graduation from Beida. Some, as we
shall see, went off to study in Europe and the United States immediately
after the events of 1919–20. While they were abroad, academic concerns
postponed their need to reckon with the incongruence between a changing self and an intractable world. But not for long.

At home, *New Tide* intellectuals such as Zhu Ziqing and Ye Shengtao
founded the Society for Literary Research, a concrete vehicle to carry on
the mission of the May Fourth literary revolution. Quite a few of those
involved with the Commoners' Education Lecture Society went on to
become active in workers' night schools and the Beida Society for the

Study of Marxist Theory. Among those who made the rapid leap from the May Fourth enlightenment to the founding of the Chinese Communist Party in 1921 were teachers such as Li Dazhao and Chen Duxiu and students such as Deng Zhongxia, Zhang Shenfu, Zhang Guotao, Gao Shangde, and Li Jun.[5]

However, in spite of the multiplicity of social and political paths traveled by members of the May Fourth generation, a shared concern with cultural change persisted into the 1920s. These young intellectuals continued to search for a more scientific, more logical worldview with which to replace their compatriots' customary and debilitating Confucian outlook. They also persisted in their attack on the ethic of subservience that made sons unquestioningly obedient to fathers, women helplessly dependent on men, individuals frightened to express themselves in a public realm dominated by status and familial obligations. Finally, they kept on borrowing, translating, and adopting Western ideas even as their contemporaries lapsed into increasingly fervent anti-foreignism. In fact, as subsequent chapters will document, May Fourth intellectuals managed to retain and augment the role of critical reason throughout the course of China's long, impassioned struggle against imperialism. Throughout that stuggle they never strayed far from the goals of the larger revolution even as they acknowledged special tasks and limitations of intellectuals like themselves.

QUEST FOR A SCIENTIFIC WORLDVIEW

Three years before the founding of the *New Tide* Society in the winter of 1918–19, Cai Yuanpei had already asserted that it was legitimate, even urgent, for young students to seek and to fashion for themselves a life perspective different from that of their elders. When he took over the presidency of Beida, Cai was already armed with a philosophical rationale for an "education for a worldview" (*shijie guan jiaoyu*).[6] His hope had been to correct the traditional literatus' contempt for knowledge about the Western world. So he offered Beida students a chance to learn from professional educators and to organize themselves into autonomous study societies where they first explored Western ideas and non-utilitarian values. Under Cai's tutelage, a group of iconoclastic teachers pressed further and called into question the most fundamental assumptions of the Confucian belief system. These intellectuals, the students' mentors, embraced Western-inspired utilitarianism as the sole criterion of a socially valid worldview.

One year before the students themselves joined the cause of an anti-

Confucian enlightenment, *New Youth* magazine sponsored a special issue on the "Problem of Existence." The purpose of the contributors was, according to editor Chen Duxiu, to weigh a variety of current world-views and to point the way to the one most suited to the needs of China today. In his own article, entitled rather boastfully "The True Meaning of Human Life," Chen proceeded to debunk all religions that had attracted his compatriots: Confucianism, Buddhism, and Christianity. They were, in his view, thoroughly inadequate because of their excessive asceticism, anti-individualism, and general lack of a realistic appraisal of social life. In the end, Chen Duxiu concluded that self-fulfillment could not become the end of a new worldview. Addressing himself to students directly, he pleaded:

If you want blessings, don't fear suffering. The sorrows of individuals today often become the blessings of the future.... An individual should leave behind a society that future individuals can enjoy as well.[7]

The new youths who were inspired by Chen Duxiu's generation did not take his counsel literally. Although they too were concerned, nearly consumed, with the problem of a new worldview, they were less willing to go on suffering in the present for the sake of some future generation. Instead, they explored a variety of thought systems that promised to bring the individual more prompt gratification in the present-day social world while enabling him or her to counter the repressive, unscientific views held by the vast majority of the Chinese people. Thus, in the very first issue of *New Tide*, published in January 1919, Fu Sinian returned to a question seemingly settled by Chen Duxiu a year earlier, namely, "What is the point of human existence after all?" Less concerned with the debilitating illusion fostered by religious belief, Fu concentrated his article on the most recent Western philosophical and scientific analyses of human life. Moving swiftly, and rather superficially, from Feuerbach to Darwin to Nietzsche, he outlined the process through which modern Western civilization came to define the meaning of existence in more *humane* terms than the unenlightened Chinese tradition had. In the end, however, Fu Sinian, like Chen Duxiu before him, was unable to break completely with the Confucian ideal of social service. Thus, he concluded that the most viable and valid worldview was one that encouraged "the free development of the individual for the common welfare."[8]

Even while holding the "common welfare" in mind, Fu Sinian and his fellow *New Tide* members went on to probe deeper and deeper into the philosophical and social prerequisites of the "free development of the individual." In the course of their explorations, they discovered the complexities of scientific reason, of analytical logic, and of modern psychology. These subjects had eluded their mentors during their struggles with the conservative intellectual establishment. Capitalizing upon their teachers' hasty victories, students were able to become more inward and more critical in their own approach to Western philosophy and religion.

Unlike older intellectuals who railed against the superstitious beliefs of their countrymen, the students focused upon the "haphazard" approach to life characteristic of Chinese tradition from its earliest Confucian origins. In search of an antidote to what Luo Jialun had called China's "chaotic mentality," they took it upon themselves to introduce "systematic reasoning," more specifically analytical logic and experimental methods, to China. Fervent believers in Socrates' injunction that "the unexamined life is not worth living," they undertook the cultivation of a scientific worldview with a fierce and single-minded devotion. It is not surprising, then, that from their ranks emerged China's first professional scientists, social scientists, and philosophers. To name just some of the more prominent examples: Wang Jingxi became founder of the Research Institute of Psychology; Fu Sinian became director of the Historical Research Institute of the Academia Sinica; and Feng Youlan, Jin Yuelin, and Zhang Shenfu pioneered a scientific approach to philosophy at Qinghua University.

Concerned with methodology (*fangfa*), *New Tide* members tried to alert their countrymen to questions of causality and of evidence, which had been long ignored by Confucian thinkers. They raised anew the question of *how* one learns (not only toward what ends) and so condemned traditional Chinese academic life as "anti-learning." Their condemnation, however, did not end with elite culture. It went on to encompass popular culture, too, which these students believed to have been poisoned by the prolonged deterioration of Chinese intellectual life. In the words of the *New Tide* manifesto of January 1919: "People with scanty learning tend to be muddleheaded about the relationship of cause and effect. Unclear about causality, their conduct is, naturally, shortsighted and irresponsible."[9] Subjective prejudice and "passive one-sidedness" was the consequence. The worst manifestation of muddled thinking, in the eyes of these intellectuals, was prejudice and passive one-sidedness. They, like the French philosophers of the enlightenment before them, had nothing but contempt for lazy acceptance of customary explanations of the world. Prejudice for them, as for Montesquieu, was "not that which renders men ignorant of some particulars, but whatever renders them ignorant of themselves."[10]

In order to precipitate their compatriots' self-awakening, *New Tide* intellectuals focused their earliest efforts on clarifying the laws of knowledge, or, more precisely, the significance of cause and effect. Scorn for causal explanations, they discovered, ran deep in Chinese culture, both elite and popular. At its most basic and most pervasive level, this prejudice was rooted in the old concept of fate. The notion that one's fortune or misfortune lay beyond the control or the understanding of the individual was, in the eyes of May Fourth youths, the essence of traditional thought among sages as well as the masses. Gu Jiegang summarized his generation's conviction that "fatalism"—an intellectual aversion to systematic exploration of cause and effect—was the source of China's moral degeneracy:

Psychological reliance on fate leads to self-indulgence, to recklessness in personal behavior.... And yet everything has its cause and effect. Those who believe in fate choose to blind themselves to the laws of cause and effect, choose to overlook how all end results are caused by our own actions.... What China needs is a more modern, Western definition of fate as the combination of inherited potential and the realization of that potential in a given environment. This is what it means to be "master of one's own fate."[11]

Mastery of fate through an understanding of the scientific laws of cause and effect thus became the aim of the *New Tide* intellectuals. Their nationalistic contemporaries, among them the editors of *Citizen* magazine, also shared this concern with China's backwardness. They, too, argued that China needed science, not as a means of self-awakening but as a way of "catching up with Japan ... a society in which the atmosphere is suffused with scientific concern."[12] By contrast, *New Tide* members' interest in scientific reasoning was both more philosophical and more personal. They probed the limitations as well as the social promise of scientific knowledge. They went beyond materialist explanations of cause and effect to explore the complex world of individual and social psychology. Their sense of the circumscribed utility of science sets them apart not only from more nationalistic fellow students but also from older enlightenment intellectuals like Ding Wenjiang, Wu Zhihui, Hu Shi, and Chen Duxiu, who believed that "*nothing* ever escapes the laws of science."[13]

New Tide intellectuals, focusing on the presuppositions of knowledge, were far more interested in how scientists reach their conclusions than in how infallible or enduring those conclusions might be. Their epistemological emphasis has been overlooked by most historians of modern China, who fail to distinguish between the "scientism" of older iconoclasts and the more scrupulous professional commitment to scientific reasoning among members of this younger generation. Both generations have been portrayed as superficial in their exploration of science and as infected with an ulterior, extrascientific obsession with the control and predictability of social events.[14] This characterization does injustice to both.

In fact, *New Youth* contributors had been explicit about their nonscientific goals from the beginning. They sought to foster a generally critical outlook through the medium of science. Even they, however, were not simply instrumental in their advocacy of a scientific worldview. Wang Xinggong, for example (the member of the teachers' generation most responsible for the complex view of scientific truth that inspired the younger May Fourth intellectuals), emphasized *psychological* factors in his overview of the origins and consequences of modern science. In an essay published in the December 1919 issue of *New Tide* (the same issue in which Luo Jialun published his "Reply to Mr. Zhang Puquan"), Wang tried to refute contemporaries who condemned science as a new form of intellectual enslavement. Raising the question "Is scientific truth truly objective or not?" he elaborated his psychological explanation of scientific curiosity. Wang Xinggong's purpose in this article was to point out that scientific truth was nothing but a "natural outgrowth of mankind's long-standing interaction with the objective world."[15] This point was difficult to accept, especially in the light of certain simplistic notions about absolute "laws of reason" prevalent among both proponents and opponents of scientism. Thus, Wang was forced to emphasize that science is a "concrete way to harmonize spiritual inner thought with the objective material world." Harking back to traditional Chinese philosophical assumptions, he concluded that "scientific knowledge is not purely objective, but rather is the result of the essential inseparability of subject and object, of self and world."[16]

Wang Xinggong's students undertook the task of elaborating the concept of a scientific worldview in more philosophical terms. Feng Youlan raised issues similar to Wang's concerns in an essay on Henri Bergson, a philosopher who also emphasized the non-objective, limited nature of scientific truth. Zhang Shenfu, in a similar article introducing Einstein's research on relativity, also wrote about the philosophical significance of this revolution in modern physics. Such essays reaffirmed the inseparability of subject and object, and the thesis that intuition is not antithetical to scientific reasoning.[17] Students, thus, made a more complex argument than their teachers for the claim that no single scientific finding is ever absolutely true or truly conclusive.

Their teachers had tried to prove the utility of science in all aspects of social life. Students, on the other hand, were more modest. They focused their efforts on making philosophy more scientific. Their modesty gave way, however, when they went on to try to prove that scientific philosophy was the culmination of all sciences. Fu Sinian, in an article written on the eve of May 4 demonstration of 1919, expressed his generation's impatience with Beida professors who claimed to be teaching philosophy while being "thoroughly ignorant of natural and social sciences." Arguing against those who would add a dash of "scientific glamor" to traditionalistic conjectures about the "eight diagram" theory, he concluded that philosophy can and must be subject to the same tests of verification and falsification as all other scientific hypotheses.[18]

He Siyuan, another *New Tide* member and, later, noted writer on subjects related to the methodology of social sciences, shared Fu Sinian's early enthusiasm for scientific philosophy. In October 1919, shortly before he went to the United States to study for his Ph.D., he published an article entitled "New Methodologies of World Philosophy." In it, he argued that philosophy can and must become not only theoretically scientific but experimental as well. The distinctive feature of modern philosophy, according to this young theorist, was its indebtedness to sociology and biology. In the end, he argued, "true philosophy" must go beyond experience to explain experience.[19] Half a year later, He Siyuan elaborated the implications of these conclusions in another *New Tide* article entitled "Philosophy and Common Sense." Trying to defend the importance, the primacy really, of philosophy for an increasingly politicized, activist student movement, he wrote:

Everyone has his own philosophy, whether it is known by that person or not. No matter how much you condemn philosophy, you have to recognize that your attack is inseparable from your own philosophical standpoint. Whoever condemns philosophy is unaware of his own philosophy. The less self-conscious [*zijue*, i.e. autonomous] one's philosophy is, the more restricted it is. If it is totally unconscious, then we are slaves of prejudice for life.

Having restated the faith of enlightenment—that prejudice is the result of ignorance of self—he went on to claim that

self-consciousness is an opportunity for philosophically aware living. . . . If our life can actualize our knowledge, then, and only then, may we say that knowledge is the guiding principle of our life. . . . Then, and only then, has theory become reality. Thus, human life can, and must, become an effort at cognition.[20]

He Siyuan's point, like that of many other *New Tide* intellectuals, was that philosophy must be based on common sense yet overcome the limitations of common sense. This enlightenment-inspired critique of ordinary, experiential knowledge brings these Chinese youths closer, in spirit, to European Marxists like Gramsci and Lukacs than to Mao

Zedong, who later attempted to identify knowledge with experience, and philosophy with common sense.

Interest in formal philosophy also deepened the May Fourth students' discontent with traditional Chinese thought. Although they were quite familiar with the texts of native philosophy, they went on to explore the alien territory of modern logic. The older iconoclasts, consumed by their strident battle with the forces of cultural reaction, had had neither time for, nor interest in, the form of their arguments against Confucianism. The students' generation, by contrast, showed a marked and persistent interest in formal rules of philosophical reasoning. For example, in May 1920, *New Youth* published Gao Yihan's overview entitled "The Philosophy of Bertrand Russell." This teacher of May Fourth youths focused his essay almost entirely on the social thought of the famous mathematical logician. A year and a half earlier, the students had already included in the first issue of *New Tide* Xu Yanzhi's lengthy, technical translation of Russell's essay "Logic as the Essence of Philosophy." Russell's argument that logic is the main problem of modern philosophy fell on particularly receptive ears among students committed to making Chinese philosophy more scientific, more rigorous, and more practical. Russell's claim that formal logic had been lost by Hegel and must now be recaptured through mathematical logic was embraced by *New Tide* intellectuals as a personal and social challenge.

Fu Sinian, voicing the conviction of his generation, wrote in March 1919: "Formal logic is the foundation of the practical philosophy that we need to borrow and to adopt in China so as to clear the muddleheaded atmosphere prevailing in contemporary Chinese thought."[21] Zhang Shenfu, who later became China's foremost Russell specialist, elaborated this conviction in a two-part essay for *New Tide* detailing the history of the connection between mathematics and philosophy. After a lucid review of the technical problems solved by mathematicians from Plato through Russell (with only one sentence about ancient Chinese mathematicians), Zhang proceeded to prove how philosophy and mathematics had moved closer and closer in the past forty years, especially in the domain of formal logic. Formal logic, Zhang argued, was also socially useful. It was, in his view, nothing less than a model of responsible, autonomous reasoning, provided that those who taught logic were "at once thoroughly expert in mathematical logic and widely read in the general problems of social philosophy.[22]

Scientific philosophy and formal logic, then, were two aspects of the new worldview sought by the *New Tide* generation. In addition to these, they also explored the uncharted field of modern psychology. This aspect of their quest, like the other two, set them apart from their mentors, who had had little energy to spare for psychological introspection. Spokesmen of the teachers' generation knew and dreaded the debilitating gloominess that overwhelmed them whenever they stopped to explore the subject of their own motivations and origins. The students, by contrast, turned eagerly to self-examination as well as to readings in technical psychology. They hunted for references beyond those that *New Youth* mentors such as Chen Daqi—the first faculty member to teach psychology at Beida—gave them in courses about modern "soul science."[23]

Among *New Tide* members, Wang Jingxi carried an interest in modern psychology the furthest. Early on, before he obtained his Ph.D. in experimental psychology from Johns Hopkins University, Wang set a markedly behavioralist tone for May Fourth discussions of "What is thought?" In an early 1919 article, he argued that "thinking"—the quintessential attribute of humankind—is nothing but an "innate instinct": that is, only a more complex, more purposeful unfolding than the instinctive behavior of other forms of life.[24] This, as well as Wang's other essays published in the *New Tide*, applied an experimental approach to the problem of consciousness. Through such writings, Wang imparted a sense of confidence to other members of his generation who had come to wonder about the *practical* significance of the "worldview" question. Thought revolution thus became a far more feasible project once "thought" was redefined in terms of behavioral psychology.

Other *New Tide* members, in time, came to share Wang Jingxi's concern. For example, Zhu Ziqing and Yang Zhensheng (who later became famous as Chinese fiction writers) took up the challenge of translating technical works in modern psychology during their studies at Beijing University.[25] He Siyuan carried this generational interest in psychology into the realm of social theory. His *New Tide* articles on sociology emphasized social psychology more than those of *New Youth* mentors such as Tao Menghe.[26] Zhang Shenfu, a member of this youthful cohort, introduced Freud's theory of psychoanalysis into China through a translation from the British magazine *Nature*. An interest in Freud, in turn, expanded the Chinese intellectuals' previously behavioralist understanding of "instincts" by calling attention to what Zhang called the "conflict between instinct and consciousness."[27] ("Scientific" introductions to Freud during and after the May Fourth period turned out to be an effective cover for an enduring interest in the "sexual instinct," long repressed as a subject of inquiry in both individual and social life in China.)

New Tide intellectuals, thus, were both more philosophical and more psychological in their quest for a scientific worldview than their teachers. They also managed to avoid the dichotomy between science and religion that had characterized their predecessors in the European enlightenment as well as their *New Youth* mentors. Members of this younger generation approached the question of religion more open-mindedly, and more sympathetically, than their forerunners. They refused to contrast science with religion and, instead, chose to view science and religion as synthesized in philosophy. In the first issue of *New Tide*, Tan Pingshan, later one of the organizers of the Communist Party, elaborated this view in an article about the complementary limitations of scientific rationality and religious faith. His detailed analysis of emotional factors at work in human intelligence contained a plea for a positive appreciation of religious belief. Such a plea would have been inconceivable to enlightenment-oriented enemies of religion both in China and abroad: "Religion is a shelter where people can feel safe, where they can set the course of their destiny and thereby achieve peace of mind.... One's worldview is based on emotion and these emotions can become reality and can change the world by deepening one's worldview.... With peace of mind, one can struggle bravely against the world as it is."[28]

More impressive than peace of mind, according to Tan, was the believer's capacity to alter the world and fight the world with the power of his or her faith. Thus, he concluded:

Those who are believers don't worry whether what they believe matches with the reality of the world or not.... Believing in their own beliefs they can stand steadfast even when tempted by wealth and rank or threatened by death.... Religion is concerned with ideals, it can fuse feelings and the subconscious ... and thus helps the individual in a very different way than science does..., Although science, which emphasizes the analysis of nature, seems to be in conflict with religion [which emphasizes ideals], these two can be reconciled by philosophy.... Philosophy, in turn, is the source of progress of all civilization.[29]

Intellectuals of the older generation, unlike Tan Pingshan, had been absolute in their opposition of science to religion. They had been obsessed with a struggle against superstitions (*mixin*) and the Chinese equivalent of religion, *lijiao* (faith in ritual). The students' generation, on the other hand, found the phenomenon of belief (*xinyang*) inspiring, especially when approached from a perspective of psychological appreciation. Having argued that Chinese thought lacked logical coherence, they went on to point out that China also lacked psychological inwardness or, more precisely, what they termed the force of belief. Gu Jiegang summarized his generation's argument as follows:

Belief is a psychological phenomenon. It is a person's conviction that originates from a subjective understanding of the world. This understanding can become an extraordinarily powerful force in the motivation of an individual or a society. Neither an individual nor a society can do without belief.... Chinese religion, by and large, is not a religion of belief but a means to achieve material prosperity. When prosperity doesn't materialize as a result of worship, belief starts to waver. This cannot be considered true belief.[30]

During the years of political activism that followed the events of 1919–20, it became harder and harder to hold on to this positive view of religious belief. Nonetheless, *New Tide* members continued to emphasize the power of belief even as they deepened their commitment to science and, in some cases, to Marxist revolution. For example, in a 1921 letter to Chen Duxiu from Paris, Zhang Shenfu (who was then actively engaged in the recruitment of Chinese Communists in France) raised once again the value of religion. Writing to the mentor noted for his hostility to all spiritual gibberish, Zhang insisted: "Many people say that Marxism is a kind of religion. Actually, if you want to accomplish anything in this world you must have some of that force of belief that is part of religion." Surprisingly, Chen Duxiu answered: "You are right. It is not only in the course of making a revolution that we need the spirit of self-sacrifice, but in doing anything truthfully one has to have this spirit. No project can be undertaken successfully without religious belief."[31]

For a brief while, then, it seemed as if the younger generation was converting its elders. In fact, however, the two groups shared the most fundamental enlightenment conviction: that a scientific worldview is inherently liberating and progressive. Although students, more than their teachers, emphasized questions about the methodology and the epistemology of science, they, too, wanted freedom of thought above all else. Thus, both generations held firm to the belief that to think scientifically means to renounce the false consolations of fatalism. To understand cause and effect, in their view, was to make the most concrete contribution possible to the revolution of thought. This mental revolution was the goal of the May Fourth enlightenment. It required both teachers and students to connect science with democracy, to link the quest for scientific method with a struggle for freedom of thought. In December 1919, this goal seemed nearly at hand when Luo Jialun wrote:

The freedom of thought is actually the freedom to express thought.... The reform of worldview must be in keeping with the spirit of science. It must be undertaken in order to develop democracy.[32]

The freedom of thought that Luo Jialun and his fellow *New Tide* members fought for was inextricably tied up with a longing to express themselves as autonomous individuals. Although they were fully committed to an informed, logical, psychologically inward notion of "science," these students never lost sight of more fundamental obstacles to free thought, namely, China's lack of "democracy." Unlike their elders who made "science" and "democracy" into slogans to connote all-encompassing alternatives to the Confucian tradition, the younger generation preferred a more circumscribed perspective. They viewed science as a *method* of interpreting, dissecting really, the world of phenomena. Democracy, by contrast, was an *attitude* of self-confidence that an individual brought to scientific inquiry.

The more these students pursued the question of the methodology of science, the more they came up against the prohibitions against self-expression that permeated Chinese society. In the end, *New Tide* members realized that their freedom to express thoughts freely was thwarted not so much by a lack of scientific knowledge among their compatriots as by their own long-standing, internalized self-repression. It was this self-repression that they called "undemocratic" and they feared would undo all their efforts to develop an alternative epistemology. The quest for a scientific worldview, thus, led them to a direct confrontation with habits of self-doubt and passivity fostered in Chinese culture through the family system.

REBELLION AGAINST THE FAMILIAL ETHIC OF SUBSERVIENCE

May Fourth students were hardly the first to call into question the mores of the traditional family system. Despite the heroic image of themselves that they projected to the rest of China's youths through publications, they were, in fact, mere consolidators of a rebellion against patriarchy that was at least two decades old at the time they joined the battle in 1919.[33] Two generations of political critics before them had already traced China's lethargy and backwardness to the crushing burden of filial piety. The students' distinctive contribution to this struggle was their willingness to acknowledge their own acquiescence in the repression of the individual. Rather than simply blame the inherited tradition for its lack of individual autonomy, they went on to probe the individual's own reluctance to take responsibility for his or her own fate. In the process of this self-examination, they uncovered the hidden comforts of subservience as well as the awful burden of genuine freedom of thought.

Before these youths could begin to wrestle with the problem of self-repression, others before them had to inaugurate the attack against the "bondage" of the family system. Such an attack began as early as 1907, when the radical anarchist journal *New Century* launched its call for an "ancestor revolution," or, more precisely, a revolution against ancestor worship.[34] The unquestioning veneration of the aged, whether dead or alive, was deemed by these early radicals to be against the dictates of science and reason, both of which they saw as key to a truly modern and powerful China. The anarchists' conviction that political revolution must begin with the family, which was the primary instrument of subjugation and inequality, was carried to an even more fervent extreme by contributors to *New Youth*. In the years immediately prior to student demonstrations of 1919, intellectuals of the teachers' generation, disillusioned with the failure of the 1911 revolution, attacked the family system on less political grounds than the pre-1911 anarchists. Victims of the abuses of patriarchy themselves, these cultural iconoclasts tried to remedy the situation for their surrogate offspring—the new youth. When these writers attacked the family system, they were, in effect, voicing their own rage at an ethical code that was easier to defy in public life than in private.

Most of the iconoclastic teachers at Beida, unlike the May Fourth students, had been forced to marry, to study, and to work according to the dictates of familial authority. During and after the events of 1919–20, they continued to live their lives in quiet, desperate acquiescence to the demands of filial piety even as they committed themselves to the liberation of the next generation. A few of these men, and Chen Hengzhe—the one female faculty member among them—dared to break off arranged marriages and start new, "free love" affairs. But most of the *New Youth* writers, such as Hu Shi, Li Dazhao, and Chen Duxiu, remained devoted to their mothers and wives, who had bound feet and little or no education. They also continued to financially support aged fathers who were hostile to the advocacy of *New Youth*.

The strident attack on the family system was thus the teachers' way of venting frustration over political revolution as well as concealing despair about their own personal emancipation. A Daoist lawyer, Wu Yu, was one of the most bitter of the *New Youth* intellectuals to accuse the family of squelching freedom of thought. His February 1917 article "The Family System as the Basis of Despotism" raised a cry of protest against filial piety. This cry grew to a deafening roar by the time the students founded the *New Tide* Society in the winter of 1918–19. Although he seemed to follow up on themes of other *New Youth* writers like Yi Baisha and Chen Duxiu, who had attacked Confucian teachings in the wake of the monarchical restoration attempts, Wu Yu in fact inaugurated a critique of despotism that went far beyond politics. He focused his attack on filial piety in order to show how the family and state collaborated to keep the individual bound and gagged emotionally, intellectually, and spiritually.

The burden of "gratitude" and the chains of "propriety" were, according to Wu Yu, the source of autocracy from the time of Confucius onward. He argued that filial devotion to parents and to ancestors had compelled individuals to forget their own selves and thereby to serve despots more readily. His conclusion was simple and drastic: The family system had rendered China's four hundred million people "slaves of the myriad dead, and thus unable to rise."[35]

Wu Yu's protest gained depth and popularity through the fiction of Lu Xun. One year after Wu Yu's indictment, Lu Xun's story "Diary of a Madman" pierced the Chinese world of letters with its shrill equation of Confucian virtue with cannibalism. By October 1919, when Lu Xun wrote his long answer to the question "How are we to be fathers today?" Wu Yu's general attack on paternal authority had evolved into a full-fledged program for emancipating one's own children from filial piety.

In this essay, Lu Xun used the authority of evolutionary biology to condemn the Chinese family system as being "against nature." To ask the young to sacrifice themselves for the old was, in his view, a grave and characteristically Chinese perversity. His argument was addressed to his own generation of "awakened" fathers on the verge of starting their own families. He asked parents to sacrifice themselves for their children, and to break the habit of demanding subservience. This was, as Lu Xun knew it would be, a difficult and slow project. Unable to obtain freedom for their own generation, champions of enlightened fatherhood had to content themselves with the hope of liberating the next one:

Burdened as a man may be with the weight of tradition, he may yet prop open the gate of darkness with his shoulder to let the children pass through to the bright wide-open spaces to lead happy lives henceforth as rational human beings.[36]

Unlike mentors such as Wu Yu and Lu Xun, radicals of the student generation were less content with sacrificing themselves for the future. They demanded a new ethical code that would make self-fulfillment a natural and widespread prerogative. Ten years younger than their teachers, members of the *New Tide* Society were markedly more impatient with the everyday manifestations of filial piety. Although they were too old to be the biological offspring of their teachers—and thus could not benefit directly from the reversal of Confucianism suggested in Lu Xun's essay "How Are We to Be Fathers Today?"—they were young enough to refuse to put up with a lifetime of arrangements made for them by Confucian-minded parents.

Their refusal, though more active and personal than that of their teachers, came after an initial period of compromise. Thus, nearly all of the *New Tide* members were married when they entered Beida. By the time of the founding of their society, these young men had fathered children, often while on vacation from their modern secondary schools in the city. Quite a few had already lost their wives in childbirth. Although some were content with the particular women chosen by their families, all felt burdened, even humiliated, by being spoken for. They longed to find their own voices and live their lives more in keeping with an enlightenment vision of autonomy.

To speak out for oneself, however, is to risk hurting those one loves the most. Not surprisingly, then, the students' enmity toward filial piety was at once personal and indirect. In the first issue of *New Tide*, for example, Fu Sinian, who had married at fifteen a girl his mother chose and who never criticized his parents publicly, wrote a bitter indictment of the family system. Calling it "the source of all evil," Fu argued that it crushed all sense of individuality (*gexing*) and dwarfed one's hope for self-fulfillment. This essay expressed, often self-indulgently, the anguish of an entire generation of recently married but disgruntled young men:

The enormous burden of the family makes it totally impossible for a Chinese person to pursue his own vocation. It pushes him, bit by bit, toward immorality.... Alas! Such is the benefit of the Chinese family system: it forces you to become a provider, it makes you muddle-headed, it forces you to submit yourself to others and lose your identity.

Not content to accuse the family of crushing modern aspirations toward individuality, Fu went on to appeal to traditional ideals as a means of proving its immorality and unfairness:

According to the doctrine of the *Daxue* (Great Learning) self-cultivation comes first, and ordering the family is second. This may have been true in ancient China, but now, those who are engaged in self-cultivation can never support a family, while those who are engaged in supporting a family can never engage in self-cultivation.... Alas! The burden of the family! The burden of the family! The burden of the family! Its weight has stifled countless heroes![37]

Fu Sinian's passionate indictment was followed by an even more thoroughgoing attack on the family by Gu Jiegang, one of the shyest and most bookish of the *New Tide* founders. Gu, whose wife by an arranged marriage had died in 1918 and who adopted the pen name Gu Chengyu in fear of his father's wrath, recorded his generation's most comprehensive critique of the family system. It was published in the *New Tide* under the title "Reflections on the Old Family System." Unable to pour out all this pent-up discontent in the first essay of February 1919, Gu Jiegang went on to write a second essay, which was not completed until May 1920 due to the author's illness. Read together, these two essays provide an intimate view of the distinctive reasons that led *New Tide* students to join their mentors' attack on the ethic of filial piety.

Lu Xun had written in a humorous, nearly abstract tone about fathers-to-be. Gu Jiegang, by contrast, describes only what he has seen personally in the Suzhou area among middle-gentry families close to his own. Disclaiming any "scientific expertise," he adopts the voice of the guilty participant. His essays dissect the addiction to dignity, honor, and status characteristic of literati offspring. Accusing his parents, his relatives, and himself, Gu writes: "We keep secret the long-standing suffering caused by the old-style family's three 'isms': fame-ism (the ceaseless, oppressive quest for worldly position), habit-ism (the belief that one must not change an iota of the Confucian ethic of filial piety), and fatalism (letting things take their course, thus inflicting upon the next generation the pains suffered by oneself)."[38]

In these essays, Gu Jiegang uncovers something older intellectuals such as Wu Yu and Lu Xun did not have time to notice: the psychological comfort, the security that is the side effect of subservience. When he came to analyze the phenomenon of "status-obsession" (*mingfen zhuyi*) Gu was criticizing one of the basic assumptions of traditional culture: that every person must fit into a specific social identity delineated by the Confucian classics.[39] His aim in this critique was to lay bare the long-standing habit of acquiescence that was the psychological underside of the parental authority decried by the older generation of iconoclasts. This more self-conscious assault on the family system took note of the benefits that accrue to the inferior as a result of prolonged subjugation to the superior.

The theft of selfhood that the teachers' generation had attributed to Confucian notions of filial piety is described by Gu Jiegang as the result of the centuries-long fear of overt confrontation. With striking inwardness, he dissects the fear of responsibility that prevents youth from grasping autonomy. "Why does the younger generation not want its individuality? Because the severity of the elders has bred into them a reverence that prevents them from expressing a personal viewpoint.... They feel more secure if the world knows them as 'so-and-so's son,' 'so-and-so's brother,' 'so-and-so's wife.'"[40] In Gu's view, the "cruelty" of the aged and the "cowardice" of the young are thus interrelated aspects of the family system. Consequently, he comes across as more pessimistic than Lu Xun, who took for granted that an end to elders' cruelty would solve the family problem. Gu, like so many of his generational cohorts, probes the mechanism of internalized oppression and then concludes: "Seeing the traditional family and the society organized on this foundation makes me desperate to the point of wanting to die. It is uncertain if the future holds a brighter promise."[41]

The alternative to playing the role of so-and-so's son, so-and-so's brother, so-and-so's wife was, in the view of *New Tide* members, to gain a positive sense of one's own individuality. They believed that even if the family "system" was deeply rooted in the social psyche, it could be eroded over time by the determined efforts of those who dared to forge for themselves an autonomous self. This quest to achieve a viable, tough self-image to withstand the pressure to become a mere social cipher led students to take further risks. They not only uncovered the psychological comforts of being an appendage in a fixed family hierarchy, but also went on to probe the strange, new realm of philosophical and ethical individualism.

Confronted with a native tradition that had labeled as "selfish" (*zisi*) all concern with and talk about the self, they looked to the world outside of China for inspiration. In their explorations of Western alternatives to the Chinese image of self, these students followed leads provided by their teachers in the *New Youth* group. Hu Shi, friend and mentor of May Fourth students, emerged as the most helpful guide. When he undertook to edit *New Youth*'s 1918 special issue on Ibsen, his aim was to provide a practical and contentious model of self-becoming.

In his own lead article, "On Ibsenism," Hu Shi quoted a passage from Ibsen's letter to Georg Brandes. This passage was to strike with the force of thunder the younger generation seeking some way out of the web of filial piety: "What I hope from you is a pure kind of egoism. It is important that there be times in which you feel that 'I' am the most important thing in the world; all the rest matters not."[42] Although Hu Shi himself remained in an arranged marriage all his life, and although, toward the end of the New Culture movement, he began, in essays such as "The Non-Individualistic New Life,"[43] to warn students about the dangers of excessive autonomy, his 1918 message that pure egoism was the highest form of true altruism was to have an enduring impact upon younger enlightenment intellectuals.

Members of the *New Tide* Society were particularly eager to embrace this new notion of self. Their philosophical and psychological interests had already led them toward a positive appreciation of the individual's inner life. Now, sanctioned by teachers such as Hu Shi and animated by their own frustration with family life, they elaborated a full-scale rationale for individualism. Wu Kang, a *New Tide* student who was to make a significant contribution to the development of modern Chinese philosophy in the 1930s, summed up his generation's aspirations in a 1921 philosophical treatise entitled "Egoism." Starting with the old questions of "What am I?" and "What is the universe?" Wu went on to criticize both materialist and idealist answers. His own point of view, carefully distinguished from the views of Stirner and Fichte, was that the self is the starting point for all knowledge of inner and outer phenomena. Thus, the self cannot be posited as either in the world or apart from it. Rather, self, according to Wu, is what brings all else together. It makes all of life both meaningful and bearable. Not content to identify the "I" with either thought or intuition, Wu Kang concluded that it "must be called self-consciousness ... and be recognized, once and for all, as free and absolute."[44]

Egoism, however, was not just a philosophical stance adopted by the younger generation. It was the essence of a worldview that enabled May Fourth students to defy the ethical norms of the society around them. To be sure, *New Tide* members were not thoroughly beyond the Confucian suspicion that self-assertion was really "selfishness." Not unlike their teachers, students continued to praise the virtue of self-sacrifice, to urge one another to personal freedom for some higher social good. Nonetheless, they embraced the ideal of self-fulfillment more directly than their teachers had. Two translations that accompany Hu Shi's article "On Ibsenism" reflect the different notions of individualism that appealed to teachers and to students. Tao Menghe, a member of the teachers' generation, translated Ibsen's play *An Enemy of the People*. Luo Jialun, later editor of *New Tide*, translated *A Doll's House*.

Cultural rebels of the teachers' generation, who, like Lu Xun, saw themselves as "vipers" in the contemporary society, welcomed Ibsen's glorification of critical conscience. Dr. Stockmann, the main character of *An Enemy of the People*, spoke directly to their need for a model of the independent-minded nonconformist. Dr. Stockmann's last words— "[t]he strongest man on earth is he who stands most alone"—summarized poignantly the predicament of the teachers' generation. Before they happened upon Ibsen, these older intellectuals had relied on such native models of defiance as Qu Yuan, the mythified ancient minister who killed himself in order to enlighten his recalcitrant lord. However, Qu Yuan's example of a "minority of one"[45] was one of martyrdom, and offered little hope of changing the status quo. At a time when *New Youth* contributors were being labeled "wild beasts" for their iconoclasm against the old order, they found a more appropriate inspiration in Dr. Stockmann's willful stance as "an enemy of the people." Hu Shi stood firmly within the camp of the teachers when he wrote that enlightened intellectuals like Dr. Stockmann must function like the white cells in the body:

> The human body is dependent on white cells in the blood; when the body encounters a sickness, the white cells go to war; only after they wipe out bacteria can the body be totally healthy and full of spirit. The health of a society and a nation also depends completely on the presence of such "white cells" who are never satisfied, never content, who battle against criminals and struggle against filthy elements.... If we want to protect the health and hygiene of society, then there must be in society people like Dr. Stockmann who function as the white cells of the human body.[46]

always questioning

The metaphor of the white cells has endured for many years, at times more subliminally than others, in the self-consciousness of May Fourth intellectuals of both generations. It continues to inspire their descendants to act as critics of society, even when cultural criticism is deemed either pernicious or irrelevant, and to take up more encompassing causes such as war mobilization in the 1930s or government-sponsored modernization in the 1970s and 1980s.

At the time of the May Fourth movement itself, however, the student generation embraced Nora, the heroine of *A Doll's House*, more readily than they did Dr. Stockmann. In search of a model of more individualistic rebellion they found that her final gesture—a door defiantly slammed shut against her assigned roles—echoed their struggle for emancipation from the family system. Nora's unequivocal answer to her husband's accusations that she was betraying her "sacred duties" as a mother and a wife engraved itself in the hearts of this generation: "I have a more sacred duty, my duty to myself."

The predicament of women thus spoke most directly to the emotional needs of young men trapped in social duties not of their own choosing. Examples of dissent drawn from the Confucian tradition of defiant but loyal ministers did not meet their need for a model of disloyal, unfilial egoism. Nora did just that. She fired the imagination of Chinese sons, who read about her, wrote about her, and even played her on the Chinese stage.[47] To identify with the nineteenth-century Norwegian playwright's heroine also meant that they could not help but identify with twentieth-century Chinese women closer to home. Members of the *New Tide* generation, thus, took up the cause of feminism in China, animated by the ardor of their identification with Nora. Young men who wanted to carve some space in the all-embracing family system for their own individuality became natural allies of daughters-in-law crushed by even heavier burdens of duty and loyalty.

The teachers' generation had taken up the cause of women's liberation as an institutional and social challenge. The students embraced this struggle more personally. In the second issue of *New Tide*, Ye Shengtao set the tone for the younger generation in his article "The Question of Women's Dignity." Following through on Fu Sinian's concern with the individuality (*gexing*) of sons destroyed by the family system, Ye protested the systematic assault on women's dignity (*renge*)—literally, human worth—throughout Chinese history. The Confucian assumption that women lacked self-consciousness was, according to this writer, the source of the image of women as "villains" and "seductresses." To retaliate against women's supposedly evil character, Confucians had come up with the ethic of the "good wife and mother," an ethic intended to enchain women through the requirements of chastity. Ye's simple, heartfelt conclusion was that "women [not unlike sons] must be allowed to regain their humanity, since they are part of humankind after all.... If women lack a positive sense of identity today, it is through no fault of their own."[48]

Once they identified with women, *New Tide* intellectuals were also able to use the voices of women to call attention to the more general predicament of youth. Many of the short stories in the students' journal turned out to be first-person accounts of young girls victimized by the demands of arranged marriages. It is to the credit of these authors that they tried to be faithful to the specific details of women's bondage, and not just project onto it their own longing for freedom. Yang Zhensheng's story "The Virgin," for example, details the sufferings of a nineteen-year-old girl forced to marry a clay statue of her husband, the young man having died after the marriage was arranged by the parents. Yang, unlike older iconoclasts who argued against such Confucian practices on ideological grounds, dwells on the girl's own feeling during the wedding ceremony with the fake husband. His indictment of the traditional code of chastity is more psychological, as he ends the story with the girl's gloomy stroll through the garden on the day after the marriage. Minutes later, her in-laws find her hanging in the marriage chamber.[49]

New Tide intellectuals did not personally face the risk of marriage to clay statues or being sold by angry in-laws (as is the fate of one young woman in Ye Shengtao's March 1919 story "She Too Is Human!"). And yet, by delving into what it felt like for women to be so thoroughly at the mercy of family arrangements, these young men deepened and sharpened their own awareness of the problem of self-emancipation. "Women's liberation" thus became for them a code word for the complex challenge that was their own self-becoming. Going beyond their teachers, who emphasized the social and political value of women's freedom, the students probed the psychological meaning of the emancipation of women. Teachers such as Li Dazhao, for example, had emphasized the ideological connection between women's liberation and democracy. Students, on the other hand, were concerned with the same problem from a different point of view. Zhang Shenfu, for example, writing in the same journal as Li Dazhao, emphasized the insulting implications of the slogan "women's liberation":

Those who respect others can't possibly say "liberate somebody." Those who have a sense of their own dignity, who value themselves, cannot possibly stand to "be liberated." Men who talk about "women's liberation" all the time are merely revealing that they still view women as not equal.... this is just like putting a pig in a pigsty.... The only correct meaning of liberation must be self-liberation.[50]

Self-emancipation, then, was the goal of younger intellectuals who were reckoning with their own problem of internalized oppression. Aware of the many excuses for avoiding the responsibility of true autonomy, they became harsh critics of the moral pieties that for centuries had sustained the ethic of subservience. Their call for "moral revolution" was less novel than they thought, however. In this undertaking, too, they had been preceded, and were sustained, by their teachers' attacks on the old morality. *New Youth* contributors like Tao Menghe and Li Dazhao had written at length about the selfishness of traditional ethics well before members of the student generation joined the enlightenment movement and demanded a new morality that would legitimate their quest for self-fulfillment.

The teachers had tried to redefine morality so as to make it beneficial to a new social order. They believed that ethics were a natural expression of mankind's effort to do good under changing historical circumstances. As Tao wrote: "The most striking characteristic of 'new morality' is that it is created rather than given.... One who assumes responsibility through free choice does not distinguish according to social roles and social status.... This way, one can, and one must, constantly create the good."[51] The students took for granted the teachers' axiom that morality changes according to the changing requirements of human life. (Wu Kang, for example, developed a mathematical formula to explain why filial piety was an outworn, irrational variable in the equation of life and morality.)[52] They were, in the end, less concerned with the narrowness of traditional morality than they were outraged by its infringement on personal happiness.

Yu Pingbo's 1919 essay "My View on Ethics" exemplifies the emphasis on self-emancipation that characterizes the writings of May Fourth youth. His generation rejected the teachers' dichotomy between old and new ethics. Instead, they insisted upon a choice between false and true morality, between outworn habits of self-repression and noble autonomy. The teachers had aimed to fight institutionalized Confucianism with ethical initiative, expecting that new knowledge would, in time, supplant old practices. The students, on the other hand, saw themselves at war with a pervasive, internalized passivity. Their participation in the "moral revolution" was spurred by a vision of active self-fulfillment. Yu Pingbo's discussion of filiality, loyalty, and chastity thus concluded with an unequivocal indictment of the "slave morality" that had, for centuries, imposed obligations on inferiors, such as youth and women, without controlling the rapaciousness of superiors, who were mostly older men:

What is "morality" in name and "custom" in fact is false morality. This conflict between true and false morality cannot be resolved through compromise.... The false must be overthrown, and we must create a free, rational, true morality. This will be no easy undertaking.[53]

To distinguish between false and true morality required a stance somewhat apart from inherited customs and traditions. Finding and maintaining that place from which one might judge what is best for oneself and for China turned out to be a more difficult undertaking than Yu Pingbo had imagined in his 1919 essay. In the years following May Fourth, he and the rest of his *New Tide* comrades had to fight off repeated accusations that they were selfish, destructive, and unpatriotic precisely because they tried to achieve a position of critical distance from the Chinese past. As they and their mentors turned to Western models of autonomy and critical consciousness, both groups risked becoming more and more alienated from China's nationalist revolution. They took that risk, during the May Fourth movement and afterward, because they were convinced, in the words of Comte and Luo Jialun, that to change politics there was no other way but to start with a change in habits of mind.

TURNING TO THE WEST AND THE ATTACK ON NATIONAL CHARACTER

May Fourth intellectuals of both generations turned to the West because it contained images of self, an ethic of rebellion, and a paradigm of

west = perspective

critical thought that corresponded to the needs of their situation. The
West did not provide either the questions or the answers for their predicament. Its function was perspective. Inquiry into Western literature,
philosophy, and science enabled these thinkers to step outside of their
own tradition and to begin to criticize it. Without an alternative place to
stand—another time, another place—they would have had no vantage
point from which to call for awakening in China. Informed curiosity
about the West enabled intellectuals to expand the limits of the Chinese
worldview more effectively. The West provided an alternative vision of
the self for enlighteners bent upon awakening their contemporaries to a
new, more autonomous sense of national community.

To try to see oneself and one's society through the eyes of another was
neither easy nor comfortable. This perspective was particularly irritating
to those who had a stake in perpetuating a more emotional, more
tradition-bound sense of national unity. Thus, May Fourth intellectuals,
by looking at China as if through foreign eyes, evoked the ire of nationalist conservatives and revolutionaries alike. To be sure, they were not the
first reform-minded intellectuals to turn to the West. Others from Zeng
Guofan through Liang Qichao had argued that China's "wealth and
power" could be regained only by borrowing from the West. Nor were
these enlightenment intellectuals novel in their obsessive desire to "catch
up to modernity," a modernity clearly informed by Western and
Japanese criteria. What was unprecedented in their turning to the West
was their use of the West's critical spirit to attack the problem of
"national character" (*guomin xing*)—or more precisely, to fight the proclivity toward credulousness fostered by long Chinese tradition.

When May Fourth intellectuals brought to Chinese culture a consciousness of the corrupting impact of prolonged gullibility, they were
accused of adopting the contemptuous attitudes toward China held by
Westerners for more than half a century. The harder they pressed the
negative comparison between China and the West, the stronger the reaction that set in. This reaction, in turn, became an unintended catalyst for
the very awakening that was the goal of the May Fourth enlightenment.

Chinese intellectuals bent upon reforming politics through a change
in Chinese habits of mind were particularly moved by Western individuals or groups who bore witness against their times and managed to
transform themselves from followers into doubters, and eventually into
fighters against convention. This quest for exemplars of spiritual
defiance led May Fourth intellectuals to turn to a variety of Western
thinkers from Descartes, Voltaire, Comte, and Ibsen to contemporaries
like Romain Rolland, Henri Barbusse, Bertrand Russell, Benedetto

Croce, and Jane Addams, the latter of whom had all signed the "Déclaration de l'indépendance de l'esprit." This manifesto, issued in March 1919, was a call to conscience addressed to fellow intellectuals around the world appealing to them to retain their spirit of independence in the face of mounting pressures to speak for nationalism or certain class interests. The "Déclaration" was translated in full, with biographies of its authors, by Zhang Shenfu in December 1919.[54]

The Russian Revolution of 1917 was similarly embraced as a model of self-emancipation in a larger social context. Intellectuals as disparate in their subsequent political orientation as Li Dazhao, Luo Jialun, and Fu Sinian hailed the Bolshevik victory as a sign of expanding possibilities of emancipation from obedience to the rules and conventions of tradition. The Russian revolution thus at first attracted, then inspired Chinese intellectuals as an enlightenment epiphany. It confirmed their belief in the possibility of a worldwide "new tide" of thought and action.[55]

In daring to see China through Western eyes, May Fourth teachers and students again worked together and sustained each other. Without this mutual support, neither generation would have been able to withstand the rage and insults of contemporary conservatives. The teachers' generation had turned to the West earlier than the students, out of a more urgent sense of need. Consequently, their attitude toward Western ideas was less informed and more impassioned. Their attitude toward things Chinese, in turn, was more strident. Because they saw China as mired in its backwardness, they kept comparing it, compulsively, to the more "progressive" West. The emotional appeal of the West for these teachers may be seen in Hu Shi's writings about "the Ibsenism in my own heart," in Zhou Zuoren's writings about the need to reform Chinese drama by "copying the West," in Lu Xun's motto, "rather than worship Confucius ... one should worship Darwin and Ibsen."[56]

The students were more relativistic when they turned to the West. Although they, too, were pained by China's backwardness, they emphasized appropriation rather than imitation. As the *New Tide* manifesto made clear, younger intellectuals were more concerned with the consequences of China's ignorance of the West than with the reasons that lay behind their compatriots' prejudice against borrowing from the West:

The fundamental problem is that our people don't realize the richness of Western culture and the impoverishment of Chinese culture. Ignorance of both makes us ashamed of our own. We believe that our people should first understand these four things: 1) what is the level of world civilization today? 2) where are modern intellectual trends going? 3) compared to world trends, what are the shortcom-

Understanding West ⟶ Broadening Overall Perspective

ings of Chinese thought? 4) which trends should we blend with our own?... To gradually bathe isolated China in the waters of world civilization is the first responsibility of our organization.[57]

The gradualist, conscientious manner in which these students went about "bathing China in the waters of world civilization" has been frequently ignored or misinterpreted by their critics and admirers alike. Those who would claim that intellectuals of the younger generation were as hasty and ill-informed as their more strident mentors in borrowing Western ideas overlook the detailed, sustained translation project that was an integral part of the *New Tide* mission. The entire last issue of the students' journal, for example, was devoted to recent books and articles that contained pathbreaking intellectual ideas. Among the works translated, either in part or full, were Einstein's relativity thesis; H. G. Wells's *The Outline of History*; John Dewey's *Reconstruction in Philosophy*; Henri Bergson's *Mind Energy*; John B. Watson's "Psychology from the Standpoint of a Behaviorist" (translated, of course, by Wang Jingxi); Bertrand Russell's "Bolshevism: Practice and Theory"; Sidney and Beatrice Webb's "A Constitution of the Socialist Commonwealth of Great Britain"; George Santayana's "Character and Opinion in the United States with a Reminiscence of William James and Josiah Royce and Academic Life in America"; E. A. Ross's "Principles of Sociology"; G. D. H. Cole's *Social Theory*; Arthur J. Penty's "A Guildsman's Interpretation of History"; J. N. Farquhar's "An Outline of the Religious Literature of India"; and *The Journal of Religion* (vol. 1, no. 1, published by the University of Chicago, January 1921).[58]

The effort involved in these translations might appear, and did so to many fellow students, as a distraction from the more immediate project of social mobilization. In fact, however, the *New Tide* students' aim in undertaking such burdensome work was nothing short of cementing the link between political activism and a change in habits of mind. Far from being derivative or imitative, the students' interest in these Western ideas grew out of their own personal experience of the May Fourth movement and out of the larger New Culture effort. Being ten years younger than their teachers meant that they were simultaneously participants in the 1919–20 national mobilization against Western and Japanese imperialism as well as a ripe audience for the lectures being given at Beijing University at this same time by visiting Western philosophers such as John Dewey and Bertrand Russell. Although members of the teachers' generation were also there, the latter were already set in their ways of thinking and hence less open to transformation by this first-hand initiation into Western philosophy. (Contributors to *New*

Youth like Hu Shi, Chen Hengzhe, and Jiang Menglin, for example, retained pre-May Fourth memories of Dewey formed in the United States and were markedly unchanged in the wake of his travels and lectures in China.) Members of the *New Tide*, by contrast, apprenticed themselves to Dewey and Russell on home territory. Translating Dewey's and Russell's talks and publishing extended bibliographies of their works, the New Tiders grappled with the complexities of these philosophers' views, even when these views defied their personal and political expectations.

Sun Fuyuan, the *New Tide* member who served as reporter and translator for both Dewey and Russell in China, wrote an article on July 11, 1921 (the day both Russell and Dewey left Beijing) which captures well the indebtedness of his generation to these two visitors:

> How much of Dewey actually "left" today? Having been in China two years, Dewey has exerted a widespread influence in our society. Thus, he has not really "left." Russell, on the other hand, driven out by illness after only a few months, is gone indeed and we feel sad. We thank both of them for not deserting a barbarian race like ours. We can only hope that we won't be the same the next time we receive them.[59]

Sun Fuyuan's use of expressions such as "a barbarian race like ours" reveals just how far the May Fourth youths had gone toward adopting Westerners' views of China. They were on the verge of turning the contempt in which China held the rest of the so-called uncivilized world into self-contempt. Such a reversal was bound to create problems for advocates of enlightenment in China. In a moment of nationalist mobilization, such as that of 1919, when the forces of cultural conservatism were still vigorous and carried clout in the public domain, radical intellectuals were often accused of betraying the national culture. While defending themselves against such charges, both teachers and students had a further opportunity to define the reasons for their turning to the West and to appropriate the West's critical consciousness more effectively to their own native circumstances.

The older generation of iconoclasts predictably drew the ire of conservatives earlier than *New Tide* students. Lu Xun was in the forefront of those who raised the issue of *guomin xing*, national character, most bitterly. Not surprisingly, he was also foremost among the "wild beasts" attacked by Confucian literati. Lu Xun's own attacks on the credulousness of the Chinese people had been gaining momentum throughout the New Culture period and culminated in his scathing short story "The True Chronicle of Ah Q." In this work of fiction, he made no attempt to hide his contempt for the self-beguiling common man, the petty thief and would-be revolutionary Ah Q. Set in the historical context of the 1911 debacle, Lu Xun's story ends without any glimmer of hope. As the author and his fellow iconoclasts in *New Youth* made it clear, the only antidote to Ah Q's disease was radical, thorough disbelief.[60]

Hu Shi, Lu Xun's friend and colleague in the May Fourth period, went on to spell out the implications of such radical disbelief. In a December 1919 article entitled "The Meaning of the New Thought Tide," he made the connection between "the problem of national character" and "critical thought" fully explicit. In this article, Hu pointed out that the aim of new thought was not to attack specific old ideas or to replace old beliefs with new ones imported from the West, but to lay bare a proclivity toward being fooled by so-called ancient wisdom. This proclivity, he argued, could be uprooted through the cultivation of a "critical attitude," a capacity for discrimination (*pipan*) or, more literally, for critique. Such an attitude was, in the view of most older iconoclasts, the opposite of blind faith in and endless compromise with tradition. Quoting Nietzsche, Hu Shi explained that this critical attitude would, in time, lead to "a transvaluation of all values." To rethink values, to bring them to the level of consciousness, and to ask whether they are still suitable to the needs of the day was thus defined as the true meaning of new thought.[61]

Intellectuals of the younger generation were also deeply concerned about the problem of national character. They, too, railed against the credulousness of their compatriots, often in terms more bitter than those used by the *New Youth* group. Fu Sinian, for example, attacked the same mental habit as Lu Xun, in his October 1919 essay "Chinese Dogs and Chinese People." Where the older iconoclast unmasked the haphazard, shallow urge for "revolution" for the gullible Ah Q, Fu turned his ire against the superficial, impulsive nationalism of his fellow students. To warn them of the dangers of scattering their intellectual and social energies in a political movement that left habits of mind unquestioned, he wrote:

The other day I asked a man who trains dogs why he chose only foreign dogs. He answered: Chinese dogs are very smart; their sense of smell is sharper than that of foreign dogs. But they are incapable of single-mindedness. If you tell them to fetch something, midway they'll run into other dogs and forget their mission. So it's no use training them.... Chinese people are not unlike Chinese dogs. It's not that they're not smart; it's just that they lack a sense of responsibility.[62]

To equate one's own compatriots with dogs, however, was to make oneself quite vulnerable to charges of cultural treason. Fu Sinian, and others, took that risk because they wanted to augment China's sense of responsibility.

FROM CRITICAL THOUGHT TO
ICONOCLASM

To have a sense of responsibility, in Fu Sinian's view, was to be willing to cultivate one's own and others' capacity for critical thought. This concern with ability to sustain single-minded doubt links Fu Sinian's generation to that of their teachers such as Hu Shi. It also sets the younger generation apart, since theirs was a more impatient doubt. It led students to despair more readily than older intellectuals about the tenacity of credulousness and ignorance in the post–May Fourth era. Fu Sinian's *New Tide* comrade Luo Jialun expressed his generation's bitter disappointment at the slow rate at which critical thought was taking hold in China in a bitter essay published in April 1920. Entitled "Three W-ism," it signals the author's frustration with native culture. Luo used foreign words to summarize the prerequisites of reasonable doubt that he found sorely lacking in China's contemporary intellectual climate:

Chinese culture and society are truly depressing these days. Not only are they depressing at the present, but they may be said to have been this way for two thousand years. Europe, on the other hand, has experienced ceaseless progress since the Renaissance. The creative force in Western civilization is, simply, the spirit of criticism.... This critical spirit has been squelched in China in two ways: by autocratic politics and by autocratic thought. Autocratic thought is rooted in Confucianism, propagated by those who don't dare deviate from the sayings of the Master.[63]

Having poured out his impatience with traditional habits of mind, Luo goes on to outline a program for those individuals who would emancipate themselves from the shackles of autocratic politics and autocratic thought:

In this setting, Chinese people can only quarrel and squabble, not criticize. Anyone who would train himself in the spirit of criticism must therefore begin with the "three W's"; one must learn to ask: what? why? how?[64]

Another *New Tide* founder, the philosophically inclined Wu Kang, also took it upon himself to define the meaning of critical thought for his generation. Unlike older iconoclasts, who had focused on cultivating one's capacity for critical discrimination (*pipan*), Wu Kang (speaking for the more impatient youth) urged his fellow students to develop their capacity for doubt (*huaiyi*). This capacity was dependent upon a strong sense of one's own subjective self, something that the teachers' generation longed for but never quite achieved for themselves. Wu Kang's confidence in arguing for the right to doubt was dependent on his mentors' rebellion against inherited beliefs but went beyond it:

Iconoclasm
Doubt

In order to eradicate the tendency to obey blindly inherited beliefs, to establish an unprecedented environment in which new thought might flourish, we must thoroughly follow through with doubt.... The starting point for all doubt is the "I." Not the selfish, narrow "I" but the more encompassing "I" capable of reasoning and action.... In order to make doubt possible, to make it socially effective, one needs to dare to doubt, to be brave enough to doubt. Descartes was such a brave, successful doubter. He can indeed serve as an example and an inspiration for us.[65]

Student radicals who took Descartes as their model of intellectual insubordination, not unlike their mentors who quoted Nietzsche to justify their re-evaluation of inherited beliefs, came under attack by cultural conservatives. Members of the younger generation, precisely because they were seen as key to the future of China, were cause for the greatest worry.

Shortly after the founding of *New Tide*, Confucian scholar Liu Shipei founded a competing journal and society called *National Heritage* or *Guogu*. An ardent anti-Manchu revolutionary before 1911, Liu emerged in 1919 as the chief spokesman against the turning to the West embodied in the *New Tide* group. In an editorial published in his new journal, he accused them of "knowing only how to Europeanize and [being] totally ignorant of the national heritage." Holding up knowledge of the native tradition as the highest virtue, Liu went on to accuse the *New Tide* group of foolishly discarding what is most precious and closest at hand. Using the analogy of paper-making, he and his fellow *National Heritage* editors argued that advocates of critical thought were nothing but thoughtless radicals who "throw away the national heritage which is like the ragged cloth books of yore, for the sake of shabbier modern paperbacks, i.e., Europeanization." To those who could still be moved by an emotional appeal to the past, they counseled: "In our rush to create new paper, that is to say a new civilization, we should be careful not to discard the cloth books that are so precious. Ragged cloth books and shabby modern ones might yet make new paper. Our research in the national heritage is not for the sake of ragged cloth only. It is truly for the creation of new paper."[66]

This impassioned appeal to preserve old culture for the sake of the new fell on deaf ears—at least among *New Tide* radicals. They had no reason to be defensive about their ignorance of the Chinese past. It surrounded them intimately in their family life as well as in their academic studies of Chinese history and literature. As to the charge of being interested only in Europeanization, they felt no need to respond, since they had been quite outspoken about the inadequacies of their own understanding of modern Western ideas. The one aspect of conservative reasoning that they paid attention to—only to dissect and attack it further—was the attempt to mask the urgent problem of "national character" with a sentimental notion of "national heritage." Whereas traditional scholars such as Liu Shipei had hoped to preserve the texts and the spirit of Confucian scholarship, advocates of enlightenment insisted on revealing the attitude of passive credulity that such texts had fostered over the centuries. To hold on, however lovingly and forward-mindedly, to the ragged cloth books of tradition was, in their view, to preempt the possibility of creating new paper altogether.

And so, these May Fourth intellectuals became further entrenched in their stance of iconoclasm against tradition. Older rebels like Chen Duxiu led the attack on sentimental attachment to tradition with slogans like "Welcome Mr. Science and Mr. Democracy" and "Down with the Rotten Band of Confucian Shopkeepers." By personalizing and juxtaposing the abstract ideals of autonomy and subservience in this way, Chen was able to rally *New Youth* intellectuals such as Qian Xuantong, Liu Bannong, and others, who had more time and interest to document the way in which outworn habits of mind were being perpetuated in modern-day China in the guise of Confucian learning.[67] While these older intellectuals raged against contemporary adherents of *kongjiao* (Confucianism), the *New Tide* members focused their attention on reshaping the *guogu* (national heritage), the textual repository of old ideas. Mao Zishui called for a "scientific spirit" in the investigation of Confucianism. Wondering aloud whether *guogu* should be equated with the "bondage of Confucian ethics," he tried to pioneer a more objective approach to historical research. It was Mao's faith that the use of Western social-science methodology would, in time, lessen the stranglehold of Confucian values on contemporary life.[68]

Gu Jiegang, working closely with Mao Zishui and, therefore, coming under direct attack in Liu Shipei's indictment of the *New Tide* group, summarized his generation's point of view in an article "What Our Attitude Ought to Be toward the National Heritage." In this manifesto, Gu takes great care to distinguish the enlightenment's critical approach to tradition from Confucian scholarship, which, he claims, was animated by a desire to find and to present moral exemplars. Criticism of tradition, however, is not synonymous with rejection of tradition. Rather, Gu argues: "We seek to find out what something meant in its original context, what was its significance back then." Trying to make the past have more historical significance was bound to further irritate those who believed it should claim present loyalties as well. Still, Gu persisted in his

call for historical relativism: "This means that we do not follow tradition, but research it. This difference between 'following' (*shixing*) and
'research' (*yanjiu*) is, in itself, simple and clear. Unfortunately, Chinese
scholars have never understood it." To squelch all doubts about the
implications of this relativism, Gu concluded: "Our methodology in
reorganizing the national heritage has four components: collection, clas-
sification, criticism, and comparison."[69]

Whether sloganeering or reflective, May Fourth intellectuals of both
generations were convinced that outworn notions endured in the minds
of men and women far beyond their utility in earlier times. Hence,
teachers and students united in their call for the systematic eradication
of what Francis Bacon called "mental idols," that is to say,

false notions which are now in possession of the human understanding, and have
taken deep root therein, not only so beset men's minds that truth can hardly find
entrance, but even after entrance is obtained, they will again in the very in-
stauration of the sciences meet and trouble us, unless men being forewarned of
the danger fortify themselves as far as they may against their assaults.[70]

In the Chinese context, "idol-smashing" was readily misinterpreted as
an arrogant and foolhardy attempt to replace old beliefs with new ideas.
In fact, it was a strategy to draw attention to the limited impact of new
ideas on old beliefs.

Chen Duxiu, in his 1918 essay "On Iconoclasm," had already tried to
fortify his generation by drawing attention to the silent, covert, awesome
power of "false notions" such as emperor worship, filial piety, and
nationalism. All these, in his view, were sustained by the "passive vanity
of idol worshipers" and prevented science from making any genuine inroads into Chinese mental life.[71] A year later, in the second issue of *New
Tide*, Fu Sinian wrote an essay simply titled "On Destruction." Unlike
Chen Duxiu, Fu did not dwell on the religious connotation of "iconoclasm." Rather, he wrote about the problem of mentality in terms of the
"new wine, old bottle" analogy, arguing that existing containers had to
be emptied first before any of the modern potions peddled by critics of
national character (such as himself) could be put into them. More willing to reckon with the limitations of rationalist iconoclasm than Chen
Duxiu, he acknowledged that "emptying old bottles" would be a difficult, perhaps uncertain undertaking. Whereas Chen had concluded
that all unreasonable beliefs of vain men from ancient times must be
considered idols and all must be destroyed, Fu simply ended with a plea
for "long-term destruction."[72]

Proponents of destruction, whether long term or short, were bound to feel isolated and lonely in a society that still valued adherence to tradition. The angrier the iconoclasts became about the mental habits of their countrymen, the harsher the attacks that were heaped upon them by cultural conservatives. In the months before the demonstration of May 4, before they were able to use the cause of national salvation to spread more widely their unorthodox ideas of intellectual awakening, critical intellectuals had only each other and their Western heroes to rely on for support. Not surprisingly, they took their opponents' accusations and transformed them into symbols of their own righteousness. Fu Sinian's April 1919 essay "Some Crazy Words" makes this strategy of self-justification clearest. Faced with charges of "bestiality" and "madness," Fu agreed that only madmen would have the courage and integrity to keep on defying an autocracy as deeply entrenched as the one enveloping China. Turning to Western paragons of spiritual rebellion, he argued: "Lunatics! Lunatics! Christ was mad, Socrates was mad, Trotsky and Nietzsche are mad. How could their contemporaries not think of them as madmen? But, after a while, didn't thousands of sane people follow in the footsteps of these madmen?" To convince himself, and others, that madmen are indeed the forerunners of innovation, Fu brought the case closer to home. He pointed out that his own country was nearly moribund precisely because of a shortage of tradition-defying lunatics:

China is nearly dead today precisely because we have too few madmen.... I myself am too sane [too conventional] and thus cannot contribute much.... Madmen are our most lovable, most cherished people. Apart from madmen, only children are worthy of love.... We should therefore follow madmen and love children: the madmen will be our teachers, the children our friends.[73]

In the weeks before the May Fourth incident, the injunction to follow madmen and to love children had an edge of despair to it. It reflected the needs and fears of a small group of radicals who felt increasingly isolated and were under increasing attack by more numerous, more vocal conservatives. Within a few short months, however, advocates of enlightenment at Beida would gain nationwide attention for their views through patriotic mobilization. As the numbers of their supporters and followers grew, they had no need to keep on portraying themselves as either madmen or innocent children. Even so, the tone of embattled defiance persists in the post–May Fourth writings of those who continued to argue for cultural awakening in the context of a social movement suffused with patriotic politics.

FROM MENTAL TRANSFORMATION TO
SOCIAL REVOLUTION

In the year after the May Fourth incident itself, students were shocked to discover how deeply old habits of thought were entrenched among their countrymen. In spite of the prompt, nationwide response to their call for patriotic mobilization—as evidenced by workers' and merchants' strikes[74]—May Fourth activists found that the vast majority of the Chinese population remained deaf to the call for mental awakening. The more they talked to audiences outside of the circle of enlightened teachers and students at Beida, the more they realized how unpopular was their message of critical self-consciousness. Frustrated in their efforts to spread enlightenment in the streets and villages outside of Beida, May Fourth students were faced with two choices: either to abandon the program of mental awakening or to retranslate its content and form to suit the needs and limitations of their audience, the *pingmin*, or common folk.

To abandon the ideals of enlightenment would have been an unthinkable alternative to young radicals convinced of the priority of mental transformation in social change. Even those students who left China after the events of 1919–20 to study abroad, who became engrossed in their own personal mental awakening, did not give up the commitment to social revolution. This commitment continued to bind them to their comrades at home—those who became directly involved in workers' education programs, Marxist study, and eventually in the founding of the Communist Party. Those in China, as well as those who went to Europe and to the United States, continued to explore—whether through collaboration, through correspondence, or independently— ways of transforming their own consciousness as intellectuals in order to more effectively communicate with the common people.

The intellectuals' effort to change their own thinking began shortly after the May Fourth event itself. During the fall and winter of 1919, *New Tide* members who had collaborated with students in the *Citizen* Society to found the Beijing University Commoners' Education Lecture Society continued to ask themselves why the enlightened minority was so hampered in its ability to awaken the Chinese population. They wrestled with this problem even as they continued their street corner lectures, augmenting these Sunday afternoon activities with periodic forays into small towns and villages outside of Beijing.

During these outings, student-lecturers set off in groups of three to five to talk about topics ranging from the need to boycott Japanese goods to the need for reforming the family system. By the spring of 1920, as the immediate urgency of national salvation diminished somewhat, student lecturers had become increasingly aware of the public's reluctance to listen to the enlightenment portions of their prepared talks. In a March 13 report about the experiences of a group of student-lecturers that included *New Tide* founder Luo Jialun and *Citizen* founder Deng Zhongxia, it becomes quite clear that the common people's initial response to the call for mental awakening was nearly total lack of interest. This disappointing discovery was made in Changxindian, the very hamlet in which Beida students would be organizing workers for the Communist Party a year later:

Today is Sunday, the day off for workers at Changxindian. Most have gone to Beijing for entertainment, and Christian believers are all in church, so only very few people came to listen to our lecture.... Although our flags fluttered and our loudspeakers roared, only some women and children were drawn to it. After hearing a few words of our speech, they began to leave. We could do nothing but announce the end of our speech.... Next, we went west to Zhaoxindian.... By 1 P.M. we had set up our flags and loudspeakers. Several women hid behind a low wall, white powder on their faces, blood-red rouge on their cheeks and lips. They wore red and green clothes; we couldn't figure out from what dynasty. Their mouths agape, they looked astonished. None dared to come close. All this was not too convenient. Well, the train to Beijing was coming anyhow, so we decided to go back; no point in wasting time there.[75]

At first, then, these students were not only not heard but were actually rebuffed by the common people. They left the hamlet having concluded that their efforts amounted to little more than wasted time. Only much later would they come to realize that while they were out lecturing, even when they were not being heard, they were in fact learning something new and important about their own countrymen. Women hiding behind low walls and made up in the fashion of past dynasties reminded students how far behind the republican mood and manners of the cities most of their non-urban compatriots were. This realization was further reinforced when another group of students from Beida lectured in rural hamlets outside the small city of Fengtai. Here, they did get an audience, but it was a forced one. It was made up of village youths captive to the authority of their Confucian teachers. These teachers, though filled with ambivalence, decided that it might be beneficial to expose their charges to some of the winds of new learning brought in by the strange students from Beida:

The village of Qilizhuang has a population of two hundred, belonging to fifty families or so. In the government-sponsored village school, the teacher's desk also serves as the kitchen chopping board. It is a dingy, dark room, a rat hole....

Every student has a copy of "Thousand Character Classic" and a fragment of Confucius' *Analects*.... The young teacher, with a cigarette hanging from his mouth, seemed to be displeased with our speech.... In his eyes, we were evil and would arouse wicked ideas in the students' mind.

At another village, Dajing, the students encountered a teacher who wore a long pigtail and held a long tobacco pipe as well as his pupil-beating ruler in his hands.

We had to beg him over and over again to let his students listen to us. Then he ordered them to stand at attention, stiffly in line, to listen to us.... Later, one of our members gave a talk on "The harm of binding feet," another on "The importance of education," another on "Why shall we study?" One young housewife who had sneaked out to listen was cursed by her mother-in-law as a whore.... Recently we have heard news that the Education Ministry wants to implement compulsory education. Isn't this ridiculous? Without understanding more clearly why people have so many misconceptions ... without training competent teachers, the situation will be no different from that in the villages where we went to give lectures.[76]

Having set out to shatter illusion and ignorance with one swift blow of enlightenment thought, May Fourth youths were now forced to understand more clearly why people had so many misconceptions. Compulsory education was not the panacea earlier reformers had envisioned. Those who would set in motion genuine social change first had to learn about the sources and tenacity of popular superstitions. Going out into villages and factories to spread the message of enlightenment, May Fourth youths began to learn about the actual conditions that fostered Chinese habits of mind. What was, in the beginning, an incidental learning experience in the course of efforts to educate and awaken the common people became, in time, the very focus of their forays in the world outside of Beida. "Social investigations" (*shehui diaocha*) thus emerged as the concrete prerequisite for effective communication with the masses. Having failed to pass on the full-blown message of May Fourth enlightenment, students began to concentrate on a few long-range projects. Instead of periodic forays into the world beyond Beida, they now engaged themselves in worker education programs launched by the lecture society. In 1920, two night schools for workers were opened by members of the society: one at Beijing University for janitors and other "extraneous people" previously excluded from the sacred halls of the academy, and another for factory workers in the village of Chang-xindian.

These two schools represented two aspects of the reinterpretation of the message of enlightenment once it spilled forth from the pages of *New*

Youth and *New Tide* onto the streets around the university. The education that youthful *wenren* (literati) received in the course of imparting knowledge to the *pingmin* was very different in these two settings: the latter led toward the founding of the Chinese Communist Party, the former toward more liberal attempts at cultural reform.

The Beijing University Common People's Night School was an outgrowth of Cai Yuanpei's motto, "Labor is sacred." Shortly after he became chancellor of Beida, Cai had begun to give speeches and to write articles about the "sanctity of work" (never workers as such). This was an integral part of his effort to counter the effete, decadent mood of old-fashioned teachers and students at the National University. A strong believer in Mencius' principle that those who "labor with their minds" should guide those who "labor with their brawn" by caring for their welfare and mental cultivation, Cai was an early and persistent supporter of the students' lecture society.

In 1920, when lecture society members decided to formalize their activities in the Beijing area, Cai Yuanpei provided the financial backing to set up a permanent lecture hall on the periphery of the campus. In this building students could sign up to give regularly scheduled lectures. Eventually these lectures replaced the itinerant Sunday street corner speeches that had begun in the spring of 1919. This institution became the Beijing University Night School. In January 1922, when the first class was formally graduated, journalists crowded in to report on the intellectual luminaries who were in attendance and who thus sanctioned the connection between the May Fourth enlightenment and workers' education. One reporter wrote, in a story filed on the seventeenth:

The day before yesterday, on the anniversary of the deaths of Karl Liebknecht and Rosa Luxemburg, martyrs of the proletarian cause and leaders of the German Communist Party, the Beida Evening School for Commoners held its first commencement.... In the Grand Auditorium of Beida, it was a solemn occasion indeed. The speeches were all serious, encouraging commoners to continue their education. A representative of the students made a valedictory address that described the difficulties commoners had to overcome in their pursuit of education. The audience was much moved. There were fourteen graduates altogether.

Then, the journalist describes the background and interests of the intellectuals who had taken upon themselves to educate this first group of worker-students:

Their teacher [a Beijing University student], being otherwise occupied that day, was not present. Everyone had words of praise for President Cai Yuanpei, who is greatly concerned about commoners' education. The Beida Evening School is far ahead of others like it in the country. This is mainly Cai Yuanpei's credit. Profes-

17.   Entrance to the first night school for workers set up by Beijing University students at Changxindian in 1920.

sor Hu Shi also helped to design the schedule, of course, and therefore the program has been very effective.... The school offers many courses in addition to basic requirements, such as boxing, dancing, sewing, painting, and drama.[77]

Much less fanfare surrounded the setting up of a "Workers' After-Hours School" at Changxindian. Founded by leftist members of the lecture society, Deng Zhongxia and Zhang Guotao among them, the school was a failure at first. Factory owners promptly set up an alternative "Trade School for Workers" to limit the impact of the Beijing University "rowdies." As one worker who attended both schools recalled:

The bosses' school attracted seven to eight hundred workers, while the Beijing University Lecture Society School had only a hundred or so at its peak. At the trade school they gave us pens and paper just for signing in at night. It was much more convenient to attend this school, since the manager would tell us "let's all go to school now" and we'd get off from work early. At the end of the year there were prizes such as watches and boxes of cigarettes for those who had memorized the most from the Confucian classics.[78]

Faced with lack of interest, lecture society members decided to rename their school the "Workers' Recreation Society." They added singing and speech-making lessons to their course offerings. In the next few years, this Recreation Society became one of the first places of effective contact between the nascent Communist Party and workers. It was the workers' school at Changxindian that did most of the propaganda work during the first Communist-led labor strike in February 1922.

In the night school attached to Beijing University, a domesticated version of the enlightenment movement flourished for a while. Ideas there were simplified and translated downward for the common people. Student-teachers who engaged in this project of translation stopped giving street corner speeches. They saw less and less of the world outside of Beida, and so had fewer and fewer opportunities to confront the disparity between what they were prepared to preach and what the common people would listen to.

The students who went to Changxindian, by contrast, continued to learn while they taught. They, too, had to reinterpret the message of enlightenment in light of commoners' initial lack of interest in critical self-consciousness. At the same time, however, they were forced to deepen their social investigation skills precisely because they were failing more obviously than their comrades lecturing at the Beijing University Night School. Those skills, in time, enabled some of the young Communist intellectuals to carry the message of the New Culture movement out into society far more effectively than Hu Shi or Chen Duxiu could have done in 1917—when they first launched the call for an intellectual and literary renaissance.

In the next half decade, the split deepened between those who would bring enlightenment to the common people and those who would learn from them. Retrospective critics of the liberal intelligentsia, however, have tended to overemphasize the implications of this split.[79] In fact, however, both groups of students used their post–May Fourth experiences in mass mobilization to educate themselves further about the sources of China's intellectual and spiritual lethargy. Not content to stay within the framework of a patriotic student movement, both groups went on to explore ways of questioning and changing popular mentality. Former student leaders at Changxindian as well as at Beida remained convinced that China's mental habits had to be transformed. Both groups worked to make that transformation take root, first and foremost, among the advocates of new thought themselves.

The most obvious way to begin that process, and the favored path of *New Tide* members, was study abroad. Distancing oneself from inherited customs and values has been, as we have seen, a long-standing goal of these student radicals. Upon graduation from Beida, they finally had the opportunity and the material means with which to translate that abstract goal into a practical research strategy. Unlike the older generation of cultural iconoclasts, members of the student generation went abroad *after* graduating from a modern university in China. As a result, their sense of intellectual purpose was stronger and more focused than that of their teachers who came back to China before 1911. The latter gravitated toward graduate study in the United States and Europe, whereas their teachers had had their formative intellectual awakening in Japan.

In the fall of 1920, the first Chinese-sponsored group of Beida students departed for graduate work in the United States. Their fellowships had been provided by Shanghai cotton manufacturer Mu Ouqu, who had negotiated this donation directly with Cai Yuanpei.[80] Retrospectively blamed as homegeneously "bourgeois" because of their sponsor, the group of May Fourth students who went to the United States was in fact quite diverse in its intellectual and political interests. It included *New Tide* luminaries such as Luo Jialun, Kang Baiqing, Wang Jingxi, Feng Youlan, and Yang Zhensheng. Their academic specialties reflected the multiplicity of their intellectual concerns in China during the May Fourth enlightenment. So, not surprisingly, Wang Jingxi focused on behavioral psychology at Johns Hopkins University and Yang Zhensheng explored personal and behavioral psychology at Columbia, where Feng Youlan too began his research, which was on "Comparative Life Ideals" under the direction of John Dewey.

In Europe, lecture society founder Xu Deheng was deeply immersed in French-language study, while Fu Sinian and Zhang Shenfu kept up an intense correspondence between London and Paris about problems in mathematical logic and psychoanalysis. Although not enrolled in formal courses of study, Fu and Zhang audited classes at the University of London and the Sorbonne respectively. Both were determined to learn "from scratch" the subjects in which they had felt so expert at home, when all they had as point of comparison was their more ignorant compatriots.[81]

This determination to focus singlemindedly on one's own education was shared by May Fourth youths who did not leave China in the years following the event of 1919. Gu Jiegang, for example (one of the few who did not study abroad at all), turned down the editorship of *New Tide* in

18. Chinese students in Berlin in 1923. Seated second from right is Zhang Shenfu. Next to him is former Beijing University president Jiang Menglin. Standing behind Jiang is Fu Sinian.

1920, begging to be left unfettered for his "other obsession"—historical research. Sun Fuyuan and Li Xiaofeng, who managed *New Tide* after the other editors left for the United States and Europe, turned the association into a study society and focused its efforts on increasing sales through publishing better vernacular fiction and more readable translations of modern social science theory.

Even as they scattered from Beida, these May Fourth youths retained a shared commitment to gain new knowledge that would force their compatriots to awaken to the inadequacies of an inherited worldview. Some expressed this commitment in the send-off poems they wrote for each other shortly before leaving the university and capital city that had first nourished their vision of enlightenment and social revolution. *New Tide* founder Kang Baiqing, for example, in a March 1920 poem dedicated to Xu Deheng (his erstwhile critic from the *Citizen* group, then fellow organizer of and ally in the lecture society), wrote about the unfinished business of May Fourth that awaited their return from study abroad:

> Fight! Strike!
> Slogans in my ears now,

of work not yet done.
Show me where in the world,
are strikes and struggle not needed!
Progress requires destruction.
As long as we stand firm,
Struggle, study, and
never, never compromise,
the forces of old culture cannot
but give way before us.[82]

Kang himself soon "gave way" to old culture and returned to writing poetry in the classical language he had opposed during his student years at Beida. Nonetheless, his 1920 poem is an accurate reflection of the mood of solidarity that prevailed among new youths in the years immediately following the the May Fourth incident. Precisely because this mood has been forgotten or misinterpreted in partisan writings about the event of 1919, it is important for us now to reconstruct it more carefully. Rather than focus upon later political differences between those students who became spokesmen for the liberal intelligentsia and those who joined the Communist effort, either as party members or fellow travelers, let us recall the determination to change popular mentality that bound these intellectuals together in the wake of the student demonstrations of 1919.

In this context, it might be useful to look at the students who, in November 1921, founded the Beijing University Society for the Study of Marxist Theory. At first glance, these intellectuals seem quite different from the students who left China a year earlier for research in the United States and Europe. Yet they too were explicit in their need for self-education before continuing the project of changing Chinese society and habits of thought. This society, a training ground for the first Communist Party cell in Beijing, included among its members Deng Zhongxia, Zhu Wushan, and Gao Shangde, student lecturers quite familiar with the problems of "commoners' education." The manifesto of the society expressed clearly the enlightenment intellectuals' conviction that they themselves needed to learn more before their social advocacy could become pervasive and effective among other social classes:

We who are joining in this research association have two concerns: (1) Marx's works being so profound and so voluminous, it may require a whole lifetime for any one individual to study them, let alone for us Chinese, with our special language difficulties. Therefore, studying Marxism alone is not possible. (2) It is important to collect Marxist books. But, at the present, the poor facilities of our library cannot satisfy this requirement. So here again is a problem that cannot be dealt with through individual effort.[83]

In the nearby city of Tianjin, another group of university students who were deeply affected by the May Fourth movement came to share the priorities of the Beida intellectuals. They set up the Enlightenment Society (*Juewu she*), whose members included Zhou Enlai, Deng Yingchao, and Liu Qingyang. The manifesto of this society also reflects and underscores the younger generation's determination to pursue self-awakening while trying to alter Chinese habits of mind:

We, as students, would never be able, would never dare to assert that we had reached enlightenment, that we are, ourselves, enlightened enough. We have, however, made up our minds to search for enlightenment. We hope that other people in our society will also become determined to march toward enlightenment.[84]

From the Commoners' Education Lecture Society at Beida through the Tianjin-based Enlightenment Society thus stretches a direct line of intellectual descent. Whether standing at street corners, traveling to nearby villages, or setting up workers' night schools, these May Fourth activists discovered that they knew too little about the society they aimed to transform. In the course of their patriotic mobilization they were confronted, simultaneously, with the superficial nature of their own grasp of enlightenment thought and with the masses' reluctance to hear (much less heed) the call for intellectual awakening. Much to their credit, the students did not abandon the commitment to link social revolution with mental transformation. In fact, the deeper they plunged into the national salvation movement, the more appreciative they became of the initial May Fourth insight: that China had to dare to think freely before it could win its enduring autonomy and sovereignty among the other nations of the world.

In the half decade after the events of 1919–20 they proceeded to translate, appropriate, and spread the ideas of enlightenment in a language more suited to the ears and sensibilities of their countrymen. They continued to act, in other words, as "dangerous men"—a self-appellation coined by *New Tide* founder Zhang Shenfu, who also went on to organize the first Communist Party cell in Beijing in 1920. In May 1919, on the eve of the patriotic demonstration itself, this champion of enlightenment had already called into question the conservatives' claim that only radical thinkers were subversive to the established social order. To counter their claim, Zhang Shenfu pointed out that all thinkers are dangerous because their activity upsets a system of privileges assumed to be "natural" by superiors bent upon oppressing their social inferiors. Thought, Zhang argued, was inherently lawless, boundless, subversive, and liberating:

If proletarians were to think freely and critically, the rich would get upset. If soldiers were to think freely, the military discipline of the warlords would fall apart. If youth were to think freely, sexual desire would sweep away all traditional morality.... You curse thought, you resist thought ... but even in the process of resisting thought, you are forced to think. The future belongs only to those who dare to think.[85]

INTELLECTUALS' DILEMMA IN THE POST–MAY FOURTH PERIOD

On the eve of May Fourth it was courageous, and perhaps a bit foolish, to imagine that "the future belongs to those who dare to think." Until the outbreak of the student demonstration, the vast majority of the Chinese population had not heard about, much less cared for, the notion of "free thought." Furthermore, conservative opponents of new culture had prevailed in public debates that forced Cai Yuanpei to try to control the *New Tide* waters before they flooded society at large. It was, thus, the patriotic event of May Fourth, rather than the power of intellectual persuasion, which precipitated the overflow of ideas from Beida into the streets and villages around the university.

The overflow of ideas itself, however, did not solve the intellectuals' twofold dilemma. It did not answer their question about how popular an enlightenment movement could ever be in China given the masses' own attachment to the ethic of subservience. Nor did it quell their doubts that intellectuals themselves were inadequate representatives of the liberating power of new thought. In the half decade after the May Fourth demonstration, the young men continued to wrestle with these problems, both inside their own psyches and through the various organizations in which they participated. In the end, it was the solidarity built up during their formative years at Beida that prevented them from giving up all hope of solving these dilemmas.

The problem of integrating new thought into the theory and practice of social revolution was not simply a post–May Fourth dilemma. Intellectuals of the teachers' generation had already wrestled with the failure of a political revolution in the aftermath of 1911. It was the distinctive challenge of the students' movement, however, to spread the ideas of enlightenment among the common people. The difficulty of their task manifested itself early. In May 1919, for example, a few days before Beida students became swept up in the fervor of the patriotic demonstration, Yang Zhongjian, a supporter of the new culture movement from the provincial capital of Xi'an, wrote a letter of warning to *New Tide* editors:

I am a great admirer of your magazine, especially of your important articles on the "Human Dignity of Women," "The Problem of Family Reform," "Free Love," etc.... But I also wonder how reasonable these ideas really are. The poor women of our country have no idea what you mean by such new terms as "worldview" and "family reform." No wonder that fewer and fewer people are able to or care to read *New Tide*.[86]

Half a year later, while most of the nation was still basking in the glow of patriotic unity, May Fourth activist and *New Tide* founder Fu Sinian wondered aloud, again, about how persuasive new ideas really were in a society such as China's. By November 1919, however, Fu had posed that question to his own generation far more critically than Yang Zhongjian had intended a few months earlier. It was Fu's agonizing conclusion that not only were poor women and other common folk not ready for enlightenment thought, students like himself were also unprepared to live up to the challenge of a new worldview. Denouncing the self-image of the student generation, which the nation at large was still willing to believe to be true, Fu wrote. "We consider ourselves to be new thinkers; others credit us with having new ideas. I think it is shameful indeed. In our lives and in our psyches we keep lugging along a three-thousand-year-old history.... We can only say that we are people who value new thought, but we have not yet displaced old ways of thinking with new ones."

Unwilling to let this indictment rest on the level of vague generalities, Fu Sinian went on to point out the particular malady that was the blight of intellectuals in modern China: an attachment to their traditional role of mentors of the masses. That role had enabled them to quarrel with autocracy for centuries without ever posing a fundamental challenge to its ideological assumptions. To awaken his own generation to its lingering sickness, Fu concluded:

We should examine ourselves often. If we were living in imperial times, would we have the courage not to become officials?... We are now brashly bragging about our enlightenment, but is it so different from the grumbling of low-level scholars in imperial times? What's so special about this feeling? Of what use is it? Therefore, new thought cannot emerge readily. We must first alter our own habits of mind.[87]

Fu Sinian's doubts about his fellow students' ability to embody enlightenment ideas, and to convey them effectively to the society at large, deepened over the next few years.

Studying abroad did not quell this self-questioning but instead accentuated it. In a long, painful letter from London addressed to Beida teacher Hu Shi, Fu Sinian criticized further the false consciousness of supposedly "new" youths. Sparked by his friend Yu Pingbo's abrupt, nearly stealthy, return to China after only two weeks in England, Fu Sinian tried to make sense of the despondency of a fellow *New Tide* member. The anxieties of an entire generation are revealed in his letter. Having pursued his friend from London to Paris and then to Marseilles and having failed either to convince him to stay or to prevent him from leaving, Fu now tried to probe beyond "homesickness" for the reasons that pulled Yu Pingbo back to China. Fu's newly found foreign term for his friend's condition, "inherited psychosis," did not answer all his questions, however. He probed deeper and eventually came up with the "family system" and "literati compulsion" as the forces that poisoned Yu Pingbo's psyche "only slightly more obviously than my own."

Yu Pingbo, who had written so confidently and reasonably about getting rid of "empty, useless thinking" during May Fourth, who had called for a "new morality" based on the individual's autonomy, now discovered, according to Fu, that his recently acquired worldview was an inadequate defense against the realities of an arranged marriage:

By and by he was trapped into setting up a household, into becoming a young master (*dashaoye*). But that's not the worst of it. Ensnared by his literary studies, he became a litteratus (*wenren*) and thus departed from the real world into a dream world. I myself have been affected by literature, and not very slightly at that. It has changed my temperament a great deal, perhaps even more profoundly than that of Pingbo. If students after us can avoid this fate, it would be good indeed.... In my own studies, I am focusing on Freudian psychoanalysis.... Lately, I have lost all desire to write.... I'm also interested in science, but would be ashamed to write about it in an empty way. My own feelings and thoughts have also gotten more complex; I'm trying to become more serious as I look into the core of things. I've grown more afraid of speaking impulsively. Finally, I am becoming more introverted and lazier in some ways.[88]

In Beijing, among their fellow *New Tide* members, Yu Pingbo and Fu Sinian had tried on a new image of selfhood, that of the *xuezhe*, the independent scholar-critic, Fu continued. This persona, however, was too abstract and too weak to undo the social and emotional network in which advocates of enlightenment were caught. The inner turmoil of such men, Fu contended, was the result of the inability to overcome the temptation to become a gentleman. Aggravating the outer corruption of acting the role of "young master," *dashaoye* (the honorific title used by servants and social inferiors to address the male offspring of elite households), Yu Pingbo had also fallen prey to the inner weakness of the *wenren*. Yu's literary interests had carried him, according to his worried yet sympathetic friend, further and further into the morass of unreality. Riddled with self-doubt, he was unable to withstand the pressure to conform. His acquiescence, in turn, made him doubt the impact of May Fourth emancipation on old social roles, old literature, and old images of self. In the end, it seems, intellectuals like Yu Pingbo had been able to rethink (or perhaps pretend to rethink) inherited notions precisely because they had been so secure in their status as offspring of traditional intellectuals.

Writing from faraway London, Fu Sinian could and did dissect the temptations faced by convention-ridden Chinese men of letters. His obsession with the tenacity of tradition was mirrored at home by the persistent self-questioning of more radical May Fourth activists. Fu's fellow students who stayed in China to press on with the cause of social revolution also grappled with the temptations to conform—in this case, to conform to public opinion, something not completely unlike what made Yu Pingbo buckle while abroad. Their dilemma was to discover how to avoid compromising cultural ideals while winning popular support for their political program. In the struggle to maintain the integrity of the May Fourth commitment to enlightenment, these May Fourth students continued to be inspired by the support and example of their Beida teachers. Chen Duxiu, for example, less than one month before the First Congress of the Chinese Communist Party in July 1921, wrote a reminder and manifesto to fellow intellectuals entitled "The Courage to Oppose Public Opinion." In this essay, he recalled for them the "blind nature of mass psychology," which, in his view, comprised most of what passed as public opinion. The main characteristic of that psychology, he argued, is fear of defying authority—the same emotion that had overwhelmed Yu Pingbo in Europe. Focusing on the social implications of this private fear, Chen Duxiu concluded: "China can never hope to advance unless there are some few who dare to publicly oppose public opinion."[89]

Those who had hoped to withstand the pressure to conform to traditional authority, be it that of literati families or of public opinion, had to hold on to and develop their identity as critical intellectuals. This was not a private undertaking but a social challenge. In the years following the event of 1919, this challenge became more concrete as May Fourth teachers and students founded organizations such as the Chinese Communist Party and the Society for Literary Research. Although these associations appear vastly different from each other when judged solely by the yardstick of social activism, they were, in fact, quite similar in function. They both consolidated and developed the identity of critical intellectuals. These organizations enabled intellectuals to resist pressures to abandon the ideals of the May Fourth enlightenment.

Both the Chinese Communist Party and the Society for Literary Research emerged out of discussions and debates sparked by the events of 1919. One year later, in October of 1920, when most of their compatriots were still basking in the afterglow of nationalistic fervor, a group of Beida students and faculty joined together to organize the first cell of the Chinese Communist Party. Its purpose was to expand the purely patriotic focus of the student movement. Among its members were *New Youth* editor Li Dazhao, *New Tide* contributors Zhang Shenfu and Gao Shangde, *Citizen* founders Deng Zhongxia and Zhang Guotao, as well as activists from the Commoners' Education Lecture Society such as Li Jun and Zhu Wushan.[90] Two months later, in December 1920, another group of students and teachers gathered together to found the Society for Literary Research. Its aim was to make literature a more active force in shaping Chinese social consciousness. Among its members were *New Youth* editor Zhou Zuoren, *New Tide* contributors Ye Shengtao, Sun Fuyuan, Guo Shaoyu, and Zhu Ziqing, as well as some friends not formally associated with Beida but sharing the ideals of its iconoclastic community, most notably Mao Dun and Zheng Zhenduo.[91]

During the half decade that passed between the patriotic mobilization of May Fourth and the next large-scale movement for national salvation, the May Thirtieth movement of 1925, both these organizations worked to keep alive the critical self-awareness engendered by May Fourth intellectuals. Within the framework of the Communist Party, organizers of workers' education, labor unions, and industrial strikes continued to talk and write about the right to rebel against feudal ethics, the need for a new, vernacular poetry, and the importance of enlightenment thought for those who would awaken their more backward masses. Similarly, budding young writers of the Society for Literary Research encouraged each other not to allow the society to become a mouthpiece for traditional pieties (*wenyi zai dao*), but, rather, to make it a mirror for the blood and tears of the trampled and insulted masses.

The gulf between organizers and writers, then, was not as important as their commonality. That commonality was not a matter of accident or circumstances but of ongoing communication and collaboration. A good example of the persistent bond between May Fourth intellectuals in the period in which their differences were supposed to be greatest is the friendship between Deng Zhongxia and Zhu Ziqing. In spite of their disparate commitment to Communist organizing and literary scholarship, these two friends stayed in close contact with each other and continued to inspire each other to be faithful to the May Fourth enlightenment. Having become friends while making speeches for the Beida Commoners' Education Lecture Society, they went on to correspond about their mutual hopes for new poets in the era of social revolution.

19. Deng Zhongxia as Communist labor organizer, ca. 1924.

Deng Zhongxia wanted writers to be more deeply involved in the practical business of social change, while Zhu Ziqing worried about the clumsiness of their artistic expression.[92]

And so, they stayed in touch with each other, not letting each other forget the twofold commitment to social and cultural awakening inaugurated during their years at Beida. In the summer of 1924, the two young men met again in Hangzhou. Zhu Ziqing commemorated that occasion in a poem that captures vividly the many-layered solidarity of writers and organizers in the post May Fourth era. In the admiration and affection of the moody writer for the practical-minded organizer, we glimpse the enduring bond between the two. That bond, in turn, kept the idea of enlightenment at the forefront of social revolution during the subsequent years in which all ideas were to be tested and charred by the flame of political violence:

> Your hands are like torches
> your eyes like waves
> your words like stones.
> What could have made me forget?...
>
> You want to build a red heaven on earth
> on an earth full of thorns
> on an earth full of sly foxes
> on an earth full of the walking dead
>
> You would make yourself into a sharp knife,
> a sword able to cut down thorns.
> You would be a roaring lion
> to set the foxes running scared
> You would be a spring thunder
> to startle into awakening the walking dead
>
> I love to see you ride ...
> I imagine you as a sand and rock stirring tornado
> that aims to blow down entrenched palaces of gold
> Blow on....
>
> Last year, I saw you on a summer day
> Why did you look so drained?
> Your eyes were parched,
> your hair too long.
> But your blood was burning.
>
> I, who had been wallowing in mud,
> was baked by your fire.
> You have the fragrance of a strong cigar
> You have the power of hard brandy
> You burn like red pepper
> How can I ever forget you?[93]

The Crucible of Political Violence: 1925–1927

The hand of blood clearly pointing at him, me, you!

The eyes of blood, encompassing all, staring at him, me, you!

The mask of blood, reviling, scolding, shouting at him, me, you!

Our heads smashed and our bellies pierced,

We remain brothers!

Our heads still on our necks, our hearts remain in our chests,

But our blood? What of our blood? It is seething!

Zhu Ziqing, "The Song of Blood," June 10, 1925[1]

In the summer of 1924, when Zhu Ziqing mused poetically about the pungent aroma of revolutionaries like his friend Deng Zhongxia, he did not imagine himself scorched by their fervor. Invigorated? To be sure. But not burned. However much he longed, metaphorically, to be set on fire by his encounter at West Lake, Zhu Ziqing was not, in fact, prepared to write about, much less deal with, the bloodiness of revolution. A year later, the political violence which had been a familiar feature of Deng Zhongxia's life ever since his graduation from Beida assaulted the thoughts and the writing of the mild-tempered, shy, almost reclusive Zhu Ziqing. The catalytic event that was to reveal to Zhu the brutal price of change was the May Thirtieth movement of 1925. Although he was rather far from the Shanghai demonstration that left twelve students and workers dead—he was teaching middle school in the coastal city of Ningbo—Zhu chose not to avert his eyes from history.

In his poem "The Song of Blood," written ten days after he heard the news from Shanghai, Zhu Ziqing tried to come to terms with the realization that history was now synonymous with violence. Pained, he wrote about his discovery that there was now no place left either on Chinese soil or in the mind where one could hide from "the hand, the eyes, the mask of blood." This harsh insight forced Zhu Ziqing, as it did his fellow May Fourth intellectuals, to re-evaluate the legacy of enlightenment. The tension between the commitment to criticize the Chinese cultural legacy from within and the determination to save the nation from increasingly bloody assaults from without deepened in the decade after May Fourth. The temptation to abandon faith in critical reason became stronger and stronger as well. And yet, most May Fourth veterans stood their ground. They continued to hold on to their interest in Western thought even when all things foreign became tainted by the negative connotations of imperialism. They continued to quarrel with native feudalism even when certain nationalist revolutionaries became inclined to compromise with it for the sake of patriotic mobilization. Throughout, they remained in touch with history, convinced, as Zhu Ziqing had put it, that in spite of smashed heads and pierced bellies—"We remain brothers."

At first glance, the twenty-eight-year-old middle school teacher, preoccupied with the private joy of having his first son born the day after the Shanghai demonstration, seems an unlikely "brother" to the publicly committed Communist organizer Deng Zhongxia. Nonetheless, Deng had come to the same conclusion as Zhu. In his view, too, it was the right time to concentrate on uniting the ranks of consciously awakened patriots. Deng Zhongxia, however, had come to adopt this view by a rather different route than Zhu Ziqing. Whereas his schoolmate spent the first half of the 1920s polishing his writing style in the context of the broadly humanist Society for Literary Research, Deng had plunged himself into the labor movement. One of the founders of the Communist Party, he stayed close to the first site where Beida students encountered workers—the hamlet of Changxindian, just outside of Beijing. There, Deng became the leader of the February 1923 railroad workers' strike. At the same time he never renounced the special concern of May Fourth intellectuals with their own self-awakening. Thus, one month after the Beijing strike, Deng took the lead in founding Shanghai University—the place where the nascent Communist organizers, in collaboration with sympathetic educators, gave young men and women a taste for both modern thought and practical social action.[2] The bloody events of 1925 found Deng closer to the scene of action than his friend Zhu. Having led the first round of anti-imperialist protest in Shanghai—the February strike against Japanese-owned textile works—he went south to take part in the Hong Kong–Canton (Guangzhou) labor mobilization against British imperialism.

The ongoing friendship and feeling of brotherhood between such disparate May Fourth veterans as Zhu Ziqing and Deng Zhongxia was facilitated by the political climate of the first United Front. In the half decade from 1922 to 1927, Sun Zhongshan's (Sun Yatsen's) Nationalist Party (Guomindang, or GMD) and the Chinese Communist Party (CCP) found it useful to collaborate in a simultaneous challenge to foreign imperialism and domestic warlords. With the guidance and material aid of the Soviet Union (sent in through Comintern advisers such as Adolf Joffe and Mikhail Borodin), the two political parties worked out a policy that enabled Communists to become members of the Nationalist Party while retaining their CCP affiliation. This "bloc within" strategy postponed, for a while, the need to choose sides. Intellectuals sympathetic to revolution but outside the formal structure of either party thus were given a respite from partisan pressures. As Zhu Ziqing's friend and fellow *New Tide* member Ye Shengtao recalled decades later: "On the eve of the May Thirtieth movement of 1925, the GMD and CCP were all mixed up in our minds. Anybody, it seemed to us, could have joined both—or so we thought in our ignorance then."[3]

During this respite, the focus of revolutionary action began to shift from Beijing southward to Shanghai and Guangzhou (Canton). Intellectuals and their proliferating literary societies followed suit, but with a growing premonition that language and culture were no longer unquestionably the front lines of the battle inaugurated in May 1919. The political issue of anti-imperialism had begun to occupy center stage as educated youths moved from a position of leadership to one of observers and followers of the nationalist revolution. This change in the role and self-perception of intellectuals was reflected in the slogans that accompanied the demonstration of 1925 as opposed to those of 1919. In 1919, workers had taken to the streets to demonstrate in support of the students arrested during the events of May Fourth with banners that read: "We are proud to be the rear guard of the great student movement." By 1925, students and teachers who joined the Communist-led labor movement marched behind workers with placards that read: "Educators for Labor, Justice, and National Salvation."[4]

Although they were present, either physically or in spirit, at the Shanghai demonstration of 1925, May Fourth intellectuals were ill-prepared for the political violence that followed. The enlightenment movement that had shaped their formative years at Beida was the product of an historical moment privileged by the absence of brutality. Educated youths who had taken to the streets in 1919 could, and did, expect that their social position would protect them from violence. A simple fact stands out in retrospect. No one was killed in the Tiananmen Square demonstration of May 4, 1919. The police were reported to have patrolled the student demonstration with benevolent neutrality. One Beida student, Guo Qinguang, died some days later of "injury and overstrain."[5]

Six years after the event of May Fourth, during the 1925 demonstration on Nanjing Road in Shanghai, idealistic students lost their immunity from violence. Joining in a demonstration four times larger than the one of 1919, educated youth became more vulnerable because they were protesting the killing of a Chinese worker in a Japanese factory. When their march passed through the British concession, Sikh police fired on the unarmed demonstrators. Twelve marchers were killed, most of them students. Less than a year later there were still more student casualties, this time closer to the home of the May Fourth movement itself. On March 18, 1926, the troops of the Beijing warlord, Duan Qirui, opened fire on a mass demonstration against government capitulation to imperialist demands. Forty-seven demonstrators were killed. Again, most of those killed were students.[6]

The specter of student deaths destroyed, once and for all, the intellectuals' expectation that thought could guide, or at least transcend, politics. The phenomenon of political violence did, however, also inspire them to adjust their ideas of enlightenment to the changing needs of China's nationalist revolution. In the prompt, impassioned response of May Fourth veterans to the events of 1925–26, we thus glimpse the resiliency of the New Culture movement. It was able to incorporate the martyrdom of youth into a worldview committed to the salvation and self-awakening of youth. The outbreak of terror in 1927, on the other hand, had no such inspiring effect. The numbers of the victims of violence escalated from tens to thousands. Most of those killed were now no longer educated youths but workers and Communist organizers. In the wake of these events, intellectuals became dispirited to the point of despair. They undertook a thorough re-evaluation of the May Fourth legacy. The bits and pieces of their faith in critical reason that they managed to salvage at this time enabled them to re-enter history in the 1930s, this time as collaborators rather than as victims of revolution.

In the process of understanding and overcoming their own despair as victims, intellectuals came to terms with the limitations of thought in revolutionary times. At the time of their graduation from Beida, many of the youths of May Fourth were already aware that the ideas they expounded had to be retranslated for communication outside the *New Youth–New Tide* circle of shared belief. Though never foolish enough to expect that their ideas would shape the outcome of the Chinese revolution, they did hope that the leaders of political revolution would not reject them. Confronted with the escalating pace and then the sudden defeat of revolution in 1927, they came face to face with the crucible of political history: Either they could react in keeping with their May Fourth ideas and blame forces beyond their control for eroding the viability of enlightenment, or they could allow themselves to be shaken and challenged by events that could not be readily assimilated into the framework of critical reason.

Those who chose this latter course of action, Zhu Ziqing among them, had to scale down, often dramatically, their sense of what intellectuals could do for revolution. On the basis of this much shrunken perception of their role, they proceeded to elaborate a new identity. No longer styling themselves as virtuous "scholars" (xuezhe), or even as members of the potentially proletarian "intellectual class" (zhishi jieji), they now called themselves simply "knowledgeable elements" (zhishi fenzi). As mere fragments of a defeated revolution, they tried to make sense of history even as their more romantic contemporaries continued to insist that the intelligentsia could still guide the revolution, provided its members acted more and thought less.

A willingness to reckon with the disturbance of history without being overwhelmed by it is, thus, the distinguishing hallmark of modern intellectuals like Zhu Ziqing. They were able to keep enlightenment concerns on the agenda of revolution precisely because they could, and did, turn the doubts that were once directed against Confucian tradition onto themselves. Throughout the events of a decade that came close to denying the utility of all ideas, they managed to re-examine and rescue those ideas that made sense out of the unheroic, fragmentary insights of the survivors of violence and terror. In the place of the encompassing critiques and grand syntheses attempted during the May Fourth enlightenment, we now find the fractured, moody reflections of the petty bourgeois zhishi fenzi. Before 1919, the language of their iconoclasm had been marked by violence of an abstract kind. It reflected the confident rage of young men at war with old ways of thinking. By 1927, the writings of May Fourth veterans had become filled with the blood and gloom of actual historical experience.

THE ROLE OF VIOLENCE IN THE EVOLUTION OF THOUGHT

Unforeseen upheavals in the real world tend to bring about an abrupt interruption in a system of ideas. Such interruptions, in turn, test, confirm, or disprove the flexibility of any community of thinkers. May

Fourth intellectuals comprised such a community. For them, the absence of violence had been the unacknowledged prerequisite for reasoned reflection. The history of their response to massacre and terror, thus, demonstrates how violence can inspire creative change in a system of ideas, as well as stun thinkers into silence.

"Neither violence nor power is a natural phenomenon...." wrote Hannah Arendt in *On Violence*. Both are consequences of "man's faculty for actions, the ability to begin something anew."[7] On the eve of the formative event of 1919, both violence and power were rejected by Chinese intellectuals, who were determined to begin something new. Disappointed with the superficial revolution of 1911 and oppressed by a dread of corrupt politics, May Fourth intellectuals had renounced the political power they could have assumed as traditional literati. In the decade before 1925, they also seemed immune to violence. Ignored by the warlords, who were preoccupied with fighting among themselves, they still commanded respect as members of an educated elite. The violence of the mid-1920s, by contrast, enlarged the scope of the enlightenment movement as it expanded the intellectuals' sense of community.

Violence strengthened what Zhu Ziqing called the "brotherhood" of doers and thinkers alike. May Fourth veterans, whether in Beijing, Shanghai, Guangzhou, or Ningbo, now glimpsed possibilities for thoughtful action that would no longer be centered on the individual capacity for reasonable doubt. Violent events antithetical to reason paradoxically strengthened their commitment to the goals of reason that May Fourth had exemplified. The anti-feudal enlightenment could just as easily have been pushed aside by the new power of the patriotically aroused masses. Instead, however, due to the painstaking honesty of intellectuals like Zhu Ziqing, it was reaffirmed. Thus, enlightenment at once shrank in ambition and gained a new resiliency.

That resiliency became apparent only after intellectuals overcame their considerable political naiveté. In time, the effort to make sense out of the political violence of the 1920s overcame political innocence. The "massacres" of 1925 were limited events and were, therefore, more comprehensible for critically minded advocates of enlightenment. They became politicized in a period of optimistic nationalism. The terror of 1927, on the other hand, was broad and diffuse. It left most May Fourth veterans demoralized. Those who survived the loss of optimism became part of an intelligentsia that took up the burden of creating a new culture in more modest terms. These *zhishi fenzi* had seen the face of death: both as inspiring martyrdom and as debilitating terror.

"Death, whether faced in actual dying or in the inner awareness of one's own mortality, is perhaps the most antipolitical experience there is," Arendt has written; "but faced collectively and in action, death changes its countenance; nothing seems more likely to intensify our vitality than its proximity."[8] The violence that lead to death in China in the 1920s was also a source of vitality to those who remained alive, provided they were able to comprehend its causes. Its comprehensibility depended on the solidarity forged among survivors.

The twelve casualties of 1925 provided a cause around which thousands could and did rally. The murder of the Chinese worker that had set off the event was, in itself, no novelty. But the murder of students demonstrating in support of a workers' movement did shock and inspire a nation responsive to the sacrifices of educated youths. For the first time in modern history, intellectuals who lost their lives were no longer seen as individual martyrs, after the manner of Tan Sitong, the impassioned philosopher who was killed at the end of the "Hundred Days of Reform" of the 1898 reform movement. Nor were they perceived to be like Qiu Jin, the revolutionary who lost her life after an unsuccessful assassination attempt in 1907. Rather, they were part of a community created by the violence itself.

In contrast to those earlier events, the White Terror of 1927 was a debilitating event. Again, Arendt's definition is useful here: "Terror is not the same as violence; it is rather the form of government that comes into being when violence, having destroyed all power, does not abdicate but, on the contrary, remains in full control.... The effectiveness of terror depends almost entirely on the degree of social atomization."[9] In China, the reaction to terror was just such social atomization. The dead in 1927 were too numerous to be seen as heroic casualties. Most of those murdered had been workers. Intellectuals did not become a direct target at first. They experienced the encroachment of political repression only later, when the press became heavily censored and when the universities were purged of subversive ideas and personalities. The Guomindang government swiftly thwarted overt resistance to government policies. As protest became outlawed in the years from 1927 on, the May Fourth spirit of rebellion thus choked on unfamiliar despair.

In retrospect, then, we can see that political violence posed a serious challenge to the evolving ideas of the May Fourth enlightenment. Before 1925, intellectuals had seen themselves and their movement as the embodiment of the "spirit of the times" (*shidai de jingshen*). After 1925, however, they became increasingly obsessed with responding to the "needs of the era" (*shidai de xuyao*). This preoccupation reflects an unprecedented doubt about their own ability to define the meaning of progress and of modernity. As history overwhelmed their ideals, May Fourth veterans began to immerse themselves in timely works that captured the meaning of concrete events. New and expanded solidarities that had developed in the half decade before 1925 continued to nurture the intellectuals' earlier commitments in circumstances that had been radically altered by political violence.

The Chinese Communist Party and the Society for Literary Research, both founded in Beijing in 1920, provided May Fourth students and teachers with an immediate opportunity to engage in such "timely" work. In the context of these organizations, intellectuals were able to put enlightenment ideas to the test through worker and peasant organizing and through conscientious experimentation with humanist fiction. Not surprisingly, more of the *New Tide* and *New Youth* members gravitated toward literary activities than toward engagement in practical politics. Nonetheless, they never lost contact with Beida friends and associates such as Li Dazhao, Chen Duxiu, Deng Zhongxia, Zhang Shenfu, and others who were taking the lead in keeping May Fourth cultural concerns in the forefront of the communist mobilization of the early 1920s. Many of these literary intellectuals also followed the shift in geographical focus from Beijing southward. For example, the main journal of the Society for Literary Research, *Short Story Monthly* (*Xiaoshuo yuebao*) started to publish in Shanghai shortly after the May Fourth movement. Mao Dun—a familiar figure in May Fourth circles even though he never attended Beida—became its editor in January 1921. From his position as editor of the *Monthly* and as employee of the largest modern publishing house, the Commercial Press, Mao Dun was able to become a point of contact, a job reference, and, eventually, a political inspiration for other May Fourth intellectuals who moved south during the 1920s.[10]

Even after the migration toward Shanghai and Guangzhou became a general trend among Beida students and teachers, however, other literary associations fostered the spirit of May Fourth in the capital. *New Tide* members Sun Fuyuan and Li Xiaofeng turn up again and again as catalysts of the intellectual community after the dispersal of their fellow students from Beida. At first, their efforts were concentrated on keeping the *New Tide* Society alive, even if to do so required a transformation in its character from active student organization to more general study society dedicated to the publication of new fiction and high-quality translations from Western social science. Once Sun and Li were able to rescue the journal from financial disaster in 1922–23, they proceeded to enlist former teachers and friends such as Lu Xun, Zhou Zuoren, Zhu Ziqing, and others to contribute their new works to the *New Tide* series. In 1923, with the society's publication of Lu Xun's collection of short stories entitled *Call to Arms*, the solvency of the society was assured for the foreseeable future. At the same time, with Sun Fuyuan serving as the able editor of the literary supplement to the Beijing *Morning News* (*Chen bao*), other *New Tide* and *New Youth* members were able to gain an ever-increasing audience for their writings about new literature and about a continued re-evaluation of the Confucian tradition.

In November 1924, Li Xiaofeng and Sun Fuyuan collaborated again in bringing together an assorted group of Beida teachers and students to found the *Spinners of Words* Society. Its members included Sun Fuyuan's brother (and *New Tide* member) Sun Fuxi; Lu Xun and his brother, Zhou Zuoren; Qian Xuantong, another Beida teacher and mentor who brought with him Gu Jiegang and Yu Pingbo, *New Tide* members with a long-standing interest in a critical history. Although some scholars have characterized the *Spinners* Society as a throwback to the "mere talk" tradition of Confucian literati,[11] this society was, in fact, crucial in perpetuating and deepening the commitment to enlightenment thought inaugurated at Beida a half decade earlier. By providing a diverse group of May Fourth veterans with concrete opportunities to stay in touch with each other, to continue to debate their views in public, and to polish their writing style in keeping with the evolving requirements of vernacular fiction, the *Spinners* Society helped turn words into deeds. This was, after all, one of the major goals of the New Culture movement. It remained a central purpose of the New North (*Beixin*) bookstore and *New North* journal, which took over the *New Tide* series in March 1925.[12] Thus, two months before the outbreak of political violence, May Fourth intellectuals had available to them, both in Beijing and Shanghai, organizations and publications that would translate their individual dismay into public indignation.

THE EXHILARATION OF BLOOD:
1925–1926

Less than two months after the May 30 shooting of workers and students in Shanghai, the Society for Literary Research published a special issue of the *Short Story Monthly* dedicated to this event. In this issue, *New Tide* members such as Ye Shengtao and Zhu Ziqing collaborated with friends like Mao Dun and Zheng Zhenduo to shape public response to the violence. Commemorating the deaths of the student martyrs, they consolidated a sense of community among themselves as well as among friends and comrades in the labor movement.

This issue of *Short Story Monthly* opened with Zhu Ziqing's poem "The Song of Blood." It voiced the guilt of survival and the exhilaration of new-found solidarity among those dedicated to avenge the massacre. Reviled by the "mask of blood," Zhu described poignantly a feeling of brotherhood that was quite unlike anything he had allowed himself to experience since his days as a university student at Beida. Watchful of his own feelings, a habit begun while reading and translating psychology at Beida, he now turned his emotions inside out. Although he had been far from the scene of the action, Zhu Ziqing felt compelled to join the chorus of public indignation with a "blood song" of an intensity he would have deemed melodramatic and false a few years earlier. His friends Ye Shengtao and Mao Dun had even fewer reservations. They had been at the massacre, having taken part in the Nanjing Road demonstration. They, too, emerged invigorated from the experience. Their response was similar to that of Zhu Ziqing. Whereas Zhu had been jolted out of the private joy of his son's birth, they also found themselves changed, unable to continue their scholarly work at the Commercial Press and less interested in the romantic affairs of comrades such as Qu Qiubai and Yang Zhihua.[13]

Blood, at once a poetic symbol and a present horror, thus impinged upon the consciousness of May Fourth intellectuals. Through their writings, they hoped to convey this trauma to their readers. In an effort to come to terms with the meaning of the event of May Thirtieth, Ye Shengtao forced himself to rewalk the path of the demonstration on the following day. His essay "In the Midst of the May 31st Downpour" was intended to imprint the message of blood onto the minds of those who had not been part of the demonstration itself. His efforts seem frustrated at first by the hard rain and the impassive crowd of shoppers moving in and out of stores on Nanjing Road. Yet Ye holds on to the memory of violence as a talisman against the unfeeling throng:

I think to myself: the blood had already penetrated the earth for good. This piece of earth where students were killed will be here forever—that will be enough! This piece of earth is blood's earth, it is the blood of our companions, it is enough to leave us with a weighty assignment. Irrigated by blood, the flowers of blood bloom here, the harvest of blood is here ...[14]

"Flowers of blood," "blood's earth," "blood's eyes," "blood's hands," were new images bursting with a vengeance into the writings of the previously sheltered *New Tide* youth. Fascinated by the community, however fleeting, created among witnesses to the massacre, they found voices they never thought they had before. Eager to be part of that com-

20.   Left to right: Zhu Ziqing, Ye Shengtao, Yu Pingbo, and Gu Jiegang, 1925.

munity and to consecrate themselves to the task of commemoration, these intellectuals were in danger of fetishizing the blood of 1925. The worry about what might happen "after the blood is washed off the streets" was expressed most openly by Zheng Zhenduo. He had been on his way to a bookstore when he arrived at Nanjing Road minutes after the shooting. The owner of the bookstore broke the news to him: "You wouldn't believe it. So many people were killed. Students were killed.... Thousands were arrested. Foreign soldiers opened fire into the crowd point blank." Zheng, like Ye Shengtao, also retraced the route of the demonstration, trying to make sense of its violence. In his essay he too describes vain efforts to draw passersby into conversation about what had happened. When he discovers that his own intensity is out of step with mood of the citizens he encounters, he curses them and the "heartless rain that is washing off the blood." Zheng's commemorative essay ends with a bitter description of those who go on "laughing as usual rather than organizing for protest."[15]

Three days later, to counter his own fear that the massacre was a mere "play staged on a live podium," Zheng Zhenduo founded the *Public Truth Daily* (*Gongli bao*), a newspaper dedicated to spreading the suppressed news of what was becoming known as the "May Thirtieth movement." Printed by striking workers from the Commercial Press and distributed at dawn out of Zheng's own house, this paper was published for three weeks.[16] Its pages were filled with contributions from Mao Dun, Ye Shengtao, and others, who sought to expose the meaning behind the "cruel truth" of May 30. Accustomed to haranguing the public for its spiritual lethargy, these May Fourth veterans were now drawn, out of concern with enlightenment, into a political position of alliance with a new generation of radical students and Communist labor organizers. This alliance, like the violence that provoked it in the first place, was short-lived. *Gongli bao* was closed on June 24. May Fourth veterans, thus, were forced to relearn a lesson they already knew: that it was difficult to present discomforting truths to the public at a time when Chinese authorities found anti-foreign organizing an embarrassment for their own efforts at compromise. The memory of this moment of community was not lost, however. It remained the foundation for the intellectuals' response to the March 18, 1926, massacre in Beijing.

Those who fired the guns into the 1926 student demonstration were not foreign Sikh mercenaries, but Chinese soldiers in the pay of the Beijing warlord Duan Qirui. This demonstration was led by Li Dazhao, one of the most prominent *New Youth* intellectuals, who had emerged as the leader of the North China branch of the Communist Party. His role in the events of 1926 was to make him more culpable and eventually more vulnerable in the eyes of northern warlords. A year later, they would succeed in killing him.

The same event that increased the culpability of Li Dazhao also augmented the fears of his student, Zhu Ziqing. Less than a year earlier, Zhu had written his impassioned and optimistic "Song of Blood" from the distance of Ningbo. Now he found himself on the street with Li Dazhao, a participant in the March 18 demonstration. Like Zheng Zhenduo in Shanghai, Zhu tried to bring the "cruel truth" of March 18 to the attention of those who had not been part of the event: readers who might have been beguiled by official press reports that the students had "attacked" Duan Qirui's guards. In no position to start a newspaper— he was a public employee at Qinghua University—Zhu settled instead for a public record of his own experiences. In his indictment, which he titled "Record of the Government's Great Massacre," he describes his view from only a few yards away from the shooting. Having heard gunshots, close up, for the first time in his life, Zhu lost the abstract fascination he had had with blood: "One or two minutes later, the red-hot blood of the person on top of me streamed down the back of my hand and onto my jacket. I understood immediately that the massacre had begun."[17]

With this concrete understanding imprinted indelibly in his mind, Zhu Ziqing goes on to describe the fear and the cowardice of the survivor: "The only thing I knew was that I did not want to die," he wrote, "I only wanted to live.... I rolled down a hill of corpses. Later, when I realized that I had walked on corpses, I shuddered with fear for a long time."[18] This experience of death was far more solitary and more dreadfilled than the one Zhu had described from a distance in 1925. So close an escape brought with it the self-questioning of the survivor. The fears confessed here would have been nearly inconceivable for students active in the May Fourth movement at Beida. Nothing in the militant language of the enlightenment, or even in the passions evoked by 1925, could have prepared Zhu Ziqing for this direct encounter with public murder. The moment that the blood of the person next to him streamed onto his hand, he knew himself to be guilty. Unable to glorify the moment as one of solidarity among the survivors, he wrote of his urge for self-preservation, a sign of "natural weakness" that, in later years, he continued to confess more honestly than other, more romantic revolutionaries.

To speak frankly of fear was to acknowledge that an individual voice, no matter how sympathetic or enlightened, could no longer sustain the righteous confidence that had been the hallmark of May Fourth iconoclasts. With a much shrunken vision of what he could accomplish, Zhu still tried to be faithful to the legacy of May Fourth. At the end of his essay, he calls the event of 1926 a unique historical moment for yet another generation of "new youths." Seeing himself displaced from the front lines, the twenty-nine-year-old *New Tide* veteran—now a university professor—continued to bear witness to the right of students to act as the critical conscience of society. In commemorating the martyrdom of these students, Zhu Ziqing showed himself more capable of learning from history than some of the older May Fourth intellectuals who were also in Beijing in March 1926.

TEACHERS RESPOND TO STUDENTS'
MASSACRE

Unlike the *New Tide* group, which had scattered after graduation to study abroad or to take teaching jobs in provincial schools and publishing houses away from Beijing, most of the older enlightenment intellectuals (with the notable exception of Chen Duxiu, who became chief of the CCP in central China) remained in and around Beida during the first half of the 1920s. The political violence of the 1920s traumatized them more than it did the veterans of the May Fourth student movement. In the pages of *New Youth*, members of the teachers' generation had written about the sacrifices fathers would be required to make for their children. The unforeseen events of 1925–27 robbed these older mentors of their opportunity for martyrdom, reversing what Lu Xun had called in 1918 the natural order of the life cycle. They had expected to shoulder the wrath of society themselves so that new youths would be able to march on, "to lead happy lives henceforward as rational human beings."[19] During the second half of the 1920s, however, they found themselves mere spectators of history, or, worse yet, unwitting accomplices to its murderous designs.

The responses of Lu Xun and Zhou Zuoren to the event of March 18, 1926, reveal the dilemma of this older generation. In 1919 the two brothers had been deeply involved with the *New Youth* group. Together, they had led the teachers' generation's attack on Confucian values and feudal-minded social practices. Their activism in the realm of new thought, however, failed to prepare them for the bloodiness of political violence. The death of their own students on March 18, 1926, forced these two advocates of enlightenment to confront the political price of their cultural vision. Both were profoundly affected by the violence and wrote at length about their feelings of personal culpability. Their essays about the deceased students reflect the guilt they felt as survivors—Zhou Zuoren through melancholic grief, Lu Xun through passionate rage.

On the day of the massacre, a day he inscribed in his journal as the "darkest day since the founding of the Republic," Lu Xun wrote a bitter essay entitled "More Roses without Blooms." News of the March 18 shooting had unleashed his pain and anger at the betrayal of the children whom he had intended to save in his May Fourth story "Diary of a Madman." At first, this direct confrontation with political violence did not change Lu Xun's negative assessment of his countrymen, nor his positive hopes for new youths. The unfeeling public that had so enraged Ye Shengtao and Zheng Zhenduo in Shanghai in 1925 makes Lu Xun, one year later, feel all the more keenly the burden of his own impotence:

China is being devoured by tigers and wolves, yet no one cares. The only ones who care are a few students, who should be devoting all their attention to study, but who are too disturbed by the situation to do so. If the authorities had any conscience at all, should they not have admitted their faults, and summoned up what remained of their sense of right? Yet they slaughtered them!... Lies written in ink can never disguise facts written in blood.

Blood debts must be repaid in kind. The longer the delay, the greater the interest.

All this is empty talk. What relevance has anything written by the pen?

Bullets shed the blood of young people, true. And this blood can neither be hidden by written lies, nor soothed by written dirges.[20]

Here, as in Zhu Ziqing's 1925 "Song of Blood," violence augments the fighting spirit of the writer while reminding him of the futility of the pen in soothing the pain of youthful martyrdom. Lu Xun, one of the older May Fourth intellectuals who had fervently believed that youth should be free to devote all their attention to study, now faces an unexpected dilemma. His own words seem to him "empty," unable to convey the horror of the students' deaths. His response, in the end, is to prepare himself, and anyone who would listen, for the eventual revenge upon the shameless murderers of youth.

Five days after the shooting, Zhou Zuoren, too, commemorated the death of the martyred students. Almost immobilized by sadness, he forced himself to write: "I cannot think, cannot talk, but had better write ..." This intense despondency depleted Zhou's earlier faith in the natural potential and social righteousness of youth. Once his faith wavered, rage weakened as well. In the end, his sympathy for the dead students turns into the self-pity of the middle-aged teacher:

We must harbor feelings of grief toward all the dead, but how much more so for the unfortunate young men and women who were slain—some our own students! I grieve because of the misery and terror of death, because of the waste of yet unfinished lives, and because I am saddened by the destruction death leaves in its wake.[21]

The day after the massacre, when Zhou Zuoren goes to the morgue to pay his respects to a young woman who had been his student, he confesses relief at being spared the shock of violence: "Fortunately I did not see the bloody wounds. I only saw their covered bodies and they seemed peacefully asleep."[22]

Zhou Zuoren's sadness, unlike Lu Xun's rage, was thus an intensely private and privatizing emotion. Sorrow and melancholia combine to make his commemoration at once empathetic and judgmental. To assuage his own guilt as a survivor—shared by his brother—Zhou circumscribes his sympathy, dwelling on his own "regret" and "pity."

Turning inward, he concludes that the student had died in vain: "Any youth who dies an early death is pitiful.... The destruction of youth by human force is even more so. However, what is most pitiful is when a youth willfully *throws* away his life to seek something larger, such as the romantic love of freedom."[23] Student deaths, once seen as lives "thrown away," cease to evoke a commitment to action among those still alive.

A very different summation of the meaning of this event appears in Lu Xun's commemorative essay for his student Liu Hezhen, written on April 1. Like his brother, Lu Xun gives vent to overwhelming grief: "In a welter of more than forty young people's blood, I can barely see, hear or breathe; so what can I say?... I shall sup deeply of the dark desolation ... and present my deepest grief to this world.... This shall be the poor offering of one still living before the shrine of the dead." Here, too, we hear the voice of a guilty survivor. But, unlike Zhou Zuoren, Lu Xun willingly indicts himself. Whereas his brother deemed it "fortunate" that he was spared the sight of blood, Lu Xun forces himself to imagine how Liu Hezhen was killed, how she was shot from the back, how the bullet pierced her heart and lungs: "The bullet entered her left shoulder and came right out to the right of her heart. She was able to sit up, but a soldier clubbed her savagely over her head and breast, and so she died."[24]

In the end, Lu Xun's sardonic rage obliterates all traces of melancholia: "The valor shown by Chinese soldiers butchering women and children and the martial prowess shown by the Allied forces in teaching students a lesson have unfortunately been eclipsed by a few streaks of blood." He railed at the "murderers" still "unaware of the bloodstains on their faces."[25] As a survivor of the event, Lu Xun chooses to blame the warlord government, and not its victims as Zhou Zuoren had. To "regret" the students' murder would have diminished the value of their sacrifice. From his perspective, the students had not "thrown away" their lives. Rather, they had been robbed of their future.

Survivors, according to Lu Xun, owed the dead more struggle, not less strife. Like the *New Tide* veterans who had witnessed the May 30 massacre in Shanghai, this *New Youth* contributor also seeks to understand why "bloodstains" might pale in time. And as a teacher who outlived his students, he pledges retribution even more bitterly than the Shanghai witnesses. Lu Xun thus concludes that "the debt of blood will be repaid in blood."[26] Blood here becomes a powerful catalyst for revenge. The murder of students, so unnatural to one who expected the aged to die before the young, fortifies a commitment to link enlightenment with social action.

Because the warlord government would not tolerate his agitational activities, Lu Xun left Beijing on August 26, a few months after the massacre. Zhou Zuoren stayed on and wrote highly personal essays; he drifted deeper into a mood of emotional privacy. His May Fourth concern for "mankind" became vanquished by "society," a force he had always deemed hostile. He withdrew from the nascent community of the "we" to the saddened and solitary "I." Still, throughout the late 1920s he continued to see himself as an enlightenment intellectual, insisting that "in my personal essays the rebel is still alive."[27]

A would-be rebel, Zhou Zuoren gradually drifted deeper and deeper into a hermit's life. His personal sadness could no longer embrace the magnitude of China's social affliction. Lu Xun, on the other hand, allowed the suffering of the many to overcome his sense of personal anguish. And yet, the two brothers continued to be solicitous of each other's familial needs and to collaborate on projects such as the journal *Spinners of Words*. This ongoing collaboration, friendship, and even intimacy among politicized intellectuals and their more melancholic comrades suggests a common concern with enlightenment that continued undiminished during the violent decade of the 1920s. Even those who, like Zhou Zuoren, shied away from embracing the exhilarating lessons of the bloody massacres continued to write passionately about "the common enemy." Neither willing nor able to take the political risk of blaming warlord authorities or foreign imperialists, such intellectuals, nonetheless, kept on dissecting the habits of mind of their own countrymen. Zhou, who as late as 1928 declared himself to be the keeper of the sacred memory of the martyred students of 1926, retained his position in the front line of those attacking Chinese feudalism.

In a particularly bitter essay published four years earlier, Zhou Zuoren took up his brother's metaphor of the madman, declaring himself to be a paranoid convinced that "ghosts and animals" had attached themselves to his compatriots. These monsters, Zhou argued, threaten to wipe out the glimmer of humanistic hope opened up by the May Fourth enlightenment. To distinguish between monsters and true men is a tough task, but not impossible. He states: "What I myself have started to do is just to look at them. If they bare their teeth, loudly suck on their own saliva and threaten to eat up people, then I know they're just that fearful thing—monsters, even if they turn out to be someone special in society, let us say bankers or other notables."[28] Unafraid to appeal to Western precedents to better mock Chinese attachment to conservative ideas—and by extension, to reactionary politics—Zhou ends up bemoaning the demise of such "fine" methods of medieval Europe as burning heathens to save their souls. In China, he argues, there is no choice but "to drive the devils out of our own bodies ourselves.... We need some whips made up of willow branches to flog those whose bodies have been taken over by devils.... Only after we have wiped out devils, may we savor the pleasure of wrestling with true men."[29]

The continued use of the metaphor of devils against men and the insistence that the pain of self-purging must precede the joys of shared struggle was, in effect, evidence of a continued commitment to the legacy of May Fourth. In spite of ideological and personal divisions, retrospectively attributed to May Fourth intellectuals by partisan historians, evidence suggests that they continued to have more commitments in common than apart. To be sure, some veterans of the New Culture movement responded to the bloody events of 1925–26 more eagerly than others. Some, like Lu Xun and Zheng Zhenduo, for example, were more vocal in worrying about fading bloodstains than Zhou Zuoren. They proceeded to dedicate themselves to challenging their countrymen's lethargy with vivid commemoration of the students' martyrdom. Others, like Zhu Ziqing, were more ready to confess their own fears and weaknesses. Yet all of them retained the conviction that the deepest, most enduring change must come from within men's souls. No momentary encounter with violence was acceptable as a substitute for the difficult, prolonged self-transformation inaugurated by the May Fourth enlightenment.

This conviction was to set *New Tide* and *New Youth* intellectuals apart from the younger generation of radicals, who knew only the inspirational power of violence. Among this new group of social activists was the writer Hu Yuzhi, who declared in 1926 that

violence is the most striking characteristic of our time. In revolutionary periods, violence is most prevalent. There are some who believe that revolution can be accomplished without violence. However, quiet revolutions, revolutions of the spirit, are lies. Today, the task of revolution is to demolish obstacles and for this, violence is our only means.[30]

May Fourth intellectuals, however, were unwilling to accept the charge that the revolution of the spirit that they had set in motion before 1920 was nothing but a "lie." Throughout the violence-ridden decade that followed, they managed to hold to the conviction which they first encountered in their reading of Nietzsche that truly "great events" are created not by "inventors of new noises," but rather by "inventors of new values" like themselves.[31]

As inventors of new values, most of the veterans of May Fourth also chose to keep alert to the tide of imperialist aggression and anti-imperialist protest that was sweeping through China in the wake of the violence of 1925–26. All along, they never lost sight of the unfinished challenge of creating new values. So, while giving full credit to young activists and martyrs for their participation in the noisy events of 1925–26, they tried to warn them against becoming addicted to the quick fix of blood and violence. Among the most persuasive of those who put forth this warning was Tao Menghe, the pioneering sociologist and longtime contributor to *New Youth*. In the midst of the mobilization following the May 30 massacre, he vividly described the dangers of becoming stuck in the emotional fervor of 1925:

> The Shanghai massacre cannot be our inspiration forever.... Imperialism cannot be countered with short-term movements.... Our resistance cannot be so haphazard or so blind.... It must be guided by a lofty vision, broad knowledge, and a determination to ally with the masses.[32]

His cautious words, however, were drowned out for a while by younger, more strident voices. Still, enough of his Beida friends and students heard him that the unity of the May Fourth commitment to *jiuguo* (national salvation) and to *qimeng* (enlightenment) was not lost in the 1920s.

ANTI-IMPERIALISM AND ENLIGHTENMENT: JOINT COMMITMENTS

Hu Yuzhi had revealed, perhaps inadvertently, the fallacy inherent in the position of those who sought merely to keep up with the violence of their times. When he decried "quiet revolution," when he claimed that "revolutions of the spirit are lies," he was in effect throwing down a gauntlet to those May Fourth veterans who had championed a thought revolution. In the heat of the May Thirtieth mobilization in Shanghai, Tao Menghe had retained his belief that there could be no patriotic mobilization without enlightenment. He was not alone in his priorities. Tao's sense that the lessons of May Fourth were still applicable to the situation of the mid-1920s was shared by other May Fourth intellectuals. A commitment to "lofty visions" and "broad knowledge" remained compelling both for older, more seasoned *New Youth* iconoclasts such as Lu Xun, Tao Menghe, and Qian Xuantong and for younger *New Tide* veterans like Zhu Ziqing, Ye Shengtao, Yu Pingbo, and Zhang Shenfu.

With the generational divide between them narrowing, both groups of May Fourth intellectuals responded eagerly to the possibility of community that was created by the political violence of 1925–26. Although most of them continued to focus their creative energies on literary and scholarly pursuits, they also started to pay more attention to politics, especially to the imperialist presence in China. Half a decade after the Beida students' indignant response to China's betrayal at the Paris Peace Conference of 1919, intellectuals were still trying to alert their countrymen to the deeper implications of imperialism in China. Excited about the possibility of mass resistance to imperialism, they nonetheless refused to be swept up in the anti-foreign fervor that colored so much of the social mobilization of 1925–26.

It would be easy although unfair to view the May Fourth intellectuals' resistance to the anti-foreign feelings of their compatriots as the result of their personal attachment to the Western values and customs that they had adopted during the culture movement at Beida. In fact, their efforts to distinguish between anti-foreignism and anti-imperialism were stimulated by a fierce determination to continue the "quiet revolution" of the spirit that Hu Yuzhi had so hastily declared to be a "lie." Thus, in the wake of political violence, these intellectuals continued to emphasize the need for the internal spiritual transformation of China. Because they were unwilling to let the project of *jiuguo*, national salvation, displace the project of *qimeng*, enlightenment, they once again risked appearing unpatriotic. They had already taken that risk earlier during the May Fourth movement. They had willingly borne the burden of the accusation that they were "un-Chinese," that they were destroying the "national heritage." The accusations during the first decade of the 1900s, however, paled in comparison to those hurled against advocates of enlightenment during the impassioned anti-foreignism of 1925–26.

In the mid-1920s, those who would develop an anti-imperialist stance consistent with the goals of enlightenment had to stand their ground amidst the far more popular anti-foreign mood that colored most anti-imperialist organizing. For example, at the same time that Ye Shengtao was in Shanghai, Zheng Zhenduo and Mao Dun published the *Public Truth Daily* (*Gongli bao*) and Qu Qiubai was in charge of editing the *Hot Blood Daily* (*Rexue ribao*). Established after the *Gongli bao*, the *Rexue ribao*, under the auspices of the Communist Party's central committee, opened with an editorial rather different in tone from the intellectuals' daily. Whereas the first paper aimed simply to bring the "cruel truth" of the massacre to the attention of educational circles, the second sought to stir up a spirit of resistance against foreigners. The opening editorial of Qu's paper made its anti-foreignism quite clear:

Cold-blooded foreigners! This is what the people of Shanghai call you. The boiling, hot blood of the people of Shanghai ... has scoured completely the shame of cold-blooded foreigners.... We should inspire all of China with the hot blood of the people of Shanghai.... The stronger ones in the world today possess cold iron, while we, the weaker ones, only have our hot blood. But we are not worried that we don't have the cold iron in our hands, since we already have the hot blood boiling in our hearts. The stronger ones are doomed, since the hot blood will overpower the cold iron.[33]

Veterans of the Beida New Culture movement, in contrast to Qu Qiubai, were less confident about the victory of blood over iron. Perhaps their proclivity toward scientific logic prevented them from embracing such farfetched possibilities. Their writings during the mid-1920s did not assume that the "hot blood" of their compatriots had "already washed clean" the insults of imperialism. Rather, they expressed publicly their worries about the "unfeeling" response of the Shanghai crowds and about the ease with which life threatened to return to normal after the shootings of 1925 and 1926.

Seeking a more enduring and deeper awakening, they were unwilling to divide the world so neatly between "us" and "them," between the "hot-blooded" and the "cold-blooded." This dualistic vision had been the hallmark of "national salvation" movements since the turn of the twentieth century. Proponents of enlightenment, from their May Fourth days onward, had tried to counter simplistic patriotism. Their efforts intensified in the wake of political violence as they persisted in discussing the problems of national character, or of *guominxing*. To remind their countrymen about the spiritual limitations of the "hot-blooded us," and the valuable elements in the worldview of the "cold-blooded them," was a risky proposition indeed.

Long accustomed to taking such risks—to affronting public opinion readily, even gleefully—*New Youth* veterans were in the forefront of those who continued to talk about native shortcomings in the midst of the anti-foreign mobilization of the mid-1920s.[34] Thus, at the same time that Qu Qiubai was railing against cold-blooded outsiders, the practiced doubter Qian Xuantong published a critical essay entitled "Anti-imperialism." While giving full credit to the young agitators who were in the process of giving practical meaning to a vague, empty slogan that had been around since the days of the May Fourth mobilization, Qian goes on to remind them of the unfinished challenge implicit in the 1919 call "to get rid of traitors within, resist outside aggression without." Like Tao Menghe and others, Qian Xuantong is concerned with the short-lived nature of a patriotic fervor animated solely by the passions of the massacre. He, too, seeks to prepare his countrymen for the long and difficult project of making China ready to genuinely defeat imperialism. Therefore, he comes back, over and over again, to the need "to awaken" (i.e., to enlighten) the Chinese masses, not just to arouse them.[35]

To clarify the distinction between genuine, self-conscious awakening and impassioned, momentary arousal, Qian Xuantong proceeds to ask his readers to reflect on why the Chinese nation has been so belated and so sluggish in its response to imperialism. In the midst of one of the most successful anti-imperialist mobilization efforts of the twentieth century, this May Fourth veteran argues that his compatriots' own habits of subservience are responsible for holding China back from its rightful position in the world. Rather than portraying his people as kept down by powerful foreign masters, Qian writes:

We have been slaves for thousands of years. Our cursed ancestors wrote for us countless "Appeals for Slavery"; that is why we are ready to be the foreigners' slaves today. How can slaves ever deal with politics? How can slaves ever resist aggression? These are citizens' tasks, not slave work.... In the twentieth century Sun Zhongshan (Sun Yatsen) rebelled and overthrew the Qing dynasty. But most Chinese people remain slaves, unfortunately. They themselves, of course, are not to blame, since they have been exposed to "Appeals for Slavery" for so long. But now the situation is becoming serious indeed. Not only are we at risk of staying slaves forever, but those few who are enlightened are about to perish along with the slaves. Therefore, awakening our countrymen is a matter of life or death.[36]

Having used the patriotic emergency of the day to remind readers of the problem of mentality—that old, unfinished business left over from the New Culture movement—Qian concludes with an updated version of the May Fourth slogans. He insists that after all the political struggle to rid China of crooked warlords and pro-imperialist traitors, the battle with enemies of science and democracy, will have to be fought all over again. The final challenge, in his view, is

to wipe out long entrenched ideas inimical to the Republic. To defend our country is to defend the Republic. This is not the same as defending "national purity" (*guocui*) which is tantamount to national traitorship (*guozui*).... In short, those who love our Republic must struggle to wipe out feudal habits of mind. And while we do this and fight foreign imperialists, the British, for example, we should continue to accept their culture. Unfortunately, most Chinese people's opinion is opposite to mine. They don't cherish the Republic, they even hate it, yet they love this odious "national purity." So our country is doomed to degeneration if we don't cherish the Republic, if we stick to the damned national purity—if we reject modern culture. We must enlighten our countrymen and overturn this psychology of degeneration.[37]

Qian Xuantong's willingness to talk about the psychology of degeneration in the midst of a patriotic mobilization was matched by younger May Fourth intellectuals who also took a public risk in reminding their countrymen about the more complex implications of anti-imperialist resistance. *New Tide* member and Communist Party founder Zhang Shenfu, for example, also wrote an article in June 1925 entitled "Imperialism." In it, he asked the Chinese people to see beyond the shame of the Shanghai killings to the deeper sources of foreign domination. Five months after he had withdrawn from the Party because of its "unrevolutionary" alliance with the Guomindang, Zhang cautioned against the use of simplistic slogans that he felt had led the masses away from the more basic challenge: a thorough reform of national character.[38] While Zhang quoted Lenin and other Marxist theoreticians to make the case for an all-out, prolonged battle against the psychology of subservience, his fellow *New Tide* member Yu Pingbo came out of his retreat into literary scholarship to publish an explosive and controversial essay entitled "Defense and Revenge." Yu Pingbo, too, tried to see beyond the "shame inflicted on us," beyond the foreigners' insults that had been the focus of the stirring editorial of *Hot Blood Daily*. Risking a controversial stance in the midst of the patriotic fervor of the May Thirtieth movement, he, like Qian Xuantong and Zhang Shenfu, went beyond the "shamefulness" of foreigners to talk about "our own shamefulness."

In his essay, Yu reminded his countrymen that the British and the Japanese had recently killed tens of Chinese in Shanghai, but Chinese warlords had killed thousands of Chinese over a longer period of time. Chinese opium merchants had harmed Chinese people more than foreign guns. His message, presented with complex quotations from the classics and examples of the economic sources of political imperialism, was direct:

Don't blame the foreigners first.... We are responsible for the way we continue to insult each other.... The national humiliation we suffered recently seems like a huge mountain. In fact it is like a drop in the ocean compared to how we have been humiliating ourselves. If we hadn't been insulting each other all along, how would they have dared to insult us so?... We must start paying attention to the lives of thousands, and not get riveted by the martyrdom of tens. We must become more conscious, more enlightened.[39]

Having made his case for the need to look within, not just shout about injuries inflicted from without, Yu Pingbo goes on to talk about the dangers of sloganeering. In times that required careful, deep reflection about the causes of self humiliation, Yu exhorted:

We must stop vain, empty appeals to Justice (*gongli*) and Humanity (*rendao*)....
Since we ourselves have yet to become humane and just, severing relations with
foreign countries is useless. So what if we shout "Down with Japan"; they still
control our economy. Cutting relations with Britain is even more useless, for its
market is the entire world.... The excitement of radical action is short-lived. We
need to be careful, calm. The National Salvation movement in our country now
is disorganized and ineffective.... We must wipe out domestic shame first, before
we can take on the wolves at our door.[40]

This insistence upon drawing attention to China's internal shortcomings and to the unfinished business of becoming "humane and just"
is the hallmark of enlightenment-centered anti-imperialism. Other patriots at this time were content to blame foreigners for all China's
troubles. May Fourth intellectuals such as Yu Pingbo, on the other
hand, kept reminding their fellow countrymen that the task of self-
transformation must precede effective resistance to outwardly inflicted
humiliation.

Yu Pingbo's warning against the dangers of an emotional response to
imperialism, against the tempting shortcut of distracting attention from
one's own shortcomings, fell on unreceptive ears.[41] Few were able or
willing to hear that China itself had yet to live up to criteria of universal
justice and humanity. It was, indeed, easier to revel in the hot blood of
martyrs than to think coolly about the social, economic, and spiritual
shortcomings of China. And yet at precisely the moment that May
Fourth intellectuals were called upon to lend their intellectual and literary talents to the stirrings of blood, most chose to dwell on the complexities of national character. Even Zhu Ziqing, one week after writing the
impassioned "Song of Blood," wrote a far more reasoned essay about the
emotional underside of anti-foreignism.

Entitled "White Man—God's Favorite," this essay represents Zhu's
own effort to get beyond the simplistic sloganeering that followed the
May Thirtieth massacre. Without denying the arrogance of Westerners
and the pain suffered by Chinese who have so long endured it, Zhu goes
on to probe the more delicate aspects of this humiliating interaction.
Describing a train ride in which he came face to face with a foreign father
and his son ("probably Americans," he guesses), he dwells on the moment when he realized the loveliness of the sleeping child "with blue
eyes and blond hair." Suddenly the child wakes up and stares at the
author with "cruel eyes," as if to say: "You, yellow Chinese, you have
no right to watch me!" Shocked and hurt by the child's look, Zhu goes
on to ask himself if it is fair to call such a small, unself-conscious creature
a "foreign devil." "To be sure," Zhu wrote:

I had been attacked, I felt very insulted. My self-esteem shaken, I was left feeling hollow. At the same time I felt so irritated, so anxious. Worries about our nation rose up inside me. Damn this tiny little brat! Immediately, however, I felt horrified: He is but a little boy, hardly ten years old. Yet he is already buried under traditions, under the weight of the ways of his world.... The new world, the pure heart of the babe—the utter innocence of the new generation which we had been expecting day and night—is showing no signs of arrival! This is a loss for you, for me, for him, and for the world![42]

Having confessed this disillusionment with the May Fourth expectation that youth will inevitably save society from its outworn habits of mind, Zhu goes on to describe the hidden lesson of the foreign child:

Though he is such a little boy, there is something in him that demands respect. His calmness, his silence, his independent determination as he walked away without turning back his head even for a moment—these are signs of those who are powerful, those fit to survive. Nothing mawkish in this, nothing dawdling about them—all is sharp, determined. These signs make the white people, "the" white people.... I, on the other hand, am a conflict-ridden man; I still believe that the most important thing is that we examine ourselves, examine our own children. No one, really, is God's favorite! In the world of the future, there will be no races ...[43]

Zhu Ziqing, the "conflict-ridden" man, sounds here very different from the editors of *Hot Blood Daily*. To be so conflicted in 1925 meant that one could not be as readily swept up in the rhetoric of the weak against the strong, of us against them. To insist that "we keep on examining ourselves, our children," meant to place "shame" on oneself as well as on others. Zhu's conclusion then, draws our attention to the ongoing significance of the May Fourth commitment to self-transformation, even when resistance to foreign aggression seemed paramount in the eyes of nationalist revolutionaries.

To hold fast to the conviction that mental emancipation from the shackles of tradition was as important as waging war against arrogant outsiders was difficult indeed. One way that May Fourth intellectuals managed to maintain their beliefs during this period was to stay in close, personal, and public contact with each other. While never alienating themselves from nationalist revolutionaries, they repeatedly turned to each other for a confirmation of the priority of cultural change. It was this need to consolidate the bonds of shared commitment, for example, that led Zhou Zuoren and Zhang Shenfu to publish an exchange of letters in August 1925. Perhaps it was the deafening roar of the call for *jiuguo*, national salvation, which threatened to drown out the need for *qimeng*, enlightenment, that led these veterans of *New Youth* and *New*

Tide to reaffirm their commitment to both. Perhaps, too, each man was afraid of being accused of lacking "patriotism" in the heat of nationalist mobilization. As Zhang confessed openly:

The thought of saving the nation keeps coming up in my mind. This does not mean, however, that I am fatalistic.... I just cannot bear to see my country subjugated.... But I want to do more ... I believe that if we want to change the world, we must change human nature. I am working hard to change human nature as a way to prepare for the changes of the world.... It is impossible to hope that once a system changes, human nature will change as well.... If we are going to be *practical*, what is most necessary today is the liberation of thinking.... Our method must be "truth," telling the truth in a scientific sense ... to rake up the faults of human beings until they are sore, to reveal the hidden, inside story of everything. The sciences are doing just this work. The emancipation of thought from prejudice and superstition is a prerequisite for enduring social change. The question is where to begin? With truth and scientific objectivity, of course.[44]

PRACTICAL ACTION AND ENLIGHTENMENT THOUGHT

To restate in such unequivocal terms the vision of the May Fourth enlightenment took courage, and arrogance as well. Zhang Shenfu, known among his colleagues and friends for his plentiful aptitude for both, emerged as a vigorous spokesman for emancipation of thought based on philosophical truth and scientific objectivity. Nonetheless, however much Zhang hoped that this program was truly "practical" in 1925, others of his *New Tide* and *New Youth* comrades continued to have doubts. Brutally awakened by the political violence of the 1920s, most May Fourth veterans could not help but re-evaluate their and Zhang Shenfu's previous faith in the power of thought. That process of re-evaluation, which began in 1925, was intensified by the outbreak of terror in 1927. Its prolonged challenge enabled these thinkers to finally consummate a change of identity from scholars (*xuezhe*) to members of a socially minded, politically humbled intelligentsia who called themselves *zhishi fenzi*, or knowledgeable elements.

Those who undertook the long, difficult process of weaning themselves away from their May Fourth certainties had to put their ideas to the concrete test of history. It was only after failing to understand irrational phenomena through critical reason that they came face to face with their own limitations as intellectuals. Events such as the massacres of 1925–26 could not be subsumed into their previous framework of interpretation and thus that frame had to be expanded. Their understanding developed now apace with historical events that hardly corresponded to their pre-1920 ideals.[45] As Ye Shengtao, in an outburst of honesty, wrote the day after the May 30 shootings, it had now become impossible to escape from history, no matter how one might try. As one who had expected to make history, Ye Shengtao now found himself at its mercy:

I was terrified to hear the sounds of yesterday, terrified to look at the sight of yesterday's massacre.... Even if one were walled in securely at home, the roar would still seek out the ear, the gun would still seek out the flesh! So you see, what is the use of hiding?[46]

This sense of the futility of hiding from history led Ye Shengtao and his fellow May Fourth veterans to re-evaluate the legacy of enlightenment. While at Beijing University, these young men had come to believe that modern thought conveyed by committed educators was the most effective means of liberating society from the burdensome tradition of subservience. In the wake of the political violence of the mid-1920s, however, they discovered another source of liberation—mass action. This discovery compelled them to reconsider the relationship between educators and agitators. Ye Shengtao's novel *Schoolmaster Ni Huanzhi* describes the saga of one young intellectual who tries to come to terms with his own past ideals in response to the political violence of 1925 and 1927.

The hero, a middle school teacher—much like the Beida graduates Ye knew personally—has fully absorbed the enlightenment credo and has an overwhelming faith in emancipation through learning. He finds himself on the streets of Shanghai in 1925. There, he confronts the unexpected, almost unimaginable event, "which ripped away the mask of civilization to reveal the beast in man." A man of ideas, like most of Ye Shengtao's fellow *New Tide* intellectuals, Ni is at first overwhelmed by the naked cruelty that he finds beneath the civilized veneer of the modern city. Before the massacre in Shanghai, he had been a practitioner of the "sacred calling" of teacher. During the cultural exhilaration of May Fourth, he had envisaged himself as a "prophet" among the people. By 1925, however, he begins to question the role of educator.

A teacher learning new lessons on the streets, Ni Huanzhi finds his faith in education ebbing. Still, he retains his sense of cultural mission and salvages the legacy of May Fourth by redefining education as an instrument for revolution.

Education for education's sake was meaningless gibberish. Today's education should take revolution as its starting point. If educators discard the principle of revolution, all their efforts will be in vain. And, if revolutionaries pay no attention to education they will have no foundation for their efforts. [Ni] had fancied himself an educator. Now, if he meant to achieve any worthwhile results, he must become an educator for the revolution.[47]

Thus Ye shows how the meaning of "revolution" had changed since the period of the New Culture enlightenment. Being *for* the revolution in 1925 meant something quite different from imagining oneself as *being* the revolution in 1919. Education and educators had now moved away from center stage.

Ye Shengtao himself, like many of his *New Tide* colleagues, tried to put into practice Ni Huanzhi's ideal of an education that would "take revolution as its starting place." Thus, on June 2, 1925, he became one of the founders of the Shanghai Educators' National Salvation Association. With thirty other intellectual leaders, Ye issued this impassioned statement:

Previously, we had not only refrained from participation in the national salvation movement ourselves, but had also restricted our students.... From now on, we commit ourselves to untying the students. We will stand behind them and with them, until this problem is thoroughly solved.[48]

The next day, Ye Shengtao and some of the more active members of the Shanghai Educators' National Salvation Association organized and published the *Gongli bao*. Putting out this short-lived newspaper enabled these intellectuals to have more concrete contacts with workers. One example was the cooperation between striking printers and editorial employees of the Commercial Press like Ye Shengtao, Mao Dun, and Zheng Zhenduo. The intellectuals won the workers' trust and were asked to represent the workers' union in negotiations with the owners and administrative officers of the publishing house.

The high point of this solidarity between intellectuals and workers came, according to Mao Dun, when the owners of the Commercial Press addressed the intellectuals present at union negotiations as follows: "You workers, why can't you be satisfied with a raise in pay?"[49] This moment of community between intellectuals and workers, although short-lived, was to have an enduring appeal for May Fourth intellectuals. Those who had engaged in such practical activity in the wake of the massacres became heroes and models to those who wished they could have been closer to the scene of the action. Zhu Ziqing, for example, wrote to his friend Yu Pingbo:

I am thinking of leaving educational work altogether. Perhaps I will get some work at the Commercial Press.... [Ye] Shengtao is trying to work out something for me. It is not clear if he will be able to do so. I really feel that in educational work one mostly suffers indignities with no concrete benefit or accomplishment at all, so I am inclined to forsake it altogether.[50]

In the end Zhu, like most of the *New Tide* intellectuals, did not forsake educational work. However, they carried on their various occupations with a more modest sense of what educators could contribute to China's social transformation. Gu Jiegang, for example, after a brief flurry of propaganda activity in support of the May Thirtieth movement (writing folksongs to arouse illiterate crowds),[51] returned to his work on *Gushibian*, a masterful compendium of critical essays on ancient Chinese history. Collaborating with his May Fourth teachers Qian Xuantong and Hu Shi, he continued to develop the principles of discriminating judgment that had been one goal of the May Fourth enlightenment. Even so, he was full of self-doubt and experienced a crisis of confidence typical of the *New Tide* generation. In his autobiography, which appeared as a preface to the *Gushibian*, he wrote:

Society says to me, "You have graduated from university, your education is presumably complete—from now on you must be of some service." When a mule is fully grown he is expected to recompense his owner by pulling a heavy cart loaded with coal, rice, bricks, or stones until the load becomes utterly intolerable. When the beast can no longer draw it, the lash is applied until his hide is laid open and the blood flows forth. But of all this the owner is oblivious—only when the animal's breath is exhausted and he falls dead in his tracks, can his work be said to be finished.... There is no day that does not seem too short, no day in which I am not behind in my work, and no day in which the circumstances of my life do not depress me.[52]

Other *New Tide* members, who felt less keenly the weight of their incomplete education, were able to throw themselves into "practical" work without resenting society's lash. For example, Luo Jialun, Gu's schoolmate at Beida and fellow *New Tide* member, had earlier been an active participant in the propaganda activities of the Commoners' Education Lecture Society. In the summer of 1926, after returning from his European studies, Luo found his May Fourth skills useful in the Guomindang's Northern Expedition, a military operation aimed at unifying China by wresting power from the warlords. In one short year, Luo became head of the editorial committee in Jiang Jieshi's staff headquarters as well as assistant in charge of political study for the Northern Expedition forces led by Dai Jitao.

For most May Fourth intellectuals, then, the mid-1920s provided an opportunity to mix practical action and enlightenment thought. The precise form of the mix depended on the temperament, skills, and immediate circumstances of the individuals involved. In spite of these differences, they emerged from this first encounter with violence more creative and focused in their purpose, more determined to make an original contribution to the new culture developing in China and the social revolution at hand.[53] Those among them who went on to deepen their commitment to enlightenment experienced history not as revelation but rather as a catalyst for fulfilling their own and their society's potential. As the schoolmaster Ni Huanzhi put it, the social revolution of the mid-1920s represented a maturation rather than a repudiation of the May Fourth legacy:

This time a much greater torrent of public emotion had been unleashed than at the time of the May Fourth movement. But the May Fourth movement was the fountainhead of this torrent. Without the awakening of consciousness at that time, people would have had no sense of the right path now and would not have been able to move in the right direction.[54]

This sense of the important but limited contribution of intellectuals to social change and of the enduring relevance of the May Fourth commitment to cultural awakening sets Ye Shengtao and his fellow *New Tide* members apart from most of their contemporaries. Those who had not shared the formative experience of the Beida-based New Culture movement responded to history rather differently. One of these was the poet Guo Moruo. He viewed the events of 1925–26 as moments of illumination that necessitated an abandonment of all previous commitments and ideals. Shortly after the Shanghai massacre, Guo put forth his call for "revolutionary literature" in a manifesto that loudly proclaimed his conversion from "art for art's sake" to "revolutionary literature." This romantic artist, who had been in Tokyo during the May Fourth period and who was an opponent of the humanistic literature proposed by the Society for Literary Research, was quite unaware that the call for "revolutionary literature" had already been put forth by Beida graduate Deng Zhongxia in 1924. Deng's appeal, however, did not repudiate the ideas of enlightenment. Guo Moruo, on the other hand, styled himself as a prophet of history and responded to its call as to a religious revelation.

On April 2, 1926, at a time when May Fourth veterans like Zhu Ziqing, Lu Xun, and Zhou Zuoren were trying to make sense of the recent grim events, Guo published his exuberant conversion, entitled "The Awakening of the Artist." Such an effort to reckon publicly with the false nature of one's own previous notions was not new. As early as 1916, Chen Duxiu had written "My Ultimate Awakening," which outlined the limitations of his earlier passion for political revolution and declared that he was now determined to pursue a more fundamental mental and cultural "awakening." But whereas Chen Duxiu had employed a touch of irony in writing of his "finally final awakening," Guo Moruo is intensely serious and self-righteous. His essay reveals his discovery of the powers of society and of the prophetic mission of the poet/intellectual. Looking around himself in the wake of the mass mobilizations, Guo is taken with the generative power of the masses, a power he had previously assumed to be the sole possession of romantic genius. Wanting to partake of that power, he decides to abandon his faith in the solitary creator and to submerge himself in the causes and the passions of the proletariat.

The argument Guo Moruo puts to himself, and by extension to all artists, is twofold: First, he points out with remarkable innocence that "a person is after all born into the world ... so, no matter what, one's spiritual life cannot help but be influenced by society." Secondly, he claims that "the poet in every society and every period of history has been a prophet.... Being more sensitive than others, he or she will feel the urgency of social oppression and the need for liberation before other mortals." On the basis of these assumptions, Guo concludes that poets and intellectuals can, and must, act as the vanguard of revolution provided they are willing to forsake the main achievement of May Fourth: critical individualism.

Friends, if you consider yourselves imbued with the spirit of rebellion, you naturally walk along this path with me. We have to sacrifice our own individuality and freedom only temporarily in order to plead the case for the freedom of the masses. Why should we grieve at the prospect of this grand alternative? Why recoil from it? Friends, friends who feel as I do, the time of our awakening is now! In our literary activities, we must grasp firmly the spirit of the times as well as our own calling.[55]

In his eagerness to grasp the spirit of the times, to lead history rather than be its contemplative interpreter, Guo Moruo divided self and world. The former had to be diminished in order for the latter to grow, develop, and change. This dichotomy, however, was inimical to May Fourth veterans who had already accepted the inseparability of self and world during their New Culture movement at Beida, and who were passionately committed to the simultaneous transformation of individual and society. Having explored in depth the problem of worldview (*rensheng guan*) in the 1910s, they continued to strive for a synthetic solution to it throughout the 1920s.[56]

Unlike Guo Moruo, May Fourth intellectuals were unwilling to style themselves as representatives of the "spirit of the times." They carried on their intellectual endeavors with a more limited, more contingent view of their contributions to social change. Writers like Lu Xun, Zhou Zuoren, Zhu Ziqing, Ye Shengtao, and Mao Dun did not embark upon Guo Moruo's "grand path," but continued to insist upon the difference between literature and revolution. Throughout the violent events of 1925–26 they continued to pursue their literary calling, infusing their writings with humanitarian concerns. However, they did not let themselves imagine that their writings could precipitate the victory of revolution—only that they could increase the discomfort of its enemies.

Thus, on the eve of the terror of 1927, while more romantic intellectuals were busy submerging themselves in the forward waves of history, members of the nascent *zhishi fenzi* were consolidating their position as critics of society. Mao Dun, one of the chief spokesmen for the humanistic realism of this group, expressed its point of view most clearly in an essay entitled "The Warrior Spirit and the Student Political Movement." Published in March 1927, this work represents the composite self-assessment of thinkers who knew that they were not, and never had been, prophets or "masters of society." Going over the history of Chinese intellectuals from the Warring States period through the Eastern Han, Mao Dun makes a persuasive case for the limited but influential role of educated men as critics of entrenched authority. Unwilling to attribute his predecessors' greatness to prophetic insight, he insists that "they gained their warrior spirit (*shiqi*) from learning to resist the threatening swords and boiling cauldrons of the powerful.... Intellectuals who had begun to evaluate the performance of ministers in the Eastern Han period now caused fear among officials. Though never constituting themselves into a mass movement, these learned men became leaders of criticism.... Their fighting spirit may be seen today whenever students participate in the political movements of the day."[57]

To be a warrior in the sense that Mao Dun used the term meant to become committed to a prolonged and informed quarrel with the powers that be. This stance constitutes an elaboration of the May Fourth legacy. It suggests that advocates of enlightenment, having survived their first encounter with the incomprehensibility of political violence, refused to see themselves either as prophets or saviors of history or as its servants. Their new sense of the limited yet important contribution of reason to social progress was, however, shattered by the terror of 1927. If they were to come to terms with the defeat of revolution in 1927, they would have to question themselves and their ideas far more thoroughly than they had done after the massacres of 1925–26.

TERROR AND THE DEFEAT OF REASON

The revolution was betrayed in the early hours of April 12, 1927. Members of Shanghai's "Green Gang," wearing uniforms marked by the character *gong* (worker), attacked labor union headquarters. The masked attackers arrested more than three hundred union leaders. The next day, a huge protest demonstration marched through Zhabei, the working class district of Shanghai. When the crowd of more than a hundred thousand (ten times that of May 1925) arrived at the head-quarters of the local Guomindang military commander, it was fired upon without warning. One account captures the bewilderment that ensued:

Lead spouted into the thick crowd from both sides. Men, women, and children dropped screaming into the mud. The crowd broke into mad flight. The soldiers kept firing into the backs of the fleeing demonstrators. From the adjacent alley-ways, the attackers fell upon the crowd, swinging bayonets, rifle butts, and broad-swords ...[58]

The victims were mostly workers, many of them Communists. Absent from the scene, and not yet the object of direct attack, intellectuals heard about the outbreak of terror only secondhand. This news turned out to be far more incomprehensible and debilitating than the reports of witnesses of the student massacres of 1925 or 1926.

The political violence of 1925 and 1926 had begun and ended in broad daylight. It had produced martyrs who, although relatively few in num-ber, evoked the survivors' commitment to retribution. The events of April 1927, on the other hand, were a bloodier prelude to a manhunt that would continue for nearly a decade. This prolonged terror engen-dered dread and despondency and left the surviving intellectuals feeling solitary, doubt-ridden, weak. The terror defied reason and slowly eroded the confidence of the proponents of reason.

The shock of vague fear turned out to be more enduring than the earlier exhilaration of bloody massacres. Two mementos in the Museum of History in Beijing make the contrast clear: from 1925, a silk handker-chief embroidered with a red heart, in the middle of which is inscribed "May 30"; and from 1927, a set of photographs of cages hung on the street corners of Shanghai containing the headless bodies of anonymous agitators.[59]

Ni Huanzhi, the hero of Ye Shengtao's novel, who might very well have sported such a silk handkerchief in 1925, is described as in despair by 1927: "The events of the past few days seemed so unreal to Ni, so unthinkable. It was as if the whole sky was overhung with an invisible announcement on which was written: 'Man is a creature more bestial than the beasts themselves!'" Two years earlier, the sight of blood had accelerated Ni Huanzhi's political awakening, but now, the reality of death called into question all his previous ideals. Earlier, the whole nation had seemed to rally around the cause of student martyrs, but in 1927, the schoolmaster is left to cope with solitary grief.

That phrase he had always been reciting to himself like a psalm—"We are together!"—wasn't it so much meaningless nonsense? If we were together, how was it that we split in two groups, one of them with rifles and guns as if facing an enemy, and the other squaring their shoulders as they provide targets for their fellow men's bullets? He could not forget how the bodies had laid intermingled in the streets until they had been loaded into carts and taken away, several of them with oozing brains and exposed guts, and how they were imprinted with a particular fierceness in his mind's eye. Wherever he looked, he saw those tragic, frightening figures—a mental picture which obtruded everywhere like a permanent backdrop.[60]

The demise of unity into "meaningless nonsense" was no mere metaphor in the spring and summer of 1927.

The events of April 1927 signaled a final breakdown of the already weakened United Front between the Communist Party and the Guomindang. The policy of collaboration that had been designed by Sun Zhongshan and the Soviet adviser Borodin no longer suited the needs of Sun's successor, Jiang Jieshi. With Jiang's war against warlords declared "completed," he turned his attention to the number one "internal enemy": the Communist Party. May Fourth intellectuals thus discovered that the historical moment that had afforded them reason for hope—the feeling of "brotherhood" that Zhu Ziqing celebrated in his "Song of Blood" in 1925—had been short-lived indeed. In 1927, they paid a heavy price for their ignorance of the forces that had been manipulating the Chinese political scene for nearly a decade. They were unprepared for the breakdown of solidarity in the revolutionary ranks, and the imminent demise of the united front hit them like a thunderclap. In their uninformed attachment to united front politics, they responded to the collapse of the united front more passionately than anyone might have expected, trying their best to salvage some semblance of unity.

After the outbreak of terror in Shanghai, for example, a number of May Fourth veterans tried to get to Wuhan, where, during the summer of 1927, the left wing of the Guomindang was still maintaining a show of collaboration with the Communist Party. In Wuhan, they tried to "save the revolution," by starting and editing a series of new publications which sought to prove to themselves, and to anyone else who might read them, that intellectuals understood politics after all. Thus, we find congregated in Wuhan during that brief, transitional summer such disparate May Fourth figures as Xu Deheng, Zhang Shenfu, and Mao Dun. Xu (founder and guiding spirit of Beida's *Citizen* group) had recently returned from Europe and his Durkheim studies and was now editing journals such as *Revolutionary Review* and *Mass Vanguard*. Zhang (Xu Deheng's Beida schoolmate and his ideological forerunner in leftist politics) was editing the Wuhan *People's Daily*. Mao Dun (having barely escaped Jiang Jieshi's wrath against Communist sympathizers in the Northern Expedition) was editing the *Hankou National Daily*.[61] Despite their all out efforts to regain national sympathy for the cause of the united front, these intellectuals failed to persuade those outside their own ranks. In the end, they too lost faith as they realized that the Guomindang political authorities were able to manipulate political forces far more craftily than belatedly politicized writers and university professors.

By August 1927, the end of the Wuhan United Front government was imminent. The Guomindang military leaders felt confident enough to press their "party purification" to the end. Expelling from its ranks all remnants of the Communist Party, the GMD abrogated for itself the sole right to speak for nationalist revolution. This purge, more than the earlier political attacks, brought home to May Fourth veterans their own impotence in shaping the outcome of the Chinese revolution. With its own goal now stated in terms of "saving the revolution" and "preserving the spirit of Sun Zhongshan," the GMD was able, in a matter of a few months, to thoroughly lay waste to the ranks of Communists and Communist sympathizers. The execution of Li Dazhao on April 22, 1927, carried out on orders from the Beijing warlord, further silenced the May Fourth voices within the ranks of the revolutionaries themselves. A few months later, Chen Duxiu, blamed for the failure of collaboration with the Guomindang, was purged from the Communist Party's leadership.

With many of their friends and teachers either purged from the ranks of the revolution or killed, intellectuals found themselves increasingly unable to make sense of the terror around them.[62] They could not assimilate this latest phenomenon of political violence. To make things worse, the Guomindang's party purification policy was accompanied by an intensified use of "revolutionary" language. Nationalist theorists such as Xu Qingyu, a familiar figure to Beida teachers and students during the May Fourth period, came to the fore in 1927 to defend the "anti-feudal revolution" of the Guomindang. Modeled on Chen Duxiu's May Fourth "Appeal to Youth," Xu's 1927 "Warning to Youth" consciously evoked the language of the enlightenment movement to demand that contemporary youth join, or at least not impede, the nationalists' struggle against "the enemies of revolution."[63]

Terror clothed in revolutionary rhetoric disoriented those intellectuals who had most fervently embraced the cause of revolution. Guo Moruo, who had tried repeatedly to appeal to the conscience of the chief of the Guomindang, published a scathing indictment of Jiang Jieshi, as an "enemy of the people." In keeping with the messianic mood of his article "Awakening," published a year earlier, Guo now condemned this false "messiah" as "scum" and a "cheat." His article ended with the following plea: "The time has come for all true patriots to rally to the true revolutionary Guomindang."[64]

In the end, unable to distinguish the true revolution from the false, Guo Moruo left for Japan and retreated into archaeological research. Other May Fourth veterans also tired of rallying around the "true revolutionary Guomindang." They tried to find some alternative position from which to observe these baffling events and very slowly start to make sense of them. Zhang Shenfu, for example, and some of his Wuhan comrades escaped into the foreign concessions of Shanghai. There, for a while, they plotted the founding of a third party—an alternative to the CCP and the GMD that never quite materialized. Other fellow travelers of the social movement of the mid-1920s, such as Ye Shengtao and Zhu Ziqing, found themselves intellectually and emotionally adrift, as the revolution split and withered before their eyes. A few, like Lu Xun, tried to analyze their own gullibility about revolutionary youth and united front politics. All had to go on living with the painful realization that their earlier confidence in the power of reason had been thoroughly unfounded.

In the midst of this despair and self-questioning, we observe the first irrevocable divisions among May Fourth veterans. In the late 1920s, advocates of enlightenment were at odds over the question of how to maintain one's identity and integrity when the times seemed bent upon eroding the very foundation of critical thought. These were seen as personal rather than ideological issues at the time. The split between *New Tide* members Fu Sinian and Gu Jiegang in 1927, for example, illustrates well a parting of ways that only much later became ideological.

Both Fu Sinian and Gu Jiegang had focused their efforts on historical scholarship since their days as roommates at Beijing University. The outbreak of terror in 1927 found Fu Sinian back in China after a prolonged stay at Berlin, University, where he had done research on the theory and practice of historicism, and rather well situated as the president of Sun Yatsen University in Guangzhou. When Gu Jiegang requested help from Fu in getting a job in the South, Fu responded enthusiastically. But even before Gu could reckon with the implications of being granted the favor, Fu asked him to deliver a letter to the elder statesmen of the GMD (a group that included such New Culture movement luminaries as Cai Yuanpei and Wu Zhihui) in support of the Guomindang's plan to root out Communists from the party.

Gu Jiegang did deliver the letter, but then he turned bitterly against Fu Sinian. Gu broke with Fu Sinian not because he disagreed with Fu's political position as such, but because he believed that his own integrity as a scholar had been compromised by Fu's political ambition and efforts to use him. Gu had joined the *New Tide* Society as a student in response to the gentle pressure of his roommate. Now he rejected the burden of Fu's influence. When Fu Sinian tried to exact yet another price for the job he secured for Gu—a heavy teaching and administrative load—Gu Jiegang began to feel overwhelmed. To make things worse, Fu insisted that he had the right to screen, and at times ban, Gu's writing on folklore, which the new GMD censorship deemed "pornographic."

In an August 1929 letter to his mentor Hu Shi, Gu Jiegang retells the story of the split while defending his right to pursue true scholarship in circumstances in which patronage had become very costly. He confesses his inability, or rather his unwillingness, to sell himself or his freedom to anyone, including erstwhile soul mates like Fu Sinian:

Ever since I got to Canton, I've been swamped with administrative tasks, and find myself unable to get any research done. Mengzhen [Fu Sinian's pen name, adopted during his editorship of *New Tide*] keeps saying, "You've got plenty of money and fame already." The sarcasm in his remarks made me realize that he has purchased me at an exorbitant price which I cannot and don't want to accept.... Mengzhen views me as a traitor, it seems. Still, I cannot bear to barter my future away to him. I don't want to sell myself to anyone.... You've advised me to be proud, not arrogant. I think I have pride, but no arrogance. In previous times, I used to shun responsibility, so people assumed I was easygoing and complacent. In the past two years, I have assumed responsibilities and have tried to deal with the implications of responsibility. I have made some enemies. This is something that I do not regret. My rivals fall into two camps: those who envy me and those who want to control me. Both seem unavoidable.[65]

Having outlined his slow coming of age after graduation from Beida, Gu Jiegang goes on to describe how he is still trying to hold on to some of the ideals of May Fourth enlightenment—most obviously, the right to one's own critical consciousness:

But I cannot give up my priorities to please others. I don't want to oppress others, or be oppressed. When oppressed, I fight back.... This has made me become more reactionary. When others are ruthless toward me, I'll be ruthless in return. Whatever I do, it seems I'll be misunderstood.

This is really not arrogance. I am all too aware of how limited my knowledge is, how much there is left to learn.... But, I must break with Mengzhen! Although extremely intelligent and affable, he cannot understand my point of view. He wants to make me live according to his designs. But I hate to be enslaved and will not trade my freedom for money or fame. What I hate the most is society trying to bribe me with fame and money.[66]

Another *New Tide* member who was far away from Guangzhou and Shanghai—and thus remote from the sites where terror was most acute—Zhu Ziqing also struggled in his own way to salvage some sense of personal integrity, to make sense of these senseless times, and to justify scholarly pursuits in a time of political opportunism. Zhu, more than Gu Jiegang, had reason to know the difficulty of maintaining one's individual critical consciousness in times dominated by avarice and unreason. He had been, inadvertently to be sure, at the center of the violence on March 18, 1926, when the blood of demonstrators spilled onto his hands. In the spring of 1927, however, when workers were killed in Shanghai, Guangzhou, and Wuhan, Zhu was teaching quietly at Qinghua University and pursuing his research on ancient Chinese poetry.

His peace of mind was shattered in the spring of 1928 when, after a trip to Shanghai, he received the first direct information about the terror. Three years earlier, news of the May Thirtieth massacre had inspired him to write "The Song of Blood." Now, news of the Guomindang White Terror left him in despair and confusion. In an essay entitled "Nowhere to Go," he describes the slow, almost imperceptible infection of terror spreading in the minds of intellectuals like himself:

Living in Beijing, I am remote from the turmoil of these times. Still, I feel its intimidating influence. I am unsure of the nature of the threat, but I cannot get rid of the feeling of dread.... Often, I am overcome with this feeling of being pressured, beleaguered. Although I personally have no reason for total panic, I feel increasingly so. It leaves me scared, stupefied.... At present, the course of revolution is all confused. Even the meaning of the word "revolution" seems totally lost. And yet, class struggle is getting more and more bitter.... To carry out attacks [on behalf of the bourgeoisie] and to struggle against the proletariat is inconceivable.... To speak on their behalf [as would proponents of the new revolutionary literature] is equally impossible for someone like me.... If I say now that I am a counterrevolutionary, it is in this negative sense. I walk, weakened, toward my own extinction. It is a dead-end path.... There seems no alternative.[67]

Like Gu Jiegang, Zhu was trying to come to terms with the implications of having nowhere to go. With ruthless honesty, he dissected his own feelings and those of other May Fourth intellectuals who shared this despondency and yet also resisted the temptation to identify with one side or the other. These "conflicted men" sought to cope with the failure that now repudiated their earlier, naive enthusiasm for revolution. In the mid-1920s, it had been possible to proclaim the need for a "psychology of revenge" (*baofu xinli*). By 1927, however, in the face of this reason-defying terror, the spheres of thought and action had shrunken considerably. With reduced horizons, these intellectuals drifted toward a gloomy reassessment of enlightenment.

The task of salvaging some part of the May Fourth commitment was assumed by those willing to bear disillusionment. Zhu Ziqing was not alone. Lu Xun, having fled Sun Zhongshan University after the outbreak of terror (and after his own loud disputes with President Fu Sinian), had also gone to Shanghai. There he grappled with the loss of his faith in Social Darwinism and his May Fourth hope that the future lay with the young. As the "new youths" of the Guomindang proved themselves so able at killing other youths, Lu Xun sank into despair, no longer certain if it was possible to "save the children."

He was shaken out of his personal despondency when a young writer, Shi Youheng, accused him of having infused youth with the false hope that enlightened thought could make a decisive contribution to revolution in China. Lu Xun responded with a public confession, written only a few months before Zhu Ziqing's despairing essay "Nowhere to Go." The older mentor's essay, entitled "Reply to Mr. Youheng," contains an explicit acknowledgment of the powerlessness of critical reason in the face of terror:

I am terrified, and it's a kind of terror I have never experienced before.... My dreams have been shattered. Up till now I have always been optimistic.... I used to see myself as attacking society, but all that was beside the point. Society did not even know that I was attacking it. If it had realized that, I would long be dead without a place to be buried.... What I have said was as *ineffective as an arrow aimed into the sea*. I feel I shall perhaps have nothing to say from now on. When the terror has passed, what then? I don't know, but it doesn't seem to be anything good.[68]

The question that Lu Xun poses to himself is the same as that of Zhu Ziqing: How does one go on living, knowing that one is so marginal, unworthy even of being killed with the other victims of the terror?

Ye Shengtao's fictional schoolmaster Ni Huanzhi, who belonged to a generation younger than Lu Xun, drifts into a more acute state of depression. He seems to crumble under the weight of terror and of his own disillusionment, and he longs for death, a quick solution to his own confusion. "Oh, let me die! Feeble energies, a vacillating mind, completely ineffective!... People like me are useless, every one of us! I am no good, no good at all!"[69]

Zhu Ziqing's confession that there "is no alternative"; Lu Xun's conclusion that his work had amounted to "an arrow aimed into the sea"; Ni Huanzhi's pathetic cry, "people like me are useless ... no good"—

these are all signs of the tragedy that was engulfing Chinese intellectuals. The political violence of the 1920s threatened to obliterate the very freedom of thought that they had longed for and worked for during the May Fourth enlightenment. In a situation that demanded extreme ideological commitment, they discovered the limitations of their own faith in Reason. Even as they began to renounce that faith, they held on to the concept of limitations—of their own marginality in the larger Chinese society. Eventually, they recovered confidence in Reason, but only after they had come to terms with the problem of class consciousness.

Before the defeat of Reason, it would have been inconceivable for May Fourth veterans to talk so despondently about "people like me." Their own vacillation and ineffectiveness in countering violence led them to discover themselves as "mere intellectuals." The novelty and significance of that discovery were grasped immediately by Mao Dun. In his essay "On Reading *Ni Huanzhi*," he criticized writers who still saw intellectuals as leaders of the proletariat's revolution. He praised Ye Shengtao's willingness to analyze "the anxious agitation of our own generation, of our own kind." "Anxieties" and "waverings" thus held the key to whatever limited contribution intellectuals might make in the future of the social revolution.

There are so many Ni Huanzhi's in our country. They cannot be considered brave heroes of the revolution, to be sure. But Ni Huanzhi knows himself; he understands his own weakness, the limitations of his own abilities. His feelings and thoughts are volatile, yet he remains a visionary throughout. For this he deserves our sympathy.... Ni Huanzhi, then, is a petty bourgeois intellectual who is the product of his times, of the last decade of social transformation moving from the countryside to the city, from burying his head in education to participation in the mass movement.[70]

In recognizing Ni Huanzhi's "failure," May Fourth intellectuals like Mao Dun and Ye Shengtao were taking their first halting steps toward class-consciousness. In time, class-conscious intellectuals would become able to reinvigorate the legacy of the May Fourth enlightenment movement, to reintroduce its concerns into the social and political movements of the 1930s.

"DOWN WITH THE INTELLECTUAL CLASS"

Spared from political violence during the May Fourth movement itself, enlightenment intellectuals had imagined history and society as a seamless whole. Their proposals for the total transformation of culture and their expectations that intellectuals would be central in that process were grounded in a classless vision of culture. In the aftermath of 1927, however, the issue of class became unavoidable. Those who, like Zhu Ziqing, resisted both romantic identification with the proletariat and the safety offered by its enemies, were left anxious and alone. Zhu writes: "The anxiety can be resolved only by either joining or opposing the revolution. If one is unwilling or unable to join this practical movement, then there is temporary escape ... to numb one's senses into forgetfulness."[71]

Yet forgetfulness was rejected. It did not answer the long-term needs of intellectuals who were trying to reckon with the failure of revolution. As May Fourth veterans like Zhu Ziqing began to realize the weakness of culture and the frailty of reason, they came face to face with their own marginality, with the class-bound nature of their concerns with enlightenment. After the outbreak of the terror, they were able to see how much of their optimism and radicalism during the New Culture period had been predicated upon an unconscious acceptance of their own privileged status in society.

During the May Fourth period, Confucianism had been damned as outworn and corrupt. To attack it as a useless political ideology, however, was easier than to admit its utility as the self-justifying worldview of educated men. In the late 1920s, Confucianism was re-examined. A new, disconcerting realization emerged among enlightenment advocates: This core aspect of Chinese tradition was the supreme, skilled achievement of intellectuals like themselves who had sought social privileges through a monopoly of the means of cultural expression. Although they had earlier attacked the traditional values fostered by scholar-officials, May Fourth intellectuals had done so in the name of a universal ideal of modernity. They had spoken to the *pingmin* (commoners) as representatives of scientific reason. They had aimed to make culture more "popular," to inject into it certain "vernacular" values. Yet they had never grappled with how unpopular ideas had served the interests of their predecessors: the scholar-officials of imperial times.

The terror that shattered the illusion of an amorphous, all-encompassing revolutionary "we" forced intellectuals to look at revolution in a new way. No longer viewed as a broadly national undertaking, now it emerged as the specter of class war. Thinkers who survived the terror and their own crisis of faith emerged with a new self-understanding. Before 1927, the social questions had centered around others, the *pingmin*. Now the intellectuals dwelt on the problems of what Zhu Ziqing called "our kind."

To be sure, elements of a class perspective had already been present in the May Fourth attacks on the Confucian tradition. The accusatory finger, however, had not yet been pointed selfward. Rage toward parasitic Confucian officials who lived off the manual labor of others and wallowed in their special relation to imperial authority had been mounting since the turn of the century. After 1927, intellectuals identified privilege as the social precondition of culture and reason. Once culture and reason lost their universality, their liberating potential became suspect as well.

Before the outbreak of terror, intellectuals had been the self-assigned spokesmen for emancipation through cultural renewal. In 1927, they came face to face with their own weakness and the impotence of culture. They discovered their class situation in the winter of 1926–27, an historical moment in which intellectuals were made superfluous to revolution. At this time, Communist propaganda teams doing advance work for the Northern Expedition found it advantageous to stir up the countryside with the slogan "Down with the Intellectual Class" (*dadao zhishi jieji*). In the villages of Central China, where "enlightenment" had never been understood, the propaganda teams found a populace ready to attack the social privileges of educated men. Thus, before the optimism of the Northern Expedition had worn off, before the actual break between the GMD and CCP, the urban intellectuals began to hear rumors about a campaign directed against their "class." As active participants in, or at least enthusiastic bystanders of, the Northern Expedition, most May Fourth veterans thought at first that this campaign was a direct outgrowth of their own initiatives during the New Culture movement. After all, the very phrase "intellectual class" (*zhishi jieji*) had been their own adaptation from the Japanese *chishiki kaikyū*.[72] But these critically minded borrowers from foreign cultures discovered that they were to be a more direct target of attack than they had imagined possible a decade earlier.

In the countryside, Communist organizers were able to mobilize an unexpectedly deep feeling of hostility on the part of *pingmin* toward all *wenren*, educated gentlemen. The privileged status and cultural authority of local notables—the not-so-distant relatives of May Fourth intellectuals—had become irritants in the eyes of those who would rouse rather than enlighten the rural masses. Extreme in their outlook and methods, these agitators were, at first, reprimanded by the Communist Party. As late as December 1926, the Central Committee of the CCP tried to stem what it believed to be "the greatest danger of the mass movement," which they termed "extreme leftism."[73] Party workers, however, especially in villages in the Zhejiang and Jiangsu areas, continued to argue for more radical assaults on traditional elites. Their goal was the total destruction of the economic and social privileges of the literati-gentry.

Urban intellectuals, who might still doubt the rumor that radicals meant what they said, were dismayed by news that Communist authorities in Zhejiang had confiscated the property of Zhang Taiyan, respected teacher of both generations of May Fourth intellectuals. To be sure, May Fourth intellectuals themselves had condemned Zhang for abdicating his revolutionary faith of the early 1900s. They too had reason to be angry with him for his defense of the old culture. Nonetheless, most of his erstwhile colleagues and students from Beida were unprepared for the personal attack on Zhang Taiyan. Having shared his social status, but not his views, they suddenly realized how readily his fate might become theirs.[74]

The first tactic used in their own defense by those who were sympathetic to revolution but worried about the implications of the campaign against the "intellectual class" was to accentuate the ideological difference between themselves and "superfluous" intellectuals like Zhang Taiyan. Zhang Xiruo, a Western-trained political scientist and long-time associate of May Fourth veterans such as Hu Shi and Zhang Shenfu, wrote one of the earliest essays in response to the Communist campaign against the intellectual class. In this work, Zhang argued for making a more careful distinction between "intelligence" (*lizhi*) and "knowledge" (*zhishi*). Defensive about the elitism implied by the notion of an "intellectual class" (*zhishi jieji*), he suggested the use of a new term, *lizhi jieji*, "intelligence class." Zhang Xiruo claimed that this new expression would more aptly describe himself and his colleagues: a community of thinkers defined by their potential for critical reason as opposed to their leisured privilege.

Looking at the China of January 1927, Zhang Xiruo focused his essay on an "intellectual class" that was neither leisured nor privileged. In fact, he wrote, intellectuals were hardly a new class at all, but an amorphous collection of artists, teachers, and scientists—all weak, penurious, and often naive. They had yet to acknowledge their ideological commonality. Only after that recognition, Zhang argued, would they be able to take up the lofty task of discovering truth, elevating thought, and promoting beauty:

The real danger to the intellectual class is not that it will be overthrown by others but that it does not consider itself a genuine intellectual class.... If [China's present-day intellectual class] remains a class only in name but not in fact, if it continues to be marred by its infantilism, then even if it is not overthrown, we must wonder what is the use of its continued existence.[75]

One month later, in February, Zhang Xiruo himself came under attack in the Shanghai press for his idealization of intellectuals. Younger radicals accused him of glossing over the historical and material interests of the intellectual class. Far from being concerned with the "expansion of knowledge" or the "propagation of culture," they charged, the intellectual class was now identified with those who had for centuries failed to "work according to their abilities and had all along been excessive in the satisfaction of their needs."[76] Once knowledge and culture became identified as products of material self-interest, the slogan "Down with the Intellectual Class" seemed to acquire a new legitimacy.

In these early phases of the debate—unlike the later, all too frequent attacks on intellectuals in the 1950s and 1960s—there was still time for moderation and for distinctions to be made. Some of the harsher implications of the slogan "Down with the Intellectual Class" could be deflected by the defense that most intellectuals were engaged in productive learning. Even Zhang Xiruo's critics could and did acknowledge that "the entire intellectual class cannot, and should not, be abolished. Those who have become addicted to idleness might be placed in asylums where they will not be so pernicious, where they can be forgotten. Those willing and able to work should be used more effectively."[77] Once "idleness" was identified as a precondition for the acquisition of knowledge, however, the modern intellectual class became less distinguishable in the eyes of its attackers from the traditional scholar-official class (*shidafu jieji*). In the countryside, especially, radical agitators were able to use the slogan "Down with the Intellectual Class" to galvanize a long-standing hatred of scholar-officials. In the eyes of poor, uneducated peasants, leisure for learning was nothing but an obvious by-product of the gentry's ownership of land.

In the cities, "self-defense" for the intellectual class was becoming synonymous with self-criticism. By the summer of 1927 those who would spare themselves the fate of Zhang Taiyan and Zhang Xiruo began to disclaim their own social and intellectual prominence by calling themselves *zhishi fenzi* (knowledgeable elements). In August, an article written by an author using the pseudonym of Xinru ("According to the heart") introduced this new self appellation for those intellectuals who were willing to acknowledge publicly the right of the dispossessed class to liberate themselves. As mere "intellectual *elements*," they had a unique and limited role to play in the emancipation of others, and thus could be excluded from the elimination of the intellectual *class* as a whole.

Xinru's argument was based upon a thorough analysis of the parasitic function of traditional intellectuals who had really been "slaves" of the ruling class but had adopted an "emperor mentality." To become part of the *zhishi fenzi*, however, intellectuals had to forsake their lucrative servility to the ruling elites. They also had to wean themselves from their traditional compulsion to lead the masses by virtue of superior insight:

If you think that although the masses have strength, they lack knowledge, that they cannot get along without your leadership—that is tantamount to wanting the emperorship and it is just as well for them to overthrow you. This is what gave rise to the slogan: "Down with the intellectual class." ... The intelligentsia (*zhishi fenzi*) which from now on expects to be spared destruction must be integrated with labor and with the masses (*laodonghua, minzhonghua*).[78]

As the White Terror gathered momentum, the question of how to integrate with labor and with the masses became increasingly unclear to intellectuals. Radical agitators in the countryside and in the cities were losing the initiative in their call for the destruction of intellectuals. The Communist Party, fighting for its own survival in the face of the Guomindang "party purification" movement, now began to court all potential sympathizers. Leftist survivors of the terror emerged with more empathy toward the very intellectual class they had so recently deemed unreliable and pernicious. Feng Xuefeng, a youthful theoretician who had been a student of both Lu Xun and Zhu Ziqing, most clearly articulated this new view toward intellectuals. In a 1928 essay, "Revolution and the Intellectual Class," he calls upon his fellow activists to help intellectuals cope with spiritual wounds inflicted by recent events. In Feng's view, the defeat of revolution in 1927 was a more disorienting event for idealistic thinkers than it had been for self-styled realists like himself:

For the intellectual class ... it was a frightful thing.... Reason was an especially frail instrument of resistance in this situation. Revolution is always heartless (*wuqing*). Its destruction is not limited to material things that protect you physically. It goes on to assault the supporting structures of your spiritual life as well. It destroys your confidence and your spirit. All that once was precious, sacred, and magnificent now becomes dead for you.[79]

Feng Xuefeng thus both sympathized with and criticized the sensibilities of May Fourth veterans. He saw intellectuals like Lu Xun stripped of their faith in reason, and full of wavering and self-doubt. Interpreting doubt as a sign of honesty, Feng went on to argue that intellectuals possessed a precious "inner vision" that could yet be harnessed for the purposes of revolution. The harsh "rationalism" of the enlightenment movement, he pointed out, had now turned inward. Reason chastened by terror, therefore, could make an important contribution to the social movement in China. Feng concluded: "The revolution must not slight the intellectual class. Rather, it must assign them an appropriate task."[80]

The revolution, of course, was in no position to assign tasks at this time. The fact, however, that some Communist Party members such as Feng Xuefeng would be willing to join with the nascent *zhishi fenzi* is significant. They stand out because they were more tolerant of intellectuals' habits of mind than the more romantic radicals that congregated around the Creation Society. Founded in 1921 by Guo Moruo and Cheng Fangwu in Japan, this society had been increasingly active in attacking fellow intellectuals since 1925. In the late 1920s, these radicals spread the ideals and prejudices of the rural "Down with the Intellectual Class" campaign into the urban tea houses and coffee shops where intellectuals met and argued with each other.

During the internecine debates that followed the failure of revolution in 1927, these romantic radicals persuaded themselves, and tried to persuade others, that it was possible to win still greater "victories." If the intellectual class could transcend itself by identifying with the proletariat, they reasoned, it could share in, even lead, the victorious struggle. Pursuing the question of self-annihilation of the intellectual class on to the level of theory, they asked intellectuals to "*aufheben*" (sublate) themselves, to leave the "bourgeoisie" and join the "proletariat."

Cheng Fangwu's essay "From Literary Revolution to Revolutionary Literature," published in the January 1928 issue of the Creation Society's journal, *Cultural Critique*, took up the motto "Down with the Intellectual Class" most explicitly. Cheng called upon his fellow intellectuals to conform to the Hegelian logic of "the negation of the negation": to leave behind the legacy of the May Fourth vernacular language movement and join in the creation of proletarian literature. Berating the leaders of the enlightenment movement (Lu Xun and his younger followers) for continuing to peddle "anaesthetic herbs" (that is, nonproletarian fiction) to a sick society in need of radical surgery, Cheng concluded:

We have fallen behind our times. We have as our mainstay a class which is soon to be sublated [*aufgehoben*].... If we still would bear the responsibility of revolutionary intelligentsia, we must negate ourselves once more.... We must endeavor to acquire class-consciousness.... Overcome your own petty bourgeois qualities; turn your back on the class which is soon to be sublated. Start walking toward the ragged mass of workers and peasants![81]

Cheng Fangwu's bombastic call for the intellectual class to annihilate itself for the sake of the revolution did not evoke a sympathetic response from May Fourth veterans. It was not that they felt themselves to be particularly worthy of preservation. Rather, they, unlike the romantics of the Creation Society, were unable to believe themselves capable of leading the masses once again. Even if they could have submerged themselves in the "ragged mass of workers and peasants"—not a realistic option considering their own struggle for survival in terror-ridden cities such as Guangzhou and Shanghai—they doubted whether they were fit for the lofty calling of prophet-revolutionary. Out of that doubt they forged slowly and painfully their new identity, that of mere "knowledgeable elements," *zhishi fenzi*.

DOUBT-RIDDEN REALISTS

Members of the intelligentsia, reduced in numbers and sobered by history, thus rejected Cheng Fangwu's slogan "Revolutionary intelligentsia unite! Don't worry about losing your chains!"[82] At the same time, they could not help but adopt his terminology in their own self-defense. Thus, in the weeks and months following the April 1927 outbreak of the terror, we note an increasing reliance on Marxist categories among intellectuals previously quite immune to or uninformed about Marxism. It was in this period of outward attack and internal despair that May Fourth intellectuals began to describe themselves as *xiao zichan jieji zhishi fenzi*—that is, petty bourgeois intellectuals. As they groped for an appropriate characterization of the limitations of their class consciousness, they drifted further and further from the position of the romantic radicals that "sublated" intellectuals could still lead the proletarian revolution close at hand.

Lu Xun's own response to those who pursued the "Down with the Intellectual Class" campaign after the defeat of revolution is put forth in his February 1928 essay "Befuddled Wooliness." Mocked by Cheng Fangwu for his petty bourgeois class background, for the leisure-laden life that enabled him to go on writing, Lu Xun replies with a biting mockery of romantic pretensions. By acknowledging that he is merely an intellectual, Lu Xun draws attention to the other side's hasty and wishful use of class analysis and class transcendence. More precisely, he states:

My class status has already been settled by Cheng Fangwu ... "the unawakened petty bourgeoisie." ... [H]ad I been more active I might have escaped being *au-fu-he-bi-an*'ed. [This is the Creation Society's phonetic translation for *aufheben*, to sublate.] I don't know why they choose such difficult words which must be all the more difficult for the proletariat.... But because they keep on asking us [petty bourgeois intellectuals] why we don't resort to the "art of weapons," we must answer them: Because the other side has the "art of weapons," we only have the weapons of art.[83]

Even these so-called weapons of art, Lu Xun pointed out, were not as powerful as what the enemies of revolution had at their command. To imagine that one could counteract through writing what the Guomindang was accomplishing with guns was, in the view of this hardened May Fourth veteran, "nothing but a simplistic 'illusion.' "[84]

Lu Xun's point of view was restated even more emphatically in July 1928 by Mao Dun. Writing from Tokyo, where he had taken refuge from the White Terror, he continues the argument against romantic revolutionaries by pleading with fellow writers to give up the chimera of leading the masses. Uncovering the deepest of the May Fourth ambitions— that the works of intellectuals would finally be read by the masses—Mao Dun now asked himself, and others, to face the facts. No one was interested in their work but intellectuals like themselves. Raising this simple fact to the level of theory, he claimed that the only art that was going to be truly revolutionary in the future was the one that painstakingly dissected the experiences and the perplexities of the author. He therefore concluded: "For the sake of the future development of revolutionary literature, the first step now is—to enter into and gain a firm footing among the petty-bourgeoisie."[85]

Mao Dun later went on to write a novel entitled *Pursuit*, which captured the emotions of petty bourgeois youths traumatized by the defeat of revolution in 1927.[86] His friends Ye Shengtao and Zhu Ziqing, in their own ways, took up the challenge of publicly delving into the class situation of intellectuals in order to dissect its limitations. In the process, they tended to blame themselves far more than they blamed their accusers. Having had class consciousness thrust upon them by history, they experienced it, at first, as personal defeat.

Zhu Ziqing's essay "Nowhere to Go" written two months after Cheng Fangwu's exhilarated proposal calling for the intellectual class to transcend itself, took up that challenge most explicitly. It continued the self-dissection begun by Zhu in 1926 when he discovered his own weakness in the presence of blood and violence. A year later, faced with the vague fear of terror, Zhu Ziqing confessed his weakness even more obsessively:

I am not a remarkable man, I cannot transcend my times. I have lived in the petty bourgeoisie for thirty years. My feelings, thoughts, actions are all those of a petty bourgeois.... To leave the petty bourgeoisie would mean for me to have no flesh and blood.[87]

The implications of this confession were more depressing for Zhu Ziqing than for many of his other May Fourth comrades. Having shared their assumption that culture, the key instrument of enlightenment, was

21. Zhu Ziqing as Qinghua University professor, 1928.

universal—classless—he now struggled to come to terms with its reality as a product of social privilege. At a time when both the Guomindang and the romantic leftists wanted to monopolize culture, Zhu insisted on writing about what it felt like to defend it against the political claims of both sides. Realizing that his defense limited the social utility of culture even further, he wrote: "They are destroying our finest possession: culture. We damn them.... But our words show that we are using our criteria to determine value, and our criteria are rooted in our class-consciousness.... Our curses and our rage are merely ours."[88]

To acknowledge publicly that culture was nothing but a private hobby of intellectuals like himself was difficult indeed. But Zhu Ziqing had been making it clear for quite a while that he was not afraid to look at his own attachments and prejudices with the same cold eye of reason that he had previously turned on his scholar-official ancestors. In the wake of the terror of 1927, he chose to write about the culpability of his "own kind." His essay "Nowhere to Go" goes over the familiar ground of his association with other May Fourth writers and scholars, especially Lu Xun, Hu Shi, and Gu Jiegang. Confessing on behalf of all of them an urge to retreat from the sphere of politics into scholarly pursuits, Zhu asks that this urge be mercilessly exposed. To expose it, however, was not the same as to curb its attraction. Rather, exposing was a way of turning an addiction to culture into a socially useful activity. Those who would be useful in this way could not help but dissect the class limitations of petty bourgeois intellectuals, and thereby hasten their own demise:

Those who claim that the destruction of the bourgeoisie is just a matter of time know that the petty bourgeoisie will suffer the same fate.... In fact, we are already in the midst of extinction. To offer all kinds of petitions and excuses on our own behalf is useless. It is best, therefore, to speak for oneself alone, to exert ourselves in exposing our own selves.... To attack on behalf of our own class is not possible. It is also equally inconceivable to struggle against the proletariat. Thus, if I say I am a counterrevolutionary it is in the negative sense. I walk weakened toward the path of my own extinction.... It is a dead-end path.... Still, I walk gladly toward it.[89]

What Zhu Ziqing imagined as a "dead-end path" in 1928 turned out to be the most promising option for May Fourth intellectuals. Once they gave up the grandiose ambitions of the initial enlightenment movement and managed to withstand the temptation of becoming proletarian prophets, they were able to take up the challenge of cultural change again. During the 1930s, they helped shape a new enlightenment movement, which was built upon the sober self-assessment of May Fourth intellectuals.

FIVE

Toward a New Enlightenment, 1928–1938

The heroes of May Fourth have undergone so many changes!...
History has shaken up everything in front of them. The cart of time
has remorselessly pushed aside the weak-boned ones. Only those with
sturdy feet were able to keep up with it. Nevertheless, few have
become outcasts.

Mao Dun, "On Reading Ni Huanzhi"[1]

Filled with the despair that followed the outbreak of terror in 1927, Zhu Ziqing set out to walk toward the extinction of his own class. At the time, he felt it to be the only alternative for weakened, dispirited petty bourgeois intellectuals like himself. Within a couple of years, however, Zhu himself and fellow May Fourth veterans such as Ye Shengtao and Mao Dun came to realize that the determination to keep on walking— that is, to keep on writing from the limited perspective of a petty bourgeois *zhishi fenzi*—was no small victory. Those who would learn to walk and to write anew in the decade after 1928 could not help but forsake their May Fourth image of themselves as "heroes." Instead of the prophetic visionary who soars ahead of and above his time, they turned to the more modest figure of the long distance hiker who earns his calluses by keeping up with what Mao Dun called "the cart of time."

Not all May Fourth veterans, however, were willing or able to develop such sturdy feet. Many, sensing that terror and the failure of revolution posed too great a threat to their vision of May Fourth enlightenment, held on to their earlier ideals and cursed the history that followed. Their curses further eroded the links between abstract thought and the social problems at hand. On the other hand, those who refused to become outcasts from history had no choice but to delve into their own despondency. In the course of their seemingly self-indulgent exploration of despair, they found new ground on which to stand. They acknowledged the very limited utility of philosophy and literature in revolutionary times and thus could continue their work with a renewed but circumscribed purpose. These "gloomy idealists"[2]—Zhu Ziqing's 1930 description of his friend Ye Shengtao—were humbled but not defeated by history. In a decade in which the two political parties, the Guomindang and the Communist Party, vied with each other to dismiss the relevance of May Fourth, they managed to keep the challenge of intellectual emancipation from fading into the background.

The 1930s, as we shall see, at once thwarted and facilitated the re-emergence of May Fourth concerns. Politically, these were inauspicious times: the Guomindang pursued a policy of extreme cultural conservatism, while the Communist Party fanned the flames of a fervent national salvation movement. In 1931, the GMD brought back the worship of Confucius and escalated its mop-up operations against Communist remnants in the city and the countryside. By the spring of 1934, the Japanese had set up the puppet state of Manchukuo, fully equipped with a Confucian "emperor." At the same time, Jiang Jieshi was launching his New Life movement to restore Confucian virtues to the lives of ordinary Chinese citizens. Two years later, under pressure from patriotic students and a disgruntled Manchurian warlord, Jiang was persuaded to call off his extermination campaign against the Communists and to achieve unity against Japan. This confluence of cultural reaction and nationalist mobilization was not unlike the one in which the May Fourth movement had erupted in the first place. Not surprisingly, the idea of enlightenment surfaced again.

The re-emergence of such May Fourth concerns as the role of language in thought transformation and the responsibility of intellectuals for a nation-wide awakening was affected by new historical circumstances. By the 1930s it was no longer possible for the educated elite to speak to the commoners, the *pingmin*, with the same authority as they had in the 1910s. No longer so confident in their ability to interpret, much less direct, the course of history, May Fourth veterans chose to focus on a much smaller sphere of cultural activity. Having accepted the limitations of their fragmentary insights, the intellectuals now calling themselves "knowledgeable elements" started to reach out, slowly and carefully, toward the "masses" (*dazhong*).

These intellectuals were just a fragment of a larger whole. Their effort to communicate with those outside their own community was greatly facilitated by the political crises of the mid-1930s. Threatened by Japan,

China was once again ready to listen to educated young men and women who sought to combine national salvation with a deeper commitment to intellectual emancipation. As in the May Fourth movement at Beida, a vocal minority arose to do battle with cultural conservatives, both those inside and outside the Guomindang. Against the claims of those who tried to revive the emotional appeal to "national essence" (*guocui*), a new generation of cultural radicals upheld the notion of enlightenment. They argued for more rather than less liberation from the shackles of feudal tradition.

Mao Zedong later called this revival of enlightenment concerns a "deepening of revolution in the midst of the counterrevolution." Recalling the ability of urban intellectuals to maintain a vision of new culture at a time when Communist soldiers were barely surviving Jiang Jieshi's encirclement campaigns, Mao seems frankly surprised:

The most amazing thing of all was that the Guomindang cultural encirclement and suppression campaign failed completely in the Guomindang areas as well, although the Communist Party was in an utterly defenseless position in all the cultural and educational institutions there. Why did this happen? Does it not give food for prolonged and deep thought?[3]

What surprised Mao was not at all a mystery for May Fourth veterans, however. They knew only too well that the defenseless position of the Communist Party in the decade of the White Terror provided intellectuals with an opportunity to think critically for and about themselves. At a time when there were no clear ideological directives from above, they were able to recover their confidence and rejoin history as collaborators, not just followers, of revolution.

By the spring of 1937, however, circumstances had changed considerably. A new united front policy between the CCP and the GMD had been officially adopted. At the same time, a debate about what kind of resistance war China should fight against Japan, and toward what ends, gained vitality in intellectual circles. For a brief interval, there was a common cause between intellectuals who were convinced that China must pursue internal self-emancipation simultaneously with resistance to external aggression and activists whose top priority was national salvation. The New Enlightenment movement of 1936–39 was born out of this shared concern. Its leaders were May Fourth veterans and young Communist theoreticians. Together, they tried to convince themselves and their countrymen that anti-feudal cultural criticism was necessary and legitimate even in times of national crisis. In the end, they persuaded very few ordinary citizens and even fewer leaders in the Guomindang and the CCP. Nonetheless, their attempt to revive the May Fourth legacy kept the problem of enlightenment in the minds of nationalist revolutionaries who were all too willing to compromise with China's feudal heritage.

RENEWED SENSE OF COMMUNITY IN THE LATE 1920s

The worst consequence of the terror for May Fourth intellectuals had been the shattering of their earlier hopes for solidarity among themselves as a minority of enlighteners, as well as with the larger Chinese nation struggling for awakening in the mid-1920s. With the end of the first united front in 1927, intellectuals drifted into solitary discontent. Each, for a while, experienced history as a personal defeat; each viewed his or her own fears as a sign of individual weakness exacerbated by the class foibles of the petty bourgeoisie. Within a couple of years after the outbreak of the terror, these May Fourth veterans learned to see and accept their commonality once again. The survival and reinvigoration of a sense of intellectual community, in turn, enabled them to recommit themselves to the ideals of the New Culture movement inaugurated at Beida a decade earlier.

Survival as a *community*, however, was not easy in the late 1920s and early 1930s. It required a recovery of confidence in critical reason and in intellectuals as spokesmen for enlightenment. Disheartened by the anonymous executions and wanton persecution of the White Terror, the veterans of May Fourth reached out to each other slowly and cautiously. But they did reach. They re-established contacts, both personal and institutional, that enabled them once again to have a collective, public voice. The rediscovery of that voice was, in time, accompanied by a willingness to use it in the defense of liberal activists as well as Communist martyrs. Once these May Fourth intellectuals were able to mobilize in defense of specific victims of Guomindang policies, the White Terror lost its stranglehold over them. They became public members of a new intelligentsia and were able to do something about history rather than just witness its unfolding in mute dismay.

The first place where the re-emergence of intellectual community became noticeable was Qinghua University in Beijing. In 1928, with the arrival of Luo Jialun as its new president, this previously private university became incorporated into the system of national, public institutions of higher learning. The brief tenure of this *New Tide* veteran's presidency—from 1928 to 1930—was marked by ongoing disputes with students and faculty. Ironically, Luo, who had been a May Fourth activist and was one of the most vocal defenders of the political rights of students and faculty in 1919–20, emerged in the late 1920s as an opponent of a faculty-run university. Despite his conservative position on the sharing of administrative responsibilities, however, Luo Jialun was able to make Qinghua a great center of liberal learning. In fact, during the 1930s, the spirit of intellectual inquiry at Qinghua was much freer than at the officious and by now quite reactionary Beida.[4]

Luo Jialun's key to success at Qinghua was not unlike that of Cai Yuanpei at Beida during the May Fourth era—faculty hiring. Like Cai, Luo brought to the newly established national university key members of his earlier intellectual coterie: in this case, veterans of the *New Tide* group. Thus, in 1928, the new president invited to Qinghua two of his schoolmates from his studies in the United States: the philosopher Feng Youlan and the literary scholar Yang Zhengshen. These two, in turn, brought other *New Tide* veterans such as Zhu Ziqing, Yu Pingbo, Zhang Shenfu, and others into the Qinghua faculty. Once they had begun to congregate in sufficient numbers, May Fourth veterans were able to shape the unique atmosphere and history of Qinghua to their own design. In contrast to Beida, which was marked by its origin in 1898 as the Imperial University, Qinghua had originally been a preparatory school for students going to study abroad, especially to the United States. Inspired by American models from its inception, the new national university fostered a spirit of community by its location in the suburbs and by its resident faculty. Throughout the late 1920s and the 1930s, Qinghua University was thus able to nurture a spirit of critical scholarship that sometimes went beyond what Luo Jialun deemed safe in this new era of Guomindang hegemony.

In Shanghai, May Fourth intellectuals re-established their bonds of community under more dangerous circumstances. The Guomindang authorities here were more alert to "subversive" forces, even after the crushing defeat suffered by the Communist Party in 1927. They persecuted cultural institutions more directly. In spite of this political and ideological vigilance, however, Shanghai became the center for radical intellectuals' organizing efforts. The League of Left Wing Writers, for example, was founded here in February 1930. Under the protective mantle of Lu Xun, May Fourth intellectuals ranging from Mao Dun to Guo Moruo, as well as some younger radicals recently returned from Japan and the Soviet Union, gathered together to try to update and to radicalize the legacy of enlightenment. Even for less polemically inclined *New Tide* veterans such as Ye Shengtao, who did not formally join the League of Left Wing Writers, its existence provided a network for renewing friendships. Once in touch with each other, these intellectuals were able to recommit themselves to the May Fourth vision of cultural change.[5]

More prominent, though no less vulnerable to Guomindang persecution than the leftists sheltered by Lu Xun, were the older May Fourth luminaries who congregated around the Shanghai League for Civil Rights. Its members included Hu Shi and Cai Yuanpei, as well as Madame Sun Zhongshan, the widow of China's first revolutionary leader. Set up to investigate the fate of political prisoners and to provide a public defense for the freedom of the press, this organization, like the League of Left Wing Writers and Qinghua University, helped redefine May Fourth ideals in the changing political climate of the White Terror.

The re-emergence of organizational ties among May Fourth veterans did not, by itself, cement a sense of community. This sense was strengthened by the ongoing repression by the Guomindang, which led to the public martyrdom of intellectuals. Only when the victims of terror were members of their own community—unlike the anonymous Communist organizers and workers killed in 1927—were intellectuals able to rally in a public defense of their common beliefs.

The first of such "martyrs" were five members of the League of Left Wing Writers killed on February 7, 1931. Relatively undistinguished during their lifetimes, the deaths of these young writers strengthened the feeling of community among the survivors of the White Terror.[6] Lu Xun, who in 1927 had been so dejected by the arrest and murders of his students in Canton, was thoroughly optimistic about the historic "significance" of these five deaths half a decade later. He chose to interpret their martyrdom as a sign "that the force of our cultural movement is no longer weak and that it has become an important part of the revolutionary movement.... Our comrades' blood testifies that the revolutionary literature of the working class suffers from the same oppression and terror as the toiling masses, that it is fighting the same battles, shares the same destiny."[7] Whether the deaths of these young writers "proved" what Lu Xun asserted is not the issue. The point is that these deaths enabled him to express publicly a grief that linked intellectuals to each other as well as to other "sufferers" in Chinese society.

In a similar manner, the efforts of liberal intellectuals mobilizing for national salvation in 1935 and 1936 crystallized around the case of the "Seven Gentlemen." These prominent educators, all leaders of the National Salvation Association, were arrested in December 1936. The youngest among them, the thirty-year-old Wang Zaoshi, himself a May Fourth intellectual, also interpreted this "martyrdom" as a link between

patriotic intellectuals and the rest of Chinese society: 'We love our nation sincerely. Our conscience is pure. We only advocate what so many
others feel equally strongly about, that is to say: national salvation.
Should political leaders be inclined to listen, we tell them: Rise up! Let
us not enslave ourselves willingly [to the Japanese].[8]

To be sure, the selective persecution by the Guomindang had a
numbing as well as an inspiring effect on intellectuals. In June 1933, for
example, when the executive secretary of the League for Civil Rights,
Yang Xingfo, was assassinated in broad daylight, the league stopped all
its activities. Similarly, the solitary execution of May Fourth luminaries
such as Deng Zhongxia in 1933 and Qu Qiubai in 1935 diminished, for
a while, the fighting spirit of intellectual survivors. Hearing news of
the loss of their comrades months, sometimes years, after the actual
events, May Fourth veterans often were unable to react constructively.
By contrast, the arrest of Chen Duxiu in October 1932 created a great
stir among May Fourth intellectuals. Although the concerted efforts of
the intellectual community did not lessen Chen's sentence (he remained
jailed until 1937), those efforts did precipitate a recommitment to May
Fourth ideals. Even Zhang Shizhao, the prominent critic who had
opposed Chen Duxiu's enlightenment program during the May Fourth
movement, came to Chen's defense in 1932. As chief lawyer for the accused, Zhang made possible a widely publicized trial in which Chen
continued to denounce the GMD. At the same time, *New Tide* veteran Fu
Sinian also came out strongly in defense of Chen Duxiu. Fu called his
Beida teacher an "ardent liberal" who had dared to oppose the old,
corrupt morality that formed the foundation of autocracy in China. Fu
Sinian went on to praise Chen's "great contribution during May Fourth
... his unparalleled defense of the spirit of the French Revolution, which
is the spirit of freedom itself."[9] By de-emphasizing Chen's Bolshevik
ideas, Fu recast him as the leader of the Chinese enlightenment and
asked all supporters of that legacy, especially Hu Shi, to help in Chen's
case. Although Hu Shi did not do much in the public defense of Chen
Duxiu, he continued to correspond with his jailed *New Youth* comrade, to
discuss May Fourth ideas with him, and to send him books on linguistics
and philosophy, in which they shared an interest.[10]

FROM DESPAIR TO RENEWED
CONFIDENCE

Public renewal of May Fourth bonds was the first step in the intellectuals' recovery from private despair. Beyond it lay the challenge of arti-

culating a new definition of critical thought. Unlike the eighteenth-century philosophers of Europe, who delighted in the discovery of a rational knowledge wrested from religious authorities, the May Fourth intellectuals could not rest with the claims of systematic reason. Without recourse to the coherent worldview shared alike by eighteenth-century iconoclasts, they had to make do with bits of reason salvaged from their own disillusionment. To recover confidence in these circumstances required something more than a reassertion of scientific truth over superstition. It required patient practice in the discipline of systematic doubt.

The notion of doubt—including self-doubt—embraced by May Fourth veterans like Zhu Ziqing also stands in stark contrast to the certainties and fears of their more romantic Chinese contemporaries. For example, at the same time that Zhu was wrestling with the "dead-end" path of the petty bourgeois *zhishi fenzi*, another group of literary intellectuals had gathered around the *Crescent Moon* Society to implement a more flamboyant recovery of confidence. Founded in 1923 as a private club for students returning from England and America, the *Crescent Moon* group emerged in the late 1920s as the most vigorous voice defending the transcendent values of reason and culture. Its members, also shocked by the outbreak of terror, tried to shake off the burden of self-doubt by reasserting the supremacy of ideals over reality. Inspired by the words of Genesis: "And God said: Let there be light, and there was light," they defined their mission as bringing the "radiance of true thought" to shine upon the "market place of ideas" polluted by "decadents, aesthetes, utilitarians, obscenists, fanatics, etc." The manifesto of the *Crescent Moon* Society, published in March 1928—the same month *Yiban* magazine published Zhu Ziqing's "Nowhere to Go"—reaffirmed the absolute validity of pure thought:

We believe that the first requirement of human life is the creation of pure and genuine thought. This pure and genuine thought is full of vigor and can resist, even conquer and destroy, all symptoms of disease.... We speak of intellectual liberation because we do not doubt it is the source of the vitality of life.[11]

To have "no doubt" about the prowess of thought in the midst of terror and in the face of constant censorship, to assert that "pure and genuine thought" was "the first requirement of human life" was, in effect, to elevate reason to the level of absolute faith. This faith was predicated upon the expectation that reason could "resist, even conquer and destroy" unreason. Nevertheless, the GMD began to persecute, and in time nearly silenced, the more vocal members of the *Crescent Moon* Society.[12]

Hu Shi, a seasoned veteran of May Fourth, at first supported and joined the *Crescent Moon* but ended up articulating a strategy different from that adopted by his younger, more romantic colleagues. By 1929, when the White Terror was well entrenched, Hu Shi chose to use the legacy of enlightenment as a mirror to reflect the prejudices of its contemporary enemies. In a sharply worded essay entitled "The New Culture Movement and the Guomindang," he undertook a defense of May Fourth ideas in light of the present human rights problem. Hu Shi was particularly incensed by the GMD's propaganda chief, who had begun to glorify Confucius and the "Golden Age" before the foreigners had come with their corrupting ideas. Hu Shi portrayed the current government as an enemy of freedom of thought by recalling, with bitter historical precision, the May Fourth attack on blind belief. Whereas he and his *New Youth* colleagues had tried to liberate the Chinese people from superstition, Hu Shi argued, the Guomindang was actively crushing all signs of skeptical attitudes and the spirit of criticism.

In his view, the very antithesis of the May Fourth program for liberation was the current campaign to suppress freedom of thought and speech: "One may still denounce the emperor, it's true, but one cannot criticize Sun Zhongshan. One is not yet forced to worship Confucius, although his birthday has become sacred again. And of course, one must not miss the daily readings of injunctions from our President." Hu traced these reactionary policies to the GMD's cultivation of uncritical nationalism. After he detailed various ways in which the GMD was using patriotism in its current campaign of party purification, he concluded:

These are not isolated facts. Neither can they be seen as accidental. The attitude of the Guomindang toward new and old culture has its historical background and theoretical foundation. In its essence, the activity of the Guomindang is motivated by extremist nationalism. From its very beginning this was a conservative ideology, and it has continued to engender conservative theories. These theories, in turn, provide the basis for current reactionary thought and action.[13]

Hu Shi was not alone in his pointed indictment of government-sponsored cultural conservatism. Although it was more direct in tone and content than other liberals' evocations of the May Fourth legacy, his critique was frequently echoed by Hu Shi's colleagues on the left. The most bitter among them was Lu Xun, a fellow *New Youth* member who took it upon himself to attack conservatives who defended the superiority of Chinese culture. He, too, continued to redefine the meaning of critical thought in the changing circumstances of Guomindang reaction. The object of Lu Xun's rage, however, was not the propaganda office of the

GMD, but the community of younger idealists in the *Crescent Moon* Society itself. With characteristic satire, he mocked their efforts to recover from the terror by retreating into a realm of art that they believed to be above class and history. His own interest in Soviet literary theories. Lu Xun said, was a continuation of the May Fourth interest in foreign ideas for the sake of liberating critical reason in China. At a time when many intellectuals were trying to recover from despair with the aid of new and absolute beliefs, Lu Xun, like Hu Shi, reaffirmed, from a more explicitly leftist point of view, the need for an unsentimental, doubt-filled approach to cultural criticism:

Revolutionaries are often compared to the legendary Prometheus, because in spite of the torture to which Zeus exposed him, he had so much love and fortitude that he never regretted stealing fire for mankind. I stole fire from abroad in the hope that if the taste proved agreeable those who tasted it would benefit, and my sacrifice would not have been in vain. I was driven by sheer individualism, mingled with the ostentatiousness of a petty-bourgeois [intellectual].... Still, I too wanted to be of some use to society, for then onlookers could at least see my fire and light.[14]

"Onlookers" of all sorts did indeed see Lu Xun's "fire and light." Inspired by the older writer's conscientious study of Marxist theory and his courageous resistance to the terror, more than fifty young writers joined in February 1930 to form the League of Left Wing Writers. They had previously been divided over the question of how petty bourgeois intellectuals could contribute to the proletarian struggle. Now, such writers as Mao Dun and Guo Moruo called off their war of words to unite against the GMD. Lu Xun was both a symbol and an incarnation of this new sense of community among leftist intellectuals, His modest interpretation of the role of the revolutionary and his awareness of Prometheus as a self-destructive hero stood in contrast, however, to the optimism of the younger members of the league. Their "Resolution of Views Adopted" resuscitated the May Fourth spirit of righteous rebellion, this time in a more historical, class-bound context:

The facts about the true development of society and of social progress are for us not mere abstract knowledge.... So, we attack all reactionary and conservative elements and foster the development of oppressed and progressive elements. This is a natural conclusion for us to reach.... If the poet is to be a prophet among men and the artist a guide, they cannot but stand in the front line of history and take upon themselves the responsibilities of liquidating the power of conservatives on behalf of the evolution of human society.[15]

Thus, for these younger, less seasoned comrades of Lu Xun, the recovery of confidence depended upon the revival of the intellectual's prophetic role. By assuming that they had a natural right to speak on behalf of oppressed and progressive elements, this new generation of cultural rebels were to imagine themselves in the front lines of history. In fact, their new righteousness was so pervasive and so loud that some of their contemporaries perceived it as oppressive. In 1932, for example, in a journal entitled *Les Contemporains*, two young essayists, Hu Qiuyuan and Su Wen, mounted a campaign on behalf of the "third type"—that is, intellectuals drawn to the cause of the left but unable to subordinate themselves to it. Appealing to the beleaguered leftists to "set writers free" from the obligations of class alliance and to "liberate art from the burden of constant class warfare," they attempted to prove that "freedom of creativity" was being squelched not only by the violent oppression of the GMD but also by the theoretical vigilance of the left.[16]

Intellectuals of the "third type" such as Hu Qiuyuan and Su Wen were, in effect, doing the same thing as younger members of the League of Left Wing Writers. They, too, sought to recover their nerve. Not unlike their opponents on the left, they were drawn to the theory of dialectical materialism as a way of explaining the "facts of the true development of society." What made their strategy of recovery different, however, was their infatuation with abstract knowledge and with absolute criteria of beauty. Unhappy in their present social circumstances, they tried to call themselves Marxists while upholding the "nobility of art" and its right to transcend the present in order to bear witness to "the eternal truth of beauty." They discredited the May Fourth legacy, although unwittingly perhaps, by lifting it out of time and place.[17]

In contrast to young, ambivalent Marxists like Hu Qiuyuan and Su Wen, middle-aged *New Tide* intellectuals tried to recover their confidence by coming to terms with history rather than by separating themselves from it. They did not blame the Communists for *not* "letting them be," and continued to analyze their own characters. They tried to locate the source of their own artistic and political lassitude in the class predicament of the writer. Zhu Ziqing, for example, writing in 1931 just as he was getting ready to go abroad for the first time, described the "silenced" writer rather differently from contributors to *Les Contemporains*. In an essay entitled "On Having Nothing Left to Say," he recalled and mocked his own pretensions as poet-prophet in the May Fourth period. Identifying the urge to be a spokesman (*daiyan ren*) as the core of his youthful ambition, he reflected on what it means to grow older, to have no choice but to accept the constraints of one's own history and class circumstances. In 1931, Zhu argued, it no longer made any sense to speak of "the human condition," of "human nature," or even of abstract "freedom." Rather, all that one could do was

> to find one's own path ... to take a cold, hard look at one's own needs.... You see, a middle-aged man is a man of little courage. The more he hears others talk, whether good words about him or bad, the less he has to say.... From our middle-aged perspective, so much of what is said these days seems empty talk. Should a middle-aged man, however, fancy himself as a spokesman still, should he imagine that all that he says represents others, then he will be left with no words of his own.[18]

Having moved beyond his gloomy silence in the late 1920s, Zhu Ziqing now sought some authentic, albeit limited, words of his own. Even in the early 1930s, however, he remained careful not to overestimate the power or the truthfulness of the words of intellectuals like himself. Therefore he concluded:

> For my generation, it is uncertain if there will be any future way out of our tragic and presumptuous arrogance. For now, we have even less to say than ever. Recently, however, reading an essay called "Literary Theory and Historical Materialism," I realized that the French expression *rien à dire* means all is well. Alas, this does not hold true for me, for my time![19]

Zhu Ziqing's willingness to talk publicly about having nothing left to say and about his diminishing creative energies, thus, sets him apart from youthful romantics of the "third type." He did not blame his muteness on the ideological vigilance of the left. Closer to Lu Xun than to Hu Qiuyuan, he renounced the prophetic pretensions of "spokesmen" and declared himself ready to take a tough, rational look at both himself and his bleak times. This was a thoroughly relativist estimate of the human condition—one shared by several other of Zhu Ziqing's fellow *New Tide* members, most notably Feng Youlan and Gu Jiegang.[20]

The emergence of a coherently articulated position of philosophical and historical relativism was, thus, a direct consequence of the May Fourth intellectuals' own abdication of their earlier faith in absolute verities. Feng Youlan, for example, who had already begun to explore the cultural relativity of worldviews in the 1920s, continued in the 1930s to write about the time-bound nature of all philosophical truths. It was Feng Youlan's conviction, which he shared with Gu Jiegang, that no truth may be said to transcend history and, by implication, that no thinker is above the limitations of his times. A ceaseless critic of Confucian historiography, Gu continued to unmask its ideological foundations in the 1930s. Once he recovered from the despair of the late 1920s, he was able to focus his scholarly work on the problem of how the class interests of Confucian literati had shaped the corpus of official historical documents.[21]

This sense of relativism, then, distinguished middle-aged *New Tide* intellectuals from younger writers like Hu Qiuyuan and Su Wen, who still longed for transcendent truths. The former also refused the consolations of the ahistorical praise of May Fourth that was prevalent among younger contributors to *Les Contemporains*. The veterans' contextual approach to their own history represents a significant development. During the May Fourth movement itself, they too had tried to distance themselves from history, Chinese and Western alike. Now, their relativism included themselves, as well as history. Earlier New Tiders had taken pride in being able to doubt (*yigu*) Confucian values, to challenge superstitions; now they moved toward explanations (*shigu*) of themselves and of their own past.[22] In the course of re-explaining history, they recovered a modest confidence in reason and in themselves as intellectuals. With a circumscribed yet firm commitment to critical rationality, these intellectuals were able to revive May Fourth concerns in a changed, yet still unenlightened age.

THE MASS LANGUAGE MOVEMENT

The first sign of an explicit revival of May Fourth commitments appeared, not surprisingly, in a renewed interest in the issue of language. This aspect of cultural change had caught the attention of advocates of enlightenment early on in their iconoclastic years at Beida. It retained its appeal and its urgency throughout the turbulent decades that followed. During the early period of the May Fourth enlightenment, intellectuals had discovered that language reform touched the most sensitive nerves of the still-Confucian society around them. More than their new ways of doubting or reasoning, their quest for new ways of *saying* things had brought them in conflict with defenders of traditional values. Advocates of enlightenment had appeared odious because, while pursuing the *baihua* vernacular movement, they had begun to expose the selfish attachment of *wenren*, the literati, to *wenyan*, the classical language. That attachment became even more transparent as May Fourth students shifted their concern with language from the pages of their journals to the streets of Beijing. The activities of the Commoners' Education Lecture Society brought them face to face with their own ignorance of the language and the values already prevalent among the masses.

Understanding those values as well as changing them became the goal of *baihua* advocates after May Fourth. In order to press on with language reform at this more complex level, they had to recognize their own limitations as intellectuals. Those who would instruct the common people had first to divest themselves of the privileges of their literati ancestors. A new literature based on a new language could only be created, not discovered somewhere out there in the recesses of popular culture.

The efforts of the Commoners' Education Lecture Society had brought intellectuals into contact with illiterate workers and peasants. The masses, however, had remained "common," in their view, an inert body to be acted upon. After the political violence of the 1920s, however, intellectuals changed their views of themselves and of the masses. As a result, literary reform became both more feasible and more compelling. One sign of this new effort was the "Proletarian Literature movement" launched by the League of Left Wing Writers in the early 1930s. Based upon the May Fourth concern with vernacular fiction, this movement went beyond it as well. At first, the league's campaign for "proletarian literature" echoed the May Fourth commitment to create a "common people's literature" (pingmin wenxue). It, too, was urban-oriented, or more precisely city-bound. Thus, it risked falling victim to the same naive, ignorant enthusiasm for the masses that had thwarted the initial effort in 1919–20.[23]

The proletarian literature of the 1930s, called also the "literature of the rising class," was meant to depict the lives, thoughts, and feelings of the working classes. Shortly after the founding of the league, it was obvious even to its most optimistic members that proletarian literature lacked popularity among the "masses." The problem of "popularizing" new fiction was now confronted more directly than during the May Fourth movement. In 1930 intellectuals were able to directly question their special, restrictive attachment to language. In an open forum on proletarian literature the young playwright Shen Duanxian pointed out that "revolutionary culture" had become abstract, alienated from the very people whose predicament it was supposed to depict and share. He compared revolutionary literature to an indigestible delicacy offered to a starving man:

Just at the time when the masses of workers and peasants need dark-floured dumplings to survive, we consider it adequate to send them honey biscuits.... We must not merely mirror the moods and feelings of a minority of the intellectual class. At the present, so-called "fans" of the left-wing merely add fragrance to already refined honey biscuits.[24]

Shen conluded that in order to be intelligible and useful, "proletarian literature" had to be produced by writers who transformed themselves and became the masses' own "flesh and blood."[25]

Shen Duanxian's emphasis on "the intellectuals' self-transformation," however, did not sit well with the more romantic radicals, who were ready to write for and about the proletarian masses.[26] If it had not been for the trusted voice of Lu Xun, who joined the debate on Shen's side, this initial effort to revive the May Fourth legacy would have deteriorated into a hollow propaganda campaign. Lu Xun, however, chose to be "simple-minded" enough to remind his fellow writers that the masses had an even more basic problem than the lack of their own proletarian literature: illiteracy. Denied access to the simplest tools of literary expression, they could hardly be expected to be enthusiastic readers of the latest fads in "working class fiction." Therefore, Lu Xun argued, intellectuals had before them a task far more modest than the one envisioned by idealistic prophets of this new literature. First, they had to teach the masses how to read.

Lu Xun then went further. He also warned intellectuals who went out among the masses to be on guard against their own sycophancy. He asked them to curb their urge to please the masses so that they would be accepted as "teachers" and "guides." Always suspicious of the prejudices carried through the veins of popular culture, Lu Xun worried about a proletarian literature that might become popularized too fast, that might "too easily placate the masses, flatter the masses. But to placate and to flatter is not the same as to benefit the masses."[27] Lu Xun was, in effect, recalling for fellow intellectuals one of the more easily forgotten lessons of May Fourth. He reminded them that those who would become agents of language transmission must renounce not only their monopoly over language but also the false modesty that covers up unreformed attachment to their role as teachers and guides of wordless commoners.

Lu Xun's pupil and friend, the Communist literary critic Qu Qiubai, was even more suspicious of the intellectuals' urge to "guide" the masses. In an essay entitled "Who's 'We'?" written on May 4, 1932, he pointedly unmasked this remnant of May Fourth arrogance. Qu Qiubai was convinced that the 1930 popularization campaign, like the *baihua* movement of May Fourth, did nothing about the gulf between intellectuals and the masses, between owners of the tools of literary expression and those in need of them for their own emancipation. Therefore, he warned: "The proletarian literary movement ... is still an intellectual clique and not a mass movement. These revolutionary intellectuals ... still view themselves as teachers of the people and do not dare to go to the people to learn.... This posture not only separates them from the masses, but also compels the masses to look askance at them."[28]

The chasm between those who would teach the masses and the

masses themselves was as undeniable in the 1930s as it had been in 1919. The question remained: what should be done about the chasm? Younger leftist critics argued that condescension toward existing popular culture in itself signaled an urge to control the masses.[29] Thus, by 1932, Qu was ready to accuse the May Fourth *baihua* movement of exacerbating the linguistic oppression of the masses, and of creating a Europeanized language even more opaque than its classical Chinese predecessor.

Condemned as unintelligible, the May Fourth language was in danger of becoming a foil against which a new mass language would be defined. Qu Qiubai, leading the attack, wrote: "The so-called vernacular language (*baihua*) of the May Fourth period ... is a half-classical language which when read aloud does not resemble in the least the speech of living people; thus it is a half-dead language. Therefore, the question is hardly whether it is difficult but whether the language used is or is not Chinese—the speech of living Chinese people, the speech of China's masses."[30] For those intellectuals who had already struggled with accusations that they were being "un-Chinese" during the May Fourth movement, this indictment was hardly new. What was surprising was that critics on the left should echo so closely charges leveled against advocates of enlightenment during their days at Beida. These charges also aggravated the attack on May Fourth from the right.

By 1934, a Guomindang-sponsored movement to bring back the use of a "more Chinese" language was well under way. Its leaders argued for a return to *wenyan* as a language of instruction in primary schools on the basis of the "fact" that May Fourth literature was "un-Chinese." Like the leftists, they claimed: "The context of *baihua* is entirely foreign, not Chinese. Its sentence structure cannot be understood by even the average literate Chinese.... Those who understand it ... do not consider themselves Chinese."[31] The combined effect of these attacks was to revive the fighting spirit of May Fourth veterans. From its inception, the enlightenment program and its proponents had been vulnerable to charges of being unpatriotic. Now, assaulted from both sides, defenders of the May Fourth legacy were forced to come together. Their show of unity bore the imprint of recent history and of their own reflections on the limitations of *baihua*. They were no longer defending the vernacular as such, but the right of access to language.

Thus, there was a subtle but significant shift in the concern with language change in the 1930s: Whereas the May Fourth goal had been the *discovery* of a plain-talk (*baihua*) language, now the goal became the *creation* of a mass-language (*dazhong yu* or *dazhong yuyan*). Unlike the earlier emphasis upon writing *for* the common people, in this round of language reform the reformers focused upon listening *to* them. To listen to the masses led to engagement in complex debates about local *dialects* versus one *national language*, slang versus ordinary speech, a latinized alphabet versus ideographs. May Fourth luminaries such as Wu Zhihui, Lu Xun, and Hu Shi and their younger students Ye Shengtao, Sun Fuyuan, Mao Dun, and others emerged from various literary corners to wrestle with these rather specialized linguistic problems. Their involvement in the language movement of the 1930s meant that the debate would not remain "merely linguistic" for long. Unrepentant about their May Fourth conviction that language and thought are inseparable, they succeeded in unmasking the reactionary ideas behind this new wave of concern with the purity of Chinese culture:

The various May Fourth intellectuals—some of whom had become each other's political enemies—were brought together by the confidence that they could criticize native Chinese culture precisely because they were part of the masses. The movement they had earlier pioneered had been an instrument of emancipation from both corrupt popular culture and the elitist tradition of literati culture. In 1934, this emancipation came under attack again by those who called for a return to the language of tradition, for a "popular" revival of Confucian values. Wang Mouzu, a long-time critic of enlightenment and one of the chief spokesmen for the revival of the classical language, made this attack on the May Fourth legacy:

The *baihua* movement was an outgrowth of the New Culture movement.... It spawned a host of vernacular fiction that encouraged and indulged in the self-realization of the individual, the quest for personal freedom. It licensed the total expression of personal feeling.... These writings led the younger generation astray, filled them with new ideas at the expense of their moral cultivation. Thus, they degenerate.... Now, if materials written in classical language were to be completely wiped out from textbooks of middle school students, it would surely lead to a further decrease in nationalist consciousness (*minzu yishi*).[32]

In response to such accusations, May Fourth intellectuals spoke up in support of the new mass language movement as a way to safeguard some of the gains of the enlightenment. Before they could affirm the value of self-realization and personal freedom for themselves and the common people, they had to reaffirm the need to break with the classical language that had repressed such ideas. Defenders of the May Fourth legacy, however, did not speak with a unified voice. Wu Zhihui, for example, who had pioneered the study of the scientific method during the New Culture period and who was by 1934 one of the elder statesmen of the GMD, was at once boisterous and circumscribed in his defense of the

May Fourth language reforms. His often-quoted essay "Long Live the Mass Language!" was concerned primarily with the problem of communication between intellectuals and the uneducated public and therefore argued for a mass language based on *baihua*. Aware of the current lack of popularity of *baihua*, Wu appealed for the "spontaneous creation of a mass language out of the common language spoken by the masses themselves." He asked the literate minority, including both leftists and cultural conservatives, to cease restricting the forms of "national expression." He called on them to unite to create a common spoken language.[33]

Whereas Wu Zhihui spoke up primarily for language reform, his friend and colleague Hu Shi defended the connection between language reform and cultural awakening. Having put forth the New Culture call for a "renaissance movement," Hu Shi was now outraged by those who called for a "*wenyan* renaissance." Sensing that conservatives were motivated by something more than a solicitude for schoolchildren's "moral habits," he attacked them for their contempt for common people. Wanting to retain some cultural initiative in the hands of those so long cut off from the classical tradition, he restated his May Fourth credo: "We still oppose the reading of classics."[34]

Of the older May Fourth intellectuals who came out in support of the mass-language movement, Lu Xun was the most explicit in his defense of the enlightenment goal of language reform. In an essay ostensibly about the history of written characters, he allowed himself to wonder again, as he had done often since 1927, about the forced silence of the masses. Lu Xun saw them not only as illiterate but also as lacking essential knowledge of the world. Although he mocked the traditional literati's contempt for the "stupid common people," he went on to point out that the masses possessed only experiential knowledge. That knowledge needed to be placed on a firmer foundation with the aid of new knowledge. More than Wu Zhihui or Hu Shi, Lu Xun reaffirmed the efficacy of *baihua* in bringing new knowledge to the masses. The goal of a genuine mass language, he believed, could be achieved only by self-conscious intellectuals, not by those on either the right or the left who pandered to the masses:

They all fly the flag of "the masses" and say things are not good because they cannot be understood by the masses.... They even go so far as to argue that, for the sake of the masses, we must get rid of all new and difficult terms....

They fail to see however that some of the masses' ideas are less enlightened than those of intellectuals who are conscious of their needs.... History teaches us that all reforms are first tackled by intellectuals. But those intellectuals must study, think hard, use their own judgment, and have perseverance.[35]

Lu Xun's willingness to acknowledge the special connection between intellectuals, language, and new knowledge thus reflects his own sense of responsibility for bringing enlightenment to the masses. Fortunately, he was not alone in this commitment. His views echoed closely those of younger May Fourth figures who took the lead in a more coordinated and self-conscious response to proponents of the classical renaissance.[36] These *New Tide* veterans were familiar with the commoners' education project since their college years at Beida. Now, they turned to the task of creating a mass language with a new sense of judgment and perseverance.

Outraged by the neo-classicists who were "trying to stop time," these May Fourth veterans were quick to detect that the uproar in 1934 was not over new language but new ideas. *New Tide* member Ye Shengtao was particularly acute in pointing out that advocates of the *wenyan* renaissance would "gladly accept *baihua* if they could fill the heads of young people and of the masses with old ideas."[37] To unmask the social meaning of the language revival movement going on around them, these intellectuals made good use of the tools of historical and class analysis they had acquired in the post-May Fourth decade. They now distinguished between *baihua* and a yet-to-be-created *dazhong yuyan*, and tried to anticipate the changes they would have to make in *baihua* in order for it to reflect mass consciousness more effectively.

At once serious and modest about their role as intellectuals, they believed that reflecting the consciousness of the masses was an active undertaking. As part of the masses, these "knowledgeable elements," *zhishi fenzi*, were now determined to contribute more directly to shaping popular culture. Thus Ye Shengtao wrote in 1934, in a very different mood from his dejected voice in *Ni Huanzhi* in 1927: "Which one of us is not part of the masses? Who among us does not need mass language and mass literature?"[38]

This definition of need was more concrete and more socially informed than the vision that had inspired advocates of enlightenment fifteen years earlier. It compelled some of the younger May Fourth activists to take a leading role in the mass education movement that was an outgrowth of the mass language debate. One *New Tide* member who emerged in the front line of the mass education movement of the 1930s was Sun Fuyuan. He was not hesitant to continue using the old May Fourth slogan of *pingmin wenxue*, literature for the common people, put forth by his mentor Hu Shi. In the 1930s, working closely with Tao Xingzhi and others to solve the practical problem of developing a language of the masses, Sun described himself as a "language worker." He was committed to spreading new knowledge among the masses while recording the masses' own use of language. Determined to bring the New Culture movement to the village level, Sun argued that the May Fourth legacy was quite relevant, provided it could be adjusted to the needs of rural education: "Our work is based on the needs of the peasants. We are not limited by word usage in this aspect of our work.... The textbooks we are designing for rural use include science, social science, and applied science.... It is our conviction that science is the most effective cure for the ignorance and foolishness that still pervade so much of the Chinese countryside."[39]

The language work of intellectuals like Sun Fuyuan threatened to stir up the countryside and to bring "enlightenment" to the places most troublesome for the Guomindang. As the debate about mass language moved out of the circle of the urban intelligentsia, it raised the specter of new constituencies clamoring for social justice, not just for access to a language so long denied to them. In 1934, as the GMD was fighting its fifth encirclement campaign against Communist bases in Jiangxi, it attempted to counter more directly this explosive connection between language and social rebellion. To meet the broader challenge of a potentially mass-based enlightenment, the Guomindang designed its own more encompassing ideological campaign: the New Life movement. This government-sponsored cultural reaction, when augmented by Japanese efforts to revive traditional Confucian culture, provoked May Fourth veterans to defend and to update the enlightenment legacy even more vigorously.

CULTURAL COUNTER-REVOLUTION: JIANG JIESHI AND THE JAPANESE

In the spring of 1934, as May Fourth intellectuals debated the merits and problems of a mass language, Jiang Jieshi launched his own movement to reform the physical and mental habits of the Chinese masses. The New Life movement was meant both to echo and to surpass the May Fourth concern for a new *rensheng guan*, a new worldview. Like the earlier movement it sought to depose, the New Life movement emphasized China's backwardness in knowledge and ethics. In a tone that rivaled the May Fourth intellectuals' attack on the "problem of national character" (*guomin xing*), Jiang Jieshi's inaugural speech chastised the Chinese people for being "dejected" (*tuitang*) physically and spiritually, for being "barbaric" (*yeman*) and "devoid of reason" (*bu heli*). Using the metaphor of animal life (not unlike advocates of enlightenment who had compared Chinese dogs to Chinese people), he, too, claimed that Chinese people behaved no better than "cows, horses, pigs, or sheep":

Their clothes and homes were in utter disarray; they spat and urinated wherever they pleased. Having no principles, they smoked, gambled, and whored their lives away. When they talked, they looked half dead with a demeanor reminiscent of "zombies" (*huosi ren*).[40]

But whereas the vision of a half-dead China had led to a call for iconoclasm during May Fourth, Jiang Jieshi looked at the same predicament and called for a return to the Confucian virtues of *li* (propriety), *yi* (right conduct), *liang* (honesty), and *chi* (integrity). He, like earlier critics of the problem of mentality, called for a renaissance movement in China. But in contrast to those who had emphasized individual emancipation, Jiang was concerned with the individual's submission to the goal of national regeneration. Renaissance for him connoted a return to native morality, to those Confucian values that required obedience to authority.

Jiang Jieshi was a nationalist leader thoroughly suspicious of the foreign origin of the May Fourth vision of modernity. Therefore he tried to make the New Life program intelligible to those who had seemed so befuddled by the language and the ideas of May Fourth. Aiming to popularize his program for spiritual reform, Jiang Jieshi emphasized behavioral change. By 1936, however, Jiang's initial plan to transform habits of mind had been reduced to a hygiene campaign. Proud that there was "no wandering or shuffling in the streets, no stopping in the middle of the road, no gaping about and no blocking the traffic, no smoking or spitting in public places," Jiang declared the New Life movement a great success.[41]

This deterioration of the New Life movement into an etiquette campaign did not, however, signal a shift in Jiang's conviction that a change in behavior could bring about a change in mental outlook. Spiritual regeneration remained his goal as he continued to call the New Life movement an "awakening" (*juexing*) movement. The awakened citizen, he hoped, would be a politicized and disciplined person. A person with internalized prohibitions against spitting in public places was, in this view, presumed to be less vulnerable to Communist propaganda about land reform in the countryside and freedom of speech in the cities—both concrete problems for the Guomindang in 1934. New Life "awakening," thus, became synonymous with obedience, with following orders from above. As such, it represented the opposite of May Fourth, all the while using the May Fourth legacy skillfully, and even, at times, sincerely. New Life awakening was a negative foil for the New Culture idea of *juewu*—which was something more like enlightenment—a goal to be reached through increased autonomy and the use of critical reason.

As the abuse of enlightenment ideas in the New Life movement became more apparent, some of the May Fourth intellectuals closest to the Nationalist Party were compelled to speak out against Jiang Jieshi. Hu Shi, who had attacked conservative nationalism in 1928, emerged once again as a critic of the New Life movement. Although he himself had warned Beida youths against the excesses of individualistic emancipation as early as 1920, he now spoke out in support of the right of the individual to question inherited beliefs. The same *New Youth* mentor who had earlier warned students about the temptation to flee social responsibility was, by 1934, trying to safeguard their right to seek a "meaningful new life."[42] A meaningful life, in Hu Shi's view, had to depend on knowledge and on acquired learning far more than on rote conformity to the rules of public hygiene.

Hu Shi's student from Beida, Fu Sinian, also wrote about the false echo between the New Life movement and May Fourth. Having risen in the officially sanctioned scholarly world, and now director of the Institute of History and Philology of the Academia Sinica, Fu used his public position to quarrel with the historical amnesia of the Guomindang. He recalled his own earlier opposition to public mores during the enlightenment movement in order to denounce more effectively the ethics of submission reinforced by the Guomindang. The New Life movement thus appeared to Fu Sinian as an obstacle to the acquisition of truly emancipating new knowledge. Outraged by the political corruption that he had witnessed during a trip in 1934 at the height of the New Life mobilization, he wrote:

I am ashamed to say that from Nanjing to Beijing there was no sign of progress. Everywhere, I saw only complacency and confusion. It is impossible to overlook the grave national crisis, the desperate condition of the people's lives and to see only the proliferation of cars of the Public Works Department, the numerous appointments made by public officials, the welcoming of foreign guests. Everywhere, irrelevant things are being made to look good, and the government declares that all is just fine. Still, I wonder, how can such a government pretend to be creating a new morality for the people?[43]

Critics of the New Life movement from within the Guomindang thus tried to uphold the need for new learning, in the face of Jiang's view that traditional morality was enough for national regeneration. Again, as in the 1910s, they became susceptible to charges of being "un-Chinese," of being alienated from the organic sources of native culture. This time, the attack came from a group of leading professors who, in January 1935, issued a manifesto entitled "Declaration for Cultural Construction on a Chinese Basis." Dedicated to stemming the "wholesale Westernization" always blamed on May Fourth, they called for a "nationalistic approach" to foreign ideas that would spare China from having to "absorb the dregs" of the West.[44]

Hu Shi, in his "Criticism of the 'Declaration for Cultural Construction on a Chinese Basis,'" restated the assumptions of the enlightenment movement. Again, he pointed out how those concerned with "traditional culture" were really speaking for conservative political interests. More explicitly than before, he explained the meaning of his earlier advocacy of "Westernization" as an antidote to the inherent inertia of all cultures. Precisely because Chinese culture would always remain Chinese, to nudge it forward one had to bring to it a relativizing, comparative perspective:

This declaration is a most fashionable expression of a reactionary mood prevalent today.... The professors advocated discarding the dregs and preserving the essence.... This is the most fashionable tune of compromise.... The fundamental error ... lies in their failure to understand the nature of cultural change.... Culture itself is conservative.... When two different cultures come into contact, the force of competition and comparison can partially destroy the resistance and conservatism of a certain culture ... it can never completely wipe out the conservative nature of an indigenous culture.... Simply stated, it is the people —all the people—who are the "basis." There is no worry that this basis will be destroyed.... The Chinese are still Chinese.[45]

Hu Shi's unequivocal defense of cultural relativism was in keeping with the May Fourth interest in borrowing from the West. The fact that he was willing to restate this cosmopolitan faith at a time of intense national anxiety made him more vulnerable to Guomindang criticism. In the end, what spared him from the worst of the ire of reactionary politicians was the abuse of traditional Chinese values by Japanese aggressors. When the enemies of China began to portray themselves as "true defenders of Confucianism," Hu Shi's point finally became more compelling.

In March 1934, two years after consolidating their conquest in Manchuria, the Japanese enthroned the last Qing ruler, Puyi, as Confucian "emperor" of the new state of Manchukuo. Placed at his side as prime minister was the noted Confucian poet and calligrapher Zheng Xiaoxu, a man who had long proven himself skilled in harmonizing Japanese interests with the Confucian kingly way (*wangdao*). At the very time that Jiang Jieshi was pursuing native Communists and calling for a return to "native morality," Zheng was claiming that Chinese values were most faithfully upheld in the new Northern Empire. The question of who were the true defenders of China and of Chinese values thus became more acute and more embarrassing. The fact that both a puppet government and the Nationalist regime appealed to Confucian values increased the likelihood that a patriotic outburst would turn anti-Confucian. This likelihood did indeed materialize in 1935–36, when the old fighters of May Fourth joined a new generation of patriotic students to create a new anti-feudal national salvation movement.

The spark that facilitated this coming together of two generations was the December Ninth incident of 1935. Starting out as a protest march organized by students and faculty from several universities in Beijing, it became one of the largest anti-government demonstrations since the Japanese occupation of Manchuria. Pained by the specter of a weak, humiliated China not unlike the May Fourth students before them, educated youths once again set in motion an awakening movement that spread far beyond the geographical location and social constituency of their own comrades in Beijing. What became known as the December Ninth movement was a complex of organizational activity focusing on the need for national salvation. Eventually, activists in the movement gathered enough momentum to force the Guomindang to call off its campaign against the Communists and join in the formation of the second United Front.

The December Ninth movement was, in the eyes of many participants, the result of skillful collaboration between May Fourth veterans and a new generation of patriotic students. *Citizen* Society founder Xu Deheng, for example, has repeatedly underscored the importance of his own and his colleagues' contribution to the student movement of 1935–36. Xu himself took an active part in organizing support for striking students and even risked his job as university professor to ensure visible public involvement of May Fourth intellectuals in the patriotic mobilization. In his view, the December Ninth movement was a direct outgrowth and fulfillment of the aspirations of the original student movement of 1919.[46]

To other observers such as Nym Wales (Edgar Snow's wife at the time), May Fourth intellectuals appeared markedly absent from the scene of student activism in 1935–36. From her position as mentor and friend of the Yanjing University students involved in the December Ninth demonstration, she wrote:

The cycle of the May Fourth Nationalist Movement seems to have turned its wheel.... A new generation is in the schools today.... On May 4, 1919, ten thousand earnest young students in Beijing staged a patriotic demonstration that was the signal for the outburst of the tremendous nationalist movement which reverberated throughout China.... On this May 4th anniversary those "earnest students" are only seventeen years older. But ... during the December Ninth

Movement in 1935 when the students went to these men who are now their professors and begged them to join in the national united front against Japan and to help struggle for the elementary democratic rights that the Chinese people have never won for themselves, not only did nearly all of them refuse to cooperate, but instead joined with the Japanese controlled authorities working against the patriotic movement.[47]

Nym Wales's claim that "nearly all" of the May Fourth veterans who held faculty positions refused to aid the student movement thus stands in marked contrast to the testimony of Xu Deheng. It appears, however, that even though they were seventeen years older than they had been in 1919, these intellectuals did not view the situation so differently from the student activists of 1935–36.

A few of them, most notably Luo Jialun and Hu Shi—administrators by now—did try to temper youthful activists by counseling them to return to study and to be more patient in their approach to the problem of national salvation. Most May Fourth intellectuals, however, did join the December Ninth movement publicly and forcefully. *New Tide* members Gu Jiegang and Zhang Shenfu, for example, were quite outspoken in their support of the student movement and paid dearly for their open defiance of the Guomindang policy of compromise with Japan.[48]

Even Yu Pingbo, their fellow *New Tide* member at Beida who had retreated into ancient history and literary criticism, came out to lend his voice to the national salvation movement. Although Yu was one of the university professors whom Nym Wales may have seen as an escapist from the urgent issues of the day, he had, in fact, been quite attentive to the problem of national salvation. As early as September 1931, he had written to his May Fourth mentor and friend Hu Shi to ask him to become more involved in the work of patriotic mobilization. Disappointed by Hu's lack of response, Yu Pingbo published his own view about the "preconditions" of national salvation. As he had during the May Fourth enlightenment, he emphasized the need to think critically, to consciously expand one's awareness of a national entity beyond the selfish, comfort-oriented "I." Less hopeful than he had been in 1919, he concluded: "I don't see anybody in the intellectual class who is ready to sacrifice himself for such a vision of national salvation."[49]

By 1935–36, intellectuals knew their limitations and their potentials better. Having struggled with the problem of class consciousness and with how to communicate their ideas in a language intelligible to the masses, they were now better prepared to contribute to a mass-based national salvation movement. Traces of self-doubt and dejection, however, lingered. At this moment of need for intellectual leadership,

Nie Gannu, a young Communist theoretician, wrote an essay intended to help intellectuals overcome this crisis of self-confidence. Modeled on Feng Xuefeng's 1928 work "Revolution and the Intellectual Class," it was entitled simply "On Intellectuals" ("Guanyu zhishi fenzi"). In this work, Nie tried to lift the crushing weight of guilt still carried by May Fourth veterans by asking them to contribute their vision and their skills to the social movement at hand: "Society truly needs us. There are too few intellectuals as it is.... We must attack our own syphilis; we must not mask it with fine-sounding verbiage. But if by recognizing mistakes we become pessimistic and self-denying, then we would have gone from the evil of syphilis to incurable melancholia. The latter is a more crippling disease."[50]

In 1935–36, intellectuals who had overcome their own "syphilis" were moving to the forefront of the student-initiated patriotic movement. Without their contributions in the realm of thought, the nationalist fervor might have remained merely an anti-Japanese, anti-government passion, lacking any clear sense of China's destiny during and after the war with Japan. With their leadership and support, it became a movement for national regeneration as well as national salvation. In Beijing, Gu Jiegang, who had wrestled long with the dangers of "incurable melancholia," launched a new journal called *Knowledge for the Masses (Dazhong zhishi)*. Intended to provide clear, lively information about political events in Europe, Asia, and the United States, this journal realized Yu Pingbo's hopes of 1931: to stir up an informed resistance against Japan, to continue to open up minds while mobilizing for national salvation. Gu's first editorial made explicit the gulf between intellectuals and the masses. This gulf, however, could be crossed in the emergency at hand: "We hope to become united with the masses, to stand together at the war front so that our joint strength might be broader and more resilient. Only thus can we defeat our common enemies. By that time, you and ourselves will have become inseparable; your work and ours will be one."[51]

In Shanghai, meanwhile, another group gathered around a journal entitled *Intellectual Life (Dushu shenghuo)*. Closer to the Communist Party than to the May Fourth intellectuals active in Beijing, their goal was to popularize Marxism. In 1936, at the same time as Gu launched his magazine *Knowledge for the Masses*, Ai Siqi, the most philosophically inclined among the Shanghai Marxists, published an influential little book entitled *Philosophy for the Masses*. Ai was "deeply influenced by the fervor of the student movement and by his contacts with the scholars who became known as the 'seven gentlemen.'"[52] He aimed to inject theoretical concerns into the emotional, action-oriented atmosphere that swept over China after December 9. He also tried to move beyond the narrow, immediate requirement of national salvation to outline the mental preconditions for a resistance movement to Japan. Like the middle-aged May Fourth veterans, Ai Siqi, too, felt a conflict between his own scholarly interests and the ideas that could be intelligibly communicated to the masses. His postscript to the article "How I Came to Write *Philosophy for the Masses*" was unusually candid about the linguistic, conceptual, and personal difficulties encountered by an enlightenment-oriented intellectual addressing himself to an unfamiliar constituency:

In trying to convey complex ideas like that of dialectics.... I had to find illustrative expressions closer to the readers' lives. I had to discard my own style as a specialist researcher.... Because I knew so little about the readers' lives, I could not but write a touch naively at times.... In linguistic matters, I was even less experienced, so I made the text simple, repetitious, not touching on things that would be too complex.[53]

Having confessed a temptation to simplify ideas for the sake of popularizing his message, Ai Siqi went on to question that strategy as well:

This was a negative, formalistic way to try to come closer to readers, a long way from a more positive, content-centered way to link my work with the readers' lives.... My only consolation is that with all its problems, *Philosophy for the Masses* ... would enable many of those who are researching specialized scholarly problems (myself among them) to understand better what the Chinese masses need in terms of knowledge. Only then will we know what we should write for them.... If my book can be like a "stone cast in the water to bring up jade," I will be satisfied indeed.[54]

"Jade" did indeed seem to be sprouting up everywhere in China. By 1936, educated young men and women in both Shanghai and Beijing were exploring ways of bringing knowledge and philosophy to the masses. The organizational collaboration of the national salvation movement and the new enlightenment movement was not far behind. In May, in the midst of the celebrations, for the seventeenth anniversary of May Fourth, the All China National Salvation Association was founded in Shanghai. A year later, as an outgrowth of the eighteenth anniversary celebration, the New Enlightenment Association was founded in Beijing. It would be historically justifiable and yet simplistic to interpret this convergence of concern as Communist-sponsored activity in support of the second United Front. Although there can be no doubt that the Communist Party needed and relied upon patriotic intellectuals to bring pressure on the Guomindang, political needs do not account for such complex intellectual commitments. In fact, the political priorities of the

United Front necessitated a postponement of enlightenment concerns for the sake of national salvation. And yet the call for an enlightenment movement grew louder rather than weaker at this time. Participants in the proletarian culture movement and in the mass language movement proved themselves ready and willing to tackle the dilemma of a new, truly popular May Fourth.

The convergence of the national salvation and the New Enlightenment movements in the year between May 1936 and May 1937 represents a victory for intellectuals, even if a short-lived one. After the outbreak of war, advocates of enlightenment were, like the rest of China, swept away by the passions of a national emergency. Their faith in their mission waned again, and they were compelled to identify enlightenment with national salvation. In that process, as we shall see below, they came close to renouncing the very concept of intellectual autonomy.

THE NEW ENLIGHTENMENT MOVEMENT OF 1936–1937

In May 1936, an obscure young history teacher began to call at the home of a prominent philosopher to discuss problems of dialectical materialism. The personal friendship that developed between Chen Boda and Zhang Shenfu provided the catalyst for the New Enlightenment movement. Only ten years apart in age, the two men could not have been more different. Zhang Shenfu, offspring of a gentry-elite family and a *New Tide* member, was well known for his writings about Bertrand Russell. One of the three founders of the Chinese Communist Party, Zhang had traveled and studied in Europe, broken with the Party in 1925, and survived the fall of Wuhan in 1927. By the 1930s, he was a key figure in the Qinghua new philosophy circles. A leader in the December Ninth movement, he was arrested on suspicion of being a Communist. Shortly after he was released from jail in May 1936, he began his conversations with Chen Boda, a poverty-stricken, stammering instructor in ancient Chinese history at China University. Chen, a Communist veteran of the Northern Expedition, had just returned from a short stay in Moscow. Zhang, having taught for a number of years at China University, had many friends and students there. These acquaintances brought the two men together.[55]

Before they met one another, Chen Boda and Zhang Shenfu had independently considered ways to revitalize the May Fourth legacy. While in jail, Zhang used his time for philosophical reflection toward this end. In the midst of the national crisis, he called for continued attention to goals

22. Zhang Shenfu as Qinghua University professor, 1934.

of Chinese survival, not only to means of assuring this survival. At the same time, Chen Boda was in close contact with young leftist intellectuals such as Ai Siqi, Hu Sheng, Hu Feng, and He Ganzhi, who were editing *Dushu shenghuo*. Like them, Chen was beginning to explore ways to expand the national salvation movement into a broader cultural movement, on the model of May Fourth.

Longing to be heard by those younger than his own generation, Zhang Shenfu was quite open to appeals for guidance and collaboration from a young man eager to call himself "a son of the May Fourth."[56] Zhang provided what Chen Boda needed: an informed voice about past history and contemporary philosophy, a baseline, as it were, for an appropriation of and departure from the legacy of May Fourth.

In the fall of 1936, Zhang Shenfu and Chen Boda began to collaborate on a concrete plan for a new enlightenment. The older man, an acknowledged leader of the December Ninth movement, began to write public manifestos about the shortcomings of the national salvation movement. He called the political leaders to task for their insufficient attention to cultural problems and to China's need for a cultural emancipation movement. To further his case, Zhang tried to show how problems of logic, of dialectics, and of philosophy more generally, were anything but extraneous to China's national survival. At the same time, Chen Boda put forth an explicit call for a culture-oriented national salvation movement, modeled on May Fourth but drawing upon new philosophical developments in the study of dialectics and logic.[57] In the spring of 1937, the eighteenth anniversary of May Fourth provided both Zhang and Chen with the symbolic occasion to formally launch the New Enlightenment movement.

Having prepared the groundwork for others to join them, the two men parted. After the Japanese invasion of North China in July 1937, Chen went on to Yan'an, Mao Zedong's Communist base in the Northwest, while Zhang, unable to secure the secret connections necessary for the passage to the Northwest, headed south into Sichuan. For the next two years (though not in direct contact with each other), both Zhang and Chen continued to propagandize on behalf of the new movement. Both tried to find new ways to popularize the idea of enlightenment.

The revival of May Fourth orchestrated by Zhang Shenfu, Chen Boda, and others was anything but a naive return to the past. All participants were acutely sensitive to the political priorities of the national salvation movement. They were also well informed about Marxist theory of history. Using the ideas of dialectical materialism, they argued for a *new* enlightenment movement. This argument both built upon and departed from May Fourth. Unlike the romantic radicals of the late 1920s (such as Cheng Fangwu, who had also talked about surpassing May Fourth but became mired in borrowed words such as *aufheben* and fuzzy ideas about the "negation of the negation"), advocates of the new enlightenment proceeded on surer ground. Using the domesticated expression *fangqi* (meaning, literally, to discard in order to set free), they were able to articulate clearly why China needed to both preserve and transcend the May Fourth legacy. *Fangqi*, in 1936–37, carried the connotation of *fanfu*—a return to May Fourth. Those who used this expression now seemed less anxious about being engulfed and compromised by the past. They proceeded more surefootedly on a new road out of the past. As a prominent participant in the original May Fourth movement, Zhang Shenfu took on the task of distinguishing between the new and old enlightenment movements. In his May 1937 anniversary speech, he pointed to the present cultural backwardness of China as a sign of the inadequacies of May Fourth. Recalling the "ill-informed borrowing from the West" that marked the original enlightenment movement, he called for a more systematic and rational synthesis of Chinese and Western cultures. Although he did not exclude himself from those who had been hasty in the earlier movement, Zhang concluded:

The major shortcoming of May Fourth was that it was shallow. Trying to attack too many problems, it ended up being confused. In the past eighteen years we have matured and made progress.... The new enlightenment must be clearer, deeper. It must be able to make practical, scientific evaluation of both Chinese and Western cultures.... It needs to be much more thorough in its understanding of natural and social sciences.... Finally, it must forsake its complete ignorance of and disregard for philosophy.... The central task of our new enlightenment movement is to recognize the significance of May Fourth, to spread the influence of May Fourth, to compensate for the inadequacy of May Fourth....[58]

Communist advocates of enlightenment shared Zhang's critical appreciation of May Fourth. Although they had been too young to participate in the event of 1919, they had developed a profound attachment to its spirit of cultural iconoclasm. They, too, had to break with their own previous assumptions before they could make a credible case for the new enlightenment. Chen Boda made his own first appeal for new enlightenment in an essay entitled "The Self-Critique of a New-Style Philosopher," written after he began his conversations with Zhang Shenfu. Chen, like Zhang, emphasized the lack of a systematic, informed approach in the anti-feudal stance of May Fourth. Concerned in particular with the shortcomings of Marxist theory and its hasty use by Chinese Marxists, he discussed a similar problem: "There is in general a lack of a systematic, penetrating critique of China's old traditional thought, and this millennia-old ruling ideology has today become a powerful tool that imperialists (especially the Japanese imperialists) and traitors are using to enslave the consciousness of the Chinese people."[59]

Proponents of the new enlightenment, thus, tried to keep their contemporaries from forgetting the cultural significance of May Fourth in the midst of a patriotic fervor to which they themselves were not immune. When national emergency seemed to require nothing but action, they insisted on the importance of thought. As loyalty to authority became all-important to the war mobilization, they continued to warn against slavish adherence to any single official point of view. Theirs was a complex recommitment to reason in circumstances least favorable to reasoned reflection. As Zhang Shenfu made clear in his June 1937 essay "What Is the New Enlightenment Movement?," rationalism—the use of reason to evaluate all creeds, truths, and assumptions—was the first priority. Closely related to this was the emancipation of thought. This was to be achieved through a systematic attack on superstition and arbitrary authority, and through the popularization of new knowledge, especially scientific information, among the masses.[60]

Younger Communist intellectuals who elaborated these ideas were well-informed about their historical and philosophical background. More than May Fourth veterans, they aimed to make the new enlightenment relevant to the political circumstances of the day. Hu Sheng, for example, in his essay "On Rationalism," emphasized the need to moderate the passions of patriotism through the use of reason. At the same time, he insisted that reason had to "take different forms in different historical circumstances" and that eighteenth-century rationalism had to be relegated to the "bourgeois past."[61] Ai Siqi, in a 1937 essay, equated reason with criticism (*pipan*) and concluded that the most appropriate use of criticism was to improve one's own thought. He concluded, therefore, that the May Fourth attempt to use the spirit of critique to evaluate the native historical inheritance "was extreme in its own time and is even more inappropriate for us today."[62]

Chen Boda also advocated a moderate view of intellectual emancipation in his 1937 essay "To Think Is No Crime." Reaffirming the enlightenment notion that all thought is by nature critical, and therefore subversive of arbitrary authority, Chen went on to outline the limits of critical thought. Unlike May Fourth iconoclasts who had used reason to unmask tradition, he emphasized an historical critique of tradition. He pointed out that May Fourth rationalism could only pose problems, not solve them. Recalling with positive admiration Hu Shi's

May Fourth dictum, "slaves cannot build a democratic country," Chen Boda went on to argue that a critique of slave mentality had to come out of patient investigation rather than self-righteous repudiation of traditional culture. To carry out this project, Chen called on May Fourth intellectuals like Gu Jiegang to lend their skills in historical relativism to the new enlightenment.[63]

Although holding different views on critical reason, May Fourth veterans and younger Communist theoreticians were united by a concern about the two key problems raised by May Fourth: How widespread could a rationalist enlightenment ever be among the masses? And, is it possible to develop a patriotic critique of feudalism? The first question, they hoped, could be answered by continuing the literacy work begun during the mass language movement. The second was thornier because it probed, again, the relationship of educators to the masses by questioning the motives of those who took it upon themselves to impart new knowledge to the common people.

In response to these dilemmas, enthusiasts of New Enlightenment reasserted the social significance of philosophy and philosophers. Zhang Shenfu's own profound attachment to rationalism led him to assert that "it is the task of intellectuals to train people to choose reason over feeling and to prefer ideals over the satisfactions of material life."[64] Younger Communist intellectuals, for a while at least, also shared the conviction that philosophers were integral to the new enlightenment. He Ganzhi was most explicit in his appreciation of philosophers and of the special depth of insight they bring to social problems:

We sometimes cannot help sighing: Where are our philosophers? It is time for us to play our roles. To be sure, many people still think that philosophy is nothing but empty talk, without being aware that there must be a methodology behind thought and action. We should use our sharpest tool for thought—philosophy— to analyze all the subtle questions of the past six years [1931–37] ... to hold fast to our today so that we may pursue our tomorrow more effectively.[65]

Having praised the unique contribution that philosophers bring to social action, He Ganzhi imagined what the result of a truly popular May Fourth might be in the Chinese context. Thus, he concluded:

Only when [through the systematic popularization of philosophy] our millions are liberated from their hazy superstitions and prejudice, from their worship of the ancient and submission to arbitrary authority, may we say that our country has been saved from destruction.[66]

In contrast to these devotees of philosophy, the *New Tide* philosopher Feng Youlan did not join in the cause of New Enlightenment. He voiced his suspicion of its elitist assumptions many years later. Finally free to recall his own past without the guidance of ideology, he argued that those in the forefront of the New Enlightenment movement had been "too arrogant" in their determination to bring light to the broader masses: "They seemed to me convinced that life was lived better and more fully with philosophical awareness. I, myself, on the other hand, always believed that there is philosophy everywhere that there is human life, that everyone has a philosophy of life and does not need the high and mighty help of professional philosophers to tell them so."[67]

Many of those who believed in what Feng Youlan had termed the "high and mighty" mission of philosophy were unable to hold on to such convictions for long. Under the pressure of war mobilization, they began to feel the attractions of "nationalist faith," an emotion more readily spread among the masses than the concept of reasoned reflection. He Ganzhi, who had earlier praised the role of philosophers, now argued that "faith can generate reason, much as reason can generate faith." Forsaking some of his enthusiasm for eighteenth-century advocates of enlightenment, he now echoed the words of seventeenth-century European rationalists as well as May Fourth intellectuals who were fascinated by the phenomenon of *xinyang*, belief. To perpetuate an uneasy synthesis between reason and faith thus became the short-lived goal of the New Enlightenment movement.[68] War destroyed this synthesis, forcing most advocates of enlightenment to become spokesmen for patriotic "faith."

The compatibility of faith and reason turned out to be as tenuous as that between patriotism and anti-feudalism. Long accused of being "un-Chinese," advocates of the new enlightenment naturally tried to make their program less abrasive in the eyes of those joining them under the national salvation banner. Aware of the limitations of May Fourth anti-feudalism, they tried to appear more moderate in their criticism of tradition. Zhang Shenfu's writings in 1937 reflect this need to create a *synthetic* modern culture, one that would combine elements of both Western and Chinese traditions. Unlike conservative nationalists, he believed that "modernity" could not be *either* Chinese or Western, but had to be *both*. His own research in ancient Chinese thought and modern Western philosophy led him to add ,to the May Fourth slogan "Down with Confucianism" another one: "Save Confucius."[69]

This distinction between Confucius and Confucianism could not have been made so confidently before the New Enlightenment movement. Only after the social history debates of the late 1920s, after the intellectuals had come to terms with their scholar-official ancestors, could they turn to a more historical critique of Confucianism. To mobilize the masses in a national salvation movement, Confucianism had to be understood before it could be rooted out. As Chen Boda put it: "The Japanese, with the aid of traitors, are trying to fool us with the rotten ideology of Confucianism. Therefore, an in-depth, critical evaluation of Confucius and Confucianism is urgently needed.... The greatest achievement of May Fourth was its criticism of Confucianism. Chen Duxiu, Yi Baisha, Wu Yu, and Lu Xun spearheaded that attack. Lu Xun tore off China's mask of hypocrisy ... and yet he could not see that Confucianism was nothing but an historical reflection of the social structure of feudalism in China."[70]

Although they claimed that it was now finally possible to deepen the anti-feudal critique of May Fourth, advocates of new enlightenment in 1937 fell prey to the pressures of patriotism. Perhaps they trusted their Marxist theory too much. Believing themselves adept at historical materialist analysis, they were convinced that they could be more effective critics of tradition than the May Fourth intellectuals.

In the end, however, they became obsessed with the need to prove the Chineseness of their cultural movement. This need led them to abdicate May Fourth criticism of national character (*guomin xing*). As the requirements of patriotism became more and more urgent, the determination to root out native shortcomings weakened as well. By 1938, with the war effort well under way, Chen Boda defined what he hoped would be the meaning of *patriotic* enlightenment:

As genuine Marxists, we know that new culture is never irrelevant to the old. We must become more effective at improving Chinese culture, bringing in positive aspects of the Chinese past.... We need a new understanding of "national essence." What reactionaries want to preserve is ridiculous, gaudy: the cruelty of the past. Our concept of national essence is different.... We suggest that old forms can and must be used to create a new culture.[71]

This call to reuse native, old bottles for the new wine of modern thought was, in effect, a reversal of May Fourth priorities. Earlier advocates of enlightenment had experienced first-hand the contaminating power of traditional culture and had consciously embraced the creed of cosmopolitan iconoclasm. Chen Boda, on the other hand, faced with different historical circumstances, retreated into a nationalist defense of tradition. Even Chen, however, was not totally immune to the warning implicit in the May Fourth iconoclasm. Therefore, he concluded:

To be sure, proponents of new culture can also fall prey to the temptations of the old.... As Lu Xun warned, new youth is all too prone to indulge in old books and old ideas. Our task should be to guard against such tendencies.[72]

Far from being able to guard against the tendencies that Lu Xun had warned them about, advocates of patriotic enlightenment developed rationalizations for them. Having forsaken the right to raise the problem of "national character," *guomin xing*, they were left to rationalize its short-comings. "Sinification" became their code word for those many-sided rationalizations.

WAR AND THE PRESSURE FOR SINIFICATION

Until 1937 it seemed possible, even necessary, to pursue China's internal cultural self-transformation along with the external challenge of political survival. With the outbreak of war in July 1937, however, the disparity between internal emancipation from feudalism and outward pursuit of national security grew too great. As China suffered defeat after defeat in the crucial years from 1937 to 1939, the intellectuals' faith in enlightenment waned. They were unable to justify to themselves, much less to their countrymen, the need to continue criticism of native traditions while the fight for national survival was so perilous. Not surprisingly, most became propagandists for national salvation. Their lingering attachment to the legacy of May Fourth was reflected in their frequent, often clumsy, efforts to identify *qimeng* (enlightenment) with *jiuguo* (national salvation).

At first, when war with Japan was imminent, intellectuals viewed it as a facilitator of enlightenment. The awakening that intellectuals had hoped to bring about through the mass education movement and through the new enlightenment movement seemed to be progressing much faster than before in the early months of war mobilization. One of the younger proponents of the new enlightenment, Zhou Zhi, expressed this exhilaration about war most clearly when he wrote in March 1937: "In 1919, the masses were still stuck in a world of dreams. May Fourth liberated quite a few workers but very few peasants or self-employed artisans.... The present national danger has created a great change. It has emancipated the minds of a majority of our compatriots."[73]

This expectation that political calamity might accelerate cultural awakening was shared by middle-aged May Fourth veterans as well. Eager to reach out to the masses, they viewed war as a golden, although painful, opportunity. Naturally enough, few of them stopped to question the implications. On the eve of the war, Gu Jiegang, a *New Tide* member who was not directly involved with the new enlightenment group but shared their expectations, used his journal *Knowledge for the Masses* to

create a climate of opinion in which thought change and national salvation might be seen to be interdependent. In an article entitled "Two
Kinds of Thinking Which Are Most Desirable to Eliminate," he turned
to ancient Chinese history to document his case for expunging national
and individual tendencies toward "decadent pleasures" and "corrosive
fears." Gu's advocacy of mental preparation for war was so effective that
he and his journal ended up high on the "most wanted list" of the
Japanese army as it prepared to invade China in July 1937.[74]

With the outbreak of war, however, opportunities for the transformation of thought seemed to diminish rapidly. Fear and self-centered concern with immediate survival threatened to overwhelm the sense of
national unity that the new enlightenment advocates believed to have
existed a few months earlier. These intellectuals began to emphasize the
need for collective identity rather than individual consciousness. As Ai
Siqi put it, there was not time left for May Fourth priorities in war-torn
China: "The cultural movement before May Fourth had been grounded
in self-transformation. Patriotism then began with the emancipation of
the self. Now, however, with the enemy attacking us so directly, so
viciously, the leisure for self-transformation is no more."[75]

When self-transformation became seen as a leisure-time activity, the
entire rationale for enlightenment changed. What had been an end now
became a means to an end. This sense of the mere instrumentality of
qimeng in the larger framework of national survival (jiuguo) comes
through most clearly in He Ganzhi's conclusion that "the New Enlightenment movement is nothing but patriotism in the realm of cultural
thought." Whereas earlier He Ganzhi had acknowledged the need for
autonomy in the realm of cultural criticism, now he believed that the
May Fourth iconoclasm had to be left behind: "The cultural movement
from now on must have as its most direct, most immediate aim the cultivation of patriotism."[76]

When enlightenment came to be seen as a tool for fostering patriotism, its capacity to call into question the basis of national identity, to
redefine it in keeping with the spirit of anti-feudalism, was lost. May
Fourth concern with individual and national autonomy (zijue) began to
fade into the background during the war years. Instead, all emphasis
was on zixin—confidence—on the national level. The need to defend a
collective identity at all costs thus overshadowed the earlier commitment
to individual autonomy. In this process, other May Fourth commitments were transformed as well. The right to doubt collective beliefs, a
right that had been upheld through the cultivation of individual conscience during May Fourth, withered from lack of use. Reason, which

had been employed to call into question inherited values, was now seen to be a tool of foreign origin, corrosive of national confidence.

As the pressure of contemporary events intensified in the late 1930s, May Fourth intellectuals began to generate mythologized versions of the past. Gu Jiegang and Fu Sinian, two *New Tide* members who had pioneered the methodology of critical historiography, now churned out glorified stories of national unity and resistance. During the early years of the war, Gu, the arch-doubter of antiquity and of ideological history, turned his talents to nationalist propaganda. While touring Moslem areas, he tried to prove the common identity of the various races in China. He developed this argument in his new journal, *Admonitions to Virtuous Deeds*, which was published from his refuge in the Southwest. Fu Sinian, the historian who had written during May Fourth about the "burden of a garbage can full of thousands of years of useless histories" and had attacked the ethic of subservience perpetrated through famil-ism, now declared: "We Chinese people ... are a real family.... Of all the races in the world, we are the largest and of all histories, ours is the longest. This is natural and not accidental. 'The Chinese people are united' is a fact of history, even more a fact of today."[77]

Arriving in the Southwest around the same time as Gu Jiegang and Zhang Shenfu, Fu Sinian felt the same pressures to make this "fact" of unity plausible to the masses. He set out to write *A Revolutionary History of the Chinese Nation* to prove that Chinese people have always been united and capable of resisting foreign aggression. Although he never finished this work, the commitment to undertake the project illustrates the com-mon passion of these May Fourth veterans. Reunited in the wartime capital of Chongqing, they all immersed themselves in the various tasks of war mobilization, forgetting for a while that they had meant to awaken and not just arouse their compatriots.

"Revolutionary histories" such as the one envisioned by Fu Sinian constituted, in effect, a renunciation of critical historiography. Obsessed not only with *jiuguo* (national salvation) but more immediately with *wangguo* (national extinction), Fu, like so many other May Fourth intel-lectuals, was ready to compromise his commitment to enlightenment. During his days at Beida as the editor of *New Tide*, he had believed it was legitimate to question authority. Now he argued that if China was to avoid the dreadful fate of national extinction, it must follow a strong leader. It was such a leader and not some vague thought trend that was expected to transform China from a weak nation into a strong one.[78]

It would be too easy to see Fu Sinian's abdication of the enlighten-ment creed as a concession to the Guomindang and to Jiang Jieshi, the "strong leader" of wartime China. In fact, his renunciation mirrors similar shifts of commitment among intellectuals on the left. Zhang Shenfu and Chen Boda, the two men who had been so firm in their commitment to cultural criticism in the context of national salvation, also backed down from their confidence in critical thought at about the same time as Fu Sinian. They, too, began to shift their priorities from *qimeng* to *jiuguo* by emphasizing China's "national self-awakening." As "self" and "nation" became synonymous, the May Fourth emphasis on individual emancipation became part of a forgotten, nearly irrelevant past. Chen Boda began to acknowledge this when he traced the sources of the new enlightenment to nationalist upheavals *before* May Fourth: "The New Enlightenment movement really began with the 1911 revolution, and may be traced back further still to the Taiping rebellion.... These events constituted armed criticism.... Through war, people became aware of the national crisis.... The anti-Japanese war is bound to solve the problems of the past hundred years."[79]

As war broke out in earnest in 1937–38, the appeal of cultural iconoclasm diminished further. The idea of "armed criticism" became more and more attractive, even to such a rationalist as Zhang Shenfu. He too began to forget about the May Fourth spirit of criticism as he professed his new-found "faith" in a collection of wartime essays entitled *I Believe in China* (*Wo xiangxin Zhongguo*). Zhang Shenfu's shift from destroyer of idols, including the idol of "nation," during May Fourth, is striking indeed. Trying to hold on to some part of that earlier commitment, Zhang wrote in May 1938: "The purpose of our current enlightenment movement must be to combine reason and action on the national level.... Philosophy must augment national self confidence (*minzu zixin*)."[80] With collective identity dominating all concerns, enlightenment was judged solely by how much it increased national confidence.

Under the stress of patriotic mobilization, any attack on tradition could easily be seen as an assault on the collective spirit of the nation. Judged from the standpoint of these extreme conditions, iconoclasm stood in stark opposition to the masses' own feelings of loyalty to the motherland. It came to be seen as a knife wielded against the very emotions that might be mobilized for national resistance against Japan. As Chen Boda wrote: "They [May Fourth iconoclasts such as Hu Shi and Chen Duxiu] did not go beyond unmasking the irrationality of Confucian morality. They judged it to be unreasonable [contrary to reason], but failed to see its roots in social life.... They did not have sympathy and pity for people who suffered from hunger, harsh labor, misery, who led dark lives of slavery beneath the symbolic man-eating society de-

scribed by Lu Xun.... This was the greatest weakness of the May
Fourth anti-feudal movement."[81]

Viewed as unsympathetic toward the masses and lacking in compas-
sion for their feelings and values, May Fourth anti-feudalism was condemned as useless. Those who now tried to awaken the masses, to unite
them for the war, fell into the very trap Lu Xun had warned about in the
early 1930s: Their appeals to the masses verged on flattery. Intellectuals
on both the right and the left moved toward an uncritical acceptance of
popular culture. Ai Siqi spelled out the implication of this retreat: "Once
we understand that only what benefits the cause of national collective
survival matters for now ... then we must be ready to compromise with
[literally, hold hands with] certain feudal elements. This really is not so
bad or regrettable."[82]

Ai Siqi's proposal to "hold hands with feudal elements" appeared to
many May Fourth veterans as a practical, reasonable alternative. In
1938–39, when China as a whole seemed on the verge of extinction, to
question native traditions became less and less possible. To be squeam-
ish about alliances with "feudal elements" was to risk being seen as
unpatriotic by the very masses whom intellectuals hoped to mobilize for
national salvation.

"Sinification" emerged at this time as the code word for a complex of
efforts to make every ideology and political commitment more Chinese.
It was the most concrete way to legitimize holding hands with feudal
elements. In the Communist base area, Chen Boda first introduced this
concept in his July 23, 1938, essay, "The National Character of Our
Cultural Movement." Responding to the same pressures that had led Ai
Siqi to call for compromise with feudal elements, he called for a "selective reliance on national forms." While still portraying himself as a true
follower of Lu Xun, he concluded that cultural workers (a new term for
intellectuals) were required to use traditional (i.e., old) cultural forms to
create a new national culture—one that would be truly sinified (*Zhongguo hua*).[83]

Chen Boda's idea of a sinified cultural movement in China—a new
May Fourth with its iconoclastic edge blunted—fell on the receptive ears
of his political patron, Mao Zedong. Mao had by this time won top
position in the Communist Party and was eager to consolidate his experiences as a guerrilla leader into a body of nationalist political theory.
Thus, he found the notion of sinification quite useful. It enabled him to
raise his own practical experience of adjusting Communist ideas to
Chinese realities to the level of a universal principle. In his October 1938
speech "On the New Stage [of China's and the party's struggle for vic-

tory]," he went on to call for a "sinification of Marxism," which he believed would free China from the dogma of foreign theories. Sinified Marxism, according to Mao, was nothing less than the "revolutionary science" of the Chinese revolution.[84]

Writing from Chongqing in February 1939, Zhang Shenfu picked up Mao's ideas with open enthusiasm. He went on to elaborate their implication for a "sinification of enlightenment." In an essay entitled simply "On Sinification" (published in the journal he edited, *Wartime Culture*—an echo of Chen Boda's Yan'an publication *Cultural Front Line*), Zhang praised "Mr. Mao Zedong's ... positive appreciation of the rich inheritance we have from our ancestors" and "his wise warning against blind application of abstract theories." For a philosopher who had for decades introduced complex, technical Western philosophy into China, this was a radical departure. Zhang explained his turnabout through the metaphor of medicine. He argued that "if the medicine of enlightenment is to be applied to China, the cure cannot be effective without adjusting it to the needs of the patient, without considering the patient's capacity to absorb the medicine."[85]

Zhang's image of intellectuals as doctors and of enlightenment as medicine was not new. May Fourth intellectuals had been using this metaphor since the New Culture movement. In war-torn China, however, curing present ills with criticism of tradition was a risky proposition. The "medicine" now was deemed harmful to national confidence. Therefore, Zhang concluded that an enlightenment movement that would be popular and would contribute to unifying the nation must have as its goal the sinification of Western ideas.

To illustrate his point, Zhang focused on the most important idea to be sinified by the New Enlightenment movement: science. By arguing that it was possible and even necessary to make science more Chinese, to give it a "Chinese color," Zhang backed himself into an untenable position. As an informed philosopher of science and a follower of Bertrand Russell, he must have known that the one idea that cannot be said to have "national form" is science. And yet, under pressure to demonstrate his patriotism, Zhang tried to compromise. His essay concluded with a series of assertions that must have appeared simplistic to himself and to others:

Chinese society is Chinese. Therefore enlightenment and revolution in China must be different from other nations.... Until recently, most of our intellectuals only studied and believed in Western ideas; overlooking, ignoring, slighting Chinese thinkers. We should study more of the thought of Sun Zhongshan—the man who pioneered the new enlightenment movement.... Our revolution must be neither capitalist nor proletarian but for the people, the nation, the country ... as conceived by Sun Zhongshan forty years ago.[86]

Trying to turn history back, however, was not a viable alternative. Zhang Shenfu, as well as his readers, knew that Sun Zhongshan was not the founder of the enlightenment; that no revolution, much less an intellectual one, could dodge the issue of ideology for long. And yet, the compulsion to dodge illustrates how confused revolutionary rhetoric had become in the late 1930s.

HISTORICALLY ENGENDERED BEFUDDLEMENT

In February 1939, Zhang Shenfu had enthusiastically welcomed Mao Zedong's call for sinification. Two months later, he argued that a sinified enlightenment movement was thoroughly compatible with Jiang Jieshi's New Life movement. The background for this political and intellectual flip-flopping was a wave of defeat suffered in the war with Japan. By the spring of 1939, as enemy armies advanced with seeming invincibility, the Guomindang and the Communist Party both became obsessed with fanning the flames of nationalism. In the Southwest, Jiang launched a "National Spiritual Mobilization"—a revised version of the New Life movement—to enhance nationalist sympathies. In the Northwest, Mao Zedong intensified his calls for the formation of a sinified Marxism with which to oppose the foreign invaders.

Situated between Mao Zedong and Jiang Jieshi and sharing their sense of national emergency, May Fourth intellectuals like Zhang Shenfu hoped to get the attention of both political leaders and to enlist their support for a waning enlightenment movement. These intellectuals were fully aware that the thought movement weakened in the face of a failing war effort. Furthermore, they felt thwarted in their attempt to carry their ideals beyond their own small circle. Thus, they tried to follow in the footsteps of earlier Confucian reformers who tried to get the ear of a "virtuous emperor" to help them spread their values to the ignorant and restless masses. During the war with Japan, the desire to popularize thought increased this long-standing tendency to rely on and to court the powerful. Thus, for example, the most prominent *New Tide* philosopher, Feng Youlan, accepted the title of Guoshi ("Teacher of the Nation") as a sign of honor from Jiang Jieshi. Hoping to influence the course of national salvation by shaping the thoughts of political leaders, May Fourth intellectuals risked becoming appendages to causes not their own.

Zhang Shenfu's predicament illustrates this danger quite clearly.

Frustrated in his efforts to get to the Northwest, Zhang decided to make the most of his circumstances in Chongqing. His April 1939 article "The New Enlightenment Movement and the New Life Movement" culminated an effort to bring his own ideology in line with the requirements of nationalist mobilization. In it, he came close to obliterating the creative tension between *jiuguo* and *qimeng*. As "national salvation" became synonymous with "enlightenment," the May Fourth legacy nearly lost its significance. Aware that his stance might provoke suspicion from both the right and the left, Zhang made it clear from the outset that he was "responding to the needs of the times."[87] This concern with adjusting enlightenment to the "needs of the times" stands in marked contrast with the claim of Zhang and other intellectuals during May Fourth that enlightenment itself could and must guide the "spirit of the times" (*shidai de jingshen*).

An endlessly flexible enlightenment movement was thus stretched to accommodate its opposite. In 1939, accommodation was described by Zhang Shenfu as a "division of labor" between the New Enlightenment movement and the New Life movement, with the former being seen as a "thought movement" while the latter was given dominion over "practical life." Furthermore, the New Life movement was described as a movement from above, sponsored by organizations of the central government, while the New Enlightenment movement was supposedly an outpouring from below. In order to enlist support from the central government, Zhang adopted the current style of quoting at length from the proclamations of Jiang Jieshi. Using the president's own words, Zhang tried to show that Jiang's definition of nationalism was no different from the vision that animated advocates of enlightenment. Both were committed to China's speedy modernization (*xiandai hua*). Dwelling on a few phrases from Jiang Jieshi's "Outline of the New Life Movement," Zhang tried to prove that the Guomindang's concept of modernization was synonymous with the May Fourth advocacy of scientific modernity, that both sanctioned a quest of truth based on critical reason:

The New Life movement advocated by Mr. Jiang and the New Enlightenment movement are, in their essence, not only compatible, but identical.... The most obvious point of convergence is that the New Life movement emphasizes science. This is precisely the most important requirement of the New Enlightenment movement.... Mr. Jiang made it amply clear how much he values the spirit of science when he said, "The basic meaning of scientific spirit is to search truth from facts."[88]

This quest for an identity, not merely a compatibility, between the New Life movement and the New Enlightenment movement was bound to distort both. On the one hand, Jiang, the well-known enemy of social revolution, emerged as an ardent supporter of scientific modernity and defender of people's rights and welfare. On the other hand, Zhang Shenfu, once an impassioned critic of feudal ethics, now portrayed himself as a true believer in Confucianism. He even went so far as to set up an equivalence between Jiang's emphasis on Confucian ritual (*li*), and the enlightenment emphasis on modern reason (*li*): "Mr. Jiang has stated that the New Life movement must start from the word 'ritual.' ... But, in turn, ritual must accord with human nature. Human nature is inherently rational. Therefore, I believe that ritual is not only appropriate to guide human nature, but that it really is the same as reason."[89]

Political casuistry complemented by logic did not, however, mask the inherent contradictions in Zhang's effort. No matter how much he tried to convince himself and others that patriotic conservatism and enlightenment thought were the same, he did not succeed.

In the end, what prevented this metamorphosis of *qimeng* into *jiuguo* from reaching its final stage—the total discrediting of the May Fourth legacy for the sake of political expediency—was that neither the advocates of enlightenment nor the cultural conservatives were able to forget the iconoclasm of May Fourth. Despite a widespread desire to "hold hands with feudal elements," there was no way to deny that the original May Fourth appeal to reason had been for the purpose of *fanlijiao*—for a critique of the religion of rites rather than a defense of it.

This realization deepened as the enemies of May Fourth grew more and more strident in the years after 1939. Once the danger of a wholesale restoration of feudal values in the midst of patriotic mobilizaton had become obvious, May Fourth veterans could not but speak out in defense of enlightenment. Even Zhang Shenfu, who seemed so willing to equate reason and ritual, had to acknowledge the difference. In a markedly sober essay entitled "Logical Critique of the National Spiritual Mobilization," he carried that difference into the realm of political debate. This essay, which is less conciliatory toward Jiang Jieshi than others he wrote at the time, emphasized China's enduring problems in the area of thought and the need to change the feudal mentality even while working for a national salvation. It concluded with a plea that was bound to displease cultural and political conservatives:

We must continue our efforts to transform old ways of Chinese thinking, which are confused, apathetic, disorganized, dreamy.... These are not just problems of thought but of everyday life as well. To be sure, they have their abstract as well as concrete implications ... but the source of all this is a remnant feudal economy which is the foundation of Chinese society and the lingering feudal habits of mind.[90]

To continue to talk about China's feudal economy and the feudal habits of mind it fostered was, in effect, to risk open disagreement with the Guomindang. Zhang Shenfu took that risk because he was, in fact, quite clear in his own mind about the true meaning of the May Fourth legacy. He then took that risk one step further when he joined in the founding of the Association for National Construction. Organized in November 1939, less than half a year after Zhang's "logical" critique of the spiritual mobilization campaign, this association went beyond advocating intellectual awakening. It accused the GMD directly of thwarting the development of democratic thought and democratic politics. With the explicit revival of the May Fourth slogans of "Science" and "Democracy," advocates of enlightenment were, once again, able to draw upon the history they knew well. They tried to distill out of that history lessons that might be of use to their contemporaries in the present.

In the four decades that followed the inauguration of the Association for National Construction, May Fourth intellectuals survived many new political upheavals. Sometimes, these upheavals turned against the May Fourth legacy, nearly crushing its spokesmen underfoot. Intellectuals, however, never quite forgot the meaning of the original enlightenment movement. Whenever it was possible, they tried to reintroduce its goals into the Chinese revolution. The importance of their effort has recently been acknowledged even by Zhou Yang, who was propaganda chief of the Chinese Communist Party until the beginning of the Cultural Revolution. An ardent defender of the imperatives of national salvation over cultural criticism since the 1930s, Zhou himself had been one of the most bitter critics of May Fourth veterans and their younger followers throughout the 1940s and 1950s. In 1983, however, recently rehabilitated himself, Zhou Yang acknowledged the enduring significance of the May Fourth enlightenment in the following terms:

Although the sound of critical thought was drowned out by the urgency of the war resistance against Japan, its message remains important.... All subsequent movements for democracy in China remain indebted to May Fourth. All have been incomplete. Although some intellectuals tried to solve the problem of feudal mentality in the 1940s, they were unsuccessful. Even the Chinese Communist Party's land reform campaign in the 1950s did not tackle the deepest aspects of the culture problem. Courage alone—the Communists' slogan "Be not afraid to have your head chopped off"—did not suffice in dealing with old habits of mind.... Superstitions persist in spite of repeated efforts to wipe out backwardness and ignorance. Enlightenment thought is still needed, you see, because the power of habits of thought is stronger than other kinds of power. It is invisible.[91]

SIX

May Fourth as Allegory

Memory's
no sin, so long as it serves some purpose.
After that
it's the laziness of moles, degradation
moldering on itself.

*Eugenio Montale, "Voice That Came in with
the Coots"*[1]

When Zhou Yang recalled the history of May Fourth more than six decades after the event, he did so for a reason. It was to remind himself and his countrymen that the goals of the enlightenment movement had yet to be achieved. As long as the force of habit and superstition remained so strong and so invisible, he argued, China could not afford to forget its debt to May Fourth. This notion of "debt" has also been upheld by intellectuals who were participants, observers, even critics of the May Fourth enlightenment. They, too, have continued to bring their memories into the public domain. Their conscientious, purposeful remembrance has not wiped out their indebtedness to history. It has, instead, contributed toward the future repayment of that debt by keeping the challenge of intellectual emancipation at the forefront of China's modernization effort.[2]

Zhou Yang's didactic use of the history of May Fourth is not unique. For decades before him, commemorators and commentators had done the same. In fact, it is hard to find an account of the event of 1919, first-hand or otherwise, that is not a distillation of the "lessons" of May Fourth. The lessons as well as the details of the history have changed over the years. Each new generation has created a different image of the May Fourth enlightenment, one that is more in keeping with its own needs and aspirations. The process of shaping a critical mirror for the present out of the past is termed, here, allegorization. An allegory, in this sense, is a reconstruction of memory for the explicit purpose of instructing the present. In the Chinese context, the didactic message of May Fourth has become clearer and clearer in recent decades as commemorators of the event of 1919 continue to war against old values and habits of mind.

This urge to instruct their compatriots through a purposeful retelling of their own experiences has been characteristic of May Fourth intellectuals since the beginning of their participation in the event of 1919. Less than three weeks after the student demonstration in Tiananmen Square, Luo Jialun tried to extract its lessons in an essay entitled "The Spirit of the May Fourth Movement." To call such a recent occurrence a "movement" and to highlight its "spirit of resistance" was, in effect, to create the first allegory of May Fourth. Luo Jialun, like Zhou Yang more than six decades later, sought to inspire his countrymen by reminding them that it was possible—and therefore necessary—to question seemingly sacred authorities. Unlike Zhou, however, Luo emphasized the social and political battle that was paramount in the minds of young students at the time: "Our movement expresses the spirit of social justice. In this dark China, there is no effective law, and politics are so reactionary that a group of traitors can feel safe having numerous guards to protect them. People feel outraged but do not dare say anything. They, too, share this belief that traitors are somehow sacred and inviolable."[3]

Having described the way the population of China shares the superstitions of its rulers, Luo went on to commemorate the victory of "empty-fisted students" like himself. With nothing less than the force of their convictions, he claimed, they were able to open a new page in history. The symbolic meaning of the student movement, according to Luo Jialun, is to show that the "idol of arbitrary authority has collapsed. After this movement, there will be many more instances of social justice. We proclaim to our people: at a time when there is no law, in a place where politics doesn't work, only social justice can change China for the better!"[4]

The tendency to make proclamations to the nation at large through a retelling of the history of May Fourth increased after the event of 1919. As the decades passed, intellectuals held on to the allegory of May Fourth as a means of keeping alive the spirit of criticism and of chastising those who would consign it to the past. Especially when the "idols of arbitrary authority" appeared most menacing, the architects of the original enlightenment movement found their memories most useful. They used these fragments of the past to console themselves as well as to arouse younger contemporaries who had not shared in the initial battle of the bare-fisted students. The allegorization of May Fourth thus became a way for intellectuals to continue their struggle for autonomy from feudal values, from authoritarian political authorities, and, at times, even from the collective superstitions of the masses.

In order to make their point about the relevance of May Fourth persuasive to their compatriots, intellectuals had to be on guard against what Montale called "the degradation of moles"; that is to say, the temptation to idealize the past and, therefore, become superfluous in the present. The allegory of May Fourth did not become a refuge from the present precisely because intellectuals did manage to maintain a critical view of history. Luo Changpei, a young scholar and disciple of May Fourth intellectuals, expressed most sharply this commitment to a critical view of May Fourth in 1949, a time of radical transition and reorientation for all of China:

The old tune of May Fourth cannot be replayed. Without May Fourth, we would not have the present. If we continue to grasp forever the spirit of May Fourth, we will have no future. May Fourth is already thirty years old. We ourselves have yet to acquire the broadness of a similar adult mentality. We must not long for the glory of the past; rather, we must plan the creation of the future.[5]

The challenge of maturing in step with a changing historical situation did not take May Fourth intellectuals by surprise. They, like all of their compatriots who participated in and survived decades of political upheaval, had become quite used to this problem. The particular aspect of this challenge that May Fourth veterans took most seriously was the ongoing criticism of political autocracy. They brought into the public domain details of their past experience and of their earlier ideals and thus challenged the politicians' monopoly over history. At different moments in China's political history, intellectuals put forth different versions of May Fourth to bear out their claims about the meaning of enlightenment and revolution. Participants, observers, and critics of the event of 1919, of course, had to learn to use their memories quite selectively. They remembered more political details whenever the pressure for *jiuguo* (national mobilization) increased, and they recalled details of the cultural battle for *qimeng* (enlightenment) whenever the climate became more favorable to the goals of intellectual emancipation.

The ensemble of all these composite images may be termed the "remembered history" of May Fourth. Such a collection, according to historian Bernard Lewis, is characterized by "statements about the past rather than history in the strict sense." It is, in effect, "the collective memory of a community or nation—what it, or its leaders, poets, sages chose to remember as significant, both as reality and symbol."[6] This type of history has been important in China for a long time. In fact, it has assumed a sacred significance in a culture that had renounced appeals to transcendent gods in the realm of public life. A commitment to voluminous and relatively accurate recording of personal, regional, and dynastic histories goes back to Confucius (551–479 B.C.) and to Sima Qian (145–87 B.C.). This commitment continues to shape the rich tradition of May Fourth veterans. Like generations of dissenting scholar-officials before them, they have been able to draw both inspiration and legitimacy for their challenges to established political authority from their appeals to history. The allegorical use of their memories, however selective, has injected a contentious note into official views of the history of May Fourth.

The remembered history of May Fourth, as we shall see below, has evolved out of two kinds of sources: *jinian* (commemorative proclamations) and *huiyi* (personal recollections). Commemorations tend to be based upon made-to-order memories closely linked with certain major political events. Personal recollections, by contrast, are based upon an individual's need to say something about contemporary politics, and often to say something against them. Participants in the May Fourth movement have produced both the *jinian* and the *huiyi* literature. They have contributed to public commemorations, lending their personal experience of the past to official praise for the accomplishments of 1919. At the same time, they have guarded some less political memories that they continue to recall in order to remind their countrymen of the unachieved goal of cultural enlightenment. An official history of the political successes of May Fourth thus coexists with a less publicized history of its incomplete cultural mission.

Commemoration (*jinian*) and remembrance (*huiyi*) have been intricately linked both on the Chinese mainland and in Taiwan. Personal memory, never immune to the demands of public history, became even less so after 1949. The two political parties, the Nationalist and the Communist Party, now uphold two different, opposing versions of May Fourth. Whenever their war of words becomes acute, the competition for the allegiance and for the remembrances of May Fourth intellectuals grows more intense as well. Few of these intellectuals were able to remain silent during the major anniversaries of May Fourth. Especially during the 1949, 1969, and 1979 anniversaries, they had to adjust remembrance to key transitions in Chinese political life. In these years, the requirements of commemoration threatened to engulf the memories of May Fourth participants.

And yet, in spite of such political pressure, May Fourth veterans have been able to keep alive a vision of enlightenment that differs from official history. Although they have lent their voices repeatedly to public commemorations which claim that event of 1919 was simply as it should have been—patriotic, progressive, mass-based—they never forgot what it was really like: iconoclastic, conflict-ridden, incomplete. Out of their memories of what their movement might have been but did not quite become, they have distilled the so-called "spirit" of May Fourth. This spirit, as we shall see, continues to animate subsequent generations of cultural radicals who had taken on the challenge of enlightenment.

OFFICIAL IMAGES OF MAY FOURTH

From the very beginning, the event of 1919 was an object of political concern. Sun Zhongshan, the chief of the Nationalist Party at that time, was just the first of the many political leaders who have wanted to use and encode May Fourth into their vision of the revolutionary past. Out of Sun's own observations of student organizing and on the basis of news reported to him directly by Beida leaders such as Luo Jialun and Xu Deheng, he began to weave his own version of the lessons of May Fourth. Jiang Jieshi, Sun's successor in the Guomindang, although just a young military officer in 1919 with little interest in cultural criticism, later on also became interested in May Fourth. He, too, needed this piece of remembered history to fit into his larger picture of the struggle for Chinese nationalism and of the preservation of China's cultural heritage. Mao Zedong, the only political leader who was actually at Beida during the enlightenment movement (as an assistant librarian working with Li Dazhao and Zhang Shenfu), used his own memories of May Fourth and those of other participants to create an image of a cultural movement that was leading all along to the political victory of the Chinese Communist Party.

Each of these political leaders knew only too well that contending versions of the present needed to be buttressed by disparate, richly documented versions of the past. Their own political practice taught them what historian J. H. Plumb has noted in a more scholarly context: that warring authorities require warring pasts.[7] In twentieth-century Chinese history, the struggle over what would emerge as the correct, official image of May Fourth unfolded along with the political battles of the Chinese revolution. Twists and turns in the course of the revolution have been reflected in the changing definitions of May Fourth elaborated by prominent political leaders. Compelled to define May Fourth, these leaders extracted from the past only what was useful, and discarded the rest. The significance they assigned to May Fourth often ran counter to the experience of May Fourth participants. At odds with experiential history, the politicians' version carried a message of warning: Intellectuals had to stay in line with current convention or risk being exiled from the revolutionary ranks.

Ambivalence about intellectuals in general, and about their proclivity toward cultural criticism in particular, permeates the various meanings imposed upon the event of 1919. For a brief moment in the late 1930s, while the second United Front between the GMD and the CCP still held, ambivalence about the legacy of May Fourth assumed the same form on both sides. Thus, the two parties agreed to commemorate the event of 1919 as national "Youth Day." Intended to consolidate the United Front and to increase patriotic feelings, this occasion emphasized the role of students in national salvation. Later, the legacy of the larger cultural movement could no longer be ignored, and May Fourth began to be commemorated as "Literature Day,"even "Culture Day."[8] But whether commemorated as Youth Day, Literature Day, or Culture Day, May Fourth was being narrowed down all the same. By excluding the questions, the doubts, and the fears that had sparked the initial enlightenment movement, official images consolidated only the answers, the victories, the certainties deemed useful for the present. This shrunken vision of May Fourth was also a tame one. It could not challenge the present as effectively as more complex recollections of the event of 1919 could and, as we shall see, did.

Tactics for domesticating May Fourth were developed early on. Sun Zhongshan, an ardent nationalist with little or no interest in the problem of enlightenment, recognized the political utility of May Fourth immediately after the outbreak of student activism in 1919. Before he could make sense of it, however, he had to overcome his own distaste for cultural radicals. After all, Sun's long-standing association with cultural conservatives such as Zhang Taiyan and Liu Shipei had led him to shape a revolutionary nationalism that was greatly influenced by concepts of "national essence." Convinced that the preservation of traditional culture was the key to national survival,[9] he was therefore ill-prepared for his encounter with the iconoclastic enlightenment movement. What prevented him from becoming an enemy of May Fourth was his prompt appreciation of the significance of student patriotism.

The Beida students who sought him out in 1919–20 tried to argue with Sun Zhongshan about his "lack of interest in the New Cultural Movement."[10] They failed to change his ideas, but found him eager for a political alliance. Sun, dismayed with his own political organization, was eager for cooperation with this new constituency, which had seemingly nationwide support. Impressed by the students' fervor, he adopted their event and codified its meaning in an address to his party followers. Singling out "new thought"—by which he meant, simply, powerful convictions—as the main force behind the "brave actions of patriotic youth," Sun urged members of the GMD to learn from the student movement: "Ever since the Beida students started the May Fourth movement, patriotic youths have used new thought to prepare themselves for the revolution.... If our party wants to accomplish the revolution it must rely upon thought transformation.... Toward this end, the New Cultural Movement might be a most useful instrument indeed."[11]

To use enlightenment as a means toward nationalist ends was one thing. To follow through with its program was another. Although Sun Zhongshan urged his followers to emulate "thought transformation," his own commitment to it remained weak. Until the time of his death in 1925, Sun remained ambivalent about the pace and cosmopolitan implications of the cultural movement advocated at Beida. He continued to write in classical Chinese, a concrete gesture of resistance to a central point of May Fourth enlightenment. Nonetheless, his early, although circumscribed, appreciation for the accomplishments of May Fourth continued to color the perceptions of the inheritors of his revolutionary mission. Because he and his ideas have been claimed as guiding principles by both the GMD and the CCP, May Fourth has become a part of the political combat between them as well.

On the side of the Nationalists, the burden of appropriating May Fourth fell upon Sun Zhongshan's self-appointed successor, Jiang Jieshi. Even more ambivalent about cultural iconoclasts than Sun had been, Jiang had to work harder to sever the political, patriotic May Fourth from the enlightenment movement that had been its original inspiration. China's war of resistance in the late 1930s and early 1940s provided him with an opportunity to consolidate his long-standing suspicion of foreign-inspired thought movements into official policy. Ironically, Jiang used the twenty-second anniversary of May Fourth to admonish a new generation of students and teachers not to be taken in by the legacy of May Fourth. In his 1941 commemorative talk, entitled "The Relationship of Philosophy and Education to Youth," he posed a series of rhetorical questions intended to narrow the significance of the event of

1919 to the single acceptable element: the students' patriotic demonstration. The other elements of the enlightenment movement, ranging from vernacular literature to interest in Western thought, were condemned by Jiang (a Methodist married to a Wellesley graduate) as dangerous rejection of China's culture and people. Unable to fully repudiate Sun's praise for the New Culture movement, he asked: "Does the New Culture movement mean the destruction of all discipline and the wanton quest for individual freedom? Or does New Culture mean blind worship of foreign countries and indiscriminate introduction and acceptance of foreign civilization? If it does, the New Culture we seek is too simple, too cheap and too dangerous!"[12]

A decade later, with the loss of the mainland still fresh in mind, Jiang became even more vigilant about the legacy of Sun Zhongshan as well as the dangers of May Fourth. In order to "compensate for the inadequacies" of May Fourth, he argued, another slogan must be added to "Science" and "Democracy." Not surprisingly, Jiang's addition was *jiuguo*, Patriotism. In a 1952 exegesis of the correct meaning of Sun's "Three People's Principles" Jiang suggested that patriotism provided the underlying unity of all three principles. Patriotism by itself, however, was insufficient. It had to be buttressed by a concrete concept of the culture that was the foundation of the political entity known as the nation. Therefore, Jiang argued that May Fourth was to have a new meaning for nationalists: it should strengthen their loyalty to Chinese culture, especially to Chinese "ethics," *lunli*. The main lesson of the event of 1919, then, was: "love for the family, the clan ... reciprocal relationships ... and self-cultivation."[13] With this definition, May Fourth became identified with Jiang Jieshi's own New Life movement, and both were drafted into the task of preserving traditional culture. Thus, the enlightenment movement was not merely tamed; it was turned into its very opposite.

On the Communist side, Mao Zedong was less afraid than Jiang Jieshi of the challenge of enlightenment. In fact, he had styled himself as a follower of the May Fourth legacy since the time he worked as an assistant librarian at Beida on the eve of 1919. In spite of his loud and consistent praise for the cultural achievements of May Fourth, however, Mao Zedong shared Sun's and Jiang's suspicions about intellectuals who made enlightenment a prerequisite of national salvation. In contrast to the other two revolutionary leaders of China, who were primarily military men, Mao had had more contact with intellectuals. Thus he had more cause both for respect and for conflict with members of the May Fourth generation. A contemporary of the students at Beida, Mao had found himself snubbed by *New Tide* luminaries like Fu Sinian, Luo Jialun, and Zhang Shenfu. His bitterness toward them only increased during his career as revolutionary leader.[14]

The points of theoretical divergence that might possibly have been worked out had Mao Zedong been accepted into the inner circle of New Culture activists were blown all out of proportion in later years. May Fourth intellectuals had interpreted "thought emancipation" (*jiefang*) as a matter of individual responsibility leading to national emancipation. Mao Zedong, both at the time of May Fourth and after, emphasized the cultivation (*xiuyang*) of individual character rather than its emancipation. Mao's goal, like that of Sun and Jiang, was China's national regeneration. Therefore, he was quite suspicious of thought movements that might distract the masses from the central task of patriotic action. Whereas advocates of enlightenment had placed doubt and reason at the heart of their definition of critical thought, Mao had always been more impressed by the power of faith and of will.[15] More interested in defiant actions than defiant thoughts, Mao was, in the final analysis, like Sun Zhongshan and Jiang Jieshi, a selective admirer of May Fourth.

The extent of his ambivalence about the event of 1919 became apparent shortly after he arrived in Yan'an. In his May 4, 1939, talk on the occasion of "Youth Day," Mao addressed himself to the heirs of May Fourth. He asked them to abandon their special claims to the event of 1919, and thereby place it and themselves in the service of the revolution. Opening his speech with explicit praise for the "revolutionary contributions of May Fourth intellectuals," Mao declared that their enlightenment movement was "historically necessary ... yet incomplete." The source of this incompleteness, he argued, was the intellectuals' own "lack of determination to merge with the masses." In the conclusion of his address, his tone was markedly commemorative and official, as he talked of the "duties of youth and cultural workers"—a description of obligations set in the context of a leader's expectations for his followers.[16] In this essay Mao made an important distinction between himself as China's current revolutionary leader and intellectuals as architects of a revolutionary movement now quite past. This distinction signaled an intensified struggle over who would inherit May Fourth: Mao Zedong or the intellectuals?

Six months after the Youth Day talk, in January 1940, Mao consolidated his version of May Fourth in a longer discourse, entitled "On New Democracy." In order to assign the event of 1919 more firmly into past history, Mao now called it the fountainhead of his own revolutionary movement. He insisted that May Fourth had been an integral part "of the world revolution of the proletarian class," along with the Russian Revolution of 1917. He defined May Fourth as a momentous demarcation between the "old democracy" period from 1911 to 1919, in which the primary struggle had been between the bourgeoisie and the feudal classes, and the period of "new democracy," marked by the leadership of the Communist Party and its proletarian vision of socialism.

May Fourth, however, was not presented as merely a milestone in a political revolution. Mao, like Sun Zhongshan before him, also took into account the cultural significance of 1919. The May Fourth attack on old ethics and old literature was enshrined here as a "great and thorough cultural revolution ... unprecedented in Chinese history." To call May Fourth a cultural revolution enabled Mao at once to glorify iconoclasm in general and to criticize the actual participants of the original enlightenment. This feat of interpretation was achieved by incorporating May Fourth into the larger epic of the Chinese revolution and by singling out for praise only one of the May Fourth thinkers: Lu Xun.

When he endowed this deceased figure with heroic qualities, Mao, in effect, condemned the others still living. Lu Xun, according to Mao, had been "correct" in his time. The 1920s and 1930s had required a sustained assault on the ethic of subservience embodied in warlord governments and the Nationalist regime. In the Communist-liberated areas, on the other hand, Lu Xun's followers were no longer encouraged to attack feudal habits of mind—least of all, feudal attitudes prevalent among Communist cadres themselves. Here, according to Mao's view, they had to forsake their May Fourth compulsion to criticize everything and learn to merge with the worker-peasant-soldier masses. To make his admonition clearer, Mao concluded his interpretation of the event of 1919 with a praise of the "June Third movement," thus taking the limelight away from Beida intellectuals and shifting it to the nationwide strikes that broke out in support of the student demonstrations. By commemorating May Fourth so selectively, Mao was able to declare the intellectuals' movement "a historically necessary failure."[17]

However much a "failure," May Fourth was encoded as "historically necessary," and was used to justify the Communist movement that followed it. In fact, it was precisely because the original enlightenment movement was bound to fail, the argument ran, that it was so effective in preparing the way for the revolution spearheaded by Mao Zedong. In dying, it brought the revolution to life. This retrospectively imposed notion of causality was also shared by leaders of the Guomindang. They, too, attributed the Chinese Communist "scourge" to May Fourth intellectuals who had been too hasty in their criticism of Chinese culture.

Their iconoclasm was directly responsible for making China vulnerable
to foreign ideologies. Thus, praised and damned by Communists and
Nationalists alike, the May Fourth legacy became part of the revolutionary history to be contested and redefined in the key moments of China's
political transformation: namely, 1949, 1969, and 1979.

In these years, it became quite evident that the battle over who was to
own the event of 1919 raged on. Neither the Communist Party nor the
Guomindang was willing to let the matter rest with "historical necessity." Each side continued to reclaim May Fourth, to use it to justify
itself in the present. Not surprisingly, the battle for the political capital
embodied in May Fourth was most acute in the 1940s and 1960s. In
these years of actual or near civil war, when political discourse was
heavily colored by metaphors of struggle and betrayal, Communists
claimed that the GMD "lost" May Fourth whereas the Nationalists
claimed the other side had "snatched" it. These conflicting diatribes
left little room for remembered history. The verbal violence of such
terms as "snatched," "smeared," "stolen" imposed on commemorative
occasions a depth of antagonism quite alien to May Fourth veterans
themselves. Their opportunity for conveying a more complex view of the
event of 1919 arose only intermittently, in the 1950s and 1970s, when the
ambivalence of both Communists and Nationalists toward intellectuals
and toward enlightenment had subsided somewhat. Only when the burden of political polemics became lighter were they able to write publicly
about the incomplete mission of the cultural May Fourth.

TESTING LOYALTIES: KEY MOMENTS IN
THE COMMEMORATION OF MAY
FOURTH

Once political leaders such as Sun Zhongshan, Jiang Jieshi, and Mao
Zedong had codified the official meanings of May Fourth, it became the
responsibility of their subordinates to guard against the proliferation of
alternative views. That responsibility was most acute at times of political
struggle, when the intellectuals' otherwise innocuous remembrances
could have been used as weapons by opposing sides. In 1949, in 1969,
and in 1979, for example, loyalty to the public image of May Fourth was
tested most rigorously. These moments represented unique opportunities to reinforce acceptable interpretations of the event of 1919 and to
screen the memories of those who might be tempted to recall something
more or something other than what was mandated by the political
requirements of the day.

The thirtieth anniversary of May Fourth occurred during the last and most bitter year of the Chinese civil war. With a Communist victory quite clearly on the horizon, intellectuals were mobilized to join in celebrations that would test their commitment to the new social order that was about to be implemented across the mainland. In the forefront of those assigned to organize the activities and the memories of May Fourth veterans was Chen Boda, promoter of the New Enlightenment movement of the late 1930s, and now serving as vice president of the Communist Party's most important school, the Marxist-Leninist Institute. On the basis of his past connections with May Fourth intellectuals, Chen was able to persuade thirty-six of the most prominent among them—including Mao Dun, Ye Shengtao, Yang Zhensheng, and Yu Pingbo—to contribute to a commemorative volume. The most concrete sign of sympathy for the new regime was to say something about the inevitable connection between May Fourth and the imminent Communist victory. In Chen Boda's own introductory essay, he restated Mao Zedong's interpretation of May Fourth as a radical thought movement that helped spread Communist ideology and organization in China. At the same time, Chen, like Mao before him, reminded intellectuals that a thought movement perpetrated primarily by intellectuals was bound to fail. Therefore, the only aspect of the event of 1919 worth commemorating at this crucial point in China's history was a "proletarian May Fourth." Whether such a thing ever existed was not an issue. What mattered most was that the present required this sort of interpretation and that Chen Boda had the power and authority to evoke it. "The most significant achievement of May Fourth," he concluded, "was the coalition of intellectuals and workers. Since only a proletarian revolution can provide new birth, the logic of China's social history and revolution from May Fourth through today inspires in us completely new hopes and shows us the actual road ahead."[18]

In this precarious moment, the "logic" of the present came close to overwhelming the logic of the past. When all that mattered was "hopes" and an "actual road ahead," history became a means of promoting optimism, not of explaining the past. This temptation to inspire faith in the new order at the cost of lucid recollection was clearest in an essay by the Communist historian Fan Wenlan. In his contribution to the Chen Boda volume, Fan makes quite transparent his determination to secure May Fourth for the winning side by further severing the event of 1919 from its original constituency: the doubt-ridden intellectuals in and around Beida. Fan's conclusion goes beyond that of Chen Boda in its polemical tone and intent: "Without doubt, the glory, the greatness, the epoch-making significance of May Fourth belongs to the Communist Party, the Chinese proletariat, and the Chinese people. Bourgeos intellectuals have ... betrayed May Fourth and have become shameful counter-revolutionaries."[19]

The question of who were the "bourgeois intellectuals" was purposefully vague. Other than such prominent figures as Hu Shi, Luo Jialun, and Fu Sinian, who had already fled from the mainland to go to the United States or to Taiwan, it was understood that those remaining had yet to prove their lack of culpability. The most effective way for them to do this was to show their willingness to reinterpret May Fourth in keeping with the dictates of present political requirements.

Participants in the event of 1919 faced this test with differing degrees of trepidation. Some were more prompt than others in announcing publicly that May Fourth was, all along, leading up to the imminent Communist victory. In the end, however, most of those who did not accept Hu Shi's offer of plane tickets out of the embattled cities came to embrace the symbolic hope depicted on the cover of yet another thirtieth anniversary commemorative volume. Published by the Communist Party's fellow travelers in Hong Kong, it shows a road sign composed of a pen emblazoned with the words "May Fourth." The sign is posted on a street named "Intellectuals' Path." It points forcefully forward. The double message was clear. On the one hand, intellectuals were invited to have a share in the glorious future ahead. On the other, they were compelled to leave May Fourth behind in order to walk along that bright, new path.[20]

Listening and adhering to such double messages was not an easy task in that transitional year from civil war to Communist victory. It was an effort that strained the intellectuals' thoughts and language. And yet, they kept on trying. A good example of the effort involved may be glimpsed in Yu Pingbo's commemorative essay solicited for the Chen Boda collection. In May 1949, the future was unfathomable for this bookish *New Tide* veteran. A brilliant critic of traditional fiction, he found himself teaching in the Beida literature department. A new student movement was raging in the university. The Communists' new social order was also imminent. In these circumstances, Yu could not refuse to contribute to the official commemoration of the thirtieth anniversary of May Fourth. Along with fellow *New Tide* members Yang Zhensheng and Ye Shengtao and other intellectuals publicly associated with the May Fourth legacy, he tried to use the familiar past to make sense of the unknown fate that awaited him in a Communist-ruled China. Clearly anxious about the treatment of intellectuals after Communist

23. Cover of a collection of essays commemorating the 30th anniversary of the May Fourth movement. This volume was edited by Mao Dun and Guo Moruo and contains Mao Dun's title essay "Zhishi fenzi de daolu" (The road ahead for intellectuals).

victory, he sought reassurance through a recollection entitled "A Backwards Glance and a Look Toward the Future."

As Ye Shengtao and Yang Zhensheng had done, Yu Pingbo also made an effort to convince himself and others that the event of 1919 had foreshadowed the present circumstances with which he had to learn to cope. This effort was more costly to Yu because he knew himself to be, and was honest enough to say so publicly, a "bystander of great events." He had not participated in the Tiananmen demonstration of 1919, and had been ambivalent about living up to the "new ethics" he himself had advocated in *New Tide*. Since it seemed unlikely that he would be allowed to remain a bystander in the years to come, Yu tried to recall the one political event he knew "by heart" in the hope that he might understand with his "mind" other events to come. His remembrance made clear his hope that the slogans and the causes of 1919 would prove to be compatible with those of 1949. So Yu Pingbo asked rhetorically: "Is not the Science and Democracy of today still the Science and Democracy of that time [i.e., the May Fourth era]?... There really is not much difference between new democracy and Communism and the things that we fought for thirty years ago!"[21]

To posit an equivalence between 1919 and 1949 was to echo the rationalizations of the late nineteenth-century Confucian reformers, who claimed that their own intimately familiar Confucian past was really quite compatible with the Western modernity feared by conservative contemporaries. Yu Pingbo, surrounded by militant students who were organizing against American imperialism and sought out by Communist cadres whose aim was to persuade him to remain in China and to stay in line, struggled to find an earlier, more comprehensible moment that foreshadowed the present. Relying on a more modern metaphor than was available to his Confucian predecessors, Yu concluded: "It is as if on May 4, 1919, a check was written. At that time it looked as if the check would bounce. But today, thirty years late, it is being cashed in."[22]

This search for antecedents to justify the outcome of the present was also at the heart of May Fourth commemorations in Taiwan in the early 1950s. Like the Communists on the eve of victory in the civil war, Guomindang authorities also turned to history. Their aim, however, unlike that of the CCP, was to explain why recent political losses were really no losses at all. To make this case, they had first to prove that the "check" Yu Pingbo had seen "cashed in" on the mainland was nothing but a forgery—that the Communists, despite their claims, had no right to inherit the legacy of May Fourth. This argument was, in fact, put forth quite stridently in an essay by the Nationalist spokesman, Chen

Guyuan. Chen's point was that pro-Guomindang heirs of May Fourth (whom he referred to by the older appellation of *wenren*, literati, rather than the more recent *zhishi fenzi*) were now expected to "battle against Communist bandits:"

> Communists use the slogans of Science and Democracy and make them into weapons of political struggle. But the basic nature of Communist bandits is anti-democratic and non-scientific. They are autocratic and dogmatic. They hide behind the talisman of Science and Democracy without investigation.[23]

In its effort to wrest away the "weapons" of science and democracy from the Communists, the Guomindang came close to negating the legacy of May Fourth altogether. Using a more conservative definition of culture to buttress Jiang Jieshi's call for patriotism, the Nationalist Party began to dampen official celebrations of the event of 1919. Just as the propaganda authorities were on the verge of forbidding all public talk of May Fourth—because of the danger that reminiscences of the political event would spill over into remembrances of its cultural iconoclasm—May Fourth veteran Luo Jialun joined the polemics. Luo had served as China's ambassador to India from 1947 to 1950, and had recently been appointed chairman of the Guomindang party history archives. His loyalty to the Nationalist cause could not be doubted. And yet, while few would question his political antipathy for the Communists, many wondered aloud about his insistent way of recalling the May Fourth movement as a warning to Guomindang "reactionaries."[24] Luo Jialun's willingness to use the legacy of May Fourth in such a manifestly allegorical fashion was unusual in the charged atmosphere that prevailed in Taiwan right after the civil war. At a time when pressures to prove one's political fidelity to traditional Chinese culture were greatest, he returned to the cause of his youth: cultural enlightenment.

Having been the first *New Tide* member to allegorize May Fourth, in his 1919 manifesto "The Spirit of the May Fourth Movement," Luo Jialun continued that project in a 1950 essay, "The True Spirit of May Fourth." Written at a time still laden with the political conflict between the Guomindang and the CCP, Luo's aim was to fight off his contemporaries' desire to forget May Fourth altogether. Because he was defying current prejudices against foreign thought and critical reason, Luo's essay strayed from other, more ambivalent commemorations of May Fourth. Capitalizing on his close connection to the event of 1919, on his prominence as a founder of *New Tide*, and on having himself written the vernacular handbill used to mobilize support for the Tiananmen demonstration, Luo argued that May Fourth had been more than an outbreak of student patriotism coupled with a vague interest in vernacular language. Beyond nationalism and language reform, May Fourth was, according to Luo, significant as a thought-awakening movement with implications for all aspects of Chinese life. Thus in his remembrance May Fourth emerges as nothing less than an enlightenment movement:

May Fourth, first and foremost, represents the awakening of new culture consciousness ... and is very similar to the eighteenth-century European enlightenment.... Enlightenment figures such as Rousseau and Diderot used fierce criticism to break through the confines of old thought. Moreover, they used a scientific attitude and the spirit of freedom not only to reconsider prevailing literary tendencies ... but also to undertake a thorough inquiry into the political and social system as well.[25]

In the decades after that transitional year of 1949–50, few May Fourth veterans were able to acclaim so publicly the cultural significance of the May Fourth enlightenment. Luo Jialun's own unique position in Taiwan and his increasing prominence as the chief Guomindang historian enabled him to return intermittently to the theme of intellectual awakening. Other intellectuals had to be more guarded about their remembrances of and sympathy for cultural criticism.

In fact, the next moment in China's history when cultural iconoclasm became sanctioned again, during the Cultural Revolution of 1966–69, May Fourth veterans were completely absent from the public arena. A new generation of university students now arose to claim the mantle of May Fourth. In 1969, the Red Guards commemorated the fiftieth anniversary of May Fourth as their own event, even as they berated, beat, and, at times, killed the Western-trained intellectuals who were their teachers. They were encouraged in this belief by Mao Zedong himself, who had been the first political leader to enshrine May Fourth as a "cultural revolution." Taking Mao's views as license, the Red Guards stated unequivocally: "May Fourth created a totally new era, just like the Cultural Revolution today. Even such rightists as Hu Shi, who represented the capitalist intelligentsia, did not dare oppose it directly."[26] The half century between themselves and May Fourth virtually disappeared as these new Radicals reasserted the absolute validity of the earlier slogan: "Down with Confucius and sons." Bent upon their own battle with "old culture," they believed themselves empowered by the new culture foreshadowed by May Fourth.

To selectively recall the slogans of May Fourth was not the same, however, as to genuinely reckon with its historical significance. And yet, leftist radicals could enforce this meaning in the public domain because May Fourth veterans had, for the moment, lost their nerve. Under pressure to confess a myriad of sins, not the least being their "bourgeois" tendencies, they came close to forgetting, or at least denying, their own contributions to the May Fourth enlightenment. One of the most prominent intellectuals to seek salvation in this new line was the philosopher Feng Youlan. Unable to write truthfully about his own complex position during the original New Culture movement, he let his connection to it be used to bolster contemporary attacks on "bourgeois revisionism." In the guise of self-criticism, he simultaneously celebrated May Fourth and distorted his own role in it:

Ever since the May Fourth movement in 1919, the question of whether to knock down or to protect the "Confucian shop" has been an important part of the struggle between two classes and the two lines in the field of ideology in China. Before the Cultural Revolution, I had all along defended the "Confucian shop." By doing so I served the big landlords, big bourgeoisie, and the Guomindang reactionaries before liberation, and after it the counter-revolutionary revisionist line of Liu Shaoqi, Lin Biao, and other political swindlers.[27]

While Beijing University professors such as Feng Youlan were forced to falsify their own history, a new generation of students in Taiwan saw their golden opportunity to wrest the legacy of May Fourth away from the Communists. Without much concrete information about the fate of intellectuals on the mainand, they, too, embraced the fiftieth anniversary of the event of 1919 as an occasion that would enable them to impose their own meaning upon the past. Having identified May Fourth with the name of Hu Shi (who held a much narrower view of the event than the one held by Luo Jialun), they interpreted the Cultural Revolution attack on Hu Shi and his followers as an attack on May Fourth. Although seemingly naive, their interpretation was, in fact, quite effective in highlighting the one-sidedness of leftists' claims about the "proletarian" origins of the Chinese enlightenment. Precisely because the mainland commemorators were willing to leave out so much of the original May Fourth in their quest for a precedent for the "totally new culture," Taiwan commemorators could now recall the forgotten parts and lay claim to the newly conceived whole. As one of the contributors to the *Daxue zazhi* (*University Monthly*) wrote: "Luckily, the power struggles induced by the Cultural Revolution leave no time for the Communist Party to truly celebrate May Fourth [true enough, since the party itself was under attack in China at the time].... Insofar as the Red Guards purge the philosophy of Hu Shi, they purge May Fourth as well."[28] A "purged May Fourth" was, in this view, a lost May Fourth. The principle of "finders, keepers" was reasserted in Taiwan and on the mainland one decade later.

24.   Feng Youlan, during an interview with the author, April 1980.

On both sides of the Taiwan straits, the sixtieth anniversary of May
Fourth in 1979 prompted new debates. The time elapsed between the
event of 1919 and contemporary events enabled orators to be more confident. Official editorials on the mainland and in Taiwan underscored
the relevance of May Fourth for the present and insisted that it legiti-
mized their respective political concerns. Each side called for a fulfillment of the May Fourth legacy in keeping with its own ideological requirements. In the People's Republic, the *Guangming ribao* commentary,
entitled "The Inevitable Road of History," asserted that the event of
1919 was nothing less than a preview of the current modernization
program:

The significance of May Fourth was to prove the inevitability of anti-imperialism
and anti-feudalism. Thereby, it opened up a new alternative for the Chinese
people.... Although there were many different people in the leadership of May
Fourth [including Hu Shi, who now was praised for his contributions in the
literary movement], they met with different fates. Why?... Because some used
Marxism [in solving China's problems] while others did not. During May Fourth
only a few people knew about Marxism. Now, sixty years later, Marxism,
Leninism, and Mao Zedong thought have become deeply rooted in the people's

minds.... Thus, we can now face up to the challenge of the four modernizations.[29]

From a diametrically opposed point of view, the Taiwan-based *Zhongyang ribao* made a similar claim about the inevitable lessons of May Fourth in its editorial entitled "Getting Rid of Internal Traitors Means Exterminating the Red Menace." The official Guomindang position, like that of the PRC, was that there was one and only one meaning to the May Fourth movement. While Beijing newspapers stressed Marxist modernization, the Taibei media reaffirmed the importance of cultural loyalty through patriotism:

The slogan of the students' patriotic demonstration—"Get Rid of Internal Traitors, Oppose External Aggressors"—is exactly the same as that of the Guomindang.... The anti-traditionalism that surfaced in the latter part of the New Culture movement represents a repudiation of May Fourth. The Communists have relied on this trend for their own purposes.... Therefore to commemorate May Fourth today is ... to get rid of internal traitors and continue the struggle for the extermination of the Communists.[30]

Sixty years after the event of 1919, however, official interpretations were more flexible than it might appear at first sight. Although the party newspapers on the mainland and in Taiwan stressed certain aspects of May Fourth that were in keeping with the political needs of the day, they could not and did not silence May Fourth veterans who had other reminiscences to add to public polemics. Because this anniversary also coincided with a mood of relative tolerance toward diverse points of view, and because some participants in the event of 1919 were still alive and lucid, 1979 marks a significant elaboration of the May Fourth legacy. For example, for the first time, architects of the original New Culture movement were invited to recall their student activities in a way that did not necessarily emphasize Marxism, modernization, or political patriotism. Thus, aged intellectuals like Yu Pingbo, Guo Shaoyu, Zhang Shenfu, Mao Zishui, He Siyuan, and Li Xiaofeng, *New Tide* members who had long been absent from official commemorations of May Fourth, now re-emerged to contribute to it and to expand its boundaries.

This time, the aged survivors of May Fourth were permitted to be more honest, and even more cantankerous, than before. Their recollections did not dwell simply on the few select, retrospectively "correct" heroes—or on the historical lessons of the events. Rather, they emphasized a host of secondary characters such as Zhu Ziqing and Xu Yanzhi, as well as the survivors' own foibles and limited vision, in 1919 as well as in 1979.[31] Among those who came forward at this time to express the delights and the shortcomings of May Fourth were Yu Pingbo in Beijing and Mao Zishui in Taibei. These veterans of the event of 1919 had both been reluctant to engage in public commemorations of May Fourth. Both had tried, unsuccessfuly, to withstand political pressures to extract from their personal past usable lessons for the present.[32] By 1979, however, the septuagenarian Yu and the octogenarian Mao had lived through too much to feel obliged to shrink memory down to the size of contemporary ideology. Their reminiscences therefore reveal the many-sidedness of May Fourth in a way that newspaper editorials could not.

Yu Pingbo, the youngest member of the *New Tide* Society in 1919, celebrated the sixtieth anniversary of May Fourth with the memory of persecution weighing heavily on his mind. A victim of various criticism campaigns from 1954 onward, he had barely escaped the beatings of the Red Guards during the Cultural Revolution. In 1979, he was able to resume his public role again, a jubilant celebrant of the May Fourth enlightenment. This time, however, in contrast to the solicited essays and confessions he wrote in 1949 and 1959,[33] his remembrance took the form of a series of poems. These were rich in personal statement about his own immaturity at the time of the student demonstration of 1919 and about his inability to withstand his parents' pressure to follow Confucian ethics. These poems also claimed public attention by identifying survival of May Fourth intellectuals with the history of the May Fourth legacy:

> We were so young, so active then.
> Members of one class,
> We founded three magazines
>   (*New Tide* being one among those started by our
>   class in the Chinese Literature Department).
> I have been living in Beijing for over sixty years now!
> Watching changes in society
> Has been like watching the waters coalesce to form
>   one great river.
> Our city will assume its rightful place in history again,
> Only when our society becomes more democratic.[34]

While Yu Pingbo celebrated his own and his generation's youthful ardor for democracy in Beijing, his fellow *New Tide* member Mao Zishui also joined the sixtieth commemoration of May Fourth in Taibei. Encouraged to write on the polemical theme "No need to fear May Fourth! The history of May Fourth is ours!," he still managed to tell his own personal story. This story makes it amply clear that Mao Zishui is no longer as concerned with taking the event of 1919 back from "Communist bandits" as he is determined to salvage bits of truth that might add up to a more complete, more critical view of the past. Like Yu Pingbo,

25.   Yu Pingbo at eighty-two.

Mao had been a minor participant in the drama of the student demonstration. Although present at the scene now enshrined in the public mind
as the essence of the patriotic May Fourth, Mao chose to recall his own
and his generation's less grandiose reasons for being swept up in demonstrations and strikes of 1919: "We were young, after all, and loved the
freedom of not going to classes." Mao Zishui dwelled on details of the
founding of *New Tide* , of how he himself came to write articles about a
scientific critique of the national heritage. The conclusion is unabashedly personal and, in contrast to public commemorations, unheroic:

On the day of May Fourth, I stayed with the demonstration until the fire at Cao
Rulin's house. Then, I got scared. I lost interest and went back to the dormitory.
That night, when there was a student meeting to decide on a strike, I felt torn.
Although I didn't like going to classes, I also disapproved of the strike. So I said
nothing.... I am temperamentally lazy. This is no good. So I didn't amount to
very much in life. As far as the occasion of May Fourth is concerned, truly I
cannot be considered a conscious participant.[35]

Both Mao Zishui and Yu Pingbo, then, were able to use the sixtieth
anniversary of May Fourth to augment public images of May Fourth.
The time that had elapsed since the event of 1919, as well as the rather
liberal mood prevailing on the mainland and in Taiwan in 1979, facilitated their efforts to use memory for something more than a test of loyalty to the contemporary political line. For such reticent, temperamentally

27. Xu Deheng at ninety-two.

26. Mao Zishui at eighty-five.

reclusive intellectuals as Yu Pingbo and Mao Zishui, only the authority of the sixtieth *jinian* (public commemoration) provided sufficient protection for the outpouring of relatively uninhibited *huiyi* (personal recollections). Other, less timid May Fourth veterans managed to inject bits of personal memory into earlier official versions of May Fourth. These intellectuals, too, had time to tailor their reminiscences to suit the needs of the present. But they managed to expand the limits of what was the "correct" interpretation of the tradition of May Fourth sooner and with more force than the belated recollections of Yu Pingbo and Mao Zishui.

MEMORY IN THE SERVICE OF TRADITION

Once the meanings of May Fourth had become officially fixed by leaders of the national revolution such as Sun Zhongshan, Jiang Jieshi, and Mao Zedong, they needed to be buttressed by the recollections of participants. This demand for made-to-order memories has been described by Bernard Lewis as characteristic of all "invented history": that is, history comprised of simplified, polemical remembrances produced whenever and wherever embattled authorities require specific versions of the past. These versions, according to Lewis, are generated on the basis of recollections evoked and "improved" by practical authorities.[36]

May Fourth intellectuals were not immune from pressures to improve their memory in keeping with changing political lines. However, their memory could still be troublesome. Far from being merely a pliant instrument in the hands of political authority, memory can, and in the case of May Fourth, did frequently backfire. Participants of the event of 1919 had been retelling their history for a long time before they were required to do so. In the process, they had become skilled in selective remembrance. Even when the purpose of public commemoration differed from their own, they managed to introduce some of their own concerns with enlightenment into politicized recollections generated on demand.

The long process of rethinking the meaning of May Fourth through the 1920s and 1930s enabled them to confront later pressures more skillfully. Even when they were compelled by contemporary authorities to add their share to the invention of history, most May Fourth veterans retained a trace of honesty. As a result, the event of 1919 has remained more complex and more ambiguous than many other events in the polemical history of the Chinese revolution.

The expansion of the official version of the "tradition of May Fourth" often occurred when relatively safe intellectuals were asked to contribute recollections to relatively non-momentous commemorations of May Fourth. The distinction between *huiyi* and *jinian* was allowed more flexibility at these times. As a result, the sum total of what was deemed commemorable was stretched to include meanings that might have been otherwise filtered out or forgotten. One example that illustrates this process well is the simultaneous publication in 1955 of an official commemorative essay by Zhou Yang and of an unofficial recollection by *New Tide* member Yang Zhensheng. At the time, Zhou was one of the most active deputy directors of the propaganda department of the Chinese Communist Party's Central Committee. He had just led a campaign against another *New Tide* intellectual, Yu Pingbo, and Yu's mentor, Hu Shi. Yang Zhensheng was chairman of the Chinese department at the newly reorganized Beijing University. The contrast between Zhou's essay, entitled "Develop the Militant Tradition of the May Fourth Literary Revolution," and Yang's "Recollections of May Fourth" illustrates how the public meanings of May Fourth could be expanded through personal recollection.

Zhou Yang made it clear from the outset that he was interested only in what was politically useful about the May Fourth tradition. His purpose was to find in the past those threads that led to the future, or more precisely, to the present as he conceived it to be. He celebrated May Fourth as "the beginning of a literature of the people, an event that led to the awakening of the masses and toward socialism." The main hero of this teleological history was Lu Xun—an awkward glorification, since Lu Xun had been a bitter critic of "national character" during the very time that Zhou Yang claimed that the Chinese people were already awake and marching toward socialism. In order to assimilate Lu Xun into the "militant tradition" of the Communist Party, Zhou emphasized the patriotic significance of May Fourth and its positive discovery of the masses, and especially the peasants. Even Lu Xun's attack on the feudal system, seen in this context, was a sign that he "understood the peasant masses profoundly... and cared for them deeply."[37] Zhou's commemorative essay, in effect, forgave Lu Xun for his tough-minded humanism. Lu Xun and the tradition he embodied were deemed correct as long as they were safely past. Therefore, Zhou concluded:

May Fourth authors bequeath to us a tragic picture of life of peasants in old China.... But now, Chinese people with their own might have overthrown old China and are just in the midst of building a new, beautiful China. We must continue the militant tradition of May Fourth ... and press it further one great step now. New works of literature must depict the new peasants.... These are the new responsibilities that the masses demand that cultural workers undertake.[38]

Once the "tradition of May Fourth" was identified with patriotic concern for peasants, it could be used to chastise those who were its original constituency, the intellectuals. Stripped of its meaning as a critique of political authority and of the ethic of subservience, the May Fourth "tradition" could be continued by requiring new kinds of obedience: this time, to the demands of the "masses" as interpreted by the most recent party spokesmen.

Yang Zhensheng's recollections of May Fourth did not exactly contradict Zhou Yang's version of the "militant tradition." In fact, six years earlier, on the eve of liberation, Yang himself had written about the achievements of May Fourth in terms similar to those of Zhou Yang. He too had been willing to see it as simply a patriotic literary movement meant to awaken the masses.[39] By 1955, however, Yang was able to sidestep the question of public virtue and retell a personal tale. Yang's detailed version of May Fourth, which appeared in the same issue of *People's Literature* as Zhou Yang's, could not but expand the official meanings of May Fourth.

Yang began his remembrance with a narrative of his childhood in Shandong and intellectual restlessness during high school. Whereas literature and Lu Xun figure prominently in Zhou Yang's commemoration, Yang's memoir focuses on the dramatic emancipation going on within Beida in the late 1910s. In this essay, Cai Yuanpei and other *New Tide* teachers are more prominent than Lu Xun. Furthermore, whereas Zhou Yang had emphasized the awakening of the peasants, Yang focused on his own awakening and that of his fellow students in the *New Tide* group.

In 1955, when fellow *New Tide* member Yu Pingbo had become a political pariah in Chinese public life, Yang Zhensheng acknowledges him, recalling their days together at Beida and their joint rebellion against the forces of cultural conservatism. To add more vivid detail to this narrative, Yang retells how he and Yu Pingbo had run into conflict with the Chinese literature department, one of the strongholds of conservatism at the new Beida: "When Yu Pingbo and I joined the *New Tide*, old-fashioned professors in the department cursed us as renegades (*pantu*).... But with our newfound vigor, we feared nothing." Tracing the source of inspiration for their rebellion no further than the teachers who edited *New Tide*, Yang placed the May Fourth enlightenment in a context of generational collaboration among intellectuals: "With the seeds of seditious rebellion (*panni*) in our hearts, implanted by *New Youth* teachers, we tore off the chains from our bodies, and shouting at the top of our voices, we stormed the fortresses of feudalism.... Convinced that we were truly the new youth ... we began publication of *New Tide*."[40]

While celebrating the fervor of young intellectuals during May Fourth, Yang, like Ye Shengtao before him, also recalled their muddled state of mind. This youthful confusion was quite unlike the militant spirit Zhou Yang had commemorated in more general terms. Thus, whereas Zhou ended with a call to continue the fighting tradition by submitting to the demands of the peasant masses, Yang concluded on a more personal note: "At the time of May Fourth, we did not understand the connection between imperialism and feudal autocracy.... We knew from history that traitors are not very different from bandits ... so we hated the warlords and organized against them merely because they were China's enemies."[41]

To acknowledge the naiveté and confusion of youth as well as its idealism was honest but potentially risky. It suggested that the May Fourth tradition had grown out of the passions of hasty, immature youths rather than the "logic of history," as had been celebrated by militant Communists. Yang Zhensheng, as chairman of the Chinese department at the newly reorganized Beida, took that risk more readily than others. Confident about his own personal connection to the political May Fourth (he had been after all, one of the thirty-two students

28. Ye Shengtao, during an interview with the author, June 1980.

arrested during the Tiananmen demonstration of 1919), Yang thus managed to expand the "tradition" of May Fourth by recalling in 1955 the more complex notions behind the original movement.

In the 1950s, the official tradition of May Fourth was also being consolidated in Taiwan. There, too, as in China, official intellectuals were asked to extract commemorable virtues from the troublesome legacy of the enlightenment movement. With campaigns against Hu Shi under way on the mainland, Hu's version of May Fourth, the "May Fourth Renaissance," became enshrined in Taiwan as public truth. To narrow May Fourth down to a "literary movement" and to "patriotism" was the main strategy of its commemorators, a strategy thwarted periodically by Luo Jialun, the most prominent *New Tide* member on the Nationalist side. Luo, as chairman of the Guomindang party history committee, was in a position similar to that of Zhou Yang in China. Both were official propagandists. But Luo, who knew the history of May Fourth more intimately, was able to augment its official meanings more directly by placing his own memories in the service of an anti-Communist interpretation.

Throughout the 1950s, Luo Jialun joined official commemorations of May Fourth to remind his fellow Guomindang members that the significance of the event of 1919 could not be narrowed down to either literary reform or patriotic protest. Although he shared his audience's hostility to the Communist's claim to May Fourth, Luo never let them forget that the goal of the original movement was nothing short of an encompassing enlightenment. This interpretation was more acceptable in quiet times of political confidence than during moments of intense polemics against the "Communist bandits." 1962 was a relatively quiet commemoration of May Fourth, and during that time Luo Jialun was able to defend his view of enlightenment once again. Reiterating his long-standing disagreement with Hu Shi over limiting the meaning of May Fourth to a language renaissance, Luo insisted that only enlightenment in the sense of the German *Aufklärung*—literally, to suffuse with the light of critical reason—was appropriate for May Fourth. In Luo's view it had been nothing short of a "thorough re-evaluation of all old values by means of scientific thought ... a process that no nation can avoid if it wants to become truly modern." As a concession to those who viewed May Fourth as simply a stage in the longer tradition of patriotic protest, he added: "The enlightenment movement and the national salvation movement are inseparable parts of May Fourth and *both* must be given their rightful, objective place in our studies of history."[42]

An unwillingness to forget about the motives and the promises behind the enlightenment movement is characteristic of *New Tide* recollections of May Fourth. As long as May Fourth veterans such as Luo Jialun and Yang Zhensheng were alive, public versions of the event of 1919, both in Taiwan and on the mainland, could not narrow history too much. With the decimation by death of the ranks of those who can recall May Fourth in its complexity, the search grows more intense for other survivors to buttress the official view. In the years during which *New Tide* members faded from public activity due to persecution or neglect, Xu Deheng emerged as the most reliable symbol of the "patriotic" May Fourth. A participant in the student demonstration in Tiananmen Square, Xu has been willing, over and over again, to retell a simplified version of the event of 1919. A prominent intellectual known for his leftist sympathies since the 1930s, Xu did not become identified with party views until he became a member in 1979. Long before the sixtieth anniversary, however, he had written more recollections than any other participant. All of his commemorative essays emphasized the political, as opposed to the cultural, significance of May Fourth. Dwelling on his own activities in the National Salvation Association (*Jiuguo hui*), on his role in founding the *Citizen* journal at Beida, and on his prominence as one of the students in the original demonstration, Xu has been able to construct a counter-history to the enlightenment versions. To justify this counter-history, he has argued that the political May Fourth was anything but a "temporary flare-up in the midst of the larger cultural blaze." Rather, he has claimed that it was the "mad intensity of the new culture movement, instigated by the *New Tide* crowd, which has obscured the true meaning of May Fourth."[43] The "true meaning," of course, is patriotism; or, more precisely, the willingness to sacrifice oneself for the masses.

At the same time, Xu Deheng's remembrances, though selective, have expanded the meanings of May Fourth. Over the years, as he has come to feel more secure in his relationship to the Communist Party, his own role in the event of 1919 has grown larger and larger. His references to the one safe *New Tide* mentor, Li Dazhao, proliferated, along with his repeated expressions of gratitude to Chairman Mao. More recently, Xu Deheng has even paid tribute to Cai Yuanpei, who, despite his "bourgeois ideology ... had created a unique atmosphere of intellectual tolerance and creativity at Beida."[44] When writing about the May Fourth students, although he has endlessly emphasized his own political patriotism in the *Citizen* magazine, as opposed to the cultural iconoclasm of *New Tide* leaders, Xu has also begun to acknowledge the positive contribution of the Beijing University Commoners' Education Lecture Society. Once the lecture society had been incorporated into remembered history, it became more and more difficult to deny the fact of active collaboration between *New Tide* and *Citizen* students.[45] Thus, although political leaders counted on him to narrow the legacy of May Fourth, he has managed to keep it complex, fluid, and full of historical detail. This version is, in the end, unassimilable to Mao Zedong's view of the event of 1919.

Another member of the Commoners' Education Lecture Society who had been counted on to confirm the party line on May Fourth was Zhu Wushan. Closer to the Communist movement than Xu Deheng, Zhu was made the official commemorator of the Society for the Study of Marxist Theory, the one group to link the event of 1919 to the birth of the Chinese Communist Party. Ironically, however, it was Zhu, the May Fourth participant who was expected to remember the details necessary for Mao's version of May Fourth, who called that version into question most directly. An historian who took his profession seriously whenever ideological restraints were relaxed, Zhu ignited a widespread debate in 1962 by publishing an article entitled "Was May Fourth a New Democratic Revolutionary Movement or Not?"

Although the title of Zhu Wushan's article was cautious and openended, his argument was not. Starting from Mao's own definition of new democracy as a revolutionary change led by the proletariat, Zhu drew upon the historical evidence to argue that May Fourth was not such a revolution. Emphasizing the role of students and intellectuals, his version of remembered history contradicted the official interpretation of a proletarian May Fourth. And yet, while quarreling with the most fundamental assumption of Mao's version—that the laboring masses had led the May Fourth movement—Zhu Wushan's essay remained couched in Maoist terminology:

It is my personal understanding that Chairman Mao never once said that May Fourth was led by the proletariat.... To say that May Fourth was a new democratic revolution is to deny historical facts.... In recent years, some people have misinterpreted historical facts by arguing that Li Dazhao had formed a communist group at the Beida library by 1918. This is an obvious case of misinterpretation, imagination, and invention. As far as I can recall, Li Dazhao and Gao Yihan did organize a study group on Marx, but the participants were only professors. There were no students in the group at all. They had no influence in society whatsoever and cannot be linked to May Fourth. Some of those in this study group thought that Marx was Malthus and that what they were studying was population theory rather than class struggle.[46]

Having reconstructed the complex, often confused ideological context that surrounded the outbreak of May Fourth, Zhu Wushan went on to call into question the larger meaning attributed to it. To acknowledge May Fourth as "revolutionary" was one thing; to imply that it was Communist-inspired suggested something altogether different. In fact, he concluded, that was an unforgivable distortion of history:

So what kind of revolutionary movement was May Fourth? Like the Paris Commune, it was a spontaneous uprising, which only later became a proletarian cause.... At the time of May Fourth, the Communist Party was not even founded. It was not the proletariat that led May Fourth, but students and intellectuals. The national bourgeoisie was also very interested in the movement. For example, the big Shanghai industrialist Mu Ouqu put up the money that enabled Luo Jialun, Fu Sinian, and Kang Baiqing to study abroad.... Those who want to make the May Fourth Movement into a new democracy revolution, unfortunately, distort historical facts.... I think this is the lingering habit of traditional Confucian moralism. This cannot be our attitude as Marxists who seek the facts as they actually were.[47]

Zhu Wushan's appeals to Marxism did not detract from the implications of his argument: May Fourth had to be granted some autonomous, pre-Communist space in history. This interpretation called into question other parts of the official version of revolutionary history as well. Zhu's point of view was attacked during the next several years as Mao's views were reasserted with increasing stridency. An unproletarian May Fourth was, as all polemicists understood only too well, an untamed May Fourth. If it were acknowledged that its primary constituency had been comprised of intellectuals, then the role of intellectuals in subsequent history would also have to be sanctioned. This, however, the party and Mao were reluctant to do.

REMEMBRANCE AND THE AUTONOMY OF INTELLECTUALS

Mao Zedong's ambivalence about intellectuals, and by extension, about the May Fourth legacy, had been apparent since the 1930s. The exigencies of broadening support of the Communist Party, however, prevented him from allowing that ambivalence to develop into outright antipathy. Power, Mao knew, had to be shared, or at least it must be presented as shareable to all patriotic, progressive Chinese if his party were to emerge victorious at the end of the civil war. Intellectuals, for a while, were also eager to prove their patriotic credentials and so went along with Mao's call that they merge with the progressive masses. All along, as Zhu Wushan's essay makes clear, they still hoped for a special role in the revolutionary ranks, one that would enable them to continue their mission of cultural enlightenment while contributing to the social transformation at hand. Recollections of May Fourth were used repeatedly by intellectuals to define their own role as critics of culture. This role became, over time, indistinguishable from the identity of intellectuals. They probed its limitations and its promises with all the passion once invested in the event of 1919 itself. Remembrance, thus, emerged as a concrete means of maintaining and developing intellectual autonomy—autonomy both in relationship to political authority and to mass culture as well.

The question—"What does it mean to be an intellectual?"—and its corollary—"What is it that we as intellectuals, and only we, can accomplish on the cultural front?"—became more and more unapproachable in the decades after 1949. As Communist Party control of education and publishing grew firmer, May Fourth veterans found themselves less able to explore their identity publicly. This change in the parameters of discourse did not take them completely by surprise. Some had been preparing for it for quite some time. Mao Dun, for example, had been prompt in taking advantage of the thirtieth anniversary of May Fourth to recall its significance in a way that provided a division of labor (perhaps even power) between intellectuals and the party. Writing in a collection of essays published from the liberated areas in 1949, he reaffirmed the need to continue the May Fourth project of cultural criticism and of emancipation from feudal habits of mind. This project was, in his view, best carried out by intellectuals, for it was they who had long been on guard against the seeds of old culture at work in the lives of their compatriots and in their own lives as well.

Mao Dun's willingness to recall the unfinished aspects of the original enlightenment movement and the intellectuals' special responsibility for its fulfillment was in keeping with his long-standing public commitment to May Fourth. Even in the midst of the war with Japan, when things were going from bad to worse and national salvation was all-important, Mao Dun had insisted that the "spirit of May Fourth" could and should be continued. Like other advocates of enlightenment, he identified that spirit with science and democracy, and went on to reaffirm the legitimacy of their "destructive" impact on inherited values. In 1938, for instance, he claimed that the most significant achievement of May Fourth was its scientific and democratic outlook, which led to the "discovery and emancipation of individuality."[48]

By 1949, to talk of the May Fourth discovery of individuality had become more difficult. Mao Dun's essay, therefore, emphasized the usefulness of the spirit of May Fourth in the collective emancipation of China. The legitimacy of cultural iconoclasm could not be reasserted, however, without an explicit acknowledgment of the peculiarities and limitations of the original iconoclasts: the young intellectuals of the May Fourth generation. Strongly identifying with the "new youths" at Beida, Mao Dun was nonetheless able to portray them critically. He imagined them, and himself, as

sitting in a pavilion with their girlfriends; with one hand they grasp the wine, with the other they bang the table shouting hysterically: "Let's go to the masses! Let's go to the masses!" Intoxicated with individualistic anarchism, these are the sons of decaying families, wearing faded but fancy clothes. They throw away the last bit of their wives' dowry and personal savings and stirring with indignation they shout: "Everything must be destroyed! Everything must be destroyed! Only then can the utopia arise!"[49]

In spite of their addiction to individualism and the frantic urge to connect with the masses, these May Fourth youths had prepared the way for what Mao Dun called in 1949 the "soldiers of the cultural front." When he described the tasks of this new generation of "soldiers," Mao Dun acknowledged their commonality with and their debt to iconoclastic intellectuals. Both had worked toward the emancipation of their countrymen. In fact, he argued, as long as Chinese culture remained mired in its past, these new "soldiers" could not help but act as the iconoclasts had before them: "The creeping vine of feudalist culture is everywhere. It is tangled in our everyday lives. To cut this creeping vine, I am afraid, will take more energy than land reform. And, I'm afraid, it will take longer."[50]

To contrast cultural transformation with land reform and to suggest that it might take longer than the transformation of political and military power was, in effect, to ask for intellectual autonomy. There was no doubt in Mao Dun's essay that "soldiers of culture" were intellectuals, and that their tasks had to be different from those of other soldiers. Therefore, he concluded, those most familiar with the achievement and the limitations of May Fourth should be allowed to carry through the unfinished enlightenment.

After 1949, the discussion of intellectual autonomy became a more risky proposition. Insofar as official authorities had now taken up the fight against the "creeping vine" of feudal culture, intellectuals could no longer rest secure in their gardening role. Furthermore, as their past associations with other iconoclasts were used to indict them as "bourgeois" intellectuals, they themselves came to doubt their special connection to, and responsibility for, enlightenment. Some survived this attack on their identity and on their memories better than others. Philosopher Feng Youlan, as was mentioned earlier, collapsed under the pressure of the Cultural Revolution and proved willing to portray himself as a defender of Confucianism.

Other May Fourth veterans, most notably Gu Jiegang, were able to criticize themselves without thoroughly abdicating their own sense of what they had stood for during the original enlightenment movement. The values of their youth, thus, continued to shape their ongoing commitment to cultural criticism. Gu Jiegang came under attack during the early 1950s, when the climate of opinion was still rather respectful toward intellectuals. His confession/recollection of May Fourth appeared in an essay entitled "Hu Shi as I See Him." Although this essay was supposed to conform to general guidelines for those suspected of "bourgeois" sympathies, Gu managed to make it quite specific and quite faithful to the details of his own past history. In fact, this "confession" stands out for its remarkably objective description of the intellectual mood at Beida during the height of the May Fourth movement. It includes information about actual course offerings as well as an overview of the new methodologies pioneered in literary and historical criticism. Gu's essay acknowledges the significant, positive influence of Hu Shi on the younger generation of May Fourth intellectuals. When he finally comes around to indicting Hu Shi, Gu does not disassociate himself from his mentor but rather, after enumerating Hu Shi's shortcomings, he confesses them to be the same as his own:

Both Hu Shi and I come from traditional literati families. Both of us were interested in history and the problems of historical proof.... He brought new methodologies from the United States that I did not know about, so I became his follower.... Now, using Marxism, I can see clearly Hu Shi's and my own misconception: pragmatism cannot save China.... In the past twenty years, I have gradually been aware of this problem. But my own petty bourgeois tenderheartedness prevented me from making the break.... Now, under the leadership of Chairman Mao, I can find the correct solution.[51]

Gu Jiegang's confession testifies to the efforts of May Fourth intellectuals to safeguard a sense of history while following the official doctrine. This was not an easy undertaking. Mao Zedong himself, and officials acting in his name, were too hungry for the remembrances, the confessions, and the commemorations of May Fourth intellectuals to let them assess their own identity apart from the dictates of political revolution. And yet, despite the repeated pressure put upon May Fourth veterans to reorganize, rewrite, even reinvent their past for the sake of the present, they managed to hold on to some bits of their personal history. After the Cultural Revolution, when the waves of political mobilization subsided, they used those bits to create a new, more complex image of May Fourth. In contrast to earlier decades, May Fourth veterans can now commemorate their Beida comrades, and by implication themselves, more openly.

A recent tribute by Gu Jiegang's fellow *New Tide* member, Guo Shaoyu, to their schoolmate Zhu Ziqing illustrates well the new possibilities for using remembrance to consolidate a sense of intellectual identity. Unlike Gu, who had been forced to denounce himself through his association with his Beida mentor Hu Shi, Guo Shaoyu was able to recall Zhu Ziqing's Confucian virtues in a more positive light. By dwelling on Zhu's difficult struggle to live up to and at the same time transcend the ethical standards of his literati ancestors, Guo Shaoyu drew attention to a challenge faced by the entire generation of May Fourth intellectuals:

Zhu Ziqing was a righteous literatus who became a warrior.... He lived according to the old classical maxim of righteous intellectuals: "There are some things that the righteous gentleman will not consent to." During the war resistance, he was unable to join the ranks of anti-Japanese fighters or to flee to the liberated base areas. Still, he never compromised his conscience by joining the other side.... Unlike others who posed as "righteous" literati but who, in reality, were all too comfortable with compromising ways of the world, who only wanted to play it safe under all circumstances, Zhu Ziqing was anything but easygoing in his effort to live up to these traditional Confucian virtues.[52]

The warmth with which Guo Shaoyu commemorated Zhu Ziqing in 1978 stands in marked contrast to Gu Jiegang's cautious recollection of Hu Shi in 1951. And yet, in spite of the disparity in tone between these two efforts at remembered history, both authors make clear their determination to probe their own identity as intellectuals through appeals to a shared past. Their increasingly complex references to the past suggest a more resilient self-image in the present. This quest for identity through remembrance links May Fourth intellectuals to a very distant soulmate: Marcel Proust. In a very different context, and for far more personal reasons, Proust had placed memory at the pinnacle of various means of self-discovery. He described the joys and the discipline of remembrance in terms quite close to those of Chinese intellectuals: "On cherche à retrouver dans les choses devenues par là précieuses, le reflet que notre âme a projeté sur elles" (We seek to recover in things, dear to us on that account, the reflection cast by our spirit upon them).[53]

In Mao's China, the memory of May Fourth grew more and more precious as intellectuals looked for their embattled spirit mirrored in its depth. *New Tide* member Sun Fuyuan's 1955 essay entitled "Remembrances of That Year of May Fourth" captures this Proustian quest most effectively. Having survived repeated waves of political mobilization, this student of Lu Xun and Zhou Zuoren now chose to tell the story of his own generation in its own terms. Sun could afford to do this because of his rather safe position in the Communist world of letters. A pioneer of mass education in the 1920s and of mass literature in the 1930s, he had been known as a fellow traveler ever since his days as professor of literature at Sichuan University in the 1940s. Protected by his reputation as a "progressive intellectual," Sun Fuyuan was thus able to explore some of the more complex aspects of the remembered history of May Fourth. To highlight the limitations of memory itself—something few others dared to do in their made-to-order recollections—Sun began his essay with an anecdote about fading impressions of May Fourth. His story, in effect, contradicted those who pretended to remember all and to know exactly what the event of 1919 meant, or should have meant:

Thirty-five years have passed since May Fourth. The historical significance of May Fourth seems to become clearer every day. Yet concrete impressions of what May Fourth was like grow hazier every year.... This brings to mind a conversation I had with Qian Xuantong twenty years ago when he told me he remembered how I and fellow students from Beida had been flogged in jail during May Fourth. Qian said: "I remember distinctly your torn summer robe and Manchurian-style hat...." In fact, nothing like this really happened. Now, if an eminent professor's memory can become so fuzzy after only fifteen years, how much more so ours thirty-five years later![54]

After this caveat, Sun goes on to disclaim the "honor" of contributing to political commemorations of the event of 1919. That glory is abundantly clear already, he tells us. His own purpose here is simply to fill out the picture with assorted concrete impressions of that year: "My intention is not to perform the tasks of the researchers. I cannot examine all the books and periodicals. All I can hope to do is to record some remembrances. Individual recollections are, to be sure, unreliable. But they may become more reliable when they are corroborated by and compared with others—such as those of Xu Deheng and others."[55]

Even while hiding behind the eminence of official commemorators like Xu Deheng, Sun Fuyuan manages to compose a memoir incomparable in detail and tone of reflection. Unlike Xu, who had repeatedly sketched a portrait of patriotic students allied with the working class, Sun describes his schoolmates as young cultural rebels materially better off than the common people and separated from them by a gulf of ideas, as well as by the difference in living standards. To explain the catalytic impact of this small group of youthful radicals, Sun presents a detailed picture of the communication network of the year 1919. Telephones, the telegraph, and even newspapers were, according to him, in a state of appalling backwardness. News and information could circulate only by word of mouth.

Able to read foreign language newspapers and full of the self-righteousness of traditional literati, Sun recalls, he and his fellow students were eager to shoulder their "special responsibilities" for enlightening the general population. Unconscious of the class nature of social injustice, they were able to respond more promptly and more passionately to the injuries to their nation than their less educated countrymen:

Pressing down on the heads of young intellectuals at the time were two great mountains: one was the huge mountain of feudalism, which the 1911 revolution had sought to oppose but did not succeed in overcoming, and the other big mountain was imperialism, which the 1911 revolution did not dare to oppose but avoided rather brazenly.... We felt that we understood national matters better than others. While all the people in the country groaned under these two mountains, we, above others, had the deepest and weightiest responsibilities.[56]

Sun Fuyuan's remembrance portrays May Fourth students full of their class and cultural peculiarities. And yet, even with their limitations, or perhaps because of them, these educated youths appear truly heroic. Whether describing their silent, tearful march back to Beida after being released from jail or their impassioned response to Lu Xun's "Diary of a Madman," Sun Fuyuan never loses sight of the qualities of heart and mind that made it possible for the students to act boldly in circumstances that left their compatriots full of despair. His conclusion reveals at once humility in the face of history and nostalgia for its glories:

> May Fourth was the source, the earliest, minuscule headwater for what became the great river of the Chinese Revolution. What I witnessed was but a fragment. There is so much that I did not see. So much I had no way of understanding. Maybe even the little bit I did see, I got all wrong. Still, in the depths of my heart I feel thoroughly content, thoroughly at peace with myself... much like a thirty-five-year-old who remembers nursing at the breast.[57]

To identify oneself so closely with May Fourth—to the point of imagining the event of 1919 not only as a source of the Chinese revolution but as a maternal breast still nourishing the aspirations of its descendants—was quite rare in Mao's China. Sun Fuyuan's tribute to May Fourth, and by extension to his own generation of cultural rebels, however, was not unique. Others, too, returned repeatedly to remembrances of this fragment of the past in order to plead for more intellectual autonomy in the present. At times when political authorities expanded the parameters of acceptable criticism, May Fourth veterans, in alliance with a new generation of university students, were able to put forward their plea more directly. And yet, even in moments such as 1957, when political and cultural dissent was briefly sanctioned in Taiwan as well as on the mainland, the urge to "nurse at the breast" of May Fourth remained strong. The very strength of the bond between intellectuals and May Fourth suggests that they had found no other way to remind their compatriots of the unfinished project of enlightenment except to recall, over and over again, their own indebtedness to the event of 1919.

1957: PASSING ON THE SPIRIT OF MAY FOURTH

May Fourth participants such as Sun Fuyuan had maintained a measure of autonomy only with great difficulty. By 1957, these intellectuals were in their sixties. They had little reason to risk contradicting official historiography. Yet some continued to take that risk and to quarrel with politics by retelling the allegory of May Fourth. While older cultural rebels had been content to use symbolic narratives, another, more impatient generation was coming of age. Inspired by the allegory of May Fourth, they took it to heart far more than the political authorities it had been intended for. The older generation had written and rewritten the "true story of May Fourth" to keep alive their earlier ideals. The students of 1957 seem to have derived their ideals from the stories themselves. They had no way of knowing the historical details of the New

Cultural movement. What they were intensely curious about was the "spirit of May Fourth." Frustrated by the ossified hierarchies of power in Taiwan and on the mainland, these younger intellectuals judged their contemporary society by the standard of an idealized May Fourth. When they found it wanting, they declared themselves ready to make society live up to the image of a nearly perfect enlightenment.

Not surprisingly, political leaders, who had been consistently more sympathetic to national salvation than to cultural enlightenment, were less than enthusiastic about the students' determination to revive the spirit of May Fourth. Nonetheless, the spirit was passed on and it proved harder and harder to crush. The allegory, then, took on a life of its own. It continued to inspire new generations ready to rebel against the arbitrary authority of more contemporary political overlords.

In Taiwan, the allegory of May Fourth broke out of the confines of generational memory in a 1957 editorial in the journal *Ziyou Zhongguo* (*Free China Fortnightly*). This magazine provided a concrete contact between luminaries of the *New Youth* generation such as Hu Shi, members of the *New Tide* such as Mao Zishui, and less prominent young writers such as Lei Zhen. Entitled "Rekindle the Spirit of May Fourth," this editorial expressed the hopes and dismay of a new generation of cultural rebels. In the 1950s' struggle for intellectual freedom, participants of May Fourth tended to make their points indirectly. Fond of quoting Bertrand Russell and John Dewey, they tried to keep the goal of a scientific enlightenment in the minds of Guomindang authorities who insisted that national salvation—this time clothed in the slogan "Recover the Mainland"—was the goal that mattered most. Younger editors of *Free China Fortnightly*, on the other hand, insisted on talking in a more pointed manner about the implications of May Fourth. In 1957, they tried to rekindle not only a mood of general tolerance for different points of view but also the spirit of active criticism. More impatient than the older intellectuals, they waved the banner of an idealized May Fourth in the face of their more timid mentors as well as conservative political authorities. Their commemorative essay proclaimed: "Thirty-eight years ago, on May Fourth, China experienced its most meaningful, most precious day. What this day shows is the ability of awakened individuals to set in motion a genuine enlightenment movement in China."[58]

Worried that the spirit of May Fourth might die out because of the timidity of surviving participants, younger intellectuals made explicit their determination to appropriate the allegory. They declared themselves ready to take on that challenge. Now, as so often before, commitment to enlightenment was couched in the language of patriotism: "This

day of May Fourth belongs to those progressives who want a renewed
China.... It also belongs to truly patriotic Chinese.... In the past seven
or eight years, this day has become an inauspicious symbol. Most young
people don't even known what occasion this is. A few scholars who
understand bury it deeply in their hearts and wish that May Fourth as a
day of commemoration would pass into oblivion."[59]

The language of patriotic devotion wore thin, however, when the progressive spirit of May Fourth was held up against "reactionary supporters
of China's venerable civilization." Carrying on the unfinished project of
enlightenment in more modern and more psychological terms, the editors of *Free China Fortnightly* argued that traditional culture had become
rotten from within. Now it could appeal only to naive and selfish
powerholders, "who understand nothing about true nationalism." Unable to name Jiang Jieshi directly, they wrote: "Those who at the present
ceaselessly talk of restoring the old take as their motto 'historical culture.' Whether they talk elegantly or officially, their views are all rooted
in an outworn self-defense mechanism."[60]

The mood of young dissenters in Taiwan in 1957 was at once bleak
and militant. May Fourth was, therefore, held up as a talisman, a sign of
hope in the face of the growing opposition to intellectual and political
reform. The editorial "Rekindle the Spirit of May Fourth" ended on a
note of cautious optimism: "The vitality of May Fourth is [presently]
being sapped by the scornful destruction of backward reactionaries....
The heroes of May Fourth seem to be spending their days in winter
hibernation. However, winter will melt, spring will return, the force of
science and democracy will once again infuse the whole free world."[61]
Winter, however, worsened before spring could come. By 1960, Lei
Zhen was jailed in Taiwan on charges of subversion and the magazine
Free China Fortnightly was suppressed despite Hu Shi's efforts to guard
it with his own prestige. Nonetheless, the spirit of May Fourth, once
rekindled, did not die out. Some years later, the newly founded journal
University Monthly (*Daxue zazhi*) again called for a revival of May Fourth.
Its editors also faced political repression.

On the Chinese mainland, the springtime of free thought also beck-
oned in the first half of 1957. The "Hundred Flowers movement" inaugurated by Mao Zedong openly invited criticism from intellectuals.
Although cautious at first, intellectuals eventually responded eagerly, far
more so than Mao had expected. For a while, the allegory of May Fourth
provided a cover for their criticism of the Communist Party's monopoly
over cultural and political life. Again, as in Taiwan, older participants in
the event of 1919 were more guarded in their appeal to May Fourth than

younger students. A unified revival of the spirit of criticism, however, made the voices of these intellectuals louder and more dangerous than either generation had anticipated. Both generations became vulnerable. Many were labeled "rightists" for their fidelity to the ideals of enlightenment.

In March 1957, less than a month after Mao's speech "On the Correct Handling of Contradictions among the People"—a speech that sanctioned criticism more officially than others had—Gu Jiegang agreed to talk publicly about his own interpretation of the slogan "Let a Hundred Flowers Bloom, Let a Hundred Schools Contend." In an article published in *Guangming ribao*, Gu called for a selective emulation of the spirit of May Fourth. Like the May Fourth intellectuals in Taiwan, he was concerned with defending freedom of speech, which he described as the primary condition for intellectual creativity during his days at Beida. With the anti-Hu Shi and anti-Yu Pingbo campaigns still fresh in mind, Gu Jiegang argued that Cai Yuanpei's policy of "broad tolerance"—the very ideal reasserted in Taiwan by Hu Shi and Mao Zishui—was still needed in China to counter the "stifling impact of dogmatism on our scholarly pursuits." Gu quoted Mao Zedong profusely, and he made it clear that he was not advocating "limitless freedom of speech"—again, an echo of Taiwan liberals who argued that free speech was not necessarily anti-Guomindang. In the end, Gu Jiegang appealed simply for "a modest, practical improvement in the material conditions of scholarly research: less time in meetings, better management of documentary collections in our libraries, and a supply of research assistants to help older, more experienced scholars carry on the work of training the next generation."[62]

A month later, in April 1957, Zhang Shenfu also wrote an article about the Hundred Flowers campaign for the *Guangming ribao*. Eager to speak out after more than seven years of enforced silence, Zhang was more optimistic than Gu Jiegang. Convinced that the time for a thorough revival of May Fourth was at hand, he entitled his polemic "Develop the Spirit of May Fourth: Emancipate Thought!" Inspired by the "wise words of Chairman Mao," he reminded his countrymen that the intellectual progress of May Fourth was inextricably bound up with freedom of speech. He emphasized "emancipation" rather than the "tolerance" advocated by Gu Jiegang, arguing that active criticism of contemporary habits of mind was legitimate and necessary. Not limiting his strictures of scholarly inquiry, Zhang took on Marxism-Leninism as an example of an ossified worldview in need of thought emancipation: "Marxism-Leninism, too must be applied critically to the needs of

29.   Zhang Shenfu, during an interview with the author, May 1980.

China. . . . It too must be infused with more of the May Fourth spirit of
intellectual emancipation." In the end, Zhang praised the Hundred
Flowers campaign because it promised to take the legacy of enlightenment one step further. "We should not be afraid of controversy. We
should not be afraid of shouting out loud. The Chinese intellectuals'
tradition of passive, negative resistance, bred out of powerlessness, must
now be put behind us."[63]

Zhang Shenfu's vaguely worded statement showed every sign of being
fulfilled by a new generation of young intellectuals during the thirty-
eighth anniversary celebration of May Fourth at Beijing University. Inspired by the allegory of enlightenment, these youths now took it upon
themselves to proclaim aloud their own interpretations of the spirit of
May Fourth. Like young dissenters in Taiwan, Beida students went
beyond the spirit celebrated by older intellectuals. They tried to break
through the timidity and the preference for indirect criticism that had
become a habit for survivors like Zhang Shenfu. Where the older intellectuals spoke of tolerance and emancipation, the students linked May

Fourth with "revolution" and "destruction." A young physics instructor, Tan Tianrong, wrote in his essay "Fragmentary Thoughts on May Fourth":

Old ways die slowly, so the new is slow in being born as well. ... The forces of the new, however, cannot wait forever, so they must set out to destroy the old. This is revolution ... but revolution is by necessity always incomplete. For the new invariably becomes old and stands in the way of what is still newer. The old says: "Why should I shed my sweat and blood in vain? I deserve to enjoy my comforts." The new says: "Your comfort is my pain. You are obstructing my path." Thus, the play is staged over and over again, and revolution seems perennially incomplete.[64]

The urge to "complete the revolution," or at least to get on with their own part of it, was at the base of the Beida students' evocation of the spirit of May Fourth. They, like the *New Tide* generation three decades earlier, tried to rebel against the ethic of submission, whether Marxist or Confucian. "After classes have finally been abolished," they asked themselves, "what ethic will be immune to the doubt of reason?"[65] In spite of their appeal to critical reason, the new intellectuals were keenly aware of their own unreasonable impatience with the values of their elders. They were more frustrated in their efforts to emancipate themselves than May Fourth intellectuals had been in their days at the Beida. Even while they proclaimed the possibility of total emancipation, they had premonitions of their own inability to live up to the allegory of May Fourth. Tan Tianrong, for example, although optimistic in his evocation of the revolutionary legacy of May Fourth, pondered its fate in the hands of his own generation in a brief meditation entitled "Failure." He wrote:

I used to have a precious plant. It had a bud, but never bloomed. Impatient, I tore it open. Then, I watched it wither day after day. I cannot make it close the way it was before. I never got to see the flower I had pried it open for.

I also had a dream. I didn't like it because it was vague. I tore it to bits, carelessly. Then, awake, I kept waiting, hoping for another dream. In vain. So I lost both chances. I can't seem to have the good dream I dream about.[66]

Not only did Tan Tianrong's dream fail to be realized, it quickly turned into a nightmare. He, and so many others who put up posters at Beijing University in 1957, were labeled "rightists" by the authorities. Their commemorations of May Fourth were collected in a volume labeled "poisonous weeds," to instruct others tempted to follow in their footsteps. Zhang Shenfu, too, was labeled a rightist and removed from public life for another two decades. Gu Jiegang, although not labeled, came under suspicion for his cautious advocacy of the lessons of May Fourth.

Still, the commitment to enlightenment would not wane. The allegory had lost its indirectness when it was appropriated by the students of 1957. From then on, May Fourth could no longer be viewed simply as an inspirational story for intellectuals. It had become a "torch" that could at any moment illuminate dark corners of Chinese political and cultural life. Those who would carry on that torch risked being burned themselves. But, as a poem by Liu Jisheng, another young instructor labeled a rightist in 1957, made clear, as long as problems exposed by May Fourth remained unsolved in "People's China," enlightenment continued to be compelling for one and all:

TORCH-OF MAY FOURTH, BURN ON!

My praise
is dedicated to the torch
My passion is dedicated to the torch-bearing madman.
Ah, flame of May Fourth
though you have been dimmed for years
the time has come
to burn again
As fiercely as thirty-eight years ago
As brilliantly as thirty-eight years ago
As magnificently as thirty-eight years ago
When you burned down the mansion of Cao [Rulin].
Today, you are needed to burn down wall-less walls
The chains of ideology
The hypocritical masks
Hearts stilled by fear
Blood frozen in timid veins ...
All need your revolutionary flame.
In this new era, burn again,
You long-dimmed torch of May Fourth.
So what if critics misunderstand your aims!
So what if cowards blame you for being extreme!
Let all those too comfortable with winter sleep,
Mock you for stirring up trouble.
Proclaim to them proudly:
Though our flame will never hurt our comrades
It will never be used
To gently bandage mankind's running sores.[67]

Conclusion:
The Enduring Challenge
of Enlightenment

Revolutions may be able to abolish despotism, profit seeking. But they are unable, by themselves, to reform ways of thinking. New prejudices, like the old ones they replaced, will emerge to enchain, to control the great unthinking mass.

Immanuel Kant, "What Is Enlightenment?"[1]

In 1784, when Kant wrote his essay "What Is Enlightenment?," political revolution was more of an abstract problem than a concrete reality. Another half a decade would pass before Kant himself would become an ambivalent spectator of the French Revolution. He observed its promises and excesses from his quiet provincial hometown in Germany. Earlier, ill-fated experiments with republican forms of government in England and the Netherlands had left a deep impact on the European philosophers of Kant's generation.[2] But the memory of failed revolution did not weight nearly as heavily on their minds as it did on those of the twentieth-century Chinese champions of enlightenment. Having participated in and survived several rounds of political upheaval from the Republican Revolution of 1911 through the Cultural Revolution of 1966–69, they had a painfully intimate understanding of Kant's warning that revolutions "by themselves" are unable to change ways of thinking. They had witnessed the re-emergence of new prejudices and superstitions masked by the language and authority of national salvation. Unlike Kant, however, Chinese intellectuals could not take refuge in blaming "the great unthinking mass." They themselves had been prey to blind belief in moments when patriotism and the pressure for political conformity had drowned out the quieter imperatives of intellectual emancipation.

And yet, looking back over the history of the May Fourth enlightenment, one cannot help but be struck by the perseverance of those who battled against the old, outworn feudal mentality. The object of their thought movement was quite different in origin from the superstitious beliefs that were the main target of attack during the European enlightenment. The Chinese ethic of self-submission turned out to be more pervasive and more deeply rooted in the minds of the people than the religious fanaticism of the European masses. Without the concept of God or the institution of the Church to enforce theological orthodoxy, Confucian China had managed to indoctrinate its population for centuries with two unquestionable absolutes: (a) that the Central Kingdom was the pinnacle of world civilization, and (b) that the conventions governing social hierarchy were ideally suited to the needs of human nature. Those intellectuals who arose in twentieth-century China to quarrel with these assumptions faced a more protracted struggle than the European *philosophes* who fought against religious superstitions.

Eighteenth-century critics of religion had the benefit of more than two hundred years of scientific thought and commercial development behind them. Long before materialist skeptics such as Voltaire or his more radical compatriot the Baron d'Holbach took it upon themselves to dismantle the structure of Christian dogma, still-faithful explorers of the natural world such as Descartes had begun to develop the principles of rational doubt. On the basis of those principles, monarchs and aristocratic subjects alike had been able to build affluent, worldly communities that had prepared the way for enlightenment. Members of these cosmopolitan subcultures managed to free themselves from the hegemony of inherited beliefs that controlled the lives and thoughts of what Kant later termed "the great unthinking mass." In China, on the other hand, a cosmopolitan worldview was more difficult to achieve and to maintain. It had to emerge out of a forcible, humiliating encounter with Western imperialism. Thus, the reorientation in the intellectuals' perspective did not have the measured pace of the European enlightenment. May Fourth participants who tried to wage war against the feudal habit of mind had to condense into mere decades a process that had taken centuries to unfold in Europe. Their intellectual as well as their material life had a quality of breathlessness best captured in the following reminiscence by Hu Shi:

And the rapidity of it all! Within my own life, I read all the beloved novels by lamp of vegetable oil; I saw Standard Oil invading my own village, I saw gas lamps in Chinese shops in Shanghai.... I travelled in sedan chairs, wheelbarrows, and small river boats rowed by men; in 1904, I saw the streets of the International Settlement in Shanghai crowded at night by sedan chairs carrying beautiful singing girls hurrying to their calls; the horse carriage was then the fashion in Shanghai, the most modern city. I saw the first tramway operated in Shanghai in 1909.... My first trip on a steamship was when I was only two years old, but I never rode in a motor car before coming to the United States in 1910, and did not travel in the air until 1928. And my people have travelled with me from the vegetable oil lamp to electricity, from the wheel-barrow to the Ford car, if not the airplane, and this in less than forty years' time![3]

Most Chinese people, in fact, did not make the leap from oil lamp to electricity and from wheelbarrow to Ford car as rapidly as Hu Shi claimed. Intellectuals did, and only metaphorically at that. As a result, their efforts toward enlightenment were hastier, more superficial than those of European *philosophes* who had been well-to-do citizens of commercial empires as well as beneficiaries of a long history of rationalist philosophy. The hastiness of the cultural movement in twentieth-century China, augmented by the pressures of political revolution, forced its participants as well as its spiritual heirs again and again to come to terms with the incomplete nature of the May Fourth enlightenment. Unfinished, the legacy of May Fourth simmers below the surface of all current claims that China finally is fully launched on the way to modernization. May Fourth continues, to this day, to serve as a reminder of the lack of freedom of thought and freedom of expression in a society in which the material trappings of modernity—motorcycles, Western-style clothes, free interaction with foreigners—are increasingly available to larger and larger numbers of people. In these circumstances, the challenge of keeping alive the spark of May Fourth grows more difficult, but not, however, impossible—especially since the changing circumstances of Chinese social life have recreated over and over again the very conditions of internal repression and outside influence that gave birth to the May Fourth movement in the first place.

In assessing the impact of this incomplete enlightenment movement on twentieth-century Chinese history, three issues have become clear: first, that the commitment to cultural criticism has long been in tension with another commitment—national salvation. This tension has forced advocates of an anti-feudal new culture to prove their patriotic credentials, often at the cost of fidelity to the ideals of the original May Fourth. Second, the fate of enlightenment in modern China has become inseparable from the fate of intellectuals. Both have been vulnerable to the charge that they erode nationalist confidence; both are an irritating reminder that mass culture and revolutionary politics remain suffused with the old ethic of subservience. Thirdly, the enlightenment movement, far from being able to eradicate the roots of the old culture and old habits of mind, has served to reveal their perseverance in all aspects of Chinese life. In fact, the more insistent the intellectuals' call for autonomy has been over the past six decades, the more tenacious the voices of political authorities opposing it.

Even so, an awareness of the burden of outworn beliefs has not been squelched over the years. In spite of frequent appeals to the greatness of Chinese tradition, a small group of critically minded intellectuals has continued to point out the shortcomings of native culture. These unrepentant critics have been inspired by the example of Lu Xun. More than two decades before the Communist victory of 1949, Lu had already warned against the temptation of lapsing back into old habits of mind. In a 1925 essay entitled "The Great Wall," Lu Xun, like Kant before him, tried to alert his readers of the fact that "prejudices"—or, in the Chinese context, unquestioned loyalty to convention—are far more resilient than champions of critical reasoning had expected:

I am always conscious of being surrounded by a Great Wall. The stonework consists of old bricks reinforced at a later date by new bricks. They have combined to make a wall that hems us in. When will we stop reinforcing the Great Wall with new bricks? A curse on this wonderful Great Wall![4]

When Lu Xun wrote about the "new bricks" used to reinforce the Great Wall, he was drawing attention to the same problem that Kant had described on the eve of the French Revolution: that the mental walls of prejudice and convention are constantly in the process of being rebuilt, even in the midst of seemingly revolutionary change. Once Lu Xun became aware of being "surrounded," "hemmed in" by the monuments and the values of a tradition that others regarded as the source of China's greatness, he became the madman he himself had written about in 1918. His choice, like that of other advocates of enlightenment in China, was either to inadvertently aid in the rebuilding or to actively curse the Great Wall within the minds of Chinese people.

ENLIGHTENMENT VERSUS NATIONAL SALVATION

Some walls had to be breached first: the wall around China, imperialism; and the wall within China, class oppression. Only then did the tenacity of other walls within the mind become fully apparent. May Fourth veterans who joined in the social movements of the 1920s and 1930s retained their commitment to enlightenment because they kept on being frustrated by these other mental walls. Even as they came to terms with political violence—first with the White Terror and then with the urgency of war mobilization against Japan—they continued to confront the cultural inertia of their countrymen. They grew suspicious of political reform and revolution even as they participated in it, even as they remade themselves from *xuezhe*, scholars, into *zhishi fenzi*, members of the intelligentsia. Enlightenment, thus, developed alongside revolution, never quite synonymous with it.

In the course of that development, advocates of enlightenment had to constantly ally themselves with as well as defend themselves against those consumed by the urgency of national salvation. Nationalist revolutionaries were and still are suspicious of intellectuals who dwell on the problem of *guomin xing* (national character). Raising high the banner of patriotism, these revolutionaries continue to attack those who would hold on to the "spirit of May Fourth" in times that, in their view, require national unity above all. This nationalist assault on the legacy of May Fourth has been going on for a number of decades already. One of the earliest critics of *qimeng* (enlightenment) in the name of *jiuguo* (national salvation) was none other than Qu Qiubai, Lu Xun's friend and disciple in Shanghai during the early 1930s. On the occasion of the thirteenth anniversary of the event of 1919 (occurring shortly after the Japanese attack on North China), Qu launched a rather typical diatribe against the foreign-inspired legacy of May Fourth. His essay "Please Take Off the Mantle of May Fourth" was addressed to young admirers of enlightenment as well as to participants in the original New Culture movement itself. Foreshadowing the tone of subsequent attacks, Qu Qiubai's essay argued that all talk of restoring the spirit of May Fourth and of continuing the unfinished tasks of May Fourth was nothing but a hindrance to the anti-imperialist mobilization of the masses:

There is no cause left over from May Fourth.... China's cultural movement must now follow the needs of the revolution. Intellectuals and students must now take off the once-brilliant mantle of May Fourth!! What is needed, and what ought to be, is that they all gather under the banner of anti-imperialism. The step forward we are about to take has nothing to do with May Fourth.[5]

As the war against Japan got under way in the late 1930s and early 1940s, Qu Qiubai's point of view gained more and more adherents. Faced with the danger of China's political annihilation, May Fourth intellectuals found that cultural criticism was increasingly difficult to legitimate to themselves, much less to others. Nonetheless, they reasserted the priority of *qimeng* in the very midst of this pressure to concentrate on *jiuguo*. This was because they could not shut their eyes to the re-emergence of feudal habits of mind that had accompanied patriotic

mobilization. *New Tide* veteran Fu Sinian, writing a decade after Qu
Qiubai, was one of the most vocal defenders of the "spirit of May
Fourth" during the war of resistance to Japan. Having refused for a
number of years to participate in official commemorations of the event of
1919, he finally came out of this self-enforced silence. Angered by the
frequent talk of "the shortcomings of May Fourth" in the newspapers
and magazines of his own party, the Guomindang, Fu was unwilling to
acquiesce to this general desire to forget about May Fourth.[6] He tried to
remind readers that national salvation and national renewal are impossible without a commitment to persevere in the cultural criticism inaugurated during the original May Fourth enlightenment:

> If we drag a four-thousand-year-old garbage can on our backs, how can we
> still have the energy to be a modern nation capable of resisting the enemy and
> working hard?... Today, there are some people who think that the kind of
> re-evaluation that took place during May Fourth harmed the nation's self-
> confidence ... but with sheltered exaggerations, how can there be confidence in
> the future?... With self-confidence commissioned from the stone age or the
> period of the "Beijing Man," how can we hope to have a shred of self-confidence
> left a hundred years from now?[7]

To talk of inherited beliefs as a "four-thousand-year-old garbage can"
and to raise doubts about the "sheltered exaggerations" that were and
still are the foundations of patriotic loyalties was to risk appearing "un-
Chinese." May Fourth intellectuals such as Fu Sinian had been taking
that risk ever since they first called for a critical evaluation of traditional
ethics during the May Fourth movement at Beida. In the interval from
the patriotic demonstration of 1919 to the Anti-Japanese War of 1937–
45, the pressure to demonstrate one's nationalist sympathies by with-
holding criticism of the cultural past increased. Those who persisted in
their commitment to enlightenment did so knowing that its foreign origins, or rather its inspiration in Western models of critical thought,
could and would be used against them. In 1949, for example, Communist theoretician Feng Naichao condemned the May Fourth intellectuals
in the following terms:

> They lack "Chineseness" (*zhongguo xing*) and "peopleness" (*renmin xing*) and
> these shortcomings lead them to commit all sorts of mistakes, to do many bad
> things. If one loses one's "Chineseness" and one's "peopleness" then one be-
> comes a slave of foreigners and dogmatic masters.... For example, May
> Fourth figures such as Chen Duxiu, who looked down upon the might of working
> people, lost their position among the people and thus drifted from the Chinese
> Revolution. Hu Shi, who only saw the glory of Western civilization but was
> blind to imperialism, ceased to be Chinese and became the house slave of for-
> eigners.[8]

Declared un-Chinese and unpopular, May Fourth became the negative model of cultural revolt—but a model nonetheless. As such, it was preserved both on the mainland and in Taiwan. To this day it continues to withstand the familiar charge of "cultural treason."[9] This charge, at first glance, seems to set Chinese advocates of enlightenment apart from their European predecessors who, though they appealed to foreign models of secular government (not infrequently Chinese), carried on their quarrel with religious authorities on native ground. In fact, however, the eighteenth-century *philosophes*, like the twentieth-century *zhishi fenzi*, had to defend themselves repeatedly against the similar accusation of being too "destructive." In Europe, as in China, rational doubt threatened the deepest certainties which most people had held quite unconsciously. Those who dared to uncover this unthinking attachment to old ideas and old superstitions had to be prepared for the rage of their compatriots. The impetuous tone of their self-defense is captured well in Peter Gay's *The Bridge of Criticism*. "You call us destructive! I have said it before and shall always say it: one must destroy in order to build.... [R]everence for the unworthy is a sign not of respect, but of slavery."[10]

"Unworthy" was an enlightenment code word for the power of outworn beliefs. In Europe it was used to describe those aspects of Christian dogma that had justified the dominance of church over laity, of the absolute monarch over the aristocracy, and of the aristocracy over the rest of society. In China, it was used to attack those Confucian values that had reinforced the subservience of the individual to the family and the state. In both settings, new scientific information about nature or society did not, by itself, suffice to challenge long-standing habits of submission to arbitrary authority. Thus, enlightenment came to connote not just new knowledge, but a reform in ways of thinking.

Intellectuals committed to changing ways of thinking about tradition have been frequently mistaken for rebels against tradition. Their righteous defense of "destruction before construction" only serves to strengthen the case of those who would portray them as totalistic, nearly thoughtless iconoclasts. In fact, European as well as Chinese advocates of enlightenment, however, posed a rather complex challenge to their contemporaries' habitual acquiescence to inherited beliefs. Both *philosophes* and *zhishi fenzi* alike had tried to historicize tradition.[11] By showing how Christianity and Confucianism had grown out of the needs and values of earlier elites, they hoped to weaken the stranglehold of these belief systems on the present. The object of their critique, then, was attachment to tradition far more than tradition itself.

In eighteenth-century Europe, this distinction between ways of think-

ing about tradition and tradition itself was easier to make and to maintain than in twentieth-century China. Post-Renaissance rationalism had
been making inroads upon blind belief long before iconoclastic *philosophes*
joined the fray with the tools of historical and cultural relativism. May
Fourth intellectuals, on the other, faced a more difficult task. They had
to telescope into one lifetime the processes of both the Renaissance and
the Enlightenment. When they took it upon themselves to "reorganize
the national heritage," they had more difficulty than their European
predecessors in persuading contemporaries that they were not out-
and-out enemies of tradition. Skeptics in an age of nationalist revolution, they faced the added obstacle of being seen as traitors of national
culture. Their repeated efforts to prove that rational doubt is not
inherently corrosive of national self-confidence consumed much of the
intellectual energy that might have gone into deepening their own
understanding of critical philosophy.

At times, these Chinese advocates of enlightenment tired of the twofold pressure. To be both vigorously thoughtful and ardently patriotic
was a tall order indeed. Fortunately, whenever May Fourth veterans
found it too exhausting to defend themselves, their spiritual heirs in China and abroad did so on their behalf. One of those heirs whose voice had
been most forceful and most consistent over the years is the historian
Zhou Cezong (Chow Tse-tsung). As early as 1947, he defended the legacy of May Fourth in an article for the national daily *Dagong bao*. Entitled
"Putting on New Clothes to Criticize the Old System," Zhou's essay was
simultaneously a criticism of the pretensions of May Fourth iconoclasts
and an appreciation of their goal to invigorate Chinese culture with ideas
and ideals from abroad.[12] In the decades after 1947, Zhou continued this
double task of explaining and defending the May Fourth legacy. His
masterful study in English, *The May Fourth Movement: Intellectual Revolution
in Modern China*, published in 1960, was unabashedly admiring of cultural
iconoclasm.[13] In 1971, commemorating May Fourth for *University Monthly (Daxue zazhi)* in Taiwan, he reaffirmed the significance of this aspect of
the May Fourth legacy. Responding directly to charges of "cultural
treason" leveled against enlightenment intellectuals in both Nationalist
and Communist historiography, he wrote:

May Fourth intellectuals have been attacked for being preoccupied with the
denial of their Chinese cultural inheritance. I think that this extreme criticism of
Chinese culture was necessary in view of the strength of traditionalism at the
time. Their skepticism served to correct blind faith in the past.... We cannot
keep on blaming others for China's own weakness. [The May Fourth type of]
skepticism can reveal the sources of that weakness. Thus, I believe that the May

Fourth intellectuals' harsh criticisms of tradition were a form of self-criticism....
Any future movement for national salvation must also embark upon this kind of
self-criticism if China is to modernize at all.[14]

By linking national salvation so firmly with cultural criticism, Zhou
Cezong has tried to make the latter cause appear less threatening to
proponents of the first. He has succeeded, somewhat.[15] His claim that
May Fourth intellectuals were really engaging in "self-criticism" rather
than "denial" of the national heritage has not been accepted by political
authorities, who remain suspicious of intellectuals in general. Although
these authorities have been willing at times to sanction cultural criticism
from the top down, they have managed to limit its impact by emphasizing the "un-Chineseness" of rebellious intellectuals. This persistent
attack on *qimeng* in the name of *jiuguo* has served to consolidate the ties
between intellectuals and enlightenment. In view of recent history, critics and defenders of the May Fourth legacy alike have had no reason to
doubt that the fate of cultural awakening in China has become inseparable from the fate of intellectuals.

ENLIGHTENMENT AND INTELLECTUALS

Long before the May Fourth movement, Chinese intellectuals had
been trying to define and to safeguard their sphere of autonomy in relation to political authorities. Modern intellectuals, the heirs of critically
minded scholar-officials, could and did look back upon native traditions
of dissent even as they borrowed new methods of critical analysis from
the West. The most direct source of inspiration was the Confucian distinction between *zhitong*—the rule of authority—and *daotong*—the rule of
virtue under the dictates of reason.[16] Traditional intellectuals who had
developed and maintained this distinction often did so because they were
disappointed with the imperial bureaucracy or unable to secure a position in it. Like the May Fourth veterans we have been describing, these
Confucian literati assumed it was their right to comment upon, even to
criticize, the society around them. In times of political disunity, they
even resorted to foreign ideas, especially those of Indian Buddhism, in
the hopes that such ideas might purge native tradition of its lethargy.
Their motto, *"buguan buzhi er yilun"*—without office or politics, continue
righteous discourse—echoes the spirit of twentieth-century intellectuals
who refused to identify the dictates of political revolution with the promise of cultural enlightenment.[17]

And yet, in spite of these similarities, critically minded literati and
modern intellectuals carried on the project of "righteous discourse"

quite differently. The former had to be content with inward, individual dissent, whereas the latter managed to develop a sense of community that enabled them to oppose arbitrary authority more directly. While traditional scholars cultivated their personal virtue and their poetic sensibility as a bulwark against status worship and the reign of ritual, members of the modern intelligentsia insisted that the best way to combat the ethic of subservience was through the public use of critical reason. In making this assertion, twentieth-century Chinese intellectuals revealed their commonality with modern intellectuals in the West and Japan.[18] Like their foreign comrades, May Fourth advocates of enlightenment used "critical reason" as a code word for activity best suited to the talents and the needs of intellectuals. Without ever expropriating reason from other social classes, they made it clear in their words and in their deeds that critical reflection was more effective when carried on by "knowledgeable elements" rather than by the masses.

Enlightenment, thus, became first and foremost a means through which Chinese intellectuals defined themselves. They became members of a modern intelligentsia by renouncing the bonds of loyalty that had tied generations of their predecessors to the imperial bureaucratic state. In the course of their prolonged struggle for autonomy, they have refined the meaning of emancipation until it has become something quite precise in the Chinese context. In contrast to what their conservative opponents have asserted, enlightenment-oriented intellectuals are not seeking to overthrow the native tradition but rather to quarrel with it on the basis of scientific fact. Rather than trying to emancipate themselves and their compatriots from all political obligations, they are committed to the proposition that politics can never provide the ultimate solution to the problem of feudal mentality. Finally, far from condemning mass culture altogether, they have tried to merge with it, revive it from within while purging it of its own version of the elite's ethic of subservience.

The self-emancipation of intellectuals thus may be seen as part of the broader cultural awakening of Chinese society. May Fourth veterans themselves have argued that their endeavor has facilitated the process of political revolution. Political revolutionaries, in turn, have been eager to portray enlightenment ideas as a prelude to political action. Leaders of revolution in twentieth-century China, in the manner of their predecessors in eighteenth-century France, have designated certain intellectuals as forerunners of their cause. The cult of Lu Xun, for example, in the age of Mao Zedong, not unlike the cult of Rousseau in the age of Robespierre, testifies to an ongoing attempt to causally link enlightenment with revolution. Some cultural iconoclasts have been readily enshrined in the pantheon of progressive intellectuals. The problem of how to evaluate the much larger group of enlightenment survivors still remains. These disconcerting remnants, unlike the safely dead, cannot be fully or safely identified as precursors of political revolution.

In the Chinese context, this dilemma of how to interpret the special link between intellectuals and enlightenment has been reflected in the convolutions of historical criticism. The problem of *pingjia*, criticism (in the sense of how to weigh the praise and the blame assigned to individual May Fourth veterans), has been particularly acute over the years. Prominent intellectuals of the teachers' generation such as Chen Duxiu, Li Dazhao, and Hu Shi have been the object of voluminous and frequently controversial evaluation on both sides of the Taiwan straits. Because they can be easily identified with the goals of one or the other of the contending political parties, their thoughts on cultural emancipation have repeatedly been shrunk down to suit the political needs of the day. Only recently, "liberals" such as Hu Shi have been acknowledged in mainland historiography for their "positive" contribution to the New Culture movement. At the same time, Chen Duxiu, Hu's friend and colleague at Beida, is finally being seen as something more than just a "renegade" from the Communist cause. Even Cai Yuanpei, mentor of the new youths and president of Beida on the eve of May Fourth, has not escaped the vagaries of *pingjia*. When the political requirement of the day was to condemn "capitalist roaders," Cai was simply designated as their cohort, whether he had anything in common with them or not. Now that China is seeking new models for its university system, he has been rehabilitated posthumously as a "pioneer of modern education."[19]

Intellectuals of the students' generation have posed a more complicated problem for political practitioners of "historical criticism." Having outlived their teachers, they have been witnesses to political revolution through several of its cycles from the 1920s through the present. Thus, they cannot be placed quite so neatly into the categories of "progressive" or "reactionary." Attacked repeatedly for their "bourgeois tendencies," they remain useful to this day. Their twin expertise in Western knowledge and traditional Chinese learning makes them a unique asset to the People's Republic. In the last five years it has become even clearer that the more China wants to modernize, the less it can risk to alienate its modern intellectuals. To avoid this, the current government has publicly rehabilitated some of the May Fourth veterans while allowing others to be mentioned in passing in the memoirs of their safer, more eminent comrades.

Selective rehabilitation and remembrance, however, cannot do justice

to the complex bond between May Fourth intellectuals and enlightenment. The question of how they came to adopt the views that they did
and how they refashioned themselves and their ideals in the face of a
history quite inimical to intellectual emancipation remains yet to be in-
vestigated. In this context, conflict-ridden figures such as Zhu Ziqing
provide the most interesting challenge to the shifting conventions of
pingjia. Inward, troubled figures, these intellectuals are not so easily
fashioned into objects of praise or blame. Zhu himself was nearly canon-
ized after his death in 1948 by Mao Zedong. Focusing on the last years
of this intellectual's life, Mao was ready to call him a patriotic hero,
worthy of emulation simply because he had refused to eat flour sent to
China by the United States. Patriotic virtue, however, is too crude a
condensation of the meaning of the life of Zhu Ziqing. For a more complex appreciation of its ambiguities, we must turn to his student, the
Communist theoretician Feng Xuefeng.

Two months after the death of Zhu Ziqing, amidst the polemics that
accompanied the civil war, Feng Xuefeng took some time to commemorate his middle-school teacher. He recalled with candor the shy, gentle
young instructor who came to teach in Yangzhou shortly after graduating from Beida. After recalling the beginnings of their friendship, Feng
went on to trace the inner obstacles Zhu had tried to overcome in his
lifelong effort to keep up with the increasing, violent pace of the Chinese
revolution. Feng Xuefeng, who had as early as 1928 expressed his
empathy for intellectuals, was still sympathetic to them two decades
later. To be sure, the intervening years had made him more critical of
the "tenderheartedness" that marked even the most strident advocates
of enlightenment. Feng now questioned their dedication to "freedom
of thought" in times when the rest of China was groaning under the
oppression of such "real" enemies of freedom as the Japanese and the
Guomindang. Still, he took time to notice and to praise the contribution
of humanistic intellectuals to the revolution at hand:

We heard through Mr. Zhu [Ziqing] the galloping and roaring sound of our own
times. His predicament lets us see what happens to those caught in the great
wheel of history. He enabled us to hear the sounds of a great army, full of soldiers
and horses, as well as the sound of the staggering footsteps of those who carried
great burdens on their backs. They advanced with great difficulty. Nowadays,
so-called progressive intellectuals like Zhu Ziqing are like those burdened by
history. In their effort to push the great wheel forward, they appear not only as
prophets, pioneers, fighters—in sum, heroic figures—but also as people who
fumble, struggle, and move forward, step by step, imperceptibly at times. When
our historical movement has achieved its mission, it will be apparent that its
victory deepened not only the fierce struggle of the masses, and their protest and

heroes; it also drew upon those who reached this destiny staggering, with heavy burdens on their backs. Precisely because his example teaches us so much about the way most intellectuals change, progress, and encourage the revolution, the life of Mr. Zhu [Ziqing] has profound historical significance.[20]

Writing in 1948, Feng Xuefeng's tribute to "tenderhearted" intellectuals like Zhu Ziqing was, by necessity, low-key. His ears filled with the "roaring, galloping" sound of political revolution, this theoretician could not help but express pity for those staggering under the burden of China's cultural legacy. For a brief moment, it seemed as if intellectuals, and only intellectuals, were shouldering that burden—almost by temperamental compulsion, as it were. Since then, however, it has become apparent that this burden is weighing on the "heroic" masses and their "prophetic" political leaders as well. May Fourth advocates of enlightenment, therefore, no longer appear as isolated rebels against the national heritage but rather as pioneers of an intellectual emancipation that has yet to be fulfilled. The more open this acknowledgment of a shared burden becomes in Communist historiography, the less it is possible, or desirable, to distinguish "tenderhearted" thinkers from "tough-minded" fighters. In this context, the historical commonality of May Fourth veterans such as literary scholar Zhu Ziqing and Communist organizer Deng Zhongxia suggests a stronger, more enduring bond between cultural and political revolutionaries.

Recently, this bond has been openly celebrated by ex-propaganda chief Zhou Yang. A more senior, more powerful figure than Feng Xuefeng, Zhou had been directly scorched by the Cultural Revolution of 1966–69. In the first major address marking his re-emergence in public life, he chose to raise anew the question of intellectual emancipation. His essay, prepared for the sixtieth anniversary of May Fourth, leaves no doubt about the enduring burden of tradition, which was previously assumed to be the obsession of iconoclastic intellectuals alone. The address, entitled "Three Great Movements of Intellectual Emancipation," is a coherent argument in favor of continuing the project of May Fourth enlightenment. It connects the event of 1919 with the Yan'an period critique of dogmatic Marxism and the current campaign of Four Modernizations. In contrast to Feng Xuefeng, who had assumed that "freedom of thought" would invariably follow the defeat of such outward enemies as the Guomindang and the Japanese, Zhou Yang points out that "intellectual emancipation" is a more elusive goal than previously imagined. An unlikely heir of the May Fourth legacy, Zhou now writes in glowing terms about the heroic qualities of those who dared to challenge entrenched habits of mind:

A great movement for intellectual emancipation is hardly a simple thing. Even if an old way of thinking is no longer suited to the new trends of historical development, it is still very difficult to change. On the one hand, it has been formed over a long period of time and thus has influenced society profoundly to the point that it has assumed the authority of tradition. On the other hand, it is hard to change because it has the considerable backing of conservative forces in society. Therefore, before the gates of intellectual emancipation are opened, tradition is taken for granted as something sacred and unapproachable.... Because of its penetration of society, it has become a heavy burden on the spirit of the people. To lift it, however, requires not only painstaking effort but a willingness to fight to the death this great entrenched power. Thus, all pioneers of intellectual emancipation [from May Fourth through the present] have had the extraordinary spirit of pursuing truth through self-sacrifice. Quite a few thinkers and scientists have exhibited this spirit throughout history. From within the realm of their own work, they have dared to break out of the prison of old thought to pursue new thought. Without their efforts, it would have been impossible to break through the dark night and see the dawn of a new era.[21]

Zhou Yang's unequivocal tribute to pioneers of intellectual emancipation echoes Lu Xun's 1918 essay "How Are We to Be Fathers Today?" Sixty years earlier, this older advocate of enlightenment had pointed out that those who would lift "the gate of darkness" must be prepared to be crushed by it. In 1979, Zhou Yang, chastised by his own experience during the Cultural Revolution, had reached the same conclusion. He, too, had been overthrown by the forces of fanaticism. In the past, Zhou himself had taken the lead in campaigns against the heirs of May Fourth. Now, he claims to have joined their ranks as a result of witnessing the reemergence of "prejudice." This, according to him, "proves that socialism cannot be built except through intellectual emancipation."[22] Endowing the Communist Party retrospectively with the wisdom he himself had acquired only recently, Zhou Yang concludes: "The consistent policy of our Party has been intellectual emancipation. This has been in keeping with Comrade Mao Zedong's frequent saying that we should emphasize 'liberation' (*fang*) and oppose 'control' (*shou*). 'Liberation' means to dare to criticize, debate, acknowledge mistakes. 'Control' is to prevent people from expressing different views, to prevent them from expressing so-called mistaken opinions. If forced to choose, we must adopt the course of liberation."[23]

Whether the Chinese Communist Party has adopted or will adopt this "course of liberation" remains to be seen. One thing that is clear, however, is that as long as some of its leaders are willing to publicly acknowledge the tenacity of old habits of mind in a presumably new society, enlightenment cannot be fully identified with revolution. The creative tension that still lingers between these two endeavors accounts for the enduring appeal of the spirit of May Fourth to each generation that comes of age in the People's Republic.

THE POST-POLITICAL ENLIGHTENMENT

In the European context, political revolution—the French Revolution of 1789, to be precise—followed the enlightenment movement. The complex relationship between these two historical phenomena remains a subject of debate to this day. In spite of the teleology later imputed by revolutionaries such as Robespierre, who claimed that the enlightenment necessarily "led up to" revolution, there is considerable evidence to suggest that eighteenth-century ideas about the emancipation of intellectuals were far more congenial to enlightened despotism than to a republican form of government. On the other hand, latter-day critics of enlightenment such as Lucien Goldman who argue that enlightened thought is a hindrance to political action also commit the error of oversimplification. They neglect the wide range of political sympathizers and the many organizational connections between the English, Dutch, and French pantheists who, jointly, forged an activist movement now called "the radical enlightenment."[24] But whether it is portrayed as oil or sand in the wheels of revolution, there is no question that the European enlightenment was inextricably linked to it.

In the Chinese context, enlightenment followed revolution, or more specifically, it was, and remains, a manifestation of disillusionment with political revolution. This pattern became apparent during the May Fourth movement itself, as advocates of enlightenment sought to transform their bitter disappointment with the Republican Revolution of 1911 into a pointed criticism of traditional ways of thinking. Their efforts to create a new culture in the period from 1915 to 1921 grew directly out of their realization that institutional reform is quite impotent to challenge long-entrenched worldviews. Horrified to discover that the emperor-worship mentality—marked by a longing to submit to familiar, ceremonial politics—was alive and well long after there was no longer a Son of Heaven on the throne in Beijing, May Fourth intellectuals began to probe more deeply into the reasons for China's prolonged adherence to the ethic of self-submission. The reappearance of servility, dogmatism, and superstition in the wake of radical political action continues to be an object of concern for May Fourth veterans as well as for their spiritual heirs in the People's Republic.

These Chinese advocates of enlightenment were as aware of the resiliency of prejudice as Kant was in his time. Without the benefit of a centuries-long tradition of rational doubt, however, they were less successful in their efforts to articulate a coherent methodology of *pipan*—of a critique of feudal mentality. Each time they tried, their efforts were severely curtailed by the exigencies of nationalist revolution and by their own desire to collaborate with political revolutionaries. Nonetheless, as the history of the May Fourth legacy outlined in this book shows, the idea of a post-political enlightenment has never died out. Quite the contrary, it has become an "idée force," a term used by historian Henri Peyre to describe those ideas that have the power to set sensibilities aflame by reminding humanity of the possibility of freedom.[25] With its emphasis on freedom yet to be achieved, the Chinese enlightenment serves as a reminder of the limitations of political revolution even today. Its message has been confirmed and reconfirmed as new prejudices have proliferated in the course of mass movement for political change. Faced with this historical evidence, no political leader in twentieth-century China has been able to rest secure in his claim that enlightenment has been fulfilled through revolution.

Even so, the willingness to acknowledge this disparity between revolution and enlightenment has, as we have seen, fluctuated over time. Recently, the death of Mao Zedong and the coup against his leftist followers in 1976 provided an opportunity for such an acknowledgment of the post-political significance of the May Fourth legacy. The new regime in power has found it useful to sanction, however briefly, a public cleansing of political wounds. In the process of this reckoning with the excesses of the Cultural Revolution, it became quite clear that the Chinese people had been led astray by something deeper and more encompassing than the irrational dictates of one leader and a few of his henchmen. A widespread habit of reverence for patriarchal authority, coupled with a desire to believe in its wisdom unquestioningly, emerged as the source of the masses' vulnerability to "contemporary superstitions," *xiandai mixin*. To acknowledge this phenomenon was, in effect, to persevere in the May Fourth criticism of the ethic of self-submission. The manifestation of this ethic in the People's Republic was quite new. It was a dogmatic faith in Marxism-Leninist Mao Zedong Thought itself.

In 1977–78 the official media took the lead in reviving concern for the unfinished business of May Fourth. In a key article entitled "The Enlightenment of Philosophy and Philosophical Enlightenment," the *People's Daily* suggested that the time was ripe for a more thorough inquiry into the origins of contemporary superstitions. The author of this piece, Xing Bisi, argued that critical reason cannot and should not be consigned to the bourgeois past. Rather, he pointed out, it must be revived in the context of a new socialist enlightenment movement. The major question posed by Xing and others at this time was: How did it happen that Marxism, which "in its essence is antithetical to obscurantism," had become a "new theology in China, even after the victory of the proletariat?"[26] To limit culpability for this predicament, Xing concluded that the so-called Gang of Four were the main designers and beneficiaries of the new theology:

They borrowed the name of Marxism so they could enchain the population to their own cause. The material damage caused by the Gang of Four, although considerable, can be estimated, measured. The spiritual damage is beyond calculation. Therefore, we need a new enlightenment movement that would reinvigorate our philosophical theory.[27]

The incalculable spiritual damage that Xing talked about cannot be traced solely to the Gang of Four. In the months following this July 1978 assault on the problem of contemporary superstition, other, less official voices arose to spread the blame more widely. Cartoonists began to depict prudish Communist cadres trying to hide their "feudal pigtails" under Maoist caps and fat officials riding in sedan chairs carried by lower officials who were carried, in turn, by a populace all too familiar with self-submission.[28] Even historians associated with the Academy of Social Sciences held a conference on "Feudalism in Contemporary Life" to explore the similarities between present-day corruption and autocracy and the traditional bureaucratic mentality which assumed that the powerful are not only above the law, but are the law themselves.[29] Finally, in 1979, during the sixtieth anniversary of May Fourth, Zhou Yang once again pointed out that "simplified, dogmatized, mythified" Marxism was the main obstacle to, as well as the target of, the latest movement for intellectual emancipation.[30] The mounting consensus, then, was that old ways of thinking were thriving in China, even after the fall of the Gang of Four.

It was against this background consensus that the post-political significance of enlightenment was reasserted explicitly by the short-lived Democracy Wall movement. Led by a generation of critical Marxists born and raised in the People's Republic, this was a movement that benefited from the liberal climate of the winter of 1978 and the spring of 1979. Its aim was to take the general indictment of dogmatism and superstition one step further: to find its origins not only in the deification of Mao Zedong Thought during the reign of the Gang of Four but also in the more pervasive habit of slavishness that preceded the Cultural Revolution and continued to endure after it. The young men and women who put forth this latest round of criticism of native habits of mind were themselves participants in and survivors of the Cultural Revolution. Their own experience had taught them to be suspicious of quick solutions to the problem of a slavish mentality. Therefore, more than the political leaders who launched the call for a "socialist enlightenment," they were unwilling to distinguish between the two components of the May Fourth legacy: science and democracy. Their insistence that genuine intellectual emancipation depended on a thorough examination of the social forces which thwarted scientific rationality and democratic politics ran counter to the government policy that fostered the former without much enthusiasm for the latter.

For a while, in the winter of 1978–79, the conflict between young dissidents who believed that China needed a more May Fourth–type discussion of *guomin xing* (national character) and political authorities who believed that all energies must be focused on *jiuguo* (national salvation, now translated as "Chinese-style modernization") was not fully apparent. In this interlude, wall posters appeared in Beijing raising the call for a "fifth modernization": democracy. An addition to the government-sponsored Four Modernizations program, these posters implied that unenlightened attitudes still prevailed among those who would portray themselves as China's modernizers. At the same time, in the southwestern province of Guizhou, another group of young veterans of the Cultural Revolution founded an unofficial journal entitled *Enlightenment (Qimeng)*. Its purpose, in keeping with government sanctions, was to engage in a critical inquiry into Marxist superstitions. The young dissidents interpreted this as license to attack the "idol of political worship, which is the enemy of democracy" and "fetishized Marxism, which is an enemy of science."[31] Joined by a variety of other Cultural Revolution youths, the authors of the "fifth modernization" posters and the editors of *Enlightenment* managed to convince themselves that the dawn of a new era was truly at hand.

As during the May Fourth movement, these advocates of enlightenment became vulnerable because of their hasty, rather naive turning to the West. When the young leaders of the Democracy Wall movement began to quote Montesquieu's *The Spirit of Laws* to argue for more freedom of political expression, and to extol the virtues of Western societies that seemed to have achieved the very human rights China was still struggling for, they provoked the ire of political authorities. An unwritten limit on criticism was breached in the spring of 1979. Dissenters now began to perceive the enemies of science and democracy closer and closer to home, higher and higher in the hierarchy of the new, supposedly enlightened government. By the fall of 1979, Wei Jingsheng, the author of the "fifth modernization" posters, had been arrested and condemned to fifteen years in jail. At the same time, the editors of *Enlightenment* had been arrested and chastised for their "anti-socialist" attitudes. By the winter of 1979, the Chinese constitution was being amended to take out the right to put up wall posters. By the spring of 1980, Democracy Wall itself had been outlawed, dismantled, and restored once again to its function as a screen for a parking lot full of buses. A government bent upon "Chinese-style modernization" now worries more about its economic program than about the enlightenment movement.

The history of the Chinese enlightenment, however, is not finished. Incomplete, the project of intellectual emancipation remains all the more pressing. As Kant, Lu Xun, and even Zhou Yang foresaw, the very durability of unfreedom ensures the re-emergence of appeals for freedom of expression. The reign of prejudice, superstition, and dogmatism is, like everything else, never as eternal or as natural as it seems. Thus, it is most appropriate to conclude this history of the aspirations and the setbacks that have characterized the May Fourth legacy with a poem that appeared in *Enlightenment* at the height of the Democracy Wall movement. Entitled "Confessions of the Great Wall," it conveys a rather optimistic sense of the possibility of liberation from old habits of mind. Although in retrospect that optimism might appear rather premature, the premises upon which it was based remain convincing even today:

CONFESSIONS OF THE GREAT WALL

The earth is small and blue
I am nothing but a small crack in it.
Under gray, low-flying clouds in the sky
I have been standing here for a long time.
My legs are numb, I am losing my balance.
I am falling down and dying of old age.
I am old.
My descendants hate me.
They hate me the way one hates a stubborn old grandfather.
When they see me they turn their face.

I divide the land into countless small pieces.
I divide the land into countless small, suffocating courtyards.
I lie among the people. I shut them off from others.

They want to destroy me, to push me down.
They are behind me and have discovered that
They are locked in by me,
Kept out by me.

I am collapsing in people's minds.
I am leaving.
I have died.[32]

Whether the ethic of self-submission has in fact collapsed in the mind of the Chinese people is very much in doubt. There can be no doubt, however, that a vision of cosmopolitanism, of liberation from provincial loyalties and from patriarchy, endures in the minds of those who, like Lu Xun, still go on cursing the Great Wall.

Appendix A

Members of the *New Tide* Society

新潮社社员名单

THE FIRST GROUP

The following list of members appeared in the first "New Tide Notice," published in the *Beijing University Daily*, December 3, 1918.

Mao Zhun (Zishui)	毛准(子水)	Gu Jiegang	顾颉刚
Yu Pingbo	俞平伯	Wan Jingxi (Jizhai)	汪敬熙(辑斋)
Zhang Songnian (Shenfu)	张崧年(申府)	Xu Yanzhi (Zijun)	徐彦之(子俊)
Fu Sinian (Mengzhen)	傅斯年(孟真)	Chen Jiaai (Hangfu)	陈家蔼(杭甫)
Pan Jiaxun (Jiequan)	潘家洵(介泉)	Liu Di (Mingyang)	刘敌(名洋)
Luo Jialun (Zhixi)	罗家伦(志希)	Tan Mingqian (Chengzhai, Pingshan)	谭鸣谦(诚斋, 平山)
Cheng Ping (Shewo)	成平(舍我)		
Gao Yuan (Chengyuan)	高元(承元)	Wu Kang (Jingxuan)	吴康(敬轩)
Chen Zhaochou (Suiting)	陈兆畴(穗庭)	Huang Jianzhong (Liming)	黄建中(离明)
Yang Zhensheng (Jinfu)	杨振声(金甫)	Kang Baiqing (Hongzhang)	康白情(洪章)
Dai Yue (Yufeng)	戴岳(毓峰)	Pan Yuangeng	潘元耿

THE SECOND GROUP

In addition to the above twenty-one names, four more were cited in the first issue of *New Tide*, volume 1, number 1 (January 1919). These four constitute the second group. They are:

Chen Dacai (Yanru)	陈达材(彦如)	Ye Lin (Shisun)	叶磨(石荪)
Ye Shaojun (Shengtao)	叶绍钧(圣陶)	Liu Binglin (Nangai)	刘秉麟(南陔)

THE THIRD GROUP

Jiang Shaoyuan	江绍原	Liu Guangyi (Shuhe)	刘光颐（叔和）
He Siyuan (Xiancha)	何思源（仙槎）		

(*New Tide*, volume 1, number 5, May 1919)

THE FOURTH GROUP

The following nine new names were listed in the "New Tide Record" in *New Tide*, volume 2, number 2, December 1919.

Wang Xinghan (Zhongchen)	王星汉（仲宸）	Gao Shangde (Junyu)	高尚德（君宇）
		Li Rongdi (Xiaofeng)	李荣第（小峰）
Meng Shouchun	孟寿椿	Guo Xifen (Shaoyu)	郭希汾（绍虞）
Zhao Chengyi (Zijing)	赵承易	Zong Xijun (Zhenfu)	宗锡钧（甄甫）
Wang Zhongqi (Boxiang)	王钟麒（伯祥）	Sun Fuyuan (Fuyuan)	孙福源（伏园）

THE FIFTH GROUP

Zhu Ziqing (Peixian)	朱自清（佩弦）	Sun Fuxi (Chuntai)	孙福熙（春台）
Feng Youlan (Zhisheng)	冯友兰（芝生）		

("Special Notice" in *New Tide*, volume 2, number 3, April 1920)

THE SIXTH GROUP

Zhou Zuoren (Qíming)	周作人（启明）

("The Second Special Notice" in *New Tide*, volume 2, number 4, May 1920)

MEMBERS WHO WITHDREW OF THEIR OWN ACCORD

According to "The New Tide Record" in *New Tide*, volume 2, number 2, December 1919, any member who did not submit any writing or make a contribution to the magazine within one year was to be considered as having withdrawn from the magazine of his own accord and would not longer be listed in the membership. The following three people were omitted from the membership list published in *New Tide*, volume 2, number 2:

Cheng Ping	成 平	Liu Di	刘 敌
Huang Jianzhong	黄建中		

Source: *Wusi shiqi de shetuan*, volume 2 (Beijing, 1979) pp. 49–50.

Appendix B
Officers of the *New Tide* Society

OFFICERS ELECTED AT THE FIRST
SESSION ON NOVEMBER 19, 1918

Chief Editor	Fu Sinian	傅斯年
Editor	Luo Jialun	罗家伦
Secretary	Yang Zhensheng	杨振声
Business Manager	Xu Yanzhi	徐彦之
Assistant Business Manager	Kang Baiqing	康白情
Secretary	Yu Pingbo	俞平伯

("New Tide Notice," *Beijing University Daily*, 3 December 1918)

OFFICERS ELECTED AT THE SECOND
SESSION ON NOVEMBER 19, 1919

Editor	Luo Jialun	罗家伦
Manager	Meng Shouchun	孟寿椿
Secretary for Circulation and Liaison	Gu Jiegang	顾颉刚
Advertising	Gao Shangde	高尚德
Proofreaders	Wang Xinghan	王星汉
	Zong Xijun	宗锡钧
	Li Rongdi	李荣第

("New Tide Record," *New Tide*, volume 2, number 2, December 1919)

OFFICERS OF THE THIRD SESSION,
ELECTED ON OCTOBER 28, 1920

Chief Editor	Zhou Zuoren	周作人
Editors	Mao Zishui	毛子水

	Gu Jiegang	顾颉刚
	Chen Dacai	陈达材
	Sun Fuyuan	孙福源
	Meng Shouchun	孟寿椿
Administrative Assistants	Wang Xinghan	王星汉
	Sun Fuyuan	孙福源
	Gao Shangde	高尚德
	Zong Xijun	宗锡钧
	Li Rongdi	李荣第
	Guo Shaoyu	郭绍虞

("New Tide Record," *New Tide*, volume 2, number 5, June, 1920)

Source: *Wusi shiqi de shetuan*, volume 2 (Beijing, 1979), pp. 51–52.

Appendix C

New Tide and *Citizen* Members in the
Beijing University Commoners' Education
Lecture Society

参加
北大平民教育讲演团的
新潮社国民社社员名单

THE FIRST GROUP: FOUNDERS OF THE
LECTURE SOCIETY IN MARCH 1919

Deng Zhongxia	邓中夏	Citizen, also member of the first Communist cell in Beijing, 1920
(Deng Kang)	（邓康）	
Yi Keyi	易克嶷	Citizen
Luo Jialun	罗家伦	New Tide
Liu Zhengjing	刘正经	Citizen
Xu Deheng	许德珩	Citizen
Chen Banzao	陈泮藻	Citizen
Kang Baiqing	康白情	New Tide
Zhou Changxian	周长宪	Citizen
Chen Baoe	陈宝锷	Citizen
Lu Shiyi	鲁士易	Citizen
Zhang Guotao	张国焘	Citizen, also member of the first Communist cell in Beijing, 1920
Huang Rikui	黄日葵	Citizen
Zhou Binglin	周炳琳	Citizen
Chen Xingba	陈兴霸	Citizen
Zhu Yie	朱一鹗	Citizen
Gao Yuan	高元	New Tide

MEMBERS OF THE SECOND GROUP:
ENTERED LECTURE SOCIETY BETWEEN
APRIL AND OCTOBER, 1919

Chen Zhaochou	陈兆畴	New Tide
Li Jun	李骏	Joined the first Communist cell, Beijing, 1920

Meng Shouchun   孟寿椿   New Tide and Citizen
Yan Caizhong   晏才钟   Citizen
Yu Pingbo   俞平伯   New Tide

MEMBERS OF THE THIRD GROUP: ENTERED LECTURE SOCIETY BETWEEN DECEMBER 1919 AND MARCH 1920

Zhu Wushan   朱务善   Member of the first Communist cell, Beijing, 1920
Gao Shangde   高尚德   New Tide, also member of the first Communist
                          cell, Beijing, 1920
Wang Xinghan   王星汉   New Tide
Liu Kejun   刘克镌   Citizen
Zhu Ziqing   朱自清   New Tide

Sources: *Wusi shiqi de shetuan*, volume 2 (Beijing, 1979), pp. 140–41. Zhou Zixin, "Beijing gongchandang xiaozu" [The Beijing Communist Party cell] *Renmin ribao* (6 October 1960):4.

Notes

ABBREVIATIONS USED IN THE NOTES

XC   *Xinchao* [*New Tide*]

XQN   *Xin qingnian* [*New Youth*]

INTRODUCTION

1. This translation follows closely that of H. B. Nisbet in *Kant's Political Writings*, ed. Hans Reiss (London, 1970), p. 54. I have, however, changed the wording in some places where it seemed the Nisbet translation rendered the German into more awkward English than was necessary. Reiss's "Notes to the Text" were particularly helpful in interpreting why, for Kant, the question "what is enlightenment" was as important as the question "what is truth?" See Reiss, p. 192.

2. The idea of this tension between modernization and social change was developed first in my article "A Curse on the Great Wall: The Problem of Enlightenment in Modern China," *Theory and Society* (May 1984).

3. Reiss, *Kant's Political Writings*, pp. 192–93.

4. "Xinchao fakan zhiqu shu" [Announcement of the publication of *New Tide*], *XC* 1:1 (January 1919):2.

5. This view of the European Enlightenment as a movement for "disenchantment" from religious superstition is based on Max Horkheimer and Theodor Adorno's *Dialectic of Enlightenment* (New York, 1972).

6. Confucius, although not the architect of state Confucianism, did elaborate a worldview that was, at its core, antithetical to the aspirations of enlightenment intellectuals. He was the first to endow the concept of *li* (ceremony) with the religious connotations of holy ritual. Fidelity to the form and the spirit of ritual was, according to the *Analects*, the best way, really the only way, to tame human emotions and civilize social intercourse. To act morally one had simply to follow the Way, the *Dao*. This *Dao*, in the words of Herbert Fingarette, was a "way without a crossroads," a path that eschewed the element of choice, which

Chinese advocates of enlightenment, like the European philosophers before them, assumed to be a prerequisite for genuine moral autonomy:

To be specific, Confucius does not elaborate the language of choice and responsibility as these are intimately intertwined with the idea of the ontologically ultimate power of the individual to select from genuine alternatives to create his own spiritual destiny.... There is no genuine option: either one follows the Way or one fails. To take any other "route" than the Way is not a genuine road but a failure through weakness to follow the route.

Herbert Fingarette, *Confucius: The Secular as Sacred* (New York, 1972), pp. 18 and 21.

7. Voltaire was most appreciative of the "religion of the Chinese men of letters" when he attacked the religious fanaticism of his contemporaries. Thus, we find the following entry in his *Philosophical Dictionary*:

Fanaticism is to superstition what delirium is to fever and rage to anger ... the malady is incurable.... Religion, far from being healthy food for infected brains, turns to poison in them.... There is only one religion in the world that has never been sullied by fanaticism, that of the Chinese men of letters. The schools of philosophers were not only free from this pest, they were its remedy.

Voltaire, "Fanatisme," *Dictionnaire philosophique*, quoted in Peter Gay, ed., *The Enlightenment: A Comprehensive Anthology* (New York, 1973), pp. 241–42.

8. For a critique of the often-used dichotomy of tradition versus modernity, see Benjamin Schwartz, "The Limits of 'Tradition' and 'Modernity' as Categories of Explanation," *Daedalus* (Spring 1972).

9. For a thoughtful critique of the limitations of nineteenth-century Chinese efforts to separate Western "means" (*yong*) from Chinese "essence" (*ti*), see Joseph Levenson, *Confucian China and Its Modern Fate* (Berkeley, 1968) vol. 1.

10. This equivalence between "national salvation" and a "human salvation" is clearest in the May Fourth–era work of Lu Xun. That is the subject of a very thoughtful analysis put forth by Zhang Dainian and Liu Yulie in their article "Wusi shiqi pipan fengjian jiu daode lishi yiyi," [The historical significance of the May Fourth attack on feudal ethics], in *Jinian wusi yundong liushi zhounian xueshu taolun hui wenxuan* (Beijing, 1980), vol. 1, pp. 507–23.

11. Luo Jialun, "Yinian lai de women xuesheng yundong de chenggong shibai he jianglai ying qu de fangzhen" [The successes and failures of our student movement and the future direction to be adopted], *XC* 2:5 (May 1920):607.

12. For Bertrand Russell's ambivalent response to the phenomenon of new culture in China see his article "Modern China—III, Chinese Amusements," *The Nation* (28 December, 1921), pp. 56–57. For Pierre Teilhard de Chardin's view of the "Chinese enlightenment" see *Letters from a Traveller* (London, 1962), pp. 108–9.

13. John Dewey, "New Culture in China," *Asia* 21:7 (1921):584.

14. For a suggestive discussion of the connotations of this traditional concept in the life and work of modern Chinese intellectuals, see Li Kan, "Wusi yiqian wushi nian jian Zhongguo zhishi fenzi suo jingli de daolu" [The path taken by Chinese intellectuals in the past fifty years], *Kexue zhanxian* 2 (July 1978).

15. This contrast between "web" and "thread" history draws upon Joseph Levenson's analysis of his own historiography in "The Genesis of 'Confucian China and Its Modern Fate,'" *The Historian's Workshop*, ed. L. P. Curtis (New York, 1970).

16. This definition appears in Lester Crocker's *An Age of Crisis* (Baltimore, 1959), p. xv.

17. This usage of the concept of "a revolution of values" refers to the slow, ongoing process of anti-feudal mental change still going on in China today. It is to be distinguished from the meaning of "cultural revolution" as a radical, hasty repudiation of traditional and so-called bourgeois values—as it was used, for instance, during the Great Proletarian Cultural Revolution of 1966–69. For a very thoughtful critique of the idea of cultural revolution see Wang Gungwu, "May Fourth and the GPCR: The Cultural Revolution Remedy," *Pacific Affairs* (Canada) 52:4 (1979–80):674–90.

In this article, Wang defines the "cultural revolution syndrome" as the antithesis of "an admission that tradition may provide the soil in which the foreign plants may grow.... There is only the tacit assumption that tradition is irrelevant (except as embodied in museum objects of national pride) and modernization is only a matter of time and will and wise leadership" (p. 689). This characterization of the "cultural revolution syndrome" clearly does not apply to the *New Tide* intellectuals considered in this book, who were scrupulously and consistently concerned with adapting enlightenment to the changing needs of Chinese history. However, Wang's conclusion that a mythified May Fourth can become a force that stymies science and democracy bears out the conclusion of this study (see chapter 5): "the greater danger from the Chinese experience of the cultural revolution remedy may be in the myths and the heroic slogans that discourage free and scientific thought. It might not be a bad idea when the Chinese are being asked to be fiercely critical of the GPCR to ask that they be critical of the May Fourth movement as well" (p. 690).

18. Friedrich Nietzsche, "On Great Events," in *Thus Spake Zarathustra* (New York, 1924), p. 158.

CHAPTER 1

1. Julian Marias, *Generations: A Historical Method*, trans. H. C. Raley (Alabama, 1970), p. 161.

2. The Confucian scholar who attacked May Fourth intellectuals most stridently for their "beastly mores" was Lin Shu (1852–1924). In the spring of 1919, he published a short story entitled "Jingsheng, the Giant" in which he mocked the major figures of the New Culture movement as nearsighted, weakminded fools. In one episode, the giant, after kicking and chasing away the irksome rebels against Confucian ethics, declares: "I'll not stain my hand to kill you beasts! Get out of here!" For a translation of this excerpt and an excellent discussion of its historical context, see Chow Tse-tsung, *The May Fourth Movement: Intellectual Revolution in Modern China* (Stanford, 1960), pp. 64–67.

3. Liang Qichao, "Ou you xinying jielu" [Reflections on my European travels], *Yinbingshi wenji* (Shanghai, 1925), vol. 72. Also translated in Joseph Levenson, *Liang Ch'i-ch'ao and the Mind of Modern China* (Cambridge, Mass., 1953), p. 200.

4. Lu Xun, "Preface to Call to Arms," in *Selected Works* (Beijing, 1980), vol. 1, pp. 37–38.

5. Lu Xun, "The Diary of a Madman," ibid., p. 54.

6. For a contemporary account of the events leading up to the May Fourth

demonstration, see Gong Zhenhuang, ed., "Qingdao wenti zhi youlai" [The origin of the Qingdao question], in *Wusi aiguo yundong ziliao* (Beijing, 1959), pp. 9–39.

7.   Translated in Chow Tse-tsung, *May Fourth Movement*, p. 106–7.

8.   Xu Deheng, interview with author, Beijing, 26 May 1983.

9.   For the original verses by William Blake, "Great things are done when men and mountains meet./Nothing is done by jostling in the streets" and for the reasons for Fu's reversal, see Fu Sinian, "Zhongguo wenyi jie zhi binggen" [The source of China's literary disease], *XC* 1:2 (February 1919):343–45.

10.   Alan Gordon Moller, "Bellicose Nationalist of Republican China: An Intellectual Biography of Fu Ssu-nien," Ph.D. diss., Department of History, University of Melbourne (February 1979), p. 43.

11.   "Yang Zhensheng," in *Zhongguo wenxue zuojia cidian*, vol. 2, (Beijing 1979), p. 344.

12.   Ibid., p. 345.

13.   Ibid., p. 346.

14.   My own translation; see also Chow Tse-tsung, *May Fourth Movement*, pp. 136–37. For a point of view quite opposite the one expressed by Xu Deheng in court, see Liang Shuming's May 18, 1919, article in the *Meizhou pinglun*. In it, this young instructor at Beida, a contemporary of May Fourth youths, took issue with the self-portrayal of student activists as innocent, righteous spokesmen for public opinion. Liang argued that the students had attempted to take the law into their own hands and were far from blameless victims of the warlord government.

Liang criticized the students' attitude, which he believed to be part and parcel of the problem, selfish arrogance: "Many people may not agree with me. If so, there is something amiss here. For ten thousand years, we, the Chinese people, have only thought of benefit for 'myself,' never for others. We have either held our heads too high or have bowed down too low. We have no sense of law, of courts.... This is a great national shortcoming indeed." Liang Shuming, "Lun xuesheng shijian" [On the students' episode], *Meizhou pinglun* (18 May 1919):1.

15.   Xu Deheng, interview with author, Beijing, 16 May 1983.

16.   Xu Deheng, "Wusi yundong liushi zhounian" [The sixtieth anniversary of the May Fourth movement], *Wusi yundong huiyi lu*, vol. 3 (Beijing, 1979), pp. 51–52.

17.   Ibid., p. 53.

18.   Ibid., p. 54.

19.   Yu Pingbo, "Wusi liushi nian jinian yiwang shizhang" [Ten poems commemorating the sixtieth anniversary of May Fourth], *Zhandi zengkan* (June 1979):5–6.

20.   Yu Pingbo, interview with author, Beijing, 20 June 1981.

21.   Zhu Ziqing, "Qijie" [Courage and propriety], *Zhu Ziqing xuanji* (Hong Kong, 1964), pp. 192–93.

22.   Luo Jialun (Yi), "Wusi yundong de jingshen" [The spirit of May Fourth], *Meizhou pinglun* (23 May 1919):1.

23.   Chen Duxiu, "Women jiujing ying bu yinggai aiguo?" [Should we be patriotic after all?], *Duxiu wencun* (Shanghai, 1922), vol. 1, pp. 648–49.

24.   Karl Mannheim, "The Problem of Generations," in *Essays in the Sociology*

of Knowledge (New York, 1952), p. 291.

25.   Ibid.

26.   This formulation of the concept of "the generation of 1919" around a central, formative event is greatly indebted to the work of Julian Marias, *Generations: A Historical Method* and to Robert Wohl's *The Generation of 1914* Wohl, with his brilliant, evocative narrative of one particular generation, enabled me to draw this characterization of May Fourth students—an otherwise diverse, politically divided, and historiographically neglected generation.

27.   Li Zehou, *Zhongguo jindai sixiangshi lun* [Essays on modern Chinese intellectual history] (Beijing, 1979), pp. 470–71.

28.   A very thoughtful argument about the limitations of intellectuals' autonomy in traditional Chinese political culture was made by Frederic Wakeman in his article "The Price of Autonomy: Intellectuals in Ming and Ch'ing Politics," *Daedalus* (Spring, 1972). Wakeman points out that the Donglin scholars active in the first half of the seventeenth century, although spiritual forerunners of modern intellectuals, had relied too much on individual self-consciousness as an instrument of warfare against corrupt politics. In the process, they had remained intellectually, and politically, dependent on the ethic of subservience to the state. They kept searching for ways of serving the declining Ming dynasty better and never quite achieved a sense of their autonomy as intellectuals. In Wakeman's view, they never became a distinctive social constituency.

29.   Alvin Gouldner, *The Future of Intellectuals and the Rise of the New Class* (New York, 1979), p. 34.

30.   For a thorough discussion of the far-ranging vision of and practical limitations faced by these early champions of Western learning, see Paul Cohen, *Between Tradition and Modernity: Wang Tao and Reform in Late Ch'ing China* (Cambridge, Mass., 1974) and Benjamin Schwartz, *In Search of Wealth and Power: Yen Fu and the West* (New York, 1969).

31.   In 1902, four of the intellectuals who later taught at Beijing University left for study in Japan: Cai Yuanpei, Chen Duxiu, Lu Xun, and Ma Xulun. Wu Yu and Zhou Zuoren went to Japan in 1905, Qian Xuantong in 1906, and Jiang Menglin in 1907. Li Dazhao, being from a poorer peasant family, could not find the means to study abroad until 1913. For all, the Japanese experience turned out to be a catalyst in their transformation into revolutionaries. Japan exposed young Chinese intellectuals to a vibrant and prosperous nation—a vibrancy that heightened their awareness of China's political and cultural backwardness. In Japan, they also came upon older revolutionaries such as Sun Zhongshan and Zhang Taiyan, who constantly talked about the future Chinese Revolution while they recruited members for nascent, clandestine organizations. Some of the intellectuals mentioned above became politically affiliated with Sun's Tongmenghui after its organization in Tokyo in 1905. Others, such as Lu Xun, remained on the periphery; sympathetic, but more immediately concerned with the spiritual crises of their nation. Japan was the primary experience for the majority, though not exclusively all, of these intellectuals. For example, Cai Yuanpei also studied in Germany and France, whereas Wang Xinggong sought advanced training in England. Two of the youngest Beida professors, Hu Shi and Chen Hengzhe, having received a modern education from teachers who had returned from Japan, bypassed the Japanese milieu and chose to study in the United States.

Liu Bannong, the second youngest intellectual in the teachers' generation, did not have the opportunity to go abroad until after 1919; thus he followed more closely the educational pattern of the student generation.

32. Wang Shuqian, "Xinjiu wenti" [The problem of new and old], *XQN* 1:1 (September 1915):49–50.

33. Eric H. Erikson, "Eight Ages of Man," in *Childhood and Society* (New York, 1963), p. 248.

34. I am indebted to Ellen Widmer for drawing my attention to Japanese precedents for the Chinese enlightenment. Her thoughtful, critical comments on an earlier version of this argument enabled me to recast it in keeping with the rich documentary materials now available about the Japanese enlightenment. For the comparison with the Chinese enlightenment the most useful text has been William Reynolds Braisted's translation and introduction entitled *Meiroku Zasshi: Journal of the Japanese Enlightenment* (Cambridge, Mass., 1976).

35. Hao Chang, *Liang Ch'i-ch'ao and Intellectual Transition in China, 1890–1907* (Cambridge, Mass., 1971), p. 144.

36. Braisted, *Meiroku Zasshi*, p. xviii.

37. Hao Chang, *Liang Ch'i-ch'ao*, p. 144.

38. Braisted, *Meiroku Zasshi*, p. xxxviii.

39. For a discussion of the Japanese *New Tide* (Shincho), see Okazaki Yoshie, ed., *Japanese Literature in the Meiji Era* (Tokyo, 1968), pp. 64, 581–608. For Luo Jialun's role in the Chinese *New Tide* (Xinchao), see Moller, "Bellicose Nationalist," p. 26.

40. Fukuzawa Yukichi, *An Encouragement to Learning*, translated and with an introduction by David Dilworth and Umeyo Hirano (Tokyo, 1969), pp. 24–25.

41. Quoted in Hao Chang, *Liang Ch'i-ch'ao*, pp. 192–93.

42. Quoted in C. T. Hsia, "Yen Fu and Liang Ch'i-ch'ao as Advocates of New Fiction," in *Chinese Approaches to Literature from Confucius to Liang Ch'i-ch'ao*, ed. A. A. Rickett (Princeton, 1978), pp. 222–23.

43. This quotation and the preceding analysis of Liang Qichao's contribution to the Chinese enlightenment are based on Satō Shin'ichi's "Shinmatsu keimō shisō no seiritsu," [The birth of late Qing enlightenment], *Kokka gakkai zasshi* 92:5–6 (1979): 1–58. In this article, Professor Satō focuses on the development of a new political philosophy in late Qing China and the process of the disintegration of the Confucian worldview. He presents Liang as a modern intellectual who was uniquely and intensely aware of his transition from a bureaucrat serving cultural interests to an enlightenment thinker shouldering the burden of critical autonomy.

44. Ernest P. Young, "The Hung-hsien Emperor as a Modernizing Conservative," in *The Limits of Change: Essays on Conservative Alternatives in Republican China*, ed. C. Furth (Cambridge, Mass., 1976), pp. 174–75.

45. This interpretation of Zhang Taiyan is drawn from Li Zehou, "Zhang Taiyan as a Revolutionary and a Thinker," (paper presented at the annual meeting of the Association for Asian Studies, Chicago, April 1982).

46. In his paper, cited above, Li Zehou emphasizes the philosophical significance of Zhang's interest in Buddhism. He views this influence as leading to subjective idealism. For another perspective of Buddhism as liberation from arbitrary notions of self and world, see works by Janice D. Willis, especially her

book *On Knowing Reality: The "Tattvartha" Chapter of Asanga's "Bodhisattvabhumi"* (New York, 1979). In this work Willis argues that medieval Chinese philosophies distorted the meaning of "consciousness only" in Buddhist thought. This argument is consistent with *New Tide* discussions of ancient Buddhism as an alternative to arbitrary, subjective, and unsystematic Confucian thought. For a further elaboration of the contributions of Buddhist logic to modern Chinese thought, see Liang Shuming's letter to the editors of *New Tide* in *XC* 1:5 (May 1919) 935–44. The positive implications of Buddhist philosophy for modern enlightenment more generally have recently been outlined by Robert Thurman in his article "The Politics of Enlightenment," *Teachings at Tushita: Buddhist Discourses, Articles, and Translations*, ed. Glen Mullin and Nicholas Ribush (New Delhi, 1981), pp. 58–75.

47.   Charlotte Furth, "The Sage as Rebel: The Inner World of Chang Pinglin," in Furth, *The Limits of Change*, pp. 122–23.

48.   See Nathan Feigon, "Ch'en Tu-hsiu and the Foundations of the Chinese Revolution," Ph.D. diss., Department of History, University of Michigan (1978), p. 42.

49.   Chen Duxiu, "Wuren zuihou zhi juewu" [My own final awakening], in Chen Duxiu, *Duxiu wencun*, p. 49.

50.   Ibid., p. 55.

51.   Immanuel Kant, "What is Enlightenment?" in H. Reiss, ed., *Kant's Political Writings* (London, 1970), p. 54.

52.   This article is discussed in Maurice Meisner, *Li Ta-chao and the Origins of Chinese Marxism* (New York, 1967), pp. 21–26. Li Dazhao, one of Chen's closest allies in the *New Youth* period, disagreed sharply with Chen Duxiu's juxtaposition of nationalism and autonomy. He argued that Chen's call for autonomy would only plunge Chinese intellectuals into a worse spiritual situation than they already confronted: "We want to see the crucial point of self-consciousness (*zijue*) ... but we have lost our way in a fog of pessimism" (Meisner, p. 22). Li's accusation that the quest for individual autonomy is harmful to national self-confidence would be repeated more stridently in the 1930s.

53.   Quoted in Xiao Chaoran et al., *Beijing Daxue xiaoshi: 1898–1949* [The history of Beijing University] (Shanghai, 1981), p. 7.

54.   Ibid., p. 6.

55.   I am indebted to John King Fairbank for drawing to my attention the unique vision of education that W. A. P. Martin brought to the Imperial University—a vision often slighted in Chinese sources on the same period.

56.   Xiao Chaoran et al., *Beijing Daxue xiaoshi*, pp. 9–11.

57.   For a thorough discussion of the role that Social Darwinism played in the life and thought of Yan Fu, see Schwartz, *In Search of Wealth and Power*, especially chapters 3 and 4.

58.   From Yan Fu's introduction to the translation of Montesquieu's *Spirit of Law*, it is clear that he, in contrast to later May Fourth intellectuals, did not identify democracy with individualism. In fact, in any instance that these two ideals might conflict, he argued, national freedom must take priority over individual emancipation: "When we view the situation in China, we realize that in China the liberty of the individual is not yet a matter of first urgency. It is rather a matter of maintaining ourselves against the aggression of other nations which

will brook no delay. The freedom of the nation state is more urgent than the freedom of the individual." Quoted in Schwartz, *In Search of Wealth and Power*, pp. 172–73.

59. I am indebted to interviews with Feng Youlan (March 1980 and June 1981) for drawing my attention to the influence of Yan Fu's translations of Mill and Jevons on May Fourth intellectuals. For Feng's own description of when and how he first encountered these translations, see chapter 2 below.

60. Xiao Chaoran et al., *Beijing Daxue xiaoshi*, p. 37.

61. Ibid.

62. Yan Fu, "Shang dazongtong he jiaoyubu shu" [Letter to the President and the Ministry of Education], from the Beijing University school archives, quoted in Xiao Chaoran et al., ibid., pp. 27–28.

63. Yan Fu, "Lun Beijing Daxue buke tingban shuotie," [On the inappropriateness of closing Beijing University], ibid., p. 28.

64. Shen Yinmo, "Wo he Beida" [I and Beida], in *Wusi yundong huiyi lu*, vol. 3, p. 158.

65. Zhu Wushan, "Beijing daxue de jingshen" [The spirit of Beijing University], *Beida ershiwu nian*, unpublished document collection from the Beijing University school history archives.

66. Chow Tse-tsung, *May Fourth Movement*, p. 47.

67. For a general overview of the pedagogical vision of Cai Yuanpei, see William Duiker, *Cai Yuanpei: Educator of Modern China*, Pennsylvania State University Studies, no. 41 (University Park, Pa., 1977).

68. Cai Yuanpei, "Wusi qianhou de Beida" [Beijing University before and after May Fourth], *Xin wenxue shiliao* no. 3 (May 1979), p. 15.

69. Chiang Monlin, *Tides from the West* (New Haven, 1947), p. 116.

70. Most recently, in February 1983, the publication in the People's Republic of a volume of essays commemorating Cai Yuanpei provided intellectuals with a public occasion to reflect on their self-chosen mentor and symbol. See, especially, Tang Zhenchang, "Cai Yuanpei xiansheng jinian ji shu hou?" [What shall we do after the publication of the commemorative volume for Mr. Cai Yuanpei?], *Renmin ribao* (8 February 1983):5.

71. Shen Yinmo, "Wo he Beida," p. 161.

72. Feng Youlan, "Zhexue huiyi lu: Wo zai ershi niandai" [Philosophical reminiscences: My experiences during the 1920s], *Zhongguo zhexue* 3 (August 1980):360–61. The same point of view was expressed even more emphatically by Feng Youlan in our interviews in March 1980 and June 1981.

73. Y. S. Teng and J. K. Fairbank, "Ts'ai Yuan-p'ei's Views on the Aims of Education 1912," in *China's Response to the West* (New York, 1966), p. 237. Cai Yuanpei restated his views on esthetic education even more forcefully during the May Fourth movement itself, when he juxtaposed its salutary benefits with the befuddlement of superstition. See, especially, his article "Yi meiyu dai zongjiao shuo" [On the replacement of religion with esthetic education] *XQN* 3:6 (August 1917).

74. The activities of the Society for the Promotion of Virtue are described in some detail in Xiao Chaoran et al., *Beijing Daxue xiaoshi*, pp. 44–45.

75. A discussion of the Society for the Promotion of Virtue from a contemporary view may be found in Kang Baiqing, "Beijing Daxue de xuesheng" [The

students of Beijing University], *Shaonian shijie* 1:1 (January 1920).

76. Xiao Chaoran, et al., *Beijing Daxue xiaoshi*, p. 45.

77. Duiker, *Cai Yuanpei*, pp. 54–55.

78. Fu Zengxiang, "Zhi Cai Yuanpei" [Letter to Cai Yuanpei, 26 March 1919], in *Wusi shiqi de shetuan*, vol. 2, p. 65.

79. Cai Yuanpei, "Zhi Fu Zengxiang" [Letter to Fu Zengxiang, 12 April 1919], ibid., p. 66.

80. Fu Zengxiang, "Jiaoyubu yanjin xuesheng youxing jihui ci" [Ministry of Education proclamation prohibiting student demonstrations, May 5, 1919] in *Wusi aiguo yundong dangan ziliao* (Beijing, 1980), p. 183.

CHAPTER 2

1. Antonio Gramsci, "On Intellectuals." *Selections from the Prison Notebooks* (New York, 1971), trans. Q. Hoare and G. N. Smith, pp. 9–10.

2. For a perceptive overview of the intellectuals' role in society as both critics and servants of the monarch, see the first two chapters in Jerome B. Grieder, *Intellectuals and the State in Modern China* (New York, 1981), pp. 1–47.

3. Li Dazhao, "Xindc! Jiudc!" [New! Old!] *XQN* 1:5 (May 1918):57.

4. "Wu Yu," in Howard Boorman, ed., *Biographical Dictionary of Republican China* (New York, 1968).

5. Chen Duxiu, "Zhi Hu Shi" [Letter to Hu Shi], in *Hu Shi laiwang shuxin xuan* (Beijing, 1979), vol. 1, p. 6.

6. Chen Duxiu, "Jinggao qingnian" [Call to youth], *Duxiu wencun*, vol. 1, pp. 1–2. Also translated in Chow Tse-tsung, *May Fourth Movement*, p. 46.

7. Gao Yihan, "Qingnian zhi di" [The enemy of youth], *XQN* 1:6 (February, 1916):46.

8. Chen Duxiu, "Xin Qingnian" [New Youth], in *Duxiu wencun*, pp. 58–59.

9. Yu Pingbo, interview with author, Beijing, June 1980. A similar emphasis on the multiplicity of student activity within Yu's own class at Beida appears in his poems commemorating the sixtieth anniversary of the May Fourth movement. See "Wusi liushi nian jinian yiwang shizhang."

10. Luo Jialun, "Qingnian xuesheng" [Young students], *XQN* 4:1 (January 1918):39.

11. Erik Erikson, "Youth: Fidelity and Diversity," in *Youth: Change and Challenge* (New York, 1963), pp. 1 and 19.

12. Chen Jiaai, "Xin" [New], *XC* 1:1 (January 1919):35.

13. Ibid., p. 37.

14. Moller, "Bellicose Nationalist," pp. 7–10.

15. Arthur W. Hummel in Ku Chieh-kang, *The Autobiography of a Chinese Historian* (Leyden, 1931), pp. 6–7.

16. Zhang Shenfu, "Zhi Hu Shi," *Hu Shi laiwang shuxin xuan*, vol. 1, p. 11.

17. Zhang Shenfu, "Yi Shouchang" [Reminiscences of Shouchang], in *Li Dazhao* (Beijing, 1980), pp. 61–66.

18. "Xinchao fakan zhiqu shu" [Announcement of the publication of the *New Tide* magazine], *XC* (January 1919) 1:1:2.

19. Li Xiaofeng, "Xinchao de shimo" [*New Tide* from the beginning to the end], *Wenshi ziliao xuanji* 61 (1979):82–128.

20. "Xinchao fakan zhiqu shu," p. 3.

21. Fu Sinian, "Xinchao zhi huigu yu qianzhan" [New Tide: Recollections of the past and future prospects], XC 2:1 (October 1919):199–205.

22. Most of the truly informative New Tide memoirs are available only in the form of oral history. In the account below, therefore, I have relied extensively on the recollections of New Tide members Yu Pingbo, Feng Youlan, Ye Shengtao, and Zhang Shenfu, whom I was privileged to meet and interview during 1979–80. Their points of view, though far from similar, offer, nonetheless, a counterbalance to the general condemnation of the New Tide as simply a "petty bourgeois organization." The official condemnation is most explicit in the introduction to Xinchao presented in Wusi shiqi qikan jieshao [An introduction to periodicals of the May Fourth era] (Beijing, 1958), vol. 1, pp. 75–97. Recently, Li Xiaofeng has finally written the first "for internal publication only" account of the history of New Tide from the point of view of a participant rather than ideological critic. See Li Xiaofeng, "Xinchao de shimo."

23. Li Xiaofeng, ibid. Author's interview with Ye Shengtao, June 1980.

24. Kang Baiqing, "Taiji tu yu Phallicism" [The Taiji diagram and Phallicism], XC 1:4 (April 1919):282.

25. "Xinchao fakan zhiqu shu," p. 3.

26. Yi Peishan, "Zhi jizhe" [Letter to the editors], XC 1:3 (March 1919):551–53.

27. Li Xiaofeng, "Xinchao de shimo," pp. 109–13.

28. Luo Jialun, "Shi qingnian zisha haishi shehui sha qingnian?" [Does youth commit suicide or does society kill youth?], XC 2:2 (December 1919):349.

Before Lin Deyang's death, proponents of the new culture had discussed suicide mainly as the dilemma of young women. Girls were seen as especially vulnerable to social oppression in the form of arranged marriages. Their suicides were condoned, even glorified, as a choice of death over life imprisonment. See: Roxane Witke, "Mao Tse-tung, Women, and Suicide," China Quarterly (September 1967).

29. Chen Duxiu, "Lun zisha" [On suicide], XQN 2:2 (January 1920): 12–13.

30. Lu Xun, "Duiyu Xinchao yi bufen yijian" [An opinion about New Tide] XC 1:5 (May 1919):944–45.

31. Fu Sinian, "Da Lu Xun" [Answer to Lu Xun], XC 1:5 (May 1919):945.

32. Ku Hung-ming, "Returning Students and Literary Revolution: Literacy and Education," Millard's Review 9:11 (16 August 1919):433.

33. I am indebted to professors Yin Xuxi and Ding Shouhe, co-authors of Cong wusi qimeng yundong dao Makesi zhuyi de chuanbo [From the May Fourth enlightenment movement to the propagation of Marxism] (Beijing, 1965, reprint 1979), and to Mr. Li Kan, author of "Wusi yiqian wushi nian Zhongguo zhishi fenzi suo jingguo de daolu," for drawing to my attention, during our conversations in China in the spring of 1980, this aspect of the May Fourth intellectuals' self-consciousness.

34. Historian Hsu Cho-yun has analyzed the process that achieved a semblance of mutuality between intellectuals and nobility in his book Ancient China in Transition (Stanford, 1960). His conclusion is as follows:

The *Chan Kuo* [Warring States] period witnessed great changes in the ideas that justified social relationships. The divine charisma of rulers and ruling groups was no longer recognized ... the familial bond between ruler and his ministers was replaced by a contractual relationship like that between employer and employee.... One manifestation of this was the gradual change in the meaning of the term *chuntzu* from a title that referred to high social station to one that referred to superiority in virtue; the name that had denoted social elite was now used for the moral elite ... social mobility helped bring about an ideological remodeling (p. 174).

35.   For a description of the function and mental outlook of the ancient *ru* conveyed from the point of view of one of their modern critics, see Hu Shi, "Shuo ru" [Speaking of the *ru*], *Hu Shi wencun* (Shanghai, 1935), vol. 4, pp. 1–81.

36.   Many of China's modern advocates of enlightenment believed that the spirit of Warring States intellectuals offered a native model of the spirit of defiant courage that they themselves aspired toward. Having forsaken the obsession with propriety (*jie*) that had characterized the ancient *ru*, the upwardly mobile *shi* were portrayed as full of courage (*qi*). These *shi* had supposedly been motivated by the same motto, "Dare to know," that inspired their twentieth-century descendants. As one of them, Zhu Ziqing, wrote:

Warring States intellectuals possessed martial courage (*shiqi*). Courage (*qi*) and propriety seem to have been very different notions from the beginning.... Courage refers to the virtues of warriors. "Propriety" is what was maintained or lost by those ancients preoccupied with rites and music. Propriety, the virtue peculiar to ritual behavior, is the essence of rites. Courage prevails when intellectuals act with a common sense of their independence. Propriety, on the other hand, is the hallmark of the behavior of individual officials.

See Zhu Ziqing, "Lun qijie" [On courage and propriety], *Zhu Ziqing xuanji*, (Hong Kong, 1964) pp. 190–93.

37.   Although language functioned as a class barrier in traditional China, it was not as absolute as it might appear at first. Especially in the late Qing period, literacy began to spread among classes previously shut off from China's literary heritage. For further discussions of the class implications of language in China, see Evelyn Sakakida Rawski, *Education and Popular Literacy in Ch'ing China* (Ann Arbor, 1979); and Perry Link, "Traditional-Style Popular Urban Fiction in the Teens and Twenties," in Merle Goldman, ed., *Modern Chinese Literature in the May Fourth Era* (Cambridge, Mass., 1977). Gramsci, in his seminal essay "On Intellectuals," makes a series of generalizations about the intellectuals' special interest in language which are particularly suggestive for the analysis developed here. His statements about China, though extreme, contain an element of historical truth:

In China, there is the phenomenon of the script, and expression of the complete separation between intellectuals and the people.... The problem of different beliefs and different ways of conceiving and practicing the same religion among the various strata of society, but particularly as between clergy, intellectuals and people needs to be studied in general, since it occurs everywhere to a certain degree.... It reaches a level of absurdity in East Asia, where the religion of the people often has nothing whatsoever to do with that of books, although the two are called by the same name (p. 23).

38.   Wang Yao, *Zhongguo xin wenxue shi gao* [Outline history of the new literature movement in China], (Hong Kong reprint, 1972), p. 34. For a more recent discussion of the implications of this gulf between elite and popular culture, see Sally Borthwick, *Education and Social Change in China* (Stanford, 1983).

39. For a comparative theoretical approach, see Ivan Illich, "Vernacular Values," in *Shadow Work* (Boston, 1981), pp. 27–52.

40. Yi Sheng, "Shishi chaoliu zhong zhi xin wenxue," [Timely new literature], *Meizhou pinglun* 19 (27 April 1919):244–45.

41. Hu Shi, "Bishang liangshan huiyi wenxue geming" [Forced into banditry—recollections of the literary revolution], *Wenhua* 1:1 (February 1934):68.

42. Qian Xuantong, "Zhongguo jinhou zhi wenzi wenti" [China's language problem today], *Zhongguo jindai sixiang shi ziliao* [Documentary history of modern Chinese intellectual history], ed. Shi Jun (Hong Kong reprint of Beijing, 1957 edition), p. 19.

43. Li Xiaofeng, "Xinchao de shimo," pp. 120–24.

44. Fu Sinian, "Gei Gu Chengyu xin" [Letter to Gu Chengyu (Gu Jiegang)] *XC* 1:4 (April 1919):709.

45. Fu Sinian, "Zhongguo wenyi jie zhi binggen," p. 345.

46. Interview with Zhu Ziqing's son, Zhu Qiaosen, Beijing, March 1980.

47. Yu Pingbo, "Shehui shang duiyu xin shi de gezhong xinli guan" [Various psychological views about new poetry prevalent in society], *XC* 2:1 (October 1919):163–71.

48. Lu Xun, "Duiyu Xinchao yi bufen yijian."

49. Wang Jingxi, "Zixu" [Introduction], *Xue ye* (Shanghai, 1925), pp. 1–5.

50. Luo Jialun, "Bo Hu Xiansu jun de Zhongguo wenxue gailiang lun" [Criticism of Mr. Hu Xiansu's views on Chinese literary reform], *XC* 1:5 (May 1919):759–82.

51. For a vehement indictment of the classical language, *guwen*, see Hu Shi, "The Chinese Literary Revolution," *Millard's Review* 8:8 (19 April 1919):279–81.

52. Xu Deheng, "Jiangyan tuan kai dierci dahui bing huansonghui shi ji" [Record of the second general meeting of the Lecture Society to send off old members], in *Wusi shiqi de shetuan*, vol. 2, pp. 155–56.

53. Chang Kuo-t'ao, *The Rise of the Chinese Communist Party, 1921–1927* (Lawrence, Kans., 1971), vol. 1, p. 49.

54. For a general discussion of the teachers' support in the organization of the *Citizen* Society, see Xu Deheng, "Huiyi Guomin zazhi" [Recollections of the *Citizen*], in *Wusi shiqi de shetuan*, vol. 2, pp. 37–38.

55. Ibid., pp. 37–38.

56. Gao Yuan, "Fei mimi zhuyi" [Anti-secretism], *XC* 1:4 (April 1919):667.

57. "Beijing daxue pingmin jiaoyu jiangyan tuan zhengji yuan qi" [Statement of purpose of associated members of the Beijing University Commoners' Education Lecture Society], in *Wusi shiqi de shetuan*, vol. 2, p. 135.

58. See full titles of street corner lectures given by members of the lecture society, ibid., pp. 142–85.

59. Ibid.

CHAPTER 3

1. Luo Jialun, "Da Zhang Puquan lai xin" [Reply to letter from Zhang Puquan], *XC* 2:2 (December 1919):366–67. In this translation, as in other texts of the same period, I translated the term *sixiang* (literally, "thought") as "men-

tality." I have taken this conceptual liberty because I became convinced that May Fourth writers used *sixiang* with two connotations: (1) as here, meaning an entrenched habit of mind that needed to be altered, or even gotten rid of, and (2) in other contexts, referring to emancipatory reason—an instrument that could be used to uproot habitual responses to the world.

2. The students derived their familiarity with Comte specifically and with positivism more generally from their mentors in the *New Youth* group. As early as February 1916, Chen Duxiu had argued that Comte and John Mill held the key to the kind of realistic view of life that was to be the model for the worldview of the New Culture movement. See Chen Duxiu, "Jinggao qingnian" (call to youth), *XQN* 6 (15 September 1915) p. 1 (also discussed in Chow Tse-tsung, *May Fourth Movement*, p. 294). Chinese intellectuals who tried to make this connection between critical thought and positivism were, in fact, following a nineteenth-century European interest in "scientism," a movement beginning with Comte that aimed to replace Christian dogma (metaphysical theology, to be more precise) with a philosophy based solely on scientifically verifiable knowledge. For a further discussion of Chinese interpretations of this positivist revolt against a priori philosophical systems, see Charlotte Furth, *Ting Wen-chiang: Science and China's New Culture* (Cambridge, Mass., 1970), pp. 14, 96, and 126.

3. Luo Jialun, "Da Zhang Puquan lai xin," p. 367.

4. These were some of the milder accusations against enlightenment intellectuals put forth by Lin Shu, the conservative scholar and translator, in his famous letter to Cai Yuanpei, 18 March 1919. Cai's equally famous reply defended Beida and its policy of academic freedom in terms of the diversity of points of view expressed. The chancellor claimed that the radical group was in no way representative of the mood of the university. The final argument was cast, not surprisingly, in the terms of Social Darwinism. "The university follows the example of the great universities of the world, adopting the principle of freedom of thought. Any theories which are reasonable and merit retention, and have not suffered the fate of being eliminated by natural selection, even though they disagree with each other, should be allowed to develop freely at the university." Chow Tse-tsung, *May Fourth Movement*, p. 71.

5. See appendix C for the overlapping membership of the Commoners' Education Lecture Society, *New Tide*, and the first cell of the Communist Party organized in Beijing in 1920–21.

6. As early as 1912, Cai had articulated his philosophy in Kantian terms:

Education for a world-view, however, is not something to chatter about every day. Moreover, this relationship to the phenomenal world cannot be described in dry, simple words. Then, in what way can we reach it? The answer is aesthetic education (or education for artistic appreciation, *meigan zhi jiaoyu*). *Meigan* is a conception combining beauty and solemnity, and is a bridge between the phenomenal world and the world of reality. This concept was originated by Kant.

Cai Yuanpei, "Views on the Aims of Education," translated in Teng and Fairbank, *China's Response to the West*, pp. 236–37.

7. Chen Duxiu, "Rensheng de zhenyi" [The true meaning of human existence], *XQN* 4:2 (February 1918):101.

8. Fu Sinian, "Rensheng wenti faduan" [The origins of the question of human existence], *XC* 1:1 (January 1919); also in *Fu Sinian xuanji*, vol. 1, p. 99.

Although the "question of human existence" remained central to *New Tide* concerns throughout the spring of 1919, it was not easy to maintain its primacy. Especially as other issues, such as literary reform and patriotic mobilization, became more pressing, the editors faced a choice of priorities. In the midst of their most turbulent month, May 1919, fellow *New Tide* member Gu Jiegang wrote a letter to remind the editors that this problem ought to be their most enduring concern:

I am disappointed by our magazine's recent shift of emphasis.... Our most urgent task remains thought change. We must not get sidetracked from that which is the foundation of all thought: the problem of a worldview. It is my hope and request that you go on to elaborate your first article on the question of worldviews and also publish more works by Western philosophers.

See Gu Jiegang (Gu Chengyu), "Gei Mengzhen (Fu Sinian)" [Letter to Fu Sinian], *XC* 1:4 (April 1919):707–9.

9.   "Xinchao fakan zhiqi shu," p. 2.

10.   Charles de Secondat, Baron de Montesquieu, "Preface," *The Spirit of Law*, trans. Thomas Nugent (Chicago, 1952), p. xxii.

11.   Gu Jiegang, "Mingyun" [Fate], in *Gu Jiegang tongsu lunzhuji*, ed. Wang Bixiang (Shanghai, 1947), pp. 24–25.

12.   "Xu Bogan xiansheng ci" [Text of a speech by Mr. Xu Bogan], *Guomin* 1:1 (January 1919), reprinted in *Wusi shiqi de shetuan*, vol. 2, p. 8.

13.   For an extreme statement of the faith of the teachers' generation in scientific certainty, see Chen Duxiu, "Kexue yu shensheng" [Science and the mysterious], *Duxiu wencun*, vol. 2, pp. 57–58.

14.   For a critique of the hasty, instrumental approach to science of May Fourth intellectuals, see D. W. Y. Kwok, *Scientism in Chinese Thought, 1900–1950* (New Haven, 1965).

15.   Wang Xinggong, "Kexue de zhenshi shi keguan de ma?" [Is scientific truth objective or not?], *XC* 2:2 (December 1919):228–29.

16.   Ibid., p. 229. For a further elaboration of Wang's views on the prerequisites for a scientific worldview see Wang Xinggong, "Kexue de qiyuan he xiaoguo" [Origins and impact of science], *XQN* 7:1 (December 1919).

17.   See Feng Youlan, "Bogesen de zhexue fangfa" [Bergson's philosophical method], *XC* 3:1 (September 1921); and Zhang Shenfu, "Kexue li de yi geming" [A revolution in science], *Shaonian shijie* 1:3 (March 1920).

18.   Fu Sinian, "Duiyu Zhongguo jinri tan zhexue zhi guannian" [Reflections on those currently concerned with philosophy in China], *XC* 1:5 (May 1919):725–30.

19.   He Siyuan, "Jinshi zhexue de xin fangfa" [New methodologies in contemporary philosophy], *XC* 2:1 (October 1919):33–35.

20.   He Siyuan, "Zhexue yu changshi" [Philosophy and common sense], *XC* 2:5 (June 1920):1067–70.

21.   Fu Sinian, "Duiyu Zhongguo jinri tan zhexue zhi guannian," p. 728.

22.   Zhang Shenfu, "Lian duoshi: Zhexue shuxue guanxi shi lunyin" [Reflections under a stone roof: Outline of a history of the relationship between philosophy and mathematics], published in *XC* 1:2 (February 1919):305–14. The second half of this discussion was published in *XC* 1:4 (April 1919):642–43. The first article included a lengthy list of names and dates of Western philoso-

phers who were prominent in bringing together mathematics and philosophy. The list ranged from Thales, Anaximander, and Pythagoras through Galileo, Novalis, and Ernst Cassirer.

23. See Chen Daqi, "Pi hunxue" [Exploration in soul science (psychology)], *XQN* 4.5 (May 1910).

24. Wang Jingxi, "Shenmo shi sixiang" [What is thought?], *XC* 1:4 (April 1919). For a more complete sense of Wang's accomplishments during the May Fourth enlightenment, see his analytic introduction to behaviorism in "Xinlixue zhi zuijin qushi" [The latest trends in modern pyschology], *XC* 2:5 (September 1920):899–902. This article was a lucid distillation of the work of Wilhelm Wundt (from original German sources), as well as a discussion of its relationship to and distinction from the psychoanalytical technique pioneered by Freud and the social psychology of William McDougall.

25. See Zhu Ziqing, trans., "Xinlixue de fanwei" ["The scope of psychology" by McDougall], *XC* 2:3 (February 1920):555–67; and Yang Zhensheng's analytical review of A. G. Tansley, "Xin xinlixue" [The new psychology], *XC* 3:2 (March 1922).

26. A sharp contrast may be seen between the concrete, politically oriented explorations of sociology undertaken by Tao Menghe in his article "Shehui diaocha daoyan" [Introduction to social investigation], *XQN* 4:3 (March 1918); and He Siyuan's "Shehuixue zhong de kexue fangfa" [Scientific methodology in sociology], *XC* 2:4 (May 1920).

27. Zhang Shenfu (Zhang Songnian), "Jindai xinli" [Modern psychology], *XQN* 7:3 (February 1920).

28. Tan Pingshan (Tan Mingqian), "Zhexue duiyu kexue zongjiao zhi guanxi lun' [Philosophical perspectives on the relationship between science and religion], *XC* 1:1 (January 1919):60.

29. Ibid., pp. 62–63.

30. Gu Jiegang, "Xinyang" [Belief], in *Gu Jiegang tongsu lunzhuji*, pp. 9–11.

31. Zhang Shenfu, "Ying Fa gongchandang—Zhongguo gaizao" [The British and French Communist parties and China's reform], *XQN* 9:3 (July 1921): 1–3.

32. Luo Jialun, "Jindai xiyang sixiang ziyou de jinhua" [The progress of freedom of thought in the modern West], *XC* 2:2 (December 1919):231.

33. For an historical overview of the revolt against patriarchy, see Judith Stacey, *Patriarchy and Socialist Revolution in China* (Berkeley, 1983), especially pp. 66–107.

34. For a discussion of the anarchist journal *New Century*'s manifesto against ancestor worship, see Robert A. Scalapino and George T. Yu, *The Chinese Anarchist Movement* (Berkeley, 1961), p. 9. As the authors point out, it was Li Shizeng, the Paris-based anarchist, who put forth the call for an "Ancestor Revolution" in the June 1907 issue of *New Century* (ibid., p. 65).

35. Quoted in A. T. Roy, "Attacks upon Confucianism in the 1911–1927 Period: From a Taoist Lawyer, Wu Yu," *The Chung Chi Journal* 4:2 (July 1965):156.

36. Lu Xun, "What Is Required of Us as Fathers Today?" *Selected Works*, vol. 2, p. 71.

37. Fu Sinian, "Wan e zhi yuan" [The source of all evil], *XC* 1:1 (January

1919):126.

38.   Gu Jiegang (Gu Chengyu), "Duiyu jiu jiating de ganxiang" [Reflections on the old family system], *XC* 1:2 (February 1919):161–63.

39.   I am indebted to Professor Frederic Wakeman for bringing to my attention the many-layered connotations of *mingfen zhuyi*. What seemed at first to be mere rage against "roles" now appears to have been a more encompassing critique of the Confucian (and Daoist) assumption that distinctions of social identity are necessary for the maintenance of social order. As the *Shangzi* (an early Confucian text) suggests, social identity must be imposed and not acquired over time. In a section entitled "Fixing Divisions," the text states explicitly: "When the merchants fill the marketplaces and the bandits do not dare to steal, then this is because *mingfen* has already been fixed" (cited in Morohashi, 3297.277).

40.   Gu Jiegang, "Dui jiu jiating de ganxiang," *XC* 1:2:168.

41.   Ibid., *XC* 2:5 (June 1920):925.

42.   Hu Shi, "Ibusheng zhuyi" [On Ibsenism], *XQN* 4:6 (June 1918):503.

43.   Hu Shi, "Fei geren zhuyi xin shenghuo" [The anti-individualistic new life], in *Hu Shi wencun*, vol. 4 (Shanghai, 1930), pp. 1043–60. For a more thorough discussion of Hu Shi's view of individualism, see Jerome Grieder, *Hu Shih and the Chinese Renaissance* (Cambridge, Mass., 1970), especially pp. 93–95 and pp. 324–29.

44.   Wu Kang, "Weiwo zhuyi" [Egoism], *Zhexue* vol. 2 (August 1921):10–14.

45.   For a new and comprehensive analysis of the function of the Qu Yuan myth in modern Chinese history, see Lawrence Schneider, *A Madman of Ch'u: The Chinese Myth of Loyalty and Dissent* (Berkeley, 1980).

46.   Hu Shi, "Fei geren zhuyi xin shenghuo," p. 506.

47.   One of the most famous Noras of this period was Zhou Enlai. For a more general discussion of Nora's impact on Chinese views about individualism, see Vera Schwarcz, "Ibsen's Nora: The Promise and the Trap," *Bulletin of Concerned Asian Scholars* (January–March 1975).

48.   Ye Shengtao (Ye Shaojun), "Nüzi renge wenti" [The question of women's dignity], *XC* 1:2 (February 1919):256–58.

49.   Yang Zhensheng, "Zhen nü" [The virgin], *XC* 2:5 (June 1920):104–8.

50.   Zhang Shenfu, "Nüzi jiefang da budang" [Women's liberation: A great injustice], *Shaonian Zhongguo* 1:4 (October 1919): 41–42.

51.   Tao Menghe, "Xin qingnian zhi xin daode" [New ethics of the new youth], *XQN* 4:2 (February 1918):96. A similar point of view was expressed by Li Dazhao in an article even more directly addressed to the new youth and published in *New Tide*. "Wuzhi biandong yu daode biandong" [Material change and change in ethics], *XC* 2:2 (December 1919):207–24.

52.   Wu Kang, "Wo guo jinri daode de genben wenti" [The basic problem of ethics in our country today], *XC* 1:2 (February 1919):332–33.

53.   Yu Pingbo, "Wode daode tan" [My view on ethics], *XC* 1:5 (May 1919):889.

54.   Zhang Shenfu's translation of the "Déclaration de l'indépendance de l'esprit" was deemed so important that it was published both in *New Youth*, *XQN* 7:1 (December 1919), and in *New Tide*, *XC* 2:2 (December 1919).

55.   See Li Dazhao, "Bolshevism de shengli" [The victory of Bolshevism],

XQN 5:5 (October 1918); Luo Jialun, "Jinri zhi shijie xinchao" [The new tide in the world today], 1:1 (January 1919); and Fu Sinian, "Shehui geming—Eguo shi de geming" [Social revolution—revolution in the Russian way], *XC* 1:1 (January 1919).

50. Lu Xun, "Suigan lu" [Random thoughts], *XQN* 2:7 (February 1919): 213. It is significant to note that Lu Xun still called for the "worship" of Darwin in spite of his own criticism of the overly scientific-minded *New Tide* members.

57. "Xinchao fakan zhiqu shu," p. 2.

58. The last issue of *New Tide*, vol. 3, no. 2, appeared in March 1922. Afterward, Li Xiaofeng and Sun Fuyuan, with the aid of their teachers Lu Xun and Zhou Zuoren, turned *New Tide* into a society for sponsoring a new literature series. See Li Xiaofeng, "Xinchao de shimo."

59. Sun Fuyuan, "Duwei boshi jinri qule" [Dr. Dewey departed today], *Chen bao* (11 July 1921):18–20.

60. For a discussion of the May Fourth background of Lu Xun's story, "The True Chronicle of Ah Q," see Huang Sung-k'ang, *Lu Hsün and the New Culture Movement in China* (Amsterdam, 1957).

61. Hu Shi, "Xin sichao de yiyi" [The meaning of the new thought tide], *XQN* 7:1 (December 1919).

62. Fu Sinian, "Zhongguo gou he Zhongguo ren" [Chinese dogs and Chinese people], *XQN* 6:6 (October 1919).

63. Luo Jialun, "Piping de yanjiu: san W zhuyi" [The study of criticism—Three W-ism], *XC* 2:3 (April 1920):601–3.

64. Ibid., p. 604.

65. Wu Kang, "Cong sixiang gaizao dao shehui gaizao" [From thought reform to social reform], *XC* 3:1 (October 1920):42–50.

66. Zhang Xuan, "Bo Xinchao Guogu he kexue de jingshen pian" [Rebuttals between *New Tide* and *National Heritage* concerning the scientific spirit], *Guogu* no. 3 (May 1919), quoted in *Beijing Daxue xiaoshi* (Shanghai, 1981), p. 57.

67. Chen Duxiu, "Kongjiao yanjiu" [Research on Confucianism], in *Duxiu wencun*, vol. 1, p. 627.

68. Mao Zishui, "Guogu he kexue de jingshen" [The national heritage and the scientific spirit], *XC* 1:5 (May 1919):731.

69. Gu Jiegang, "Women duiyu guogu ying qu de taidu" [What our attitude ought to be toward the national heritage], in *Xin wenxue yundong shi ziliao*, ed. Zhang Ruoying (Shanghai, 1944), p. 215.

70. Francis Bacon, *The New Organon*, ed. F. H. Anderson (New York, 1960), p. 47.

71. Chen Duxiu, "Ouxiang pohuai lun" [On iconoclasm], *XQN* 5:2 (August 1918):102.

72. Fu Sinian, "Pohuai" [On destruction], *Fu Sinian xuanji*, vol. 2, p. 186.

73. Fu Sinian, "Yi duan fenghua" [Some crazy words], *XC* 1:4 (April 1919):684–85.

74. For a concise discussion of the merchant and labor strikes that followed the May Fourth demonstration of 1919, see Chow Tse-tsung, *May Fourth Movement*, pp. 117–44.

75. "Changxindian jiangyan zu de baogao" [Report of the Changxindian

lecture group] (13 March 1920), in *Wusi shiqi de shetuan*, vol. 2, pp. 167–68.

76. "Fengtai jiangyan zu huodong de xiangxi baogao" [Detailed report on the Fengtai lecture group's activities] (Spring 1920), in ibid., pp. 165–66.

77. "Beida pingmin yexiao diyici biye shi canguan ji" [Impressions of the first graduation ceremony at the Beida night school], *Chen bao* (17 January 1922):35.

78. Author's interview with Hang Baohua, retired worker at the Changxindian locomotive factory, March 1980. Hang came to the factory in 1915 as a temporary laborer. He transferred from the trade school to the workers' recreation society in 1921. For a complementary story of the Workers' After-Hours School, see *Beifang de hongxing* [Red star of the north], a narrative account prepared for the sixtieth anniversary of the Changxindian factory (Beijing, 1960), pp. 57–74.

79. The contrast between *New Tide* and *Citizen* is most overdrawn in the 1958 edition of *Wusi shiqi qikan jieshao* [Introduction to the periodicals of the May Fourth era] (Beijing, 1958), edited by the Marxism-Leninism Lenin-Stalin Research Association. Published at the height of the Great Leap Forward, this edition emphasized the patriotic and, by vague implication, "proletarian" utility of *Citizen* magazine in contrast to the iconoclastic, "bourgeois" *New Tide*.

80. For an overview of the relationship between Mu Ouqu and Cai Yuanpei, see Fu Lecheng's article "Fu Mengzhen xiansheng yu wusi yundong," [Mr. Fu Mengzhen (Fu Sinian) and the May Fourth movement], *Wusi yundong lunwen ji*, ed. Wang Rongzu (Taibei, 1979), p. 273. Also see Wang Jingxi's own preface to his psychology M.A. thesis, "The Relation between Spontaneous Activity and Oestrous Cycle in the White Rat," *Comparative Psychology Monographs* (Baltimore, 1923) in which he writes, "Last but not least, I wish to acknowledge that it is due to the generosity of Mr. S. Y. Moh, a cotton manufacturer at Shanghai, that the National University of Peking was enabled to send me, along with five other students, to study abroad."

81. Author's interview with Zhang Shenfu, June 1981. In this conversation, Zhang mentioned an extended correspondence between himself and Fu Sinian in Europe. These letters were "lost"—most likely burned during the Cultural Revolution of 1966–69, when all Chinese intellectuals with contacts in Taiwan were subject to suspicion and persecution.

82. Kang Baiqing, "Song Xu Deheng" [Sending off Xu Deheng], *Xingqi pinglun* no. 41 (14 March 1920):4.

83. "Faqi Makesi xueshuo yanjiu hui qishi" [Announcement of the founding of the Society for the Study of Marxist Theory], in *Wusi shiqi de shetuan*, vol. 2, pp. 272–73.

84. "Juewu de xuanyan" [Manifesto of the Enlightenment Society], in ibid., pp. 302–3.

85. Zhang Shenfu (Chi), "Weixian sixiang?" [Dangerous thoughts?], *XQN* 6:5 (May 1919):552–54.

86. Yang Zhongjian, "Gei jizhe" [Letter to the editor], *XC* 1:5 (May 1919): 948–49.

87. Fu Sinian, "Zhongguo gou he Zhongguo ren," in *Fu Sinian xuanji*, p. 348.

88. Fu Sinian, "Zhi Hu Shi" [Letter to Hu Shi], *Hu Shi laiwang shuxin xuan*, vol. 1, pp. 102–6.

89. Chen Duxiu, "Fankang yulun de yongqi" [The courage to oppose public opinion], *Duxiu wencun*, vol. 2, p. 123.

90. The first cell of the Chinese Communist Party in Beijing included *New Tide* members Zhang Shenfu and Gao Shangde and comrades from the Commoners' Education Lecture Society such as Deng Zhongxia, Zhang Guotao, Zhu Wushan and Li Jun. Zhou Zixin, "Beijing gongchandang xiaozu" [The Beijing Communist Party cell], *Renmin ribao* (6 October 1980):4; also, author's interview with Zhang Shenfu, March and April 1980.

91. For an overview of the personalities and worldviews of this group of intellectuals, see Leo Ou-fan Lee, *The Romantic Generation of Modern Chinese Writers* (Cambridge, Mass., 1973), especially pp. 11–14. Professor Lee translates *Wenxue yanjiu hui*, "Society for Literary Research," as the "Association for Literary Studies." I have kept the literal version since it seems to convey more explicitly its members' commitment to make literature the object of "research"—every bit as serious as the "social research" undertaken by activist students during the May Fourth movement mobilization.

92. I am indebted for this interpretation of the relationship between Deng Zhongxia and Zhu Ziqing to Mr. Zhu Qiaosen, the son of Zhu Ziqing, whom I was able to meet and interview in Beijing in April 1980. For further evidence of Deng Zhongxia's ongoing concern with May Fourth ideas see the following articles published in the Communist Party journal of the early 1920s: "Xin shiren de banghe" [Rebuke of the new poets], *Zhongguo qingnian* (1 December 1923):4–6; "Gongxian yu xin shiren zhi qian" [In honor of the future of new poets], ibid. (22 December 1923):6–9; "Lianai ziyou wenti" [The problem of free love], ibid. (6 January 1924):14–16.

93. Zhu Ziqing, "Zeng A. S." [Dedicated to A. S.], in *Zhu Ziqing xuanji* (Hong Kong reprint, 1975), pp. 27–29.

CHAPTER 4

1. Zhu Ziqing, "Xuege" [Song of blood], *Xiaoshuo yuebao* 16:7 (July 1925):1.

2. Qiu Zuojian, "Shanghai Daxue" [Shanghai University], *Dangshi ziliao*, vol. 2 (Shanghai, 1980), pp. 206–7. Also see Wei Wei and Qian Xiaohui, *Deng Zhongxia zhuan* [Biography of Deng Zhongxia] (Beijing, 1981), pp. 106–16.

3. Author's interview with Ye Shengtao, June 1980.

4. Deng Zhongxia, *Zhongguo zhigong yundong jianshi, 1919–1926* [A brief history of the Chinese industrial labor movement] (Beijing, 1949), pp. 6 and 142. For a further elaboration of the relationship between May Fourth students and the labor movement, see Jean Chesneaux, *The Chinese Labor Movement* (Stanford, 1968), especially chapters 2 and 3.

5. Chow Tse-tsung, *May Fourth Movement*, pp. 113–14.

6. For historical accounts of the events of 1925–27, see Nicholas R. Clifford, *Shanghai, 1925: Urban Nationalism and the Defense of Foreign Privilege* (Ann Arbor, 1979), pp. 1–34; and Tien-wei Wu, "Chiang Kai-shek's April 12 Coup of 1927," in *China in the 1920s*, ed. F. G. Chan and T. H. Etzold (New York, 1976), pp. 147–59.

7. Hannah Arendt, *On Violence* (New York, 1969), pp. 30–31.

8. Ibid., pp. 67–68.

9. Ibid., p. 55.

10. For a detailed account of Mao Dun's early years at the Commercial Press, see Mao Dun, "Shangwu yinshuguan bianji shenghuo zhi yi" [An account of life as one of the editors at the Commercial Press], *Xin wenxue shiliao* no. 1 (1978):1–12.

11. Leo Ou-fan Lee, *The Romantic Generation*, pp. 10–11.

12. Li Xiaofeng, "Xinchao de shimo," p. 33.

13. Mao Dun, "Wusa yundong yu Shangwu yinshuguan bagong—huiyilu" [Reminiscence: The May Thirtieth movement and the strike at the Commercial Press], *Xin wenxue shiliao* no. 2 (February 1980):1–26. Mao cites the forthcoming marriage of Qu Qiubai and Yang Zhihua as one of the private, romantic concerns of this group on the eve of May 30, 1925.

14. Ye Shengtao (Ye Shaojun), "Wuyue sanshiyi ri zhi jiyu zhong" [In the midst of the May 31 downpour], *Xiaoshuo yuebao* 16:7 (July 1925):5.

15. Zheng Zhenduo (Xi Di), "Jiexue xichu hou" [After the blood has been washed off the streets], ibid., p. 18.

16. Author's interview with Zheng Zhenduo's son, Zheng Erkang, April 1980.

17. Zhu Ziqing, "Zhizhengfu da tusha ji" [Record of the government's great massacre], in *Zhu Ziqing wenji* (Taibei reprint, 1975), pp. 267–70.

18. Ibid., p. 268.

19. This phrase came into common use after Lu Xun first introduced it in his 1918 essay "How Are We to Be Fathers Today?" in *Selected Works*, vol. 2, p. 71.

20. Lu Xun, "More Roses without Blooms," *Selected Works*, vol. 2, pp. 259–60.

21. Zhou Zuoren, "Guanyu sanyue shiba ri de sizhe" [On the dead of March eighteenth], in *Zexie zhi* (Beijing, 1927), pp. 139–40.

22. Ibid., p. 141.

23. Ibid.

24. Lu Xun, "In Memory of Miss Liu Hezhen," *Selected Works*, vol. 2, p. 268.

25. Ibid., p. 269.

26. Quoted in Amitendranath Tagore, *Literary Debates in Modern China, 1918–1937* (Tokyo, 1967), p. 62. David Pollard has also discussed the theme of Zhou Zuoren's "retreat" into literature, in his essay "Chou Tso-jen and Cultivating One's Own Garden," *Asia Major* vol. 2, part 2 (1966–67):180–98. Pollard has added some important biographical information on Zhou's later years in his book on Zhou's literary theories, *A Chinese Look at Literature* (Berkeley, 1973), especially pp. iii–x and 121–39.

27. Zhou Zuoren, "San yiba de sizhe" [For those who died on March eighteenth] (a letter to *Beixin* editor Li Xiaofeng, a *New Tide* member and Zhou's student at Beida), *Beixin* 4:5 (14 January 1928):37.

28. Zhou Zuoren (Kaiming), "Women de diren" [Our enemy], *Yusi* no. 76 (22 December 1924):7.

29. Ibid., p. 8.

30. Hu Yuzhi, "Women de shidai" [Our era], *Yiban* (5 November 1926):329.

31. See introduction, n. 18.

32. Tao Menghe, "Chijiu de aiguo yundong" [The long-term patriotic movement] *Xiandai pinglun* 2:29 (10 June 1925):46.

33. Quoted in Mao Dun, "Wusa yundong," p. 13.

34. Lu Xun was the most outspoken critic of "national character" [*guomin xing*] since the May Fourth era. His 1926 essay in commemoration of his student Liu Hezhen (in *Selected Works*, vol. 2) concluded with the following restatement of his views of his own compatriots:

I am always willing to think the worst of my countrymen. Still quite a few things surprised me this time. One is that authorities acted so barbarously, another that rumor mongers could sink so low, yet another, that Chinese girls could face death so bravely (p. 269).

35. Qian Xuantong, "Guanyu fan diguo zhuyi" [On anti-imperialism] *Yusi* no. 31 (15 June 1925):1.

36. Ibid., p. 2.

37. Ibid.

38. Zhang Shenfu, "Diguo zhuyi deng" [Imperialism and so on], *Yusi* no. 32 (19 June 1925):123–24.

39. Yu Pingbo, "Xuechi yu yuwu" [Defense and revenge], in *Zabaner* (Shanghai, 1928), pp. 30–36.

40. Ibid., p. 37.

41. Even Yu Pingbo's own friends, such as Zheng Zhenduo, found it difficult to understand, much less accept, his criticism of the anti-imperialist mass fervor. For a public debate, rather bitter in tone, about Yu Pingbo's essay "Defense and revenge" see Yu Pingbo, "Zhi Xidi jun" [Questioning Xidi (Zheng Zhenduo)], *Yusi* no. 36 (20 July 1925); and Zheng Zhenduo, "Da Pingbo jun" [Answer to Yu Pingbo], *Yusi* no. 39 (10 August 1925).

In this exchange Yu Pingbo claimed that his friend had misinterpreted his point about the need to focus on internal problems, such as feudal culture and landlord politics, before becoming swept up in the passion of anti-imperialist resistance. Therefore, he concluded: "I think that before we can truly defend ourselves from outside aggression, we must wash our domestic shame first. Otherwise, it's only empty words to talk about 'defense,' 'revenge,' etc. Yet Xidi claims I don't want people to look outward ... to the point of implying that I don't want resistance to the British. This is ridiculous." Yu Pingbo, "Zhi Xidi jun," p. 9.

42. Zhu Ziqing, "Baizhongren, shangdi di jiaozi" [White people, the arrogant offspring of God], in *Zhu Ziqing xuanji* (Hong Kong, 1975), pp. 54–55.

43. Ibid., p. 56.

44. Zhang Shenfu, "Gei Zhou Zuoren" [Letter to Zhou Zuoren], *Jingbao fukan* (19 August 1925):147–48.

45. For a theoretical discussion of the role of "interruptive events" in the transformation of intellectuals' consciousness, see Edgar Morin, "L'événement Sphinx', in *Communication* no. 18 (1972):173–90; and Pierre Nora, "L'événement-monstre," ibid., pp. 166–72.

46. Ye Shengtao, "Wuyue sanshiyi ri zhi jiyu zhong," p. 7.

47. Ye Shengtao, *Ni Huanzhi* (Hong Kong, 1967), p. 166. This novel has also been translated into English: Yeh Sheng-t'ao, *Schoolmaster Ni Huan-chih*, trans. A. C. Barnes (Beijing, 1958). All citations here refer to the Chinese edition, and

the translations are my own.

48. Quoted in Mao Dun, "Wusa yundong," p. 11.

49. Ibid., p. 12.

50. Quoted in introduction to *Zhu Ziqing wenji*, p. 32.

51. For a sample of Gu Jiegang's writing style in that transitional year of 1925, see his "Shanghai de luanzi shi zenmayang naoqilai de?" [How did the mess in Shanghai come about?] *Jingpao fukan* no. 177 (12 June 1925); and his "Shangxin ge" [Song of hurt], ibid., p. 2.

52. Ku Chieh-kang, *Autobiography*, pp. 174 and 182.

53. Mao Dun describes his own discovery of greater creativity, after the event of 1925, in terms that capture the spirit of the entire student generation:

Before May Thirtieth, I busied myself only with commentaries and translations. I had not written anything that truly conveyed my own point of view. The May Thirtieth massacre enabled me to break through my own self-repression. It made me realize that assorted argumentative pieces cannot fully express one's feelings and thoughts. I then wrote eight essays, seven of them about May Thirtieth. This writing certainly precipitated the path I subsequently chose for my creative writing (Mao Dun, "Wusa yundong," p. 22).

54. Ye Shengtao, *Ni Huanzhi*, p. 169.

55. Guo Moruo, "Wenyijia de juewu" [The awakening of the artist], in *Xinwenxue shiliao* ed. Zhang Xiruo (Shanghai, 1926), p. 361.

56. In the realm of philosophy, *New Tide* members Feng Youlan and Zhang Shenfu continued this investigation in a more focused and original way. Feng Youlan's major work of this period, *Rensheng zhexue*, translated as *A Comparative Study of Life Ideals* (Shanghai, 1926 and 1927), is a complex, pragmatic synthesis of Eastern and Western thought. According to Feng, Western philosophy views man as opposed to Nature, while Eastern philosophy sees man as synonymous with Nature. Seeking to answer the May Fourth question "what is the meaning of human existence," Feng concludes that socialism is the best worldview. During this same period, Zhang Shenfu was elaborating his methodology of "pure objectivism" aimed at overcoming the dichotomy of self and world. In his major work *Suosi* [Reflections] (Shanghai, 1931), Zhang claims that with sustained philosophical responsiveness to events, the arbitrariness of objectivism as well as the one-sidedness of subjectivism could be overcome. Both Feng Youlan and Zhang Shenfu thus tried to introduce reflection where Guo Moruo could allow only an exclusive choice. Both insisted that for a worldview to be valid and resilient, it must be the result of historical experience rather than instantaneous illumination.

57. Mao Dun, "Shiqi yu xuesheng de zhengzhi yundong" [The warrior spirit and the students' political movement], *Minduo* 8:4 (1 March 1927).

58. Harold Isaacs, *The Tragedy of the Chinese Revolution* (Stanford, 1951), p. 179.

59. I am indebted to Professor Yue Daiyun who, knowing the historical problems of this project, accompanied me to the Beijing Historical Museum in May 1980 and drew the significance of these exhibits to my attention.

60. Ye Shengtao, *Ni Huanzhi*, p. 372.

61. Author's interview with Xu Deheng, May 1983, confirmed by interviews with Zhang Shenfu, also May 1983.

62. Among the intellectuals who became casualties of the White Terror was Zhao Shiyan, a close friend of Zhang Shenfu and member of the first Chinese Communist Party cell active in Paris in 1921. On December 11, 1927, Zhang

Tailei died fighting in the Canton Commune uprising. Zhang Tailei's position and responsibilities fell on the shoulders of Deng Zhongxia, a close friend of *New Tide* intellectuals from their days at Beida. Author's interview with Zhang Shenfu, March and April 1980.

63   Xu Qingyu, "Jinggao qingnian" [A warning to youth], *Zhinan* (20 April 1927):1–2. Xu had been a contributor to the May Fourth periodical *Zhexue* [Philosophy], focusing on problems in academic philosophy, especially on the work of Bertrand Russell. On March 5, 1927, when he began to edit *Zhinan* [Knowing is difficult] with Guomindang sponsorship, he explained the choice of title and focus for the magazine in terms of a classical Chinese saying, "Doing is easy; knowledge is difficult." This was one of the more reflective journals to be published on the GMD side in the turbulent period around 1927.

64.   Guo Moruo, "Qing kan jinri zhi Jiang Jieshi" [Do take a look at today's Jiang Jieshi], in *Geming chunqiu* (Beijing, 1979), pp. 123–43.

65.   Gu Jiegang, "Gei Hu Shi" [Letter to Hu Shi, 20 August 1929], *Hu Shi laiwang shuxin xuan*, vol. 1, pp. 533–35.

66.   Ibid., p. 536. When Gu Jiegang threatened to leave Canton, Fu retaliated, supposedly by declaring: "I'll debase you everywhere you go. I will ruin your reputation, so you'll have nowhere to retreat." Ibid. This vendetta between Fu Sinian and Gu Jiegang was, on a personal scale, similar to the contest being played out for much larger stakes in all of China during the late 1920s.

67.   Zhu Ziqing, "Nali zou" [Nowhere to go], *Yiban* 3:4 (March 1928): 368–69.

68.   Lu Xun, "Da Youheng xiansheng" [Reply to Mr. Youheng], in *Lu Xun quanji*, vol. 3 (Shanghai, 1948), pp. 443–46 (emphasis added). This translation differs somewhat from the one in *Selected Works*, vol. 2, pp. 346–52.

69.   Ye Shengtao, *Ni Huanzhi*, pp. 370–71 and 375.

70.   Mao Dun, "Du Ni Huanzhi" [On reading *Ni Huanzhi*], in *Zhongguo wenyi lunzhang*, ed. Li Helin (Shanghai, 1932), pp. 392, 400–401.

71.   Zhu Ziqing, "Nali zou," p. 377.

72.   Long before the slogan "Down with the Intellectual Class' had emerged, the expression "intellectual class' had been widely used with some negative connotations. The phrase *zhishi jieji*, borrowed from the Japanese *chishiki kaikyū*, was, like so many other Japanese borrowings, appropriated in a critical fashion. As early as 1919, Zhang Shenfu had warned in the pages of the *Weekly Critic* that the "intellectual class must not take itself too seriously, must not imagine itself better than other classes just because it is more educated." Zhang Shenfu (Chi), "Zhishi jieji" [The intellectual class], *Meizhou pinglun* 31 (15 July 1919):4.

Qu Qiubai, who later became a bitter critic of the pretensions of May Fourth intellectuals, wrote in 1923 that "the intellectual class has a special, lofty mission in our contemporary revolutionary circumstances." Noting that the masses had very few means available to them to express their own will, Qu argued that the "intellectual class" had the right and the responsibility to speak on behalf of the oppressed. This mandate, however, was provisional: "Today, the intellectual class lives off the surplus of production—the blood and sweat of working people.... They are the vanguard of the masses.... Behind them lies the main force.... Consequently they must not dare to be overly confident." Qu Qiubai, "Zhengzhi yundong yu zhishi jieji" [The political movement and the intellectual class], *Xiangdao* 1:17 (January 1923).

In the early 1920s, even intellectuals like Gu Jiegang, who did not share Qu Qiubai's faith in revolution, were eager to find out, to prove that the "intellectual class" shared the fate of the oppressed. Hardly "confident," judging by his bleak mood in 1925–26, Gu was reassured by his friends that in the conflict between rulers and the oppressed, "we belong to the latter." "Jiegang, my brother, your sorrow and your sadness are the sorrow and sadness of the entire intellectual class." Zhou Yutong, "Gu zhou Gushibian de du houkan" [Thoughts upon reading Gu's *Gushibian*], in Gu Jiegang, ed., *Gushibian*, vol. 2 (Beijing, 1930), p. 329.

In the months before the outbreak of the terror, Qu Qiubai's mandate was wearing thin. Liberal inheritors of the May Fourth legacy such as Hu Shi started to advocate "good government by gentlemen." In retaliation, Lu Xun began a one-man campaign against "gentlemen," mocking the "goats" at the head of a flock of sheep. Such goats, Lu Xun warned, can easily turn into "heartless hedgehogs who do not care how they prick the common people in order to keep warm. Of course, people get hurt, but that is their fault for not having quills to make others keep a suitable distance. Confucius also said, punishment does not extend to nobles. So no wonder that people want to be gentlemen." Lu Xun, "A Few Parables," in *Selected Works*, vol. 2, p. 521.

73. Quoted in James Pinckney Harrison, *The Long March to Power: A History of the Chinese Communist Party, 1921–1972* (New York, 1972), p. 88.

74. For a discussion of Gu Jiegang's response to the waning fortunes of the old Confucian elite in the late 1920s, see Laurence Schneider, *Ku Chieh-kang and China's New History* (Berkeley, 1971), pp. 115–20. For Gu, even more traumatic than the ill fortune of his former mentor, Zhang Taiyan, was the suicide of Wang Guowei, another famous scholar-historian of Zhang's generation.

75. Zhang Xiruo, "Zhongguo jinri suowei zhishi jieji" [The so-called intellectual class today], *Xiandai pinglun* (January 1927):90–92.

76. Ding Wen, "Dadao zhishi jieji" [Down with the intellectual class], *Xiandai pinglun* [February 1927):8.

77. Ibid.

78. Xin Ru, "Cong dadao zhishi jieji kouhao zhong suo renshi de" [What can be understood from the slogan "Down with the intellectual class"], *Yiban* 3:1 (August 1927), pp. 35–36.

79. Feng Xuefeng (Hua Shi), "Geming yu zhishi jieji" [Revolution and the intellectual class], in *Zhongguo wenyi lunzhan*, ed. Li Helin (Shanghai, 1932), p. 1.

80. Ibid., p. 4.

81. Cheng Fangwu, "From a Literary Revolution to a Revolutionary Literature," trans. Michael Gotz, *Bulletin of Concerned Asian Scholars* (January–March 1976):37.

82. Ibid., p. 38.

83. Lu Xun, "Befuddled Wooliness," in *Selected Works*, vol. 3, pp. 18–19.

84. Ibid., p. 20.

85. Mao Dun, "From Guling to Tokyo," trans. Chen Yu-shi, *Bulletin of Concerned Asian Scholars* (January–March 1976):44.

86. Mao Dun, in his novel *Pursuit*, described this mood of self-chastisement through the voice of a female character, Zhang Qiuliu, for whom class-consciousness also seems to be equivalent to class guilt.

Why am I so feeble? Why do I lack both the courage to be progressive and the guts to fall behind? Why so self-conflicted? ... Isn't it because the fierce struggle between the two great social forces of light and dark is reflected and rages in my soul? Isn't it because I am a so-called petty bourgeois intellectual, raised in comfortable environment and education, all this combining to make me weak? (Unpublished translation by Robert Delfs.)

87.   Zhu Ziqing, "Nali zou," pp. 374–75.
88.   Ibid., p. 375.
89.   Ibid.

CHAPTER 5

1.   Mao Dun, "Du Ni Huanzhi," p. 388.
2.   Zhu Ziqing, "Ye Shengtao de duanpian xiaoshuo" [The short stories of Ye Shengtao], in *Zhu Ziqing wenji*, pp. 349–55.
3.   Mao Tse-tung, "On New Democracy," in *Selected Works of Mao Tse-tung* (Beijing, 1967), vol. 2, p. 376.
4.   For Luo Jialun's view of Qinghua, see "Xueshu duli yu xin Qinghua" [Academic freedom and the new Qinghua] in *Shizhe rusi ji*, ed. Luo Jialun and Mao Zishui, pp. 7–14. For a perspective from the faculty's side, see Feng Youlan, "Wusi qian de Beida he wusi hou de Qinghua" [Beida before May Fourth and Qinghua after May Fourth], *Wenshi ziliao* no. 34 (October 1962).
5.   Author's interview with Ye Shengtao, June 1980.
6.   For a detailed discussion of the political background of this event, see Tsi-an Hsia, "The Enigma of the Five Martyrs," in *The Gate of Darkness* (Seattle, 1968), pp. 163–233.
7.   Lu Xun, "The Revolutionary Literature of the Chinese Proletariat and the Blood of the Pioneers," in *Selected Works*, vol. 3, p. 120.
8.   Quoted in Sun Yan, "Aiguo zhuyi zhe Wang Zaoshi" [The patriotic Wang Zaoshi], *Qishi niandai* (May 1981):76–77.
9.   Fu Sinian, "Chen Duxiu an" [The case of Chen Duxiu], *Duli pinglun* no. 24 (30 October 1932):543; also in *Fu Sinian xuanji*, vol. 5, pp. 781–89.
10.   For a sample of the correspondence between Hu Shi and Chen Duxiu, see *Hu Shi laiwang shuxin xuan*, vol. 2, pp. 143 and 268.
11.   "Xinyue de taidu" [The attitude of the *Crescent Moon* Society], in Li Helin, *Zhongguo wenyi lunzhan*, pp. 435–36.
12.   Luo Longji, a *Crescent Moon* member, was arrested in November 1930 within hours of publishing an article about the GMD's disregard for civil rights. A year later, *Xinyue* was indicted because the journal "has often published writings hostile to the Party. Recently ... it even calumniated the Constitution and vilified the Party." Lee-hsia Hsu Ting, *Government Control of the Press in Modern China, 1900–1949* (Cambridge, Mass., 1974), p. 93. As a result of this directive, *Xinyue* was declared to be "semi-reactionary," an ironic echo of leftist condemnations. See Lu Xun, "The Function of the Critics of the Crescent Moon Society," in *Selected Works*, vol. 3, pp. 60–61.
13.   Hu Shi, "Xin wenhua yundong yu Guomindang" [The New Culture movement and the Guomindang], in *Renquan lunji* (Shanghai, 1930), p. 167.
14.   Lu Xun, "Hard Translation and the Class Character of Literature," in *Selected Works*, vol. 3, pp. 92–93.
15.   Quoted in Tagore, *Literary Debates*, pp. 114–15. Lu Xun expressed his

own views at the founding meeting in considerably less exuberant terms. While he affirmed the revolutionary artist's unique contribution, he also criticized the arrogance that flows from this sense of special mission:

Needless to say, the intellectual class has its own special tasks which cannot be slighted. But certainly it is not the duty of the working class to extend to poets and writers any privileged treatment.... The fact that the position of the proletariat is so dismal in society while proletarian literature is exalted in the world of letters only proves the fact that proletarian writers have become alienated from the proletariat and have lapsed back into the old society. ("Thoughts on the League of Left Wing Writers," *Selected Works*, vol. 3, p. 106.)

16.   Hu Qiuyuan put forth his slogan "Keep Hands Off Art" in his key essay: "Wenhua yundong de wenti" [Problems of the cultural movement], in *Ziyou wenyi lunbianji*, ed. Su Wen (Shanghai, 1933), p. 310. Su Wen, more than Hu Qiuyuan, seemed fearful of the organizational power of the league. He claimed that writers who felt themselves incapable of reflecting "proletarian feelings" in their work had become so intimidated by the requirements of left-wing ideology that they remained leftists at the cost of their artistic productivity. Su attributed this self-repression of writers to the bewilderment occasioned by the changing place of art in class struggle:

At first, before the concept of class assaults the mind of the writer, he dreams of literature as a pure virgin. But soon people inform him that she is not a virgin but a whore that can be sold for money. Today she may be sold to the bourgeoisie and tomorrow to the proletariat. The writer disbelieves for a while, but eventually there is no way to deny this (p. 129).

17.   The more intellectuals like Hu Qiuyuan and Su Wen tried to lift May Fourth out of its historical context, the more they provoked the bitter attack of Marxist theoreticians of the League of Left Wing Writers. One of the most vehement opponents of Hu and Su was Feng Xuefeng, who wrote the following indictment:

People like Hu Qiuyuan are infatuated with their own peacock feathers, with petty bourgeois ideals of beauty.... They stand agitated and undecided in the light of dusk. Under the glimmer of the setting sun, they want to grasp Marxism to their bosom and whirl with intoxication. They exclaim in lilting, pathetic voices: "Let us be!"

Feng Xuefeng (Hua Shi), "Cong di sanzhong ren shuo dao Zuolian" [From the third type to the Left League], ibid., p. 41.

Qu Qiubai, responding to Su Wen's complaints about whorish art, wrote that it was the artist who prostituted himself by falsely cherishing the purity of his work:

Literature is not a whore; it always belongs to a certain class. Every class has its own literature, and it is useless for me to buy or for you to sell.... Every writer, whether consciously or unconsciously, whether active in writing or in retirement, always represents the consciousness and the attitudes of a class. In a class society undergoing tremendous changes, no matter where you run, you can never be a person of the "third type" (ibid., pp. 96–97).

18.   Zhu Ziqing, "Lun wuhua ke shuo" [On having nothing left to say], in *Zhu Ziqing xuanji*, pp. 88–89.

19.   Ibid., p. 90.

20.   Guo Zhanbo, "Feng Youlan," in *Jin wushi nian Zhongguo sixiang shi* [Chinese intellectual history of the past fifty years] (Beijing, 1936), pp. 196–232; and Schneider, *Ku Chieh-kang*.

Another promethean intellectual who, like Lu Xun, tried to "steal fire from abroad to cook his own flesh" was Zhang Shenfu. A professor of philosophy at Qinghua in the early 1930s (when Zhu Ziqing was also there), Zhang used his distance from Shanghai to find out what might be done now that there seemed to be "nothing left to say." As editor of the "World Thought" column of the Tianjin-based *Dagong bao* from 1932 to 1934, he consciously and systematically appropriated Marxist philosophy for Chinese purposes. He was aware that the revolution in 1927 failed partly because of the inadequate theoretical prepared- ness of so-called spokesmen for the revolution. So, Zhang and his circle of Qing- hua philosophers, which included his brother Zhang Dainian and a relative by marriage, Feng Youlan, sought to expand and strengthen the basis of Chinese social theory. They did so by incorporating the latest Western philosophies, especially those of Wittgenstein, Einstein, and, of course, Bertrand Russell. It was Zhang's intention, much as it was Zhu Ziqing's, to go beyond the abstract, empty May Fourth concern with the "ideal human condition." This was a dif- ficult and dangerous task in the context of Guomindang rule. Giving attention to dialectical issues in formal philosophy as well as ongoing reports on foreign scho- lars' discussion of materialism turned out to be an effective way to regain some ground for critical reason. During the New Enlightenment movement of 1936 to 1939, as we shall see, Zhang Shenfu made even bolder claims on behalf of reason.

21.   For a discussion of the problem of intellectuals' class interests in Gu Jiegang's historiography, see Schneider, *Ku Chieh-kang*, pp. 188–217.

22.   For a discussion of the historiographical implications of the transition from *yigu* (doubting of antiquity) to *shigu* (explanation of antiquity), see Arif Dirlik, *Revolution and History: The Origins of Marxist Historiography in China, 1919– 1937* (Berkeley, 1978), p. 265.

23.   The slogan "mass art" did not originate in 1930. Two years earlier, on September 20, 1928, Yu Dafu had begun to edit the journal *Mass Literature* (*Dazhong wenyi*) that was later to become one of the main organs of the League of Left Wing Writers. At its inception, the new magazine introduced the theme of mass culture in an intentionally non-partisan, almost apolitical, manner. The first issue displayed its cosmopolitan spirit on the art deco jacket with its Espe- ranto subtitle: "Literatura por Homaro." In the lead article, the editor defined the term "mass literature." Acknowledging the Japanese origins of the term "popular short story" (*dazhong xiaoshuo*), Yu went on to alter and broaden its meaning by consciously distinguishing it from the Japanese connotations of "art of the lower classes": "Our meaning is that literature is something that belongs to the masses. Unlike some people, we do not believe that it can be the property of a certain class.... We believe that literature is of the masses, for the masses, and concerns the masses" (*Dazhong wenyi* 1:1 [September 1928]:2).

24.   Shen Duanxian, "Suowei dazhonghua de wenti" [The so-called prob- lem of popularization], *Dazhong wenyi* (March 1930):630.

25.   Ibid., p. 631.

26.   This concern with the self-transformation of those who would change the language and the mental habits of the masses echoed the concerns of May Fourth activists. What was new in 1930, however, was the urgency with which the intellectuals confronted their own elitism. This "malady" was the object of Guo Moruo's attack on "Red Parnassians," radicals who understood the theory of proletarian revolution but were unwilling to engage in social practice.

Although sharp-tongued about others' foibles, Guo, an erstwhile romantic, was not above imagining an eduring prophetic role for writers willingly to join the "popularization" effort:

Fly speedily toward the masses. You must know clearly that you are not flying up to heaven but down to earth. You must go out to educate the masses ... teach them to achieve their fate as masters of the future society.... You are teachers, you are guides ... you will awaken the oppressed and dazed masses.

Guo Moruo, "Xinxing dazhonghua de renshi" [Understanding the mass art of the rising class], ibid., pp. 632–33.

27.   Lu Xun, "Wenyi de dazhonghua" [The popularization of art], ibid., p. 639.

28.   Qu Qiubai, "Who's 'We'?" trans. Paul G. Pickowicz, *Bulletin of Concerned Asian Scholars* (January–March 1976):46–47.

29.   For a thoughtful analysis of the 1930s attack on the May Fourth legacy, see Merle Goldman, "Left-Wing Criticism of the Pai-hua Movement," in Benjamin Schwartz, ed., *Reflections on the May Fourth Movement: A Symposium* (Cambridge, Mass., 1972), pp. 85–94.

30.   Qu Qiubai, "Who's 'We'?" p. 7.

31.   Quoted in Goldman, "Left-Wing Criticism," p. 88.

32.   Wang Mouzu, "Jinsi wenyan yu qiangjin dujing" [Prohibitions against the classical language and encouragement to read the classics], in *Dazhonghua, baihua, wenyan lunji* (Shanghai, 1934), pp. 7–8.

33.   Wu Zhihui, "Dazhongyu wan sui!" [Long live the mass language!], ibid., p. 233.

34.   Quoted in Cao Juren, "Dazhongyu yundong" [The mass language movement], in *Wentan wushi nian* (Hong Kong, 1969), p. 188.

35.   Lu Xun, "Menwai wentan" [Literary musings of an outsider], in *Wenxue yundong shiliao*, vol. 2 (Shanghai, 1979), pp. 463–64.

36.   See Cao Juren's description of the *New Tide* leadership of the mass language movement in Cao, "Dazhongyu yundong."

37.   Ye Shengtao, "Zatan dushu zuowen he dazhongyu wenxue" [Some remarks on reading, writing and mass language literature], in *Wenxue yundong shiliao*, vol. 2, pp. 445–46.

38.   Ibid., p. 447.

39.   Sun Fuyuan, "Pingmin wenxue gongzuo lüeshuo" [Discussion of work in the common people's literature], *Wenhua yuekan* 1:1 (February 1934):72–78.

40.   Quoted in Arif Dirlik, "The Ideological Foundations of the New Life Movement: A Study in Counterrevolution," *Journal of Asian Studies* (August 1975):950.

41.   Ibid.

42.   Ibid., p. 978.

43.   Quoted in Moller, "Bellicose Nationalist," p. 166.

44.   Sa Meng-wu, Ho Ping-song, and others, "Declaration for Cultural Construction on a Chinese Basis," in W. T. DeBary, ed., *Sources of Chinese Tradition* (New York, 1960), vol. 2, pp. 192–93.

45.   Hu Shi, "Criticism of the Declaration for Cultural Construction on a Chinese Basis," ibid., pp. 194–95.

46.   Xu Deheng, "Yi er jiu pianduan huiyi" (Fragmentary recollections of

the December Ninth movement), *Renmin ribao* (9 December 1980):4.

47. Nym Wales (Helen Snow), *Notes on the Chinese Student Movement, 1935–1936* (Stanford, 1959), p. 92.

48. Schneider, *Ku Chieh-kang*, pp. 281–82. Zhang Shenfu summed up his own role in the December Ninth movement in an unpublished manuscript entitled "Yi er jiu yundong de shizhong" [The December Ninth movement from beginning to end], completed April 1980.

49. Yu Pingbo, "Jiuguo ji qita cheng wenti de tiaojian" [National salvation and other problematic preconditions], in *Zabaner zhi er*, (Shanghai, 1933), pp. 71–73.

50. Nie Gannu, *Guanyu zhishi fenzi* [On intellectuals] (Shanghai, 1948), pp. 69–70.

51. Quoted in Hu Sheng, "Lun jin liangnian laide sixiang he wenhua" [On the thought and culture of the past two years], *Renshi yuekan* (May 1937):32.

52. Li Gongbo, "Bianzhe xu" [Editor's introduction], in Ai Siqi, *Dazhong zhexue* (Shanghai, 1936), pp. 2–3. Li was a founder of the National Salvation Association and was one of the "seven gentlemen" arrested in 1936.

53. Ai Siqi, ibid., pp. 280–82.

54. Ibid., p. 283.

55. Zhang Shenfu, interview with author, June 1981.

56. Chen Boda, "Zhexue de guofang dongyuan" [The mobilization of philosophy for national defense], *Dushu shenghuo* 4:9 (September 1936):30.

57. See Zhang Shenfu, "Jiuwang yundong de quedian" [The shortcoming of the national salvation movement], *Renren zhoubao* 31 October, 1936; Chen Boda, "Zhexue" (September 1936). For a discussion of the background and significance of these developments in the thought of Chen Boda, see Raymond Wylie, *The Emergence of Maoism: Mao Tse-tung, Ch'en Po-ta and the Search for Chinese Theory, 1935–1945* (Stanford, 1980), pp. 19–52.

58. Zhang Shenfu, "Wusi jinian yu xin qimeng yundong" [Commemorating May Fourth and the new enlightenment movement], in *Shenma shi xin qimeng yundong* (Chongqing, 1939), pp. 18–20.

59. Quoted in He Ganzhi, *Zhongguo qimeng yundong shi* [A history of the Chinese enlightenment movement] (Shanghai, 1937), p. 206.

60. Zhang Shenfu, "Wusi jinian," pp. 5–8.

61. Hu Sheng, "Lun lixing zhuyi" [On rationalism], *Renshi yuekan* (June 1937):131–32.

62. Ai Siqi, "Lun pipan" [On the concept of critique], ibid., pp. 117–20.

63. Chen Boda, "Sixiang wuzui" [To think is no crime], in *Zhenli de zhuiqiu* (Beijing, 1969), pp. 50–52.

64. Zhang Shenfu, "Zhexue yu jiuwang" [Philosophy and national salvation], *Renren zhoubao* [14 November 1936):12.

65. He Ganzhi, *Zhongguo qimeng*, pp. 256–57.

66. Ibid., p. 258.

67. Feng Youlan, interview with author, June 1981.

68. He Ganzhi, *Zhongguo qimeng*, p. 360.

69. Zhang Shenfu, "Wusi jinian."

70. Chen Boda, "Lun wusi xin wenhua yundong" [On the new culture movement during May Fourth], in *Zhenli de zhuiqiu*, pp. 35–36.

71. Chen Boda, "Lun wenhua yundong de minzu chuantong" [On national tradition in the cultural movement], ibid., pp. 74–75; for an excellent discussion of the background of the "old forms, new ideas" debate, going back to Lu Xun, Qu Qiubai, and Zhou Yang, see Wylie, *Emergence of Maoism*, pp. 19–28.

72. Quoted in He Ganzhi, *Zhongguo qimeng*, pp. 213–14.

73. Quoted in ibid., p. 209.

74. Schneider, *Ku Chieh-kang*, pp. 284–85.

75. Quoted in He Ganzhi, *Zhongguo qimeng*, p. 227.

76. Ibid., p. 228.

77. Quoted in Moller, "Bellicose Nationalist," p. 168.

78. Ibid., p. 170.

79. Chen Boda, "Lun Zhongguo de ziwo juexing" [On China's self-awakening], *Xin shiji* 1:2 (October 1936):18–24. Jiang Jieshi, too, preferred the expression *"juexing"* (awakening, as if from sleep) over the more May Fourth–laden *"juewu"* (enlightenment, more conscious responsibility for one's own autonomy). See Dirlik, "Ideological Foundations," p. 948.

80. Zhang Shenfu, "Zhanshi zhexue de biyao" [The necessity for philosophy in wartime], in *Shenma shi xin qimeng yundong*, p. 176.

81. Quoted in He Ganzhi, *Zhongguo qimeng*, pp. 134–35.

82. Ibid., pp. 210–11.

83. This text is quoted and discussed at some length in Wylie, *Emergence of Maoism*, pp. 82–84.

84. Ibid., p. 89.

85. Zhang Shenfu, "Lun Zhongguohua" [On sinification], in *Shenma shi xin qimeng yundong*, p. 257.

86. Ibid., pp. 160–62.

87. Zhang Shenfu, "Xin qimeng yundong yu xin shenghuo yundong" [The new enlightenment movement and the new life movement], in *Shenma shi xin qimeng yundong*, p. 40.

88. Ibid., p. 44.

89. Ibid., p. 49.

90. Zhang Shenfu, "Guomin jingshen zong dongyuan de luoji jieti fafan" [Preliminary logical analysis of the national spiritual mobilization], in *Shenma shi xin qimeng yundong*, pp. 181–83.

91. Zhou Yang, author's interview, May 1983.

CHAPTER 6

1. Eugenio Montale, "The Voice That Came in with the Coots," trans. William Arrowsmith, *New York Review of Books* (16 April 1981):20.

2. Zhou Yang's use of May Fourth for didactic purposes became clearest in his commemorative essay published on the sixtieth anniversary of the event of 1919. His article ("Sanci weida de sixiang jiefang yundong" [Three major thought emancipation movements], *Guangming ribao* [8 May 1979]:1 and 3) linked the enlightenment legacy of May Fourth to the 1942 Yan'an *zhengfeng* (rectification) movement and the 1978–79 thought emancipation launched after the overthrow of the Gang of Four.

3. Luo Jialun (Yi) "Wusi yundong de jingshen" [The spirit of the May

Fourth movement], *Meizhou pinglun* (26 May 1919):1.

4. Ibid.

5. Luo Changpei, "Jinian wusi de sanshi zhounian" [Commemorating the thirtieth anniversary of May Fourth], in *Wusi sa zhounian zhuanji* (Shanghai, 1949), p. 104.

6. Bernard Lewis, *History: Remembered, Recovered, and Invented* (Princeton, 1975), pp. 11–12.

7. Quoted in ibid., p. 56.

8. In 1949, during the civil war, Guo Moruo put forth the most explicit criticism of the Guomindang effort to limit May Fourth to "Literature Day." In a sharply worded essay published in Hong Kong, he wrote: "May Fourth is our national occasion for culture. To keep it a 'Literature Day' ... would be blasphemy. May Fourth is a grand theme which cannot be exhausted by the efforts of writers.... Whoever works in the realm of culture must commemorate May Fourth and make May Fourth their occasion.... Let May Fourth be May Fourth!" Guo Moruo, "Wo zai tiyi" [I want to raise this matter again], in *Zhishi fenzi de daolu* (Hong Kong, 1949), p. 8.

9. For an analysis of the connection between Sun Zhongshan's nationalism and the national essence philosophy of Zhang Taiyan, see Charlotte Furth, "The Sage as Rebel: The Inner World of Chang Ping-lin (Zhang Taiyan)," in Furth, *Limits of Change*, pp. 114–15.

10. Chang Kuo-t ao, *Rise of the Chinese Communist Party*, vol. 1, pp. 77–80.

11. Quoted in "Guofu Sun Zhongshan xiansheng dui wusi yundong de pinglun," [Founding father Mr. Sun Yatsen's evaluation of the May Fourth movement], *Zhuanji wenxue* 14:5 (May 1969):85.

12. Jiang Jieshi, "Zhexue yu jiaoyu duiyu qingnian de guanxi," [The relationship of philosophy and education to youth], translated in Chow Tse-tsung, *May Fourth Movement*, p. 344.

13. Quoted in Yang Yifeng, "Wusi jingshen shuping" [A critique of the spirit of May Fourth], in *Wusi aiguo yundong sishi zhounian jinian tekan* (Taibei, 1959).

14. Mao's bitterness about the arrogance of *New Tide* intellectuals at Beida comes through quite clearly in his autobiographical account in Edgar Snow's *Red Star over China* (New York, 1944).

15. For the role of will in Mao's thoughts and its May Fourth antecedents, see Frederic Wakeman, *History and Will: Philosophical Perspectives of Mao Tse-tung's Thought* (Berkeley, 1973), especially pp. 155–66.

16. Mao Zedong, "Wusi yundong" [The May Fourth movement], in *Zhongguo jindai zhengzhi sixiang shiliao* (Dalian, 1947), p. 116.

17. Mao Zedong, "Xin minzhu zhuyi lun" [On new democracy], in ibid., pp. 111–12. It was in this speech, too, that Mao coined that expression *wenhua geming* (cultural revolution). For a further discussion of the origins of this expression, see Wakeman, *History and Will*, p. 306. Used at first to tame May Fourth, this expression burst into public life during the Cultural Revolution of 1966–69.

18. Chen Boda, "Mao Zedong tongzhi lun wusi yundong" [Comrade Mao Zedong on the May Fourth movement], in *Wusi sa zhounian jinian zhuanji* (Shanghai, 1949), pp. 1 and 14.

19. Fan Wenlan, "Jiqi zhizhui canjia geming jianshe gongzuo" [Make haste to catch up and join the work of revolutionary construction], in ibid., p. 133.

20. See figure 23.

21. Yu Pingbo, "Huigu yu qianzhan" [A backwards glance and a look toward the future], *Wusi sa zhounian jinian zhuanji* (Shanghai, 1949), p. 176.

22. Ibid., p. 177.

23. Chen Guyuan, "Wusi yundong de shidaixing" [The historicity of the May Fourth movement], in *Wusi aiguo yundong sishi zhounian jinian tekan* (Taibei, 1959), pp. 43–44.

24. Luo Jialun's critique of Guomindang authorities who were trying to suppress commemorations of May Fourth was put forth in his essay "Wusi de zhen jingshen" [The true spirit of May Fourth], in *Wusi aiguo yundong sishi zhounian jinian tekan* (Taibei, 1959). In this essay , Luo concluded: "The more you try to stop people from remembering it, the more people will want to commemorate it. This attack on May Fourth, moreover, leaves the day to the Communist Party and gives the Guomindang the undeserved reputation as reactionary. What is most useful is a progressive attitude.... Only then can the harm of the Communists be overcome" (p. 40).

25. Ibid., p. 34. In contrast to Luo Jialun stands Yang Yifeng's 1959 essay, "Wusi jingshen shuping," which represents official Taiwan historiography on May Fourth. In it, Yang makes a careful distinction between the "narrow" May Fourth that won the victory against traitorous warlords and the "broad" May Fourth that eroded traditional values through its advocacy of "critical mentality." The political May Fourth, he claims, was the achievement of students, whereas the more encompassing, cultural May Fourth was instigated by older, less "pure" intellectuals such as Hu Shi and Chen Duxiu. In his final assessment, he describes May Fourth as "an unadulterated patriotic movement. The student activities of that time—meetings and demonstrations—were all good, their [anti-warlord] slogans were good, the boycott of Japanese goods was good.:... From all of these we can see that the student activities of that time were 'pure.' Therefore, the narrow May Fourth deserves our unqualified admiration and respect" (p. 47).

26. "Wusi yundong wushi nian" [The May Fourth movement fifty years later], *Xuexi yeshu* no. 6 (May 1969):5, 7.

27. Feng Youlan, "A Criticism of Confucius and Self-Criticism of My Own Past Veneration of Confucius," in *Selected Articles Criticizing Lin Piao and Confucius* (Beijing, 1974), p. 89.

28. Chen Shaoting, "Jinian wusi yundong de wushi zhounian" [Commemorating the fiftieth anniversary of the May Fourth movement], *Daxue zazhi* no. 17 (May 1969):4.

29. "Zou lishi biyou zhi lu" [The inevitable road of history], *Guangming ribao* (shelun) (4 May 1979):4.

30. "Neichu guozei jiushi yao xiaomie chihuo" [Getting rid of internal traitors means exterminating the red menace], *Zhongyang ribao* (shelun) (4 May 1979):2.

31. For a selection of recently published *New Tide* memoirs see Guo Shaoyu, "Wusi yundong shugan zhi er" [Some ruminations about the May Fourth movement], *Xin wenxue shiliao* no. 3 (May 1979):16–17; Zhang Shenfu, "Wusi yun-

dong de jinxi" [The meaning of the May Fourth movement today], ibid. (May 1979):47–48; Mao Zishui, "Buyao pa wusi, wusi de lishi shi shuyu women de" [Fear not May Fourth; the history of May Fourth belongs to us], in *Wo canjiale wusi yundong* (Taibei, 1979), pp. 4–6; He Siyuan, "Wusi yundong de huiyi" [Reminiscence of May Fourth], *Wenshi ziliao xuanbian* 4 (May 1979):10–12; and Li Xiaofeng, "Xinchao de shimo," pp. 86–120. Some of these *New Tide* intellectuals were invited to contribute their own versions to the official record less publicly.

For example, He Siyuan, the mayor of Beijing on the eve of liberation, told frankly how he joined *New Tide*, studied in the United States, and taught at Sun Yatsen University with Lu Xun. Most striking, in this context, was the story of Li Xiaofeng, Lu Xun's publisher in the 1920s, who told freely the history of the *New Tide*. On the mainland, where this student organization has been at best slighted and more often damned because of its connections with Hu Shi, Fu Sinian, and Luo Jialun, Li Xiaofeng's decision is a testimony to the determination of these old men, now interested only in safeguarding some of the historical truth for posterity. His 46-page memoir (longer than the more official 30-page recollection of Xu Deheng that precedes it) dealt only with the *New Tide*.

With extraordinary care, Li Xiaofeng recalled all who participated in the *New Tide*. He records in detail the shift from active student organization to study society to publishing center of new, scientific theories from abroad.

His history is rich with "secondary heroes" long forgotten in the polemic that followed: Xu Yanzhi, who first wearied of the empty talk of thought emancipation and persuaded others to make their conversation more pointed and more organizational-minded; Zhou Zuoren, who, along with Lu Xun, helped bail out the floundering publishing effort of 1920–21 when so many *New Tide* members went off to Europe and the United States to study; and finally Sun Fuyuan and Li Xiaofeng himself, who kept the spirit of *New Tide* alive in their work as publishers until 1927.

Unlike Li Xiaofeng, who published his memoir in a limited circulation journal, Guo Shaoyu and Zhang Shenfu were sought out by editors of the new mass journal *Xin wenxue shiliao* [Historical sources on modern literature]. In this forum they reminisced about their lives in the old intellectual circles. Guo's narrative focused on the literary reformers who met in Beijing during the new culture movement and organized the Society of Literary Research. He mentioned in passing the "theoretical inadequacies" of those who did not fit into Mao's Zedong "cultural army." He was coming to terms with his own long-time interest in ancient texts and how they kept him in the "ivory tower." At the end he asked a difficult question that he was no longer obliged to answer: "What difference is there between me and feudal scholars? I used the vernacular and they used classical language, that's all." Guo, "Wusi yundong shugan zhi er," p. 17.

The same journal that rehabilitated Guo Shaoyu through recollection did the same for Zhang Shenfu. Prevented from publishing his works for many years, Zhang was now invited back as one of the oldest surviving May Fourth participants. His remembrances of May Fourth, like Guo Shaoyu's, did not fit neatly into the official record of the event. Zhang too insisted on retelling details of how he, Chen Duxiu, and Li Dazhao edited the *Weekly Critic*, and of how he came to translate into Chinese Romain Rolland's "Déclaration de l'indépendance de l'esprit." In this essay, Zhang quarreled again with those who subsume May Fourth into a literary renaissance. He reasserted that the goal of the Chinese enlightenment movement then, as now, was to change the Chinese worldview and to make China more scientific-minded and more democratic in practice. These goals, Zhang concluded, still remained to be achieved. "The present reopening of contacts between China, Japan, the United States, and Western Europe is the true continuation of May Fourth. It may turn out to be a development of May Fourth." Zhang, "Wusi yundong de jinxi," p. 48.

32.   Yu Pingbo, a noted literary critic, tried to retreat from the present by claiming to have been insignificant in the past: "Every time May Fourth comes up, fellow students from Beida ask me to write a commemorative essay, but I always refuse. The reason for my procrastination is that although I had a small role in May Fourth, I was but an infantryman before the cavalry." Yu Pingbo, "Huigu yu qianzhan," p. 174. Ten years later, fellow *New Tide* member and historian Mao Zishui reluctantly accepted a request to commemorate May Fourth for the Taiwan side. Echoing Yu Pingbo's sentiments, he wrote: "Every time I have been asked to commemorate May Fourth, I have refused even though I have been a participant.... My temperament is such that I keep hoping that events that are past are truly past, gone without residue.... Furthermore, I believe that if we spend too much of our time commemorating past events, we will have no time left to plan for the future." Mao Zishui, "Wusi wushi nian" [May Fourth fifty years later], *Zhuanji wenxue* 14:5 (May 1969):6.

33.   Yu Pingbo's essay "Wusi yiwang" [Looking back on May Fourth] (1959), reprinted in *Wusi huiyi lu* (Beijing, 1979), vol. 2, was written in very different circumstances from his 1949 memoir. By 1959, he was a survivor of the 1954 campaign directed against the "bourgeois approach" in his study of *The Dream of the Red Chamber*. He had also been chastened by the anti-rightist campaign of 1957. Furthermore, he had tried to thread his way through another maze of criticism in the spring of 1958, this time against "bourgeois scholarly tendencies." By 1959, the memory of May Fourth could no longer console him. Too culpable as a literary critic and too vulnerable in his position at Beida, Yu saw no point in recollecting the complex event of 1919. He focused instead on his association with *Poetry Magazine*, a context in which he had been linked with two somewhat "safe," now dead, heroes of the students' generation, Zhu Ziqing and Zheng Zhenduo. In 1949, Yu had emphasized his role as "mere infantryman" in the larger, glorious May Fourth. In 1959, he described himself as a "mere child," confused and prone to error. What had been hasty but noble idealism a decade earlier now seemed to be a source of culpability.

At that time I was only twenty, a mere child. Although the great, deeply significant student movement brushed by me, my understanding of it was extremely immature; one could even say I didn't understand it at all. Still, all mixed up as I was, I was attracted toward the bright light, inclined a bit toward democracy, that's all. From the standpoint of today, I was like a man on a mountain, head drenched by clouds, oblivious to everything outside (p. 1000).

No longer able or willing to talk of how the slogans of May Fourth apply to the present, Yu Pingbo described how he, Zhu Ziqing, Ye Shengtao, and Zheng Zhenduo tried to compose clear, meaningful, vernacular verse. He recalled Ye Shengtao's conviction that the life of a miner or a peasant is a richer subject for poetry than the idle pleasures of the gentry. Yu had hoped that "new poetry might incline people toward the good and the beautiful." "Unprogressive" and "unrevolutionary" as his own role in the poetry movement had been, Yu offered it to the present as a warning: "I hope that young people today will look at my experiences and learn from them, as from the overturned cart that stands as a warning to the carts behind" (p. 1001).

34. Yu Pingbo, "Wusi liushi nian jinian yiwang shi shezhang," pp. 5–6. In an interview with the author a year later, Yu added more details about his authoritarian parents, who had forbidden him to go out of the house on the Sunday of the Tiananmen demonstration, just as later they had imposed their will in arranging marriage. "I was forced into an arrangement, unlike Gu Jiegang and Fu Sinian, who, being older, managed to extricate themselves, get divorced, love freely" (Yu Pingbo, interview with author, May 1981).

35. Mao Zishui, "Wusi wushi nian," p. 7.

36. Lewis, *History*, p. 56.

37. Zhou Yang, "Fayang wusi wenxue geming de douzheng chuantong" [Develop the militant tradition of the May Fourth literary revolution], *Renmin wenxue* no. 55 (May 1955):3–5.

38. Ibid., p. 6.

39. See Yang Zhensheng, "Wusi yu xin wenxue" [May Fourth and new literature], in *Wusi sa zhounian jinian zhuanji*, pp. 135–38. In this essay, Yang also claims that May Fourth had been a direct cause for the mass literature of the 1930s and the literature required for socialist construction in China after 1949.

40. Yang Zhensheng, "Huiyi wusi" [Recollections of May Fourth], *Renmin wenxue* 55 (May 1955):105.

41. Ibid., p. 104.

42. Luo Jialun, "Wusi shidai de beijing ji qi yingxiang" [The historical background of May Fourth and its influence], *Zhongyang ribao* (4 May 1962):4.

43. Xu Deheng, "Wusi yundong zai Beijing" [The May Fourth movement in Beijing], *Jinsan shexun* no. 3 (1951), reprinted in *Wusi huiyi lu* (Beijing, 1979), pp. 210–17.

44. Xu Deheng, "Wusi yundong liushi zhounian" [The sixtieth anniversary of May Fourth], in *Wusi yundong huiyu lu* (Beijing, 1979), pp. 37, 69.

45. Xu Deheng, "Huiyi Guomin zazhi," in *Wusi shiqi de shetuan*, vol. 2, pp. 37–38.

46. Zhu Wushan, "Wusi geming yundong shifou jiushi xin minzhu zhuyi geming?" [Was May Fourth a new democratic revolutionary movement or not?], in *Wusi yundong yanjiu lunji* (Hong Kong, 1975), pp. 3–7.

47. Ibid., p. 9.

48. Mao Dun, "Wusi de jingshen" [The spirit of May Fourth], *Wenyi zhendi* 1:2 (March 1938).

49. Mao Dun, "Hai xuyao zhunbei changqi er jiejue zhanzheng" [We must still prepare for a long and determined struggle], in *Wusi sa zhounian zhuanji* (Shanghai, 1949), p. 39.

50. Ibid., p. 40.

51. Gu Jiegang, "Cong wo ziji kan Hu Shi" [Hu Shi as I see him], *Dagong bao* (24 December 1951):4.

52. Guo Shaoyu, "You zhunzhe bian wei doushi" [From righteous litteratus

to warrior], *Wenjiao ziliao* no. 82 (October 1978):6–7. In this essay, Guo Shaoyu, like other intellectuals writing about Zhu Ziqing, feels free to recall his friend's ambivalence about politics. For a further confirmation of this departure from "patriotic" commemorations of Zhu, see also Yang Deji, "Zhu Ziqing xiansheng zouguo de daolu" [The road traveled by Mr. Zhu Ziqing], *Wenjiao ziliao*, pp. 12–13.

53. Germaine Bree, "Introduction" to *Combray* by Marcel Proust (New York, 1952), p. 1.

54. Sun Fuyuan, "Huiyi wusi dangnian" [Remembrances of that year of May Fourth], *Renmin wenxue* no. 55 (May 1955):118.

55. Ibid.

56. Ibid., pp. 119–20.

57. Ibid., p. 121.

58. "Chongzheng wusi jingshen" [Rekindle the spirit of May Fourth], *Ziyou Zhongguo* 16:9 (May 1957):10.

59. Ibid.

60. Ibid.

61. Ibid.

62. He Bingran, "Gu Jiegang tan fangshou guanche 'baijia zhengming'" [Gu Jiegang talks about going boldly forth with a thorough implementation of the Hundred Flowers campaign], *Guangming ribao* (23 March 1957):5.

63. Zhang Shenfu, "Fayang wusi de jingshen: Fang" [Develop the spirit of May Fourth: Emancipate thought!], *Guangming ribao* (27 April 1957):5.

64. Tan Tianrong, "Wusi de zhexiang" [Fragmentary thoughts on May Fourth], in *Beijing daxue youpai fenzi fandong yanlun huiji* (Beijing, 1957), p. 52.

65. Ibid., p. 88.

66. Tan Tianrong, "Shibai" [Failure], in ibid., pp. 52–53.

67. Liu Jisheng, "Wusi de huoju wansui!" [Long live the torch of May Fourth], in ibid., p. 163.

CONCLUSION

1. Reiss, *Kant's Political Writings*, p. 56.

2. I am indebted to Oliver Holmes, my colleague in the history department at Wesleyan University, for a series of suggestive conversations about the political background of the eighteenth-century philosophers. His comments on a paper I gave at the Wesleyan Center for Humanities, along with Margaret C. Jacob's book, *The Radical Enlightenment: Pantheists, Freemasons, and Republicans* (London, 1981), were particularly useful in developing the contrast between the Chinese and the European enlightenment.

3. Hu Shi, *The Chinese Renaissance: The Haskell Lectures, 1933* (Chicago, 1933), p. 96.

4. Lu Xun, *Selected Works*, vol. 2, p. 167.

5. Qu Qiubai, "Qing tuoyi wusi de yilan" [Please take off the mantle of May Fourth], in Su Wen, ed., *Ziyou wenyi lunbian ji* (Shanghai, 1933), p. 305.

6. Fu Sinian, "Wusi outan" [Random remarks on May Fourth], *Zhuanji wenxue* 14:5 (May 1969):89–90.

7. Fu Sinian, "Wusi ershiwu nian" [May Fourth twenty-five years later], in

Wusi aiguo yundong sishi zhounian jinian tekan, p. 31. In contrast to the "false, crippling anxiety" about national confidence that pervaded his countrymen, Fu Sinian held up the May Fourth ideal of intellectual autonomy. Frustrated in his own work as secretary-general of the Academia Sinica by "academic bureaucrats who only covet officials' pay," Fu recalled a time when it had been possible to imagine, if not exactly carry out, genuine scholarly work. The preconditions for that work, Fu argued, were still science and democracy. In the end, he not only recalled May Fourth but called for its resurrection:

> There are some liars who don't know that the first principle of science is not to lie.... The whole history of science tells us that if there is no academic freedom, the progress of science is impossible. I want to resurrect again a slogan of the May Fourth movement. This slogan is "science for the sake of pure research." Do readers feel that my words are vile? But only thus can there be true science (p. 64).

Fu Sinian's resurrection was, obviously, cautious and selective. With nationalists gearing up for civil war and on guard against talk of democracy as a cover for "communist propaganda," it was easier to talk of the other May Fourth slogan, science, and to add to it the caveat of "pure research." And yet, despite all that camouflage, neither Fu Sinian nor those he criticized doubted that science and democracy were somehow inextricably linked. "Academic freedom" now, as during May Fourth itself, was not an "academic" matter at all. The implications of intellectual autonomy for political dissent were transparent. Those implications made Fu's words "vile" at least in the minds of some readers.

8.   Feng Naichao, "Congming wu" [The folly of being smart], in *Zishi fenzi de daolu* (Hong Kong, 1949), p. 7.

9.   In Taiwan in 1974, fifty-five years after May Fourth, a similar criticism was leveled against cultural iconoclasm in the journal *Zhexue yu wenhua*. Here, as in China, May Fourth intellectuals were attacked by non-participants for the consequences of their "ignorance and shortsightedness." Once more the crime was "cultural treason." On the mainland, the errors of May Fourth were assumed to have been corrected by history; in Taiwan, their negative influences were felt to be more pernicious and more immoral, hence the attack on cultural iconoclasm was less confident: "This painful tragedy [of May Fourth] is continuously replayed in Taiwan.... We sit by while our intellectual world becomes a foreign concession of thought (*sixiang zujie*)." The same May Fourth intellectuals who troubled Feng Naichao became culprits of the Nationalists' "tragedy." But whereas Feng had mocked them as "slaves," the editors of *Zhexue yu wenhua* damned them as "compradors": "The great pioneers of that time [1919] were the first to show a blind doubt about Chinese civilization and, in the end, they screamed with a hollow voice for 'total Westernization.' These so-called pioneers are nothing but China's cultural compradors." See Tian Yu, "Wusi de lishi jiaoxun" [Historical admonitions of May Fourth], *Zhexue yu wenhua* no. 122 (May 1974):205.

10.   Peter Gay, *The Bridge of Criticism* (New York, 1970), p. 51.

11.   For this distinction between critique and iconoclasm, on the European side, see Ernst Cassirer, *The Philosophy of the Enlightenment* (Princeton, 1951). In this work, Cassirer argues:

> Nothing is more erroneous or harmful than the prejudice that historical truth can and must be accepted as a stamped coin on faith and trust.... The philosophy of the enlightenment,

accordingly, does not understand its task as an act of destruction but as an act of construction ... the Enlightenment aims only at restitution of the whole [*restitutio in tegrum*] (pp. 207, 234).

In a similar vein, the sinologist Yu Yingshi, writing about the May Fourth movement, argues that critical thought was not destroying Confucian tradition but making its historicity more explicit: "The spirit of doubt, of discernment, led [May Fourth intellectuals] to demand proof for what had been taken as truth on the basis of the classics.... The most significant achievement of May Fourth was the reorganization of the national heritage [*zhengli guogu*]." Yu Yingshi, "Wusi yundong yu Zhongguo chuantong" [The May Fourth movement and Chinese tradition], in *Wusi yanjiu lunji* (Hong Kong, 1979), pp. 123–24.

12.   In this essay Zhou tried to thread his way between condemnation and idealization of the event of 1919. Like Fu Sinian and Mao Dun, he hoped to counter the urge to forget May Fourth by drawing attention to its shortcomings and to its unfinished message. He too identified the challenge of enlightenment with the students' attack on traditional mentality and therefore focused both his praise and his criticism on them:

To understand the meaning of May Fourth, the best way is to look at some of the habits of students in the 1910s. When most youths left the countryside for the city, they would put on Western coats and then criticize the Chinese coats they used to wear.... The basic spirit of May Fourth, science and democracy, though doubtlessly foreign, represents things that modern Chinese should seek to acquire.... However, a transplanted culture, like a rootless flower, can perhaps be put in a "vase." But how long can it last?

Zhou Cezong, "Yi xinzhuang ping jiuzhi" [Putting on new clothes to criticize the old system], *Dagong bao* (4 May 1947):3.

13.   Chow Tse-tsung, *May Fourth Movement*. For a thoughtful review that recognized Zhou's contribution to the study of Chinese iconoclasm, see Joseph Levenson's review of this book in *Journal of Asian Studies* 20 (February 1961):221–26.

14.   Zhou Cezong, "Wusi yundong gaosu women shenmo?" [What does the May Fourth movement tell us?], *Daxue zazhi* 48 (4 December 1971):67.

15.   In 1979, Zhou Cezong emerged as the foremost commemorator of May Fourth among overseas Chinese intellectuals. His poem in tribute to the event of 1919 was the opening piece in a recent collection of essays published in Hong Kong. The poem, entitled "Evocation of May Fourth," concludes with the following sentiment:

> Footsteps, like countless mouths, shout out in protest
> Proclaiming: It's no crime to love one's nation
> Madmen roll their eyes, who can
> Stand still, and coolly consider the issues?
> Hang Pan Gu (the mythic hero of tradition—who separated
> Heaven and Earth)
> Suspended on the hook of questioning
> Put the East wind and the West on the scale of time
> Mr. Science and Mr. Democracy, there as well....
> This new tide, will surely
> Give birth to a new offspring, a new culture
> May Fourth, May Fourth, you are our future.

> See Zhou Cezong, "Wusi shuhuai" [Evocation of May Fourth], in *Wusi yanjiu lunwenji* (Hong Kong, 1979), pp. 1–3.

16. This interpretation of the worldview of traditional Chinese intellectuals draws upon a recent, very suggestive paper by Yue Daiyun, entitled "Some Characteristics of Chinese Intellectuals Found in Fiction" (Berkeley Center for Chinese Studies, colloquium series, February 1984).

17. Ibid.

18. See chapter 1 for a more detailed discussion of the similarities and differences between the rise of a modern intelligentsia in China, Japan, and Europe.

19. The sixtieth anniversary of May Fourth provided official sanction for the historical re-evaluation of key May Fourth personages. In the context of a broader revival of historical research, historians of modern China raised the *pingjia* problem in several of their works. Foremost among those calling for a reappraisal of Hu Shi, Chen Duxiu, and Cai Yuanpei in terms of their own *past* historical circumstances as opposed to the ideological requirements of the present has been Li Shu, director of the Modern History Institute in Beijing. See especially his article "Guanyu wusi yundong de jige wenti" (Some questions about the May Fourth movement), *Jindaishi yanjiu* no. 1 (October 1979):44–57. Historian Ding Shouhe has also been pioneering a more objective approach to the *pingjia* problem, most notably in his essay "Chen Duxiu he Xinqingnian" [Chen Duxiu and the *New Youth*] in *Zhongguo xiandaishi lunji* (October 1980). The final, most official rehabilitation of these figures has taken place in the new collection *Minguo renwu zhuan* (Biographies of personages of the republican era) edited by Li Xin and Sun Sibai. The very first volume of this large-scale work, published in 1978, already heralded the rehabilitation of Cai Yuanpei, once identified as a model of pernicious "bourgeois" thought. Zong Zhiwen's essay "Cai Yuanpei," in the above compendium (pp. 342–48), was the first to suggest that Cai's accomplishments as "progressive educator" far outweigh his later "bourgeois fallacies."

20. Feng Xuefeng, "Dao Zhu Ziqing xiansheng" [Mourning Mr. Zhu Ziqing], in *Feng Xuefeng lunji* (Beijing, 1952), p. 116.

21. Zhou Yang, "Sanci weida de sixiang jiefang yundong," p. 1.

22. Ibid., p. 3.

23. Ibid.

24. For a critique of the Goldman position see Jacob, *Radical Enlightenment*, pp. 1–27. For an earlier restatement of the historiographical question about the connection between enlightenment and revolution, see Henri Peyre, "The Influence of Eighteenth-Century Ideas on the French Revolution," *Journal of the History of Ideas* no. 10 (1949).

25. Peyre, "Influence," p. 80.

26. Xing Bisi, "Zhexue de qimeng he qimeng de zhexue" [The enlightenment of philosophy and philosophical enlightenment], *Renmin ribao* (22 July 1978):5.

27. Ibid.

28. Ralph Croizier, "The Thorny Flowers of 1979: Political Cartoons and Liberalization in China," *Bulletin of Concerned Asian Scholars* 13:3 (July–September 1981):50–59.

29. "Pipan fengjian zhuyi xueshu taolunhui" [Scholarly conference on the criticism of feudalism], *Guangming ribao* (13 November 1979).

30. Zhou Yang, "San ci weida de sixiang jiefang yundong," p. 3.

31. For a concise history of the Enlightenment Society and the larger

context of the Democracy Wall movement in China, see James D. Seymour, ed., *The Fifth Modernization: China's Human Rights Movement, 1978–1979* (Stanfordville, N. Y., 1981), especially pp. 1–30. The Enlightenment Society was founded in Guiyang, Guizhou, in October 1978. The announcement of its organization was published simultaneously with that of the Beijing Enlightenment Society in November 1978. Their joint manifesto, entitled (in an evocation of Lu Xun) "A Call to Arms," read:

> Arise, Chinese workers, farmers,
> revolutionary cadres, scientists, writers,
> artists, poets, professors, editors,
> university students, and all upright and
> conscientious people! Step out boldly and
> fight for truth!
>
> Mass democracy and human rights, which we
> have long hoped for and pursued, are
> beginning to appear on the great earth of
> China ...
>
> Arise, you people of China! Attack all
> dictators and autocrats! The time has come
> for the final reckoning, and the final
> verdict.

"Enlightenment Society" (Beijing, 24 November 1978; Guiyang, 29 November 1978), Seymour, ibid., p. 29.

Another article in the first issue of *Qimeng* (November 1978) offered more details about the interests of its members. It reveals their eagerness to stay within while at the same time expanding the parameters of officially sanctioned cultural criticism:

We are a group of common workers. Over a long period of time in the past we came together on our own accord to study social questions under the merciless oppression and cultural despotism of Lin Biao and the Gang of Four....

In our opinion, the first thing to do is to respect human rights, bring socialist democracy into full play, wipe out fascist dictatorship, feudalism, and fetishism.... We workers, farmers, and soldiers of the era have new cultural needs and have developed new interests in esthetics. We want enlightenment, enlightenment, and enlightenment! We should start a great enlightenment movement in the fields of ideology and culture.

In the spring of 1979, after issues no. 1 and 2 of *Qimeng*, the group split due to the decision of some of the more outspoken members in the Guiyang group to found the "Thaw Society." See Seymour, pp. 18 and 41. In addition to the selection available in Seymour, *Qimeng* has been translated by the U.S. Joint Publications Research Service. See JPRS 73215, no. 509 (12 April 1979): "Translations from the People's Republic of China," (This issue includes: *Qimeng* nos. 1 and 2, 1978, and no. 3, 1979).

32. This is my translation of a part of "Confessions of the Great Wall," by Huang Xiang, the best-known writer of the Enlightenment Society. The poem has also been translated in full in JPRS, "Translations," pp. 10–13.

Glossary

baihua
(plain talk, the vernacular language)　　　白话

baofu xinli (psychology of revenge)　　　报复心理

Beida (Beijing University)　　　北大

Beijing daxue pingmin jiaoyu jiangyan tuan
(Beijing University Commoners' Education Lecture
Society)　　　北京大学平民
　　　教育讲演团

bunmei kaika (civilization and enlightenment)　　　文明开化

Cai Yuanpei　　　蔡元培

Chen Duxiu　　　陈独秀

chishiki kaikyū (intellectual class)　　　知识阶级

dadao zhishi jieji
(down with the intellectual class)　　　打倒知识阶级

daiyan ren (spokesman)　　　代言人

dashaoye (young master)　　　大少爷

dazhong wenyi (literature of the masses)　　　大众文艺

dazhong yishi daiyan ren　　　大众意识代
(spokesman of mass consciousness)　　　言人

dazhong yu (mass language)　　　大众语

di sanzhong ren ("the third type," a reluctant fellow
traveler)　　　第三种人

fan lijiao
(critique of the religion of rites, anti-Confucianism)　　　反礼教

fangqi (sublate, discard, transcend)	放弃
fushupin (an appendage, lacking autonomy, servile dependence)	附属品
gexing (sense of individuality)	个性
guanhua (the language of officials)	官话
guogu (national heritage)	国故
Guomindang (Nationalist Party)	国民党
guominxing wenti (the problem of national character)	国民性问题
huiyi (remembrance)	回忆
jianrong bingbao (broad-minded and encompassing tolerance of diverse points of view)	兼容并包
jieji yishi (class consciousness)	阶级意识
Jinde hui (Society for the Promotion of Virtue)	进德会
jinian (commemoration)	纪念
jiuguo (national salvation, national survival)	救国
juewu (awakening)	觉悟
kaiming (open-minded)	开明
keguan (objective, fair, undogmatic)	客观
keimō gakusha (enlightenment scholars)	启蒙学者
Laodong buxiu xuexiao (Workers' After Hours Supplemental Study School)	劳动补修学校
Li Dazhao	李大钊
Lu Xun	鲁迅
mingfen zhuyi (role-ism, status consciousness)	名分主义
minzu yishi (nationalistic consciousness)	民族意识
pingmin (common people; the wordless, unheard masses)	平民
pingmin wenxue (literature for the common people)	平民文学
pipan (critique, judgment)	批判
pohuai ouxiang (destroy idols; iconoclasm)	破坏偶像

Qian Xuantong	钱玄同
qimeng (enlightenment)	启蒙
renge (humanity)	人格
rensheng guan (worldview, life perspective)	人生观
sangang wuchang (the three ropes and the five bonds: duties and loyalties between superiors and inferiors; the ethic of subservience)	三纲五常
shehui diaocha (social investigation)	社会调查
shidai de jingshen (the spirit of the times)	时代的精神
shidai de xuyao (the needs of the times)	时代的需要
shijieguan jiaoyu (education for a worldview)	世界观教育
Shinchō (New Tide)	新潮
Tao Menghe	陶孟和
wangguo (national extinction)	亡国
wangdao (the Confucian kingly way)	王道
wenyan (classical language)	文言
wenren (literatus, man of the word)	文人
wuduan (arbitrary, thoughtless, coercive)	武断
Wusi yundong (the May Fourth movement)	五四运动
Wu Zhihui	吴稚晖
xiandai hua (modernization)	现代化
xiandai mixin (contemporary superstitions or prejudice; reified Marxism)	现代迷信
xianzhi xianjue zhe (the first to know are the first to awaken)	先知先觉者
xiangyue (periodic village lectures)	乡日
xiao zichan jieji zhishi fenzi (petty bourgeois intelligentsia)	小资产阶级知识分子
Xinchao (New Tide)	新潮
Xin qingnian (New Youth)	新青年
xinyang (belief)	信仰

xuefeng
(the winds of learning, intellectual atmosphere)   学风

xuezhe (intellectuals, scholars)   学者

zhengli guogu
(reorganize the national heritage)   整理国故

zhishi fenzi
(knowledgeable elements, members of the modern intelligentsia)   知识分子

zhongguo hua (sinification)   中国化

zixin (confidence on the national level)   自信

zijue (autonomy)   自觉

zhuguan
(subjective, prejudiced, one-sided)   主观

Bibliography

Abbreviations Used in the Bibliography

XC   Xinchao [New Tide]

XQN Xin qingnian [New Youth]

Chinese and Japanese Sources

Ai Siqi. "Lun pipan" [On the concept of critique]. *Renshi yuekan* (June 1937).

"Beida pingmin yexiao diyici biye shi canguan ji" [Impressions of the first graduation ceremony at the Beida night school]. *Chen bao* (17 January 1922).

Beifang de hongxing: Changxindian jiche cheliang gongchang liushi nian [Red star of the north: Sixty years at the Changxindian locomotive factory]. Beijing, 1960.

Cai Yuanpei. "Yi meiyu dai zongjiao shuo" [On the replacement of religion with esthetic education]. *XQN* 3:6. (August 1917).

———. "Cai Jiemin xiansheng yanshuo ji" [Mr. Cai Jiemin's speeches]. *Guomin* 1:1 (January 1919).

———. "Wusi qianhou de Beida" [Beijing University before and after May Fourth]. *Yuzhoufeng* no. 55 (December 1937). Also reprinted in *Xinwenxue shiliao* no. 3 (May 1979).

———. *Cai Yuanpei xuanji* [Selected works of Cai Yuanpei]. Taibei, 1967.

———. Zhi Fu Zengxiang" [Letter to Fu Zengxiang, 12 April 1919]. In *Wusi shiqi de shetuan*. Beijing, 1979. Vol. 2.

Cao Juren. "Dazhongyu yundong" [The mass language movement]. In *Wentan wushi nian*. Hong Kong, 1969.

Chao Zong, ed. *Xiandai Zhongguo zuojia liezhuan* [Biographies of contemporary Chinese writers]. Kowloon, 1970.

Chen Boda. "Zhexue de guofang dongyuan" [The mobilization of philosophy for national defense]. *Dushu shenghuo* 4:9 (September 1936).

———. "Lun xin qimeng yundong" [On the new enlightenment movement]. *Xin shiji* 1:2 (October 1936).

————. "Lun Zhongguo de ziwo juexing" [The self-awakening of China]. *Xin shiji* 1:3 (November 1936).

————. "Lun sixiang wu zui" [Thinking is no crime]. *Xianshi yuebao* (9 June 1937).

————. "Mao Zedong tongzhi lun wusi yundong" [Comrade Mao Zedong on the May Fourth movement]. In *Wusi sa zhounian jinian zhuanji*. Shanghai, 1949.

————. "Lun wenhua yundong zhong de minzu chuantong"·[National traditions in the culture movement]. In *Zhenli de zhuiqiu*. Beijing, 1969.

————. *Zhenli de zhuiqiu* [In quest of truth]. Beijing reprint, 1969.

Chen Daqi. "Pi hunxue" [Exploration in soul science (psychology)]. *XQN* 4:5 (May 1918).

Chen Duxiu. "Jinggao qingnian" [Call to youth]. *XQN* 1:1 (15 September 1915).

————. "Yijiuyiliu nian" [The year 1916]. *XQN* 1:5 (January 1916).

————. "Xin qingnian" [New youth]. *XQN* 2:1 (September 1916).

————. "Rensheng de zhenyi" [The true meaning of human existence]. *XQN* 4:2 (February 1918).

————. "Ouxiang pohuai lun" [On the destruction of idols, or On iconoclasm]. *XQN* 5:2 (August 1918).

————. "Lun zisha" [On suicide]. *XQN* 2:2 (January 1920).

————. "Gongdu huzhu tuan wenti" [Questions about the Work and Mutual Assistance Corps]. *XQN* 7:5 (April 1920).

————. "Xin wenhua yundong shi shenmo" [What is the New Culture movement?]. *XQN* (April 1920).

————. "Wenhua yundong yu shehui yundong" [The culture movement and the social movement]. *XQN* 5:1 (May 1921).

————. *Duxiu wencun* [The collected works of Chen Duxiu]. 2 vols. Shanghai, 1922.

————. "Kongjiao yanjiu" [Research on Confucianism]. In *Duxiu wencun*, vol. 1. Shanghai, 1922.

————. "Fankang yulun de yongqi" [The courage to oppose public opinion]. *Duxiu wencun*, vol. 2. Shanghai, 1922.

————. "Kexue yu shensheng" [Science and the mysterious]. *Duxiu wencun*, vol. 2. Shanghai, 1922.

————. "Shian zizhuan" [Autobiography of Shian (Chen Duxiu)]. *Zhuanji wenxue* 5:3 (September 1964).

Chen Duanzhi. *Wusi yundong lishi de pingjia* [A historical evaluation of the May Fourth movement]. Shanghai, 1935 (Hong Kong reprint, 1973).

Chen Guyuan. "Wusi yundong de shidaixing" [The historicity of the May Fourth movement]. In *Wusi aiguo yundong sishi zhounian jinian tekan*. Taibei, 1959.

Chen Hengzhe. *Hengzhe sanwen ji* [Collected essays by Chen Hengzhe]. 2 vols. Shanghai, 1938.

Chen Jiaai. "Xin" [New]. *XC* 1:1 (January 1919).

Chen Lifu. "Zhonggong yu wusi che bushang guanxi" [May Fourth has nothing to do with the Chinese Communist Party]. In *Wo canjiale wusi yundong*. Taibei, 1979.

Chen Mu. *Wusi yundong yilai de lunzhan ziliao* [Source materials on intellectual controversies after the May Fourth movement]. Shanghai, 1937 (Hong Kong reprint, 1975).

Chen Pao, comp. *Wusa tong shi* [The bitter history of May Thirtieth]. Shanghai, 1925.

Chen Shaoting. "Jinian wusi yundong de wushi zhounian" [Commemorating the fiftieth anniversary of the May Fourth movement]. *Daxue zazhi* no. 17 (May 1969).

Chen Tongxiao. *Chen Duxiu pinglun* [Critical essays on Chen Duxiu]. Beijing, 1933.

Chen Wanxiong. *Xin wenhua yundong qiande Chen Duxiu* [Chen Duxiu before the new culture movement]. Hong Kong, 1979.

Chen Zizhan. "Wenyan—baihua—dazhongyu" [Classical Chinese, the vernacular, and a language of common people]. In *Wenxue yundong shiliao xuan*, vol. 2. Shanghai, 1979.

"Chongzheng wusi jingshen" [Rekindle the spirit of May Fourth]. *Ziyou Zhongguo* 16:9 (May 1957).

Dalu zazhi she, ed. *Zhongguo jindai xueren xiaozhuan* [Illustrated biographies of modern Chinese scholars]. Taibei, 1971.

Deng Zhongxia. "Xin shiren de banghe" [Rebuke of the new poets]. *Zhongguo qingnian* (December 1923).

———. "Lianai ziyou wenti" [The problem of free love]. *Zhongguo qingnian* (January 1924).

———. *Zhongguo zhigong yundong jianshi, 1919–1926* [A brief history of the Chinese industrial labour movement]. Beijing, 1949.

Ding Wen. "Dadao zhishi jieji" [Down with the intellectual class]. *Xiandai pinglun* (February 1927).

Dong Yan. "Lishi xuejia tianjue lishi" [A historian distorts history]. *Zhuanji wenxue* no. 148 (September 1974).

Ding Shouhe and Yin Xuxi. *Cong wusi qimeng yundong dao Makesi zhuyi de chuanbo* [From the May Fourth enlightenment movement to the propagation of Marxism]. Beijing, 1965.

Fan Wenlan. "Jiqi zhizhui canjia geming jianshe gongzuo" [Make haste to catch up and join the work of revolutionary construction]. In *Wusi sa zhounian jinian xuanji*. Shanghai, 1949.

Fei Zi. "Xin qimeng yundong zai Beiping" [The new enlightenment movement in Beijing]. *Xianshi yuebao* (9 June 1937).

Feng Naichao. "Congming wu" [The folly of being smart]. In *Zhishi fenzi de daolu*. Hong Kong, 1949.

Feng Xuefeng (Hua Shih). "Geming yu zhishi jieji" [Revolution and the intellectual class]. In *Zhongguo wenyi lunzhan*, ed. Li Helin. Shanghai, 1932.

———. "Cong di sanzhong ren shuo dao Zuolian" [From the third type to the Left League]. In *Ziyou wenyi lunbian ji*, ed. Su Wen. Shanghai, 1933.

———. *Guolai shidai de Lu Xun lunji qita* [Lu Xun as he used to be and other essays]. Shanghai, 1946.

———. "Dao Zhu Ziqing xiansheng" [Mourning Mr. Zhu Ziqing]. In *Feng Xuefeng lunji*. Beijing, 1952.

———. *Huiyi Lu Xun* [Recollections of Lu Xun]. Beijing, 1952.

Feng Youlan. "Bogesen de zhexue fangfa" [Bergson's philosophical method].

XC 3:1 (September 1921).

———. *Yizhong rensheng guan* [A certain worldview]. Shanghai, 1924.

———. *Rensheng zhexue* [A philosophy of life]. Shanghai, 1926.

———. "Wusi qian de Beida he wusi hou de Qinghua" [Beijing University before May Fourth and Qinghua University after May Fourth]. *Wenshi ziliao* no. 34 (October 1962).

———. "Zhexue huiyi lu: Wo zai ershi niandai" [Philosophical reminiscences: My experiences during the 1920s]. *Zhongguo zhexue* 3 (August 1980).

Fukushima Yutaka. "Chūgoku no atarashii ningenzō to seiyō teki shikō" [Western thought and new image of man in China]. *Shisō* 449 (November 1961).

Fu Sinian. "Rensheng wenti faduan" [The origins of the question of human existence]. *XC* 1:1 (January 1919).

———. Shehui geming—Eguo shi de geming" [Social revolution—Revolution the Russian way]. *XC* 1:1 (January 1919).

———. "Wan e zhi yuan" [The source of all evil]. *XC* 1:1 (January 1919).

———."Zhongguo wenyi jie zhi binggen" [The source of China's literary disease]. *XC* 1:2 (February 1919).

———. "Laotouzi he xiaohaizi" [Old men and young kids]. *XC* 1:3 (March 1919).

———. "Pohuai" [On destruction]. *XC* 1:4 (April 1919).

———. "Yi duan fenghua" [Some crazy words]. *XC* 1:4 (April 1919).

———. "Duiyu Zhongguo jinri tan zhexue zhi guannian" [Reflections on those currently concerned with philosophy in China]. *XC* 1:5 (May 1919).

———. "Suigan lu" [A selection of random thinkings]. *XC* 1:5 (May 1919).

———. "Xinchao zhi huigu yu qianzhan" [*New Tide*: Recollections of the past and future prospects]. *XC* 2:1 (October 1919).

———. "Zhongguo gou he Zhongguo ren" [Chinese dogs and Chinese people]. *XQN* 6:6 (November 1919); also in *Fu Sinian xuanji*, vol. 2.

———. "Ziran" [Nature]. *XC* 2:3 (March 1920).

———. "Chen Duxiu an" [The case of Chen Duxiu]. *Duli pinglun* no. 24 (30 October, 1932); also in *Fu Sinian xuanji*, vol. 5.

———. "Zhi Hu Shi" [Letter to Hu Shi]. In *Hu Shi laiwang shuxin xuan*. Vol. 1.

———. "Wusi ershiwu nian" [May Fourth twenty-five years later]. In *Wusi aiguo yundong sishi zhounian jinian tekan*. Taibei, 1959.

———. *Fu Sinian xuanji* [Selected works of Fu Sinian]. 10 vols. Taibei, 1967.

———. "Wusi outan" [Random remarks on May Fourth]. *Zhuanji wenxue* 14:5 (May 1969).

Fu Zengxiang. "Zhi Cai Yuanpei" [Letter to Cai Yuanpei, 26 March 1919]. *Wusi shiqi de shetuan*. Beijing, 1979. Vol. 2.

———. "Jiaoyubu yanjin xuesheng youxing jihui ci" [Ministry of Education proclamation prohibiting student demonstrations, 5 May 1919]. *Wusi aiguo yundong dangan ziliao*. Beijing, 1980.

Gao Yihan. "Gonghe guojia yu qingnian zhi zijue" [A republican nation and a self-aware youth]. *XQN* 1:1 (September 1915).

———. "Qingnian zhi di" [The enemy of youth]. *XQN* 1:6 (February 1916).

———. "Yijiuyiqi nian sixiang zhi geming" [The thought revolution of 1917]. *XQN* 2:5 (January 1917).

————. "Wo de gongchan xianyi de chengju" [Proofs of my suspected communism]. *Xiandai pinglun* (September 1927).

Gao Yuan. "Fei mimi zhuyi" [Anti-secretism]. *XC* 1:4 (April 1919).

————. "Minzhu zhengzhi yu lunchang zhuyi" [Democratic politics and moralism]. *XC* 2:2 (December 1919)

Gu Jiegang (Gu Chengyu). "Duiyu jiu jiating de ganxiang" [Reflections on the old family system]. *XC* 1:2; 2:4, 5 (February 1919; May and June 1920).

————. "Gei Mengzhen (Fu Sinian)" [Letter to Fu Sinian]. *XC* 1:4 (April 1919).

————. "Huiyi xinchaoshe" [Reminiscence of *New Tide*]. *Wusi shiqi de shetuan* (September 1920).

————. "Shanghai de luanzi shi zenmayang naoqilai de?" [How did the mess in Shanghai come about?]. *Jingbao fukan* no. 177 (12 June 1925).

————. "Gei Hu Shi" [Letter to Hu Shi, 20 August 1929]. In *Hu Shi laiwang shuxin xuan*. Beijing, 1980. Voi. 1.

————. "Women duiyu guogu ying qu de taidu" [What our attitude ought to be toward the national heritage]. In *Xin wenxue yundong shi ziliao*, ed. Zhang Ruoying. Shanghai, 1944.

————. "Mingyun" [Fate]. In *Gu Jiegang tongsu lunzhuji*, ed. Wang Bixiang. Shanghai, 1947.

————. *Tongsu lunzhuji* [A selection of popular works]. Shanghai, 1947.

————. "Cong wo ziji kan Hu Shi" [Hu Shi as I see him]. *Dagong bao* (24 December 1951).

————. "Wo shi zenmayang bianxie Gushibian" [How I came to write *Gushibian*]. *Zhongguo zhexue* no. 3 (1980).

Gu Jiegang, ed. *Gushibian*. 2 vols. Beijing, 1930.

Gu Zhaoxiong. "Yijiuyijiu nian wuyue siri Beijing xuesheng zai shiwei yundong yu guomin zhi jingshen de chaoliu" [The demonstration movement of Beijing students on May Fourth, 1919, in Beijing and the tide of our national spirit]. *Beijing chenbao* (May 1919).

"Guofu Sun Zhongshan xiansheng dui wusi yundong de pinglun" [Founding father Mr. Sun Yatsen's view of the May Fourth movement]. *Zhuanji wenxue* 14:5 (May 1969).

Guo Moruo. "Wenyijia de juewu" [The awakening of the artist]. In *Xinwenxue yundong shiliao*, ed. Zhang Xiruo. Shanghai, 1926.

————. "Qing kan jinri zhi Jiang Jieshi" [Do take a look at today's Jiang Jieshi]. First published in 1927 and reprinted in *Geming chunqiu*. Beijing, 1979.

————. "Xinxing dazhong wenyi de renshi" [Understanding the mass art of the rising class]. *Dazhong wenyi* (March 1930).

————. "Wo zai tiyi" [I want to raise this matter again]. In *Zhishi fenzi de daolu*. Hong Kong, 1949.

Guo Shaoyu. "You zhunzhe bian wei doushi" [From righteous literatus to warrior]. *Wenjiao ziliao*, no. 82 (October 1978).

————. "Wusi yundong shugan zhi er" [Some ruminations about the May Fourth movement]. *Xin wenxue shiliao* no. 3 (May 1979).

Guo Zhanbo. *Jin wushi nian Zhongguo sixiang shi* [Chinese intellectual history of the past fifty years]. Beijing. 1936.

He Bingran. "Gu Jiegang tan tangshou guanche 'baijia zhengming'" [Gu

Jiegang talks about the slogan "Let a hundred schools of thought contend"].
Guangming ribao (23 March 1957).

He Ganzhi. *Zhongguo qimeng yundong shi* [A history of the Chinese enlightenment movement]. Shanghai, 1937.

————. *Lu Xun sixiang yanjiu* [Studies in the thought of Lu Xun]. Beijing, 1950.

He Siyuan. "Jinshi zhexue de xin fangfa" [New methodologies in contemporary philosophy]. *XC* 2:1 (October 1919).

————. "Shehuixue zhong de kexue fangfa" [Scientific methodology in sociology]. *XC* 2:4 (May 1920).

————. "Zhexue yu changshi [Philosophy and common sense]. *XC* 2:5 (June 1920).

————. "Wusi yundong de huiyi" [Reminiscence of May Fourth]. *Wenshi ziliao xuanbian* 4 (May 1979).

Hu Feng. "Cong yuantou dao hengliu" [From a trickle to a flood]. In *Wusi sa zhounian jinian zhuanji*. Shanghai, 1949.

Hu Qiuyuan. "Wenhua yundong de wenti" [Problems of the cultural movement]. In *Ziyou wenti lunbian ji*, ed. Su Wen. Shanghai, 1933.

Hu Sheng. "Lun jin liangnian laide sixiang he wenhua" [On the thought and culture of the past two years]. *Renshi yuekan* (May 1937).

————. "Lun lixing zhuyi" [On rationalism]. *Renshi yuekan* (June 1937).

Hu Shi. "The Chinese Literary Revolution." *Millard's Review* 8:8 (19 April 1919).

————. "Xin sichao de yiyi" [The meaning of the new thought tide]. *XQN* 7:1 (December 1919).

————. "Fei geren zhuyi de xin shenghuo" [The anti-individualistic new life]. *XC* 2:3 (April 1920). In *Hu Shi wencun*. Shanghai, 1930. Vol. 4.

————. *Hu Shi wencun* [Collected essays of Hu Shi]. 4 vols. Shanghai, 1930.

————. "Xin wenhua yundong yu Guomindang" [The New Culture movement and the Guomindang]. In *Renquan lunji*. Shanghai, 1930.

————. "Bishang liangshan huiyi wenxue geming" [Forced into banditry— recollections of the literary revolution]. *Wenhua* 1:1 (February 1934).

————. "Jinian wusi" [Commemorating May Fourth]. In *Wusi aiguo yundong sishi zhounian jinian tekan*. Taibei, 1959.

————. *Hu Shi laiwang shuxin xuan* [Selected letters to and from Hu Shi]. 3 vols. Beijing, 1980.

Hu Yuzhi. "Women de shidai" [Our era]. *Yiban* (5 November 1926).

————. "Guanyu dazhongyu" [About the language of the common people]. In *Wenxue yundong shiliao xuan*, vol. 2. Shanghai, 1979.

Hua Gang. *Wusi yundong shi* [History of the May Fourth movement]. Beijing, 1954.

Hua Guofeng. "Zai jinian wusi yundong liu shi zhounian dahui shang de jianghua" [Speech at the sixtieth anniversary of May Fourth]. *Renmin ribao* (4 May 1979).

Huang Chuntong. "Ji Sun Fuyuan" [Remembering Sun Fuyuan]. In *Xiandai Zhongguo zuojia qianying*. Hong Kong, 1973.

Huang Rikui. "Zai Zhongguo jindai sixiang shi zhong yanjin de Beida" [Beida's place in modern Chinese intellectual history]. In *Beijing daxue ershiwu zhounian jinian kan*. Unpublished document, Beijing University school history archives. December 1923.

Huang Yin, ed. *Xiandai Zhongguo nü zuojia* (Women writers in contemporary

China]. Beijing, 1931.

Ichiko Chūzō. *Kindai Chūgoku no seiji to shakai* [Politics and society in modern China]. Tokyo, 1971.

Iwamura Michio. *Chūgoku gakusei undō shi* [A history of the Chinese student movement]. Tokyo, 1949.

Jinian wusi yundong liushi zhounian xueshu taolun hui wenxuan. [Essays from the conference commemorating the sixtieth anniversary of the May Fourth movement]. 3 vols. Beijing, 1980.

Jia Yichun, ed. *Zhonghua minguo mingren zhuan* [Eminent persons of the Chinese Republic]. Beijing, 1937.

Jiang Menglin. "Xuechao hou qingnian xinli de taidu ji lidao fangfa" [Psychological attitudes of students after the "school storm" and ways of treating them]. *Xin jiaoyu* 2:2 (October 1919).

———. *Guodu shidai zhi sixiang yu jiaoyu* [Thought and education in an era of transition]. Shanghai, 1933.

Jiang Menglin and Hu Shi. "Women duiyu xuesheng de xiwang" [Our hopes for the students]. *Xin jiaoyu* 2:5 (May 1920).

Jin Yaoji. *Zhongguo xiandai hua yu zhishi fenzi* [Intellectuals and China's modernization]. Hong Kong, 1971.

Jun Ping. "Xin qimeng yundong he Yang Likui" [The new enlightenment movement and Yang Likui]. *Xianshi yuebao* (9 June 1937).

Kang Baiqing. "Lun Zhongguo zhi minzu qizhi" [On the Chinese national temperament]. *XC* 1:2 (February 1919).

———. "Taiji tu yu Phallicism" [The Taiji diagram and Phallicism]. *XC* 1:4 (April 1919).

———. "Beijing Daxue de xuesheng" [The students of Beijing University]. *Shaonian shijie* 1:1 (January 1920).

———. "Yi wen" [Doubt]. *XC* 2:3 (March 1920).

———. "Song Xu Deheng" [Sending off Xu Deheng]. *Xingqi pinglun* no. 41 (14 March 1920).

Kumano Shōhei. *Gendai Chūgoku shisō kōwa* [Lectures on modern Chinese thought]. Tokyo, 1974.

Lao Xiang. "Sun Fuyuan." In *Xiandai zuojia zhuanlie*, ed. Cao Juren. Hong Kong, n.d.

Li Dazhao. "Qingnian yu laoren" [Young people and old people]. *XQN* 3:4 (April 1917).

———. "Jin" [Now]. *XQN* 4:4 (April 1918).

———. "Xinde! Jiude!" [New! Old!]. *XQN* 1:5 (May 1918).

———. "Bolshevism de shengli" [The victory of Bolshevism]. *XQN* 5:5 (October 1918).

———. "Wuzhi biandong yu daode biandong" [Material change and change in ethics]. *XC* 2:2 (December 1919).

———. *Shouchang wencun* [Collected essays by Li Dazhao]. Shanghai, 1933.

Li Dazhao. Beijing, 1980.

Li Gongbo. "Bianzhe xu" [Editor's introduction]. In *Dazhong zhexue*, by Ai Siqi. Shanghai, 1935.

Li Helin, ed. *Zhongguo wenyi lunzhan* [Literary debates in China]. Shanghai, 1932 (Hong Kong reprint, 1957).

———. *Jin ershi nian Zhongguo wenyi sichao lun* [Chinese literary thought of the past twenty years]. Shanghai, 1947.

Li Kan. "Wusi yiqian wushi nian jian Zhongguo zhishi fenzi suo jingguo de daolu" [The path taken by Chinese intellectuals in the past fifty years]. *Kexue zhanxian* 2 (July 1978).

Li Shu. "Guanyu wusi yundong de jige wenti" [Some questions about the May Fourth movement]. In *Jindai shi yanjiu* no. 1 (October 1979). Also reprinted in *Jinian wusi yundong liushi zhounian xueshu taolunhui wenxuan*, vol. 1 (Beijing, 1979).

Li Xiaofeng. "Xinchao de shimo" [*New Tide* from the beginning to the end]. *Wenshi ziliao xuanji* 61 (*neibu* publication, 1979).

Li Xin. "Cong wusi dao siwu" [From May Fourth to April Fifth]. In *Jinian wusi yundong liushi zhounian xueshu taolunhui wenxuan*, vol. 1. Beijing, 1979.

Li Yunhan, ed. *Cong yonggong dao qingdang* [From alliance with the Communists to party purification]. 2 vols. Taibei, 1966.

Li Zehou. *Zhongguo jindai sixiangshi lun* [Essays on modern Chinese intellectual history]. Beijing, 1979.

Lian Zhu. "Hu Shi zhuyi de gende" [The basis of Hu Shi-ism]. *Mengya* (November 1929).

Liang Qichao. "Ou yu xinying jielu" [Reflections on my European travels]. In *Yinbingshi wenji*. Shanghai, 1925.

Liang Shiqiu. "Wenxue yu geming" [Literature and revolution]. In *Zhongguo wenyi lunzhan*, ed. Li Helin. Shanghai, 1932.

———. "Wusi yu wenyi" [May Fourth and literature]. In *Wusi aiguo yundong sishi zhounian ji*. Taibei, 1959.

———. "Wo kan wusi" [My view of May Fourth]. In *Wo canjiale wusi yundong*. Taibei, 1979.

Liang Shuming. "Lun xuesheng shijian" [On the students' episode]. *Beijing guomin gongbao* (May 1919); also in *Meizhou pinglun* (May 1919).

———. "Yinming dazheng" [A debate about Buddhist logic]. *XC* 1:5 (May 1919).

Liu Bannong. *Bannong wenxuan* [Selected works of Liu Bannong]. Taibei, 1969.

Liu Caifu. "Xuesheng wu zui" [Students are not guilty]. *Meizhou pinglun* (May 1919).

Liu Jisheng. "Wusi de huoju wansui!" [Long live the torch of May Fourth!] In *Beijing daxue youpai fenzi fandong yanlun huiji*. Beijing, 1957.

Liu Shousong. "Pipan Hu Shi zai wusi wenxue geming yundong zhong de gailiang zhuyi sixiang" [Criticize Hu Shi's reformist thought in the May Fourth literary revolutionary movement]. In *Hu Shi sixiang pipan*, vol. 2. Beijing, 1955.

Lu Xun (Zhou Shuren). "Suigan lu" [Random thoughts]. *XQN* 2:7 (February 1919).

———. "Duiyu Xinchao yi bufen yijian" [An opinion about *New Tide*]. *XC* 1:5 (May 1919).

———. "Women xianzai zenmayang zuo fuqin" [How are we to be fathers today?] *XQN* 6:6 (November 1919).

———. "Shuiyan zhong de menglong" [The haziness of inebriation]. In *Zhongguo wenyi lunzhan*, ed. Li Helin. Shanghai, 1930.

———. "Da Youheng xiansheng" [Reply to Mr. Youheng]. In *Lu Xun quanji*, vol. 3. Shanghai, 1948.

———. "Wenyi de dazhonghua" [The popularization of art]. *Dazhong wenyi* (March 1930).

———. *Lu Xun quanji*. 10 vols. Beijing, 1956.

———. "Menwai wentan" [Literary musings of an outsider]. In *Wenyue yundong shiliao*, vol. 2. Shanghai, 1979.

Luo Changpei. "Jinian wusi de sanshi zhounian" [Commemorating the thirtieth anniversary of May Fourth]. In *Wusi sa zhounian jinian xuanji*. Shanghai, 1949.

Luo Jialun. "Qingnian xuesheng" [Young students]. *XQN* 4:1 (January 1918).

———. "Jinri zhi shijie xinchao" [The new tide in the world today]. *XC* 1:1 (January 1919).

———. "Shi aiqing hai shi tongku?" [Is this love or pain?]. *XC* 1:3 (March 1919).

———. "Qu shi?" [To die?] *XC* 1:4 (April 1919).

———. "Bo Hu Xiansu jun de Zhongguo wenxue gailiang lun" [Criticism of Mr. Hu Xiansu's views on Chinese literary reform]. *XC* 1:5 (May 1919).

———. "Wusi yundong de jingshen" [The spirit of the May Fourth movement]. *Meizhou pinglun* (26 May 1919).

———. "Funü jiefang" [Women's liberation]. *XC* 2:1 (October 1919).

———. "Tiananmen qian de dong ye" [Winter evening in front of Tiananmen]. *XC* 2:1 (October 1919).

———. "Da Zhang Puquan lai xin" [Reply to letter from Zhang Puquan]. *XC* 2:2 (December 1919).

———. "Jindai xiyang sixiang ziyou de jinhua" [The progress of freedom of thought in the modern West]. *XC* 2:2 (December 1919).

———. "Shi qingnian zisha haishi shehui sha qingnian?" [Does youth commit suicide or does society kill youth?] *XC* 2:2 (December 1919).

———. "Piping de yanjiu: San W zhuyi" [The study of criticism—Three W-ism]. *XC* 2:3 (April 1920).

———. "Yinian lai de women xuesheng yundong de chenggong shibai he jiang-lai ying qu de fangzhen" [The successes and failures of our student movement and the future direction to be adopted]. *XC* 2:5 (May 1920).

———. "Jindai Zhongguo wenxue sixiang zhi bianqian" [The change in literature of modern China]. *XC* 2 (October 1920).

———. *Xin rensheng guan* [A new worldview]. Chunqing, 1942.

———. "Wusi de zhen jingshen" [The true spirit of May Fourth]. In *Wusi aiguo yundong sishi zhounian jinian tekan*. Taibei, 1959.

———. "Wusi shidai de beijing ji qi yingxiang" [The historical background of May Fourth and its influence]. *Zhongyang ribao* (4 May 1962).

———. *Shizhe ru siji* [Biographies of past friends]. *Zhuanji wenxue* series, no. 14. Taibei, 1962.

Luo Jialun and Mao Zishui. "Guoli Beijing daxue" [National Beijing University]. In *Zhonghua minguo daxue shi*, vol. 1. Taibei, 1954.

Luo Shuhe. "Wusi yundong de huigu ji qi zhuanxing de xin shidai" [May Fourth in retrospect and its new era of transformation]. *Xin chuangzao* 1:1 (May 1932).

Ma Xulun. *Wo zai liu shi sui yiqian* [Before I was sixty]. Shanghai, 1947.

———. *Ma Xulun xueshu lunwen ji* [Scholarly essays by Ma Xulun]. Beijing, 1958.

Mao Dun (Shen Yanbing). "Shiqi yu xuesheng de zhengzhi yundong" [The warrior spirit and the students' political movement]. *Minduo* 8:4 (1 March 1927).

————. "Du Ni Huanzhi" [Reading *Ni Huanzhi*]. In *Zhongguo wenyi lunzhan*, ed. Li Helin. Shanghai, 1932.

————. "Wusi de jingshen" [The spirit of May Fourth]. *Wenyi zhendi* 1:2 (March 1938).

————. "Hai xuyao zhunbei changqi er jiejue zhanzheng" [We must still prepare for a long and determined struggle]. In *Wusi sa zhounian zhuanji*. Shanghai, 1949.

————. "Zhishi fenzi de daolu" [A path for the intelligentsia]. In *Zhishi fenzi de daolu*. Hong Kong, 1949.

————. *Mao Dun wenji* [Collected works of Mao Dun]. 9 vols. Beijing, 1958–61.

————. "Shangwu yinshuguan bianji shenghuo zhi yi" [An account of life as one of the editors at the Commercial Press]. *Xin wenxue shiliao* no. 1 (1978).

————. "Wusa yundong yu Shangwu yinshuguan bagong—huiyilu" [Reminiscence: May Thirtieth movement and the strike at the Commercial Press]. *Xin wenxue shiliao* no. 2 (February 1980).

Mao Zedong. "Wusi yundong" [The May Fourth movement]. In *Zhongguo jindai zhengzhi sixiang shiliao*. Dalian, 1947.

————. *Zai Yan'an wenyi zuotan hui shang de jianghua* [Yan'an talks on art and literature]. Beijing, 1972.

Mao Zishui. "Guogu he kexue de jingshen" [The national heritage and the scientific spirit]. *XC* 1:5 (May 1919).

————. "Wusi wushi nian" [May Fourth fifty years later]. *Zhuanji wenxue* 14:5 (May 1969).

————. "Buyao pa wusi; wusi de lishi shi shuyu women de" [Fear not May Fourth; the history of May Fourth belongs to us]. In *Wo canjiale wusi yundong*. Taibei, 1979.

Maruyama Matsuyuki. "Ri Taishō no shisō to sono haikei: Shisō no taikeika to jissen to no kankei ni tsuite" [Background to the thought of Li Dazhao: The relationship between systematic thought and experience]. *Rekishi hyōron* 87 (August 1975).

Meng Shouchun. "Ban she zhishi" [A record of the (*New Tide*) Society]. *XC* 2:5 (September 1920).

Mu Ouqu. "Shiyejie duiyu xuesheng zhi xiwang" [The hopes of business for the student (movement)]. *Xin jiaoyu* 2:5 (May 1920).

"Neichu guozei jiushi yao xiaomie chihuo: Wusi shidai yiyi" [Getting rid of internal traitors means exterminating the red menace: The epoch-making significance of May Fourth]. *Zhongyang ribao* (4 May 1979).

Nie Gannu. *Guanyu zhishi fenzi* [On intellectuals]. Shanghai, 1948.

————. *Gannu zawen xuan* [Selected critical essays]. Beijing, 1955.

Nomura Kōichi. *Kindai Chūgoku no seiji to shisō* [Modern Chinese politics and thought]. Tokyo, 1964.

————. *Chūgoku kakumei no shisō* [Theories of the Chinese revolution]. Tokyo, 1971.

Ōjima Sukema. *Chūgoku no kakumei shisō* [Revolutionary theories in China]. Tokyo, 1961.

"Pipan fengjian zhuyi xueshu taolunhui" [Scholarly conference on the criticism of feudalism]. *Guangming ribao* (13 November 1979).

Qian Bingji, ed. "Huiyi women fuqin: Qian Xuantong" [Recollections of our father Qian Xiantong]. *Xin wenxue shiliao* no. 3 (May 1979).

Qian Xuantong. "Guanyu fan diguo zhuyi" [On anti-imperialism]. *Yusi* no. 31 (15 June 1925).

Qiu Zuojian. "Shanghai Daxue" [Shanghai University]. In *Dangshi ziliao*, vol. 2. Shanghai, 1980.

Qu Qiubai. "Zhengzhi yundong yu zhishi jieji" [The political movement and the intellectual class]. *Xiangdao* 1:17 (January 1923).

———. "Qing tuoyi wusi de yilan" [Please take off the mantle of May Fourth]. In Su Wen, ed., *Ziyou wenyi lunbian ji*. Shanghai, 1933.

———. *Luan dan* [Random shots]. Shanghai, 1949.

———. *Qu Qiubai wenji* [Collected literary works of Qu Qiubai]. Beijing, 1953–54.

Qu Qiubai, ed and intro. *Lu Xun zagan xuanji*. Shanghai, 1950.

Sanmin zhuyi yanjiu suo, ed. *Wusi yundong lunye* [Essays on the May Fourth movement]. Taibei, 1966.

Satō Shin'ichi. "Shinmatsu keimō shisō no seiritsu" [The birth of the late Qing enlightenment]. *Kokka gakkai zasshi* 92:5–6 (1979).

Shen Duanxian. "Suowei dazhonghua de wenti" [The so-called problem of popularization]. *Dazhong wenyi* (March 1930).

Shen Yinmo. "Wusi duiwo yinxiang" [How May Fourth has influenced me]. In *Wusi yundong huiyi lu*, vol. 1. Beijing, 1979.

———. "Wo he Beida" [I and Beida]. In *Wusi yundong huiyi lu*, vol. 3. Beijing, 1979.

Shi Jun, ed. "Zhongguo jindai sixiang shi ziliao" [Documentary history of modern Chinese intellectual history]. (Hong Kong reprint of Beijing, 1957 edition.

Su Wen (Dai Kechong), ed. *Ziyou wenyi lunbian ji* [Debates on artistic freedom]. Shanghai, 1933.

Sun Fuxi. "Qing yi wo weilie gei Taiwan laopengyou de yifeng xin" [Take me for example: A letter to an old friend in Taiwan]. *Renmin wenxue* (July 1957).

Sun Fuyuan. "Duwei boshi jinri qule" [Dr. Dewey departed today]. *Chen bao* (11 July 1921).

———. "Pingmin wenxue gongzuo lüeshuo" [Discussion of work in the common people's literature]. *Wenhua yuekan* 1:1 (February 1934).

———. "Huiyi wusi yundong zhong de Lu Xun xiansheng" [Reminiscence of Mr. Lu Xun during the May Fourth movement]. *Zhongguo qingnian* 9 (1953).

———. "Huiyi wusi dangnian" [Remembrances of that year of May Fourth]. *Renmin wenxue* no. 55 (May 1955).

Sun Yan. "Aiguo zhuyi zhe Wang Zaoshi" [The patriotic Wang Zaoshi]. *Qishi niandai* (May 1981).

Takahashi Yūji. "Kindai Chūgoku runessansu: Hanjukyō undō o chūshin to shite" [Renaissance in modern China: The anti-Confucian movement]. *Shakai kagaku kenkyū* (July 1950 and January 1951).

Tan Liu. "Buyong qufeng Chen Duxiu" [There is no need to praise Chen Duxiu]. In *Wusi yundong yanjiu*. Hong Kong, 1975.

Tan Pingshan (Tan Mingqian). "Zhexue duiyu kexue zongjiao zhi guanxi lun" [Philosophical perspectives on the relationship between science and religion]. *XC* 1:1 (January 1919).

Tan Tianrong. "Wusi de zhexiang" [Fragmentary thoughts on May Fourth]. In *Beijing daxue youpai fenzi fandong yanlun huiji.* Beijing, 1957.

Tang Yijie, Zhuang Yin, and Jin Chunfeng. "Lun zhitong yu daotong" [Political rule and moral rule]. *Beijing daxue xuebao* no. 2 (1964).

Tang Zhenchang. "Cai Yuanpei xiansheng jinian ji shuhou?" [What shall we do after the publication of the commemorative volume for Mr. Cai Yuanpei?]. *Renmin ribao* (8 February 1983).

Tao Menghe. "Xin qingnian zhi xin daode" [New ethics of the new youth]. *XQN* 4:2 (February 1918).

———. "Shehui diaocha daoyan" [Introduction to social investigation]. *XQN* 4:3 (March 1918).

———. "Chijiu de aiguo yundong" [The long-term patriotic movement]. *Xiandai pinglun* 2:29 (10 June 1925).

———. *Menghe wencun* [Collected essays of Tao Menghe]. 3 vols. Shanghai, 1925.

———. *Shehui wenti* [Problems of society]. Shanghai, 1927.

Tao Qingsun. "Dazhong hua wenti" [The problem of popularization]. *Dazhong wenyi* (March 1930).

Tao Xisheng. "Huoshao Cao gongguan" [Setting fire to the Cao mansion]. In *Wo canjiale wusi yundong.* Taibei, 1979.

Tian Yu. "Wusi de lishi jiaoxun" [Historical admonitions of May Fourth]. *Zhexue yu wenhua* no. 122 (May 1974).

Wang Bixiang, ed. *Gu Jiegang tongsu lunzhuji* [An anthology of popular essays by Gu Jiegang]. Shanghai, 1947.

Wang Jingxi. "Shenmo shi sixiang" [What is thought?]. *XC* 1:4 (April 1919).

———. "Xinlixue zhi zui xin qushi" [The latest trends in modern psychology]. *XC* 2:5 (September 1920).

———. *Xue ye* [Snowy night]. Shanghai, 1925.

———. *Kexue fangfa mantan* [Discourse on the scientific method]. Shanghai, 1940.

Wang Mouzu. "Jinxi wenyan yu qiangjin dujing" [Prohibitions against the classical language and encouragement to read the classics]. In *Dazhonghua, baihua, wenyan lunji.* Shanghai, 1934.

Wang Rongzu, ed. *Wusi yundong lunwen ji* [Research essays on May Fourth]. Taibei, 1979.

Wang Ruoshui. "Wusi yundong zhong de Hu Shi he Duwei" [Hu Shi and Dewey during the May Fourth movement]. In *Hu Shi sixiang pipan*, vol. 1. Beijing, 1955.

Wang Shuqian. "Xinjiu wenti" [The problem of new and old]. *XQN* 1:1 (September 1915).

Wang Xinggong. "Kexue de qiyuan he xiaoguo" [Origins and impact of science]. *XQN* 7:1 (December 1919).

———. "Kexue de zhenshi shi keguan de ma?" [Is scientific truth objective or not?]. *XC* 2:2 (December 1919).

———. "Wu he wo" [Self and matter]. *XC* 3:1 (October 1921).

Wang Yao. *Zhongguo xinwenxue shigao* [Outline history of the new literature movement in China]. Hong Kong reprint, 1972.

Wei Wei and Qian Xiaohui. *Deng Zhongxia zhuan* [Biography of Deng Zhongxia]. Beijing, 1981.

"Wenyi dazhong hua wenti zuotan hui" [Conference on the problems of popularization of art]. *Dazhong wenyi* (March 1930).

Wu Kang. "Wo guo jinri daode zhi genben wenti" [The basic problem of ethics in our country today]. *XC* 1:2 (February 1919).

———. "Weiwo zhuyi" [Egoism]. *Zhexue* vol. 2. (August 1921).

———. "Cong sixiang gaizao dao shehui gaizao" [From thought reform to social reform]. *XC* 3:1 (October 1921).

Wu Qiyuan. *Zhongguo xin wenhua yundong gaikan* [Survey of the Chinese New Culture movement]. Shanghai, 1934.

"Wusi aiguo yundong dangan ziliao" [Archival materials of the May Fourth patriotic movement]. Beijing, 1980.

"Wusi jiangtanhui" [A seminar about May Fourth]. *Zhanshi wenhua* 1:1 (May 1938).

Wusi shiqi de shetuan [Student societies of the May Fourth period]. 4 vols. Beijing, 1979.

Wusi shiqi qikan jieshao [Introduction to the periodicals of the May Fourth era]. 4 vols. Beijing, 1958.

"Wusi yundong wushi nian" [The May Fourth movement fifty years later]. *Xuexi yeshu* no. 6 (May 1969).

Wusi yundong zai Shandong. Jinan, 1980.

Wusi yundong zai Tianjin. Tianjin, 1979.

Wusi yundong zai Wuhan. Wuhan, 1979.

Wu Zhihui. *Wu Zhihui xiansheng wencun* [Essays by Mr. Wu Zhihui]. Edited by Tao Leqin. Shanghai, 1928.

———. "Dazhongyu wan sui!" [Long live the mass language!]. In *Dazhonghua, baihua, wenyan lunji.* Shanghai, 1934.

———. *Wu Zhihui xiangsheng xuanji* [Selected works of Mr. Wu Zhihui]. 2 vols. Taibei, 1964.

Xiao Chaoran et al. *Beijing Daxue xiaoshi: 1898–1949* [The history of Beijing University]. Shanghai, 1981.

Xin Ru. "Cong dadao zhishi jieji kouhao zhong suo renshi de" [What can be understood from the slogan "Down with the intellectual class"]. *Yiban* 3:1 (August 1927).

Xinchao [New Tide]. Vols. 1–5, 1919–21. Taibei reprint, 1972.

"Xinchao fakan zhiqu shu" [Announcement of the publication of the *New Tide* magazine]. *XC* 1:1 (January 1919).

Xing Bisi. "Zhexue de qimeng he qimeng de zhexue" [The enlightenment of philosophy and philosophical enlightenment]. *Renmin ribao* (22 July 1978).

"Xinyue de taidu" [The attitude of the Crescent Moon society]. In *Zhongguo wenyi lunzhan.* Edited by Li Helin. Shanghai, 1932.

Xu Deheng. "Wusi ershijiu zhounian" [At the twenty-ninth anniversary of May Fourth]. *Beida banyuekan* (May 1948).

———. "Wusi yundong zai Beijing" [The May Fourth movement in Beijing]. In *Jiusan Shexun* no. 3, 1951. Reprinted in *Wusi yundong huiyi lu.* Beijing, 1979.

————. "Huiyi Guomin zazhi" [Recollections of the *Citizen*]. 1958. In *Wusi shiqi de shetuan*, vol. 2. Beijing, 1979.

————. "Wusi yundong liushi zhounian" (The sixtieth anniversary of the May Fourth movement]. In *Wusi yundong huiyi lu*, vol. 3. Beijing, 1979.

————. "Yi er jiu pianduan huiyi" [Fragmentary recollections of the December Ninth movement]. *Renmin ribao*, (9 December 1980).

Xu Qingyu. "Jinggao qingnian" [A warning to youth]. *Zhinan* (20 April 1927).

Xu Yanzhi. "Xingshi zhe zhexue zhi jing" [The essence of formal philosophy]. *XC* 1:1 (January 1919).

————. "Xuexiao diaocha" [Investigation of our schools]. *Shaonian shijie* 1:1 (January 1920).

Yang Deji. "Zhu Ziqing xiansheng zouguo de lu" [The road traveled by Mr. Zhu Ziqing]. *Wenjiao ziliao* no. 82 (October 1978).

Yang Yifeng. "Wusi jingshen shuping" [A critique of the spirit of May Fourth]. In *Wusi aiguo yundong sishi zhounian jinian tekan*. Taibei, 1959.

Yang Zhensheng. "Zhen nü" [The virgin]. *XC* 2:5 (June 1920).

————. "Xin xinlixue" ["The New Psychology," by A. G. Tansley]. *XC* 3:2 (March 1922).

————. "Wusi yu xinwenxue" [May Fourth and new literature]. In *Wusi sa zhounian jinian zhuanji*. Shanghai, 1949.

————. "Huiyi wusi" [Recollections of May Fourth]. *Renmin wenxue* 55 (May 1955).

"Yang Zhensheng." In *Zhongguo wenxue zuojia cidian*, vol. 2. Beijing, 1979.

Yang Zhongjian. "Duiyu Xinchao zhi pinglun" [Critique of *New Tide*]. *XC* 1:5 (May 1919).

————. "Gei jizhe" [Letter to the editor]. *XC* 1:5 (May 1919).

Ye Shengtao (Ye Shaojun). "Nüzi renge wenti" [The question of women's dignity]. *XC* 1:2 (February 1919).

————. "Zhe ye shi yige ren" [She, too, is a person]. *XC* 1:3 (March 1919).

————. "Wuyue sanshiyi ri zhi jiyu zhong" [In the midst of the May 31 downpour]. *Xiaoshuo yuebao* 16:7 (July 1925).

————. "Zai minjian" [Among the people]. *Xin nüxing* 1:1 (January 1926).

————. *Ye Shengtao duanpian xiaoshuo xuanji* [Selected short stories by Ye Shengtao]. Beijing, 1954.

————. *Ye Shengtao wenji* [Collected essays by Ye Shengtao]. 3 vols. Beijing, 1958.

————. *Ni Huanzhi*. Hong Kong, 1967.

————. "Zatan dushu zuowen he dazhongyu wenxue" [Some remarks on reading, writing, and mass language literature]. In *Wenxue yundong shiliao*, vol. 2. Shanghai, 1979.

Yi Baisha. "Kongzi pingyi" [A critique of Confucius]. *XQN* 2:1 (September 1916).

Yi Peishan. "Zhi jizhe" [Letter to the editors]. *XC* 1:3 (March 1919).

Yi Sheng (pseudonym). "Shishi chaoliu zhong zhi xin wenxue" [Timely new literature]. *Meizhou pinglun* no. 19 (27 April 1919).

Yin Xuxi and Ding Shouhe. *Cong wusi qimeng yundong dao Makesi zhuyi de chuanbo* [From the May Fourth enlightenment movement to the propagation of Marxism]. Beijing, 1963.

Yokoyama Suguru. "Goshi undō no shisō to sono keishō" [The ideology of the May Fourth movement and its legacy]. *Rekishigaku kenkyū* 362 (July 1970).

Yu Dafu. "Dazhong wenyi ze ming" [The choice of the name "mass art"]. *Dazhong wenyi* 1:1 (September 1928).

Yu Pingbo. "Dapo Zhongguo shenguai sixiang yizhong zhuzhang—Yanjin yin-li" [Forbidding the lunar calendar strictly: Destroy superstition in China]. *XC* 1:3 (March 1919).

———. "Wo de daode tan" [My view on ethics]. *XC* 1:5 (May 1919).

———. "Shehui shang duiyu xin shi de gezhong xinli guan" [Various psychological views about new poetry prevalent in society]. *XC* 2:1 (October 1919).

———. "Feng de hua" [Words of wind]. *XC* 2:3.

———. "Xian xinhun zhi de pianmian piping" [Criticism of the current, unfair marriage law]. *XC* 3:1 (November 1920).

———. "Zhi Xidi jun" [Questioning Xidi (Zheng Zhenduo)]. *Yusi* no. 36 (20 July 1925).

———. "Xuechi yu yuwu" [Defense and Revenge]. In *Zabaner*. Shanghai, 1928.

———. "Jiuguo ji qita cheng wenti de tiaojian" [National salvation and other problematic preconditions]. In *Zabaner zhi er*. Shanghai, 1933.

———. "Huigu yu qianzhan" [A backwards glance and a look toward the future]. In *Wusi sa zhounian jinian zhuanji*. Shanghai, 1949.

———. "Wusi yiwang" [Looking back on May Fourth]. *Wenxue zhishi* 5 (1959). Also reprinted in *Wusi huiyi lu*, vol. 1 (Beijing, 1979).

———. "Wusi liushi nian jinian yiwang shizhang" [Ten poems commemorating the sixtieth anniversary of May Fourth]. *Zhandi zengkan* (June 1979).

Yu Yingshi. "Wusi yundong yu Zhongguo chuantong" [The May Fourth movement and Chinese tradition]. In *Wusi yanjiu lunji*. Hong Kong, 1979.

Zhang Chunsu. "Wusi he women zhedai zhishi fenzi" [May Fourth and us, the intelligentsia of today]. *Daxue zazhi* 48 (December 1971).

Zhang Dainian and Liu Yulie. "Wusi shiqi pipan fengjian jiu daode lishi yiyi" [The historical significance of the May Fourth attack on feudal ethics]. In *Jinian wusi yundong liushi zhounian xueshu taolun hui wenxuan*. Beijing, 1980.

Zhang Dongsun. "Zhongguo zhishi jieji de jiefang yu gaizao" [The liberation and the transformation of the intellectual class]. *Jiefang yu gaizao* 1:3 (October 1919).

Zhang Jinlu, comp. and annot. *Zhongguo xiandai chuban shiliao* [Source materials for the publication history of contemporary China]. 3 vols. Shanghai, 1954.

Zhang Kepiao. "Jibai zhishi de mixin he zhishi jieji" [The myth of the sacredness of knowledge and the intellectual class]. *Yiban* (July 1928).

Zhang Lianfeng. *Wusi yundong yu zhishi qingnian* [The May Fourth movement and intellectual youth]. Shanghai, 1947.

Zhang Shenfu. "Lian duoshi: Zhexue shuxue guanxi shi lunyin" (Reflections under a stone roof: Outline of a history of the relationship between philosophy and mathematics]. *XC* 1:2 (February 1919).

———. "Lian duoshi: Shu zhi zheli" [Reflections under a stone roof: The philosophy of mathematics]. *XC* 1:4 (April 1919).

———. "Weixian sixiang" [Dangerous thoughts]. *XQN* (May 1919).

———. "Nüzi jiefang da budang" [Women's liberation: A great injustice]. *Shaonian Zhongguo* 1:4 (October 1919).

————— "Jingshen duli xuanyan" [The declaration of independence of the spirit]. *XQN* 7:1 (December 1919). Also in *XC* 2:2 (December 1919).

—————. "Jindai xinli" [Modern psychology]. *XQN* 7:3 (February 1920).

—————. "Kexue li de yi geming" [A revolution in science]. *Shaonian shijie* 1:3 (March 1920).

—————. "Tongxin: Ying Fa gongchandang—Zhongguo gaizao" [An exchange of letters—the British and French Communist parties and China's reform]. *XQN* 9:3 (July 1921).

—————. "Diguo zhuyi deng" [Imperialism and so on]. *Yusi* no.32 (19 June 1925).

—————. "Gei Zhou Zuoren" [Letter to Zhou Zuoren]. *Jingbao fukan* (19 August 1925).

—————. "Zhongyu tou yi piao" [An election at last]. *Jingbao fukan* (10 February 1926).

—————. "Zhixu yu jilu" [Order and discipline]. *Wuhan minbao* (22 May 1927).

—————. *Suosi* [Reflections]. Shanghai, 1931.

—————. "Zhexue yu jiuwang" [Philosophy and national salvation]. *Renren zhoubao* (14 November 1936).

—————. *Wo xiangxin Zhongguo* [I have faith in China]. Wuhan, 1937.

—————. *Shenma shi xin qimeng yundong* [What is the New Enlightenment movement?]. Chongqing, 1939.

—————. "Wusi jinian yu xin qimeng yundong" [Commemorating May Fourth and the new enlightenment movement]. In *Shenma shi xin qimeng yundong*. Chongqing, 1939.

—————. "Fayang wusi jingshen—fang" [Develop the spirit of May Fourth— Emancipate thought!]. *Guangming ribao* (27 April 1957).

—————. "Wusi yundong de jinxi" [May Fourth movement: Its past and its present]. *Xin wenxue shiliao* no. 3 (May 1979).

—————. "Yierjiu yundong de shizhong" [The December Ninth movement from beginning to end]. Unpublished manuscript, April 1980.

Zhang Shenfu (Chi). "Zhishi jieji" [The intellectual class]. *Meizhou pinglun* 31 (15 July 1919).

Zhang Xiruo. "Zhongguo jinri suowei zhishi jieji" [The so-called intellectual class today]. *Xiandai pinglun* (January 1927).

Zhang Xuan. "Bo Xinchao Guogu he kexue de jingshen pian" [Rebuttals between *New Tide* and *National Heritage* concerning the scientific spirit]. *Guogu* no. 3 (May 1919).

Zheng Boqi. "Zhongguo xinxing wenxue de yiyi" [The meaning in China of "Literature of the rising class"]. *Dazhong wenyi* (March 1930).

Zheng Zhenduo. "Da Pingbo jun" [Answer to Yu Pingbo]. *Yusi* no. 39 (10 August 1925).

Zheng Zhenduo (Xi Di). "Jiexue xichu hou" [After the blood has been washed off the streets]. *Xiaoshuo yuebao* 16:7 (July 1925).

—————. *Zheng Zhenduo wenji* [Collected works by Zheng Zhenduo]. 2 vols. Beijing, 1959–63.

Zhong Qingwen. "Yisheng chunlei" [Spring thunder]. *Renmin wenxue* 55 (May 1955).

Zhongguo jindai renwu zhuanji ziliao [Index to biographical materials on leaders of modern China]. Taibei, 1973.

Zhou Cezong. "Yi xinzhuang ping jiuzhi" [Putting on new clothes to criticize the old system]. *Dagong bao* (4 May 1947).

———. "Wusi yundong gaosu women shenmo" [What does the May Fourth movement tell us?]. *Daxue zazhi* 48 (4 December 1971).

———. "Wusi shuhuai" [Evocation of May Fourth]. In *Wusi yanjiu lunwenji*. Hong Kong, 1979.

Zhou Yang. "Fayang wusi wenxue geming de douzheng chuantong" [Develop the militant tradition of the May Fourth literary revolution]. *Renmin wenxue* no. 55 (May 1955).

———. "Sanci weida de sixiang jiefang yundong" [Three major thought emancipation movements]. *Guangming ribao* (8 May 1979).

Zhou Yutong. "Gu zhou Gushibian de du hougan" [Thoughts upon reading Gu's *Gushibian*]. *Gushibian*, ed. Gu Jiegang. Vol. 2. Beijing, 1930.

Zhou Zixin. "Beijing gongchandang xiaozu" [The Beijing Communist Party cell]. *Renmin ribao* (6 October 1980).

Zhou Zuoren. "Women de diren" [Our enemy]. *Yusi* no. 76 (22 December 1924).

———. "Guanyu sanyue shiba ri de sizhe" [On the dead of March eighteenth]. In *Zexie zhi*. Beijing, 1927.

———. "San yiba de sizhe" [For those who died on March eighteenth]. *Beixin* 4:5 (14 January 1928).

———. *Zhou Zuoren wenxuan* [Selected essays by Zhou Zuoren]. Edited by Shao Hou. Shanghai, 1936.

Zhu Guangxi and Ding Qingtang, eds. *Zuolian wulie shi yanjiu ziliao bianmu* [Collected materials on the history of five left-wing martyrs]. Shanghai, 1962.

Zhu Shuxin and Bi Jing. "Geming laoren de huiyi jiyu" [Memories and hopes of a veteran revolutionary (Xu Deheng)]. *Renmin ribao* (May 1981).

Zhu Wushan. "Beijing daxue de jingshen" [The spirit of Beijing University]. In *Beida ershiwu nian*, collection of unpublished documents from the Beijing University school history archives. Beijing, 1923.

———. "Wusi geming yundong shifou jiushi xin minzhu zhuyi geming?" [Was the May Fourth revolutionary movement a new democratic-type revolution or not?]. In *Wusi yundong yanjiu lunji*. Hong Kong, 1975.

Zhu Xizu. "Jinggao xin de qingnian" [Warning to new youth]. *XQN* 7:3 (February 1920).

Zhu Ziqing. "Zhexue de fanwei" ["The scope of philosophy" by William McDougall]. *XC* 2:3 (February 1919).

———. "Baizhongren, shangdi de jiaozi" [White people, the arrogant offspring of God]. In *Zhu Ziqing xuanji*. Hong Kong, 1964.

———. "Xuege" [Song of blood]. *Xiaoshuo yuebao* 16:7 (July 1925).

———. "Nali zou" [Nowhere to go]. *Yiban* 3:4 (March 1928).

———. "Ye Shengtao de duanpian xiaoshuo" [The short stories of Ye Shengtao]. In *Zhu Ziqing wenji*. Beijing, 1953.

———. *Zhu Ziqing wenji* [Collected works of Zhu Ziqing]. Beijing, 1953.

———. *Zhu Ziqing xuanji* [Selected works of Zhu Ziqing]. Hong Kong, 1964.

———. "Zhizhengfu da tusha ya" [Record of the government's great massacre]. In *Zhu Ziqing wenji*. Beijing, 1953.

———. "Zeng A. S." [Dedicated to A. S.]. In *Zhi Ziqing xuanji*. Hong Kong, 1964.

———. "Lun wuhua ke shuo" [On having nothing left to say] In *Zhu Ziqing xuanji*. Hong Kong, 1964.

Zong Shiwen. "Cai Yuanpei." In *Minguo renwu zhuan*. Li Xin and Sun Sibai, eds. Beijing, 1978.

"Zou lishi biyou zhi lu" [The inevitable road of history]. *Guangming ribao* (4 May 1979).

Western Language Sources

Alitto, Guy S. *The Last Confucian: Liang Shu-ming and the Chinese Dilemma of Modernity*. Berkeley, 1979.

Bastid, Marianne. *Aspects de la Réforme de l'Enseignement Chine au Début du 20ᵉ siècle, d'Apres des Écrits de Zhang Jian*. Paris, 1971.

Arendt, Hannah. *On Violence*. New York, 1969.

Arima, Tatsuo. *The Failure of Freedom*. Cambridge, Mass., 1969.

Bacon, Francis. *The New Organon*. Edited by F. H. Anderson. New York, 1960.

Bauman, Zygmunt. *Culture as Praxis*. London, 1973.

Boorman, Howard, ed. *Biographical Dictionary of Republican China*. 4 vols. New York, 1968.

Borthwick, Sally. *Education and Social Change in China*. Stanford, 1983.

Braisted, William Reynolds. *Meiroku Zasshi: Journal of the Japanese Enlightenment*. Cambridge, Mass., 1976.

Bree, Germaine. "Introduction" to *Combray*, by Marcel Proust. New York, 1952.

Cassirer, Ernst. *The Philosophy of the Enlightenment*. Princeton, 1951.

Chan, F. G., and T. H. Etzold, eds. *China in the 1920s*. New York, 1976.

Chan, Wing-tsit. *A Source Book of Chinese Philosophy*. Princeton, 1963.

Chang, Hao. *Liang Ch'i-ch'ao and Intellectual Transition in China, 1890–1907*. Cambridge, Mass., 1971.

Chang Kuo-t'ao. *The Rise of the Chinese Communist Party, 1921–1927*. 2 vols. Lawrence, Kans., 1971.

Cheng Fangwu. "From a Literary Revolution to a Revolutionary Literature." Translated by Michael Gotz in *Bulletin of Concerned Asian Scholars* (January–March 1976).

Chesneaux, Jean. *The Chinese Labor Movement*. Stanford, 1968.

Chiang Monlin. *Tides from the West*. New Haven, 1947.

Chow Tse-tsung. *The May Fourth Movement: Intellectual Revolution in Modern China*. Cambridge, Mass., 1960.

———. *Research Guide to the May Fourth Movement*. Cambridge, Mass., 1963.

Church, William F. *The Influence of the Enlightenment on the French Revolution*. Boston, 1964.

Clifford, Nicholas R. *Shanghai, 1925: Urban Nationalism and the Defense of Foreign Privilege*. Ann Arbor, 1979.

Cohen, Paul. *Between Tradition and Modernity: Wang Tao and Reform in Late Ch'ing China*. Cambridge, Mass., 1974.

Crocker, Lester. *An Age of Crisis*. Baltimore, 1959.

Croizier, Ralph. "The Thorny Flowers of 1979: Political Cartoons and Liberalization in China." *Bulletin of Concerned Asian Scholars* 13:3 (July–September 1981).

Curtis, L. P., ed. *The Historian's Workshop*. New York, 1970.

Darnton, Robert. *The Business of Enlightenment*. Cambridge, Mass., 1979.

DeBary, William T., ed. *Sources of Chinese Tradition*. 2 vols. New York, 1960.

DeFrancis, John. *Nationalism and Language Reform in China*. Princeton, 1950.

Devereux, George. *From Anxiety to Method in the Behavioral Sciences*. Paris, 1967.

Dewey, John. "New Culture in China." *Asia* 21:7 (1921).

Dirlik, Arif. "The Ideological Foundations of the New Life Movement: A Study in Counterrevolution." *Journal of Asian Studies* (August 1975).

————. *Revolution and History: The Origins of Marxist Historiography in China, 1919–1937*. Berkeley, 1978.

Dolezelova-Velingerova, Milena. *The Chinese Novel at the Turn of the Century*. Toronto, 1980.

Duiker, William. *Cai Yuanpei: Educator of Modern China*. Pennsylvania State University Studies, no. 41. University Park, Pa., 1977.

Eastman, Lloyd. *The Abortive Revolution: China under the Nationalist Rule, 1927–1937*. Cambridge, Mass., 1974.

Eber, Irene. "Thoughts on Renaissance in Modern China: Problems of Definition." In *Studia Asiatica*, ed. L. G. Thompson. San Francisco, 1975.

Erikson, Erik H. "Eight Ages of Man." In *Childhood and Society*. New York, 1963.

————. "Youth: Fidelity and Diversity." In *Youth: Change and Challenge*. New York, 1963.

Feigon, Lee Nathan. "Ch'en Tu-hsiu and the Foundations of the Chinese Revolution." Ph.D. diss., University of Michigan, 1978.

————. *Chen Duxiu: Founder of the Chinese Communist Party*. Princeton, 1983.

Feng Youlan. *A Comparative Study of Life Ideals*. Shanghai, 1927.

————. "A Criticism of Confucius and Self-Criticism of My Own Past Veneration of Confucius." In *Selected Articles Criticizing Lin Piao and Confucius*. Beijing, 1974.

Fingarette, Herbert. *Confucius: The Secular as Sacred*. New York, 1972.

Foucault, Michel. *The Archaeology of Knowledge*. Translated by A. M. Smith Sheridan. New York, 1972.

Fukuzawa Yukichi. *An Encouragement to Learning*. Translated and with an introduction by David Dilworth and Umeyo Hirano. Tokyo, 1969.

Furth, Charlotte. *Ting Wen-chiang: Science and China's New Culture*. Cambridge, Mass., 1970.

Furth, Charlotte, ed. *The Limits of Change: Essays on Conservative Alternatives in Republican China*. Cambridge, Mass., 1976.

Gay, Peter. *The Enlightenment: An Interpretation*. Vol. 1: New York, 1966; vol. 2: New York, 1969.

————. *The Bridge of Criticism*. New York, 1970.

Gay, Peter, ed. *The Enlightenment: A Comprehensive Anthology*. New York, 1973.

Goldman, Merle. *Literary Dissent in Communist China*. Cambridge, Mass., 1967.

————. "Left-wing Criticism of the Pai-hua Movement." In *Reflections on the May Fourth Movement: A Symposium*. Benjamin Schwartz, ed. Cambridge, Mass., 1972.

Goldman, Merle, ed. *Modern Chinese Literature in the May Fourth Era*. Cambridge, Mass., 1977.

Gotz, Michael. "Introduction to Cheng Fang-wu's 'From a Literary Revolution to a Revolutionary Literature.'" *Bulletin of Concerned Asian Scholars* (January–March, 1976).

Gouldner, Alvin. "Prologue to a Theory of Revolutionary Intellectuals." *Telos* 26 (Winter 1975–76).

———. *The Future of Intellectuals and the Rise of the New Class.* New York, 1979.

Gramsci, Antonio. "On Intellectuals." In *Selections from the Prison Notebooks.* Translated by Q. Hoare and G. N. Smith. New York, 1971.

Grieder, Jerome B. *Hu Shih and the Chinese Renaissance.* Cambridge, Mass., 1970.

———. *Intellectuals and the State in Modern China.* New York, 1981.

Harrison, James P. *The Long March to Power: A History of the Chinese Communist Party, 1921–1972.* New York, 1972.

Horkheimer, Max, and Theodor Adorno. *Dialectic of Enlightenment.* New York, 1972.

Hsia, C. T. *A History of Modern Chinese Fiction.* New Haven, 1971.

Hsia, Tsi-an. *The Gate of Darkness.* Seattle, 1968.

Hsu Cho-yun. *Ancient China in Transition.* Stanford, 1960.

Hu Shih. *The Chinese Renaissance: The Haskell Lectures, 1933.* Chicago, 1933.

Huang Sung-k'ang. *Lu Hsün and the New Culture Movement in China.* Amsterdam, 1957.

Illich, Ivan. *Shadow Work.* Boston, 1981.

Isaacs, Harold. *The Tragedy of the Chinese Revolution.* Stanford, 1951.

Isaacs, Harold, ed. *Five Years of Kuomintang Reaction.* Shanghai, 1932.

Jacob, Margaret C. *The Radical Enlightenment: Pantheists, Freemasons, and Republicans.* London, 1981.

Keenan, Barry. *The Dewey Experiment in China.* Cambridge, Mass., 1972.

Kiang Wen-han. *The Chinese Student Movement.* New York, 1948.

Ku Chieh-kang. *The Autobiography of a Chinese Historian.* Translated and annotated by A. W. Hummel. Leyden, 1931.

Ku Hung-ming. "Returning Students and Literary Revolution: Literacy and Education." *Millard's Review* 9:11 (August 1919).

Kwok, D. W. Y. *Scientism in Chinese Thought, 1900–1950.* New Haven, 1965.

Lee, Léo Ou-fan. *The Romantic Generation of Modern Chinese Writers.* Cambridge, Mass., 1974.

LeFebvre, Georges. *The French Revolution.* Translated by E. M. Evanson. London, 1962.

Levenson, Joseph. *Liang Ch'i-ch'ao and the Mind of Modern China.* Cambridge, Mass., 1959.

———. *Confucian China and Its Modern Fate.* Berkeley, 1968.

———. "The Genesis of 'Confucian China and Its Modern Fate.'" In *The Historian's Workshop,* ed. L. P. Curtis. New York, 1970.

———. *Revolution and Cosmopolitanism.* Berkeley, 1971.

Lewis, Bernard. *History: Remembered, Recovered, and Invented.* Princeton, 1975.

Li Zehou. "Zhang Taiyan as a Revolutionary and a Thinker." Paper presented at the annual meeting of the Association for Asian Studies, Chicago, April 1982.

Li Zehou and Vera Schwarcz. "Six Generations of Modern Chinese Intellectuals." *Chinese Studies in History* (Winter 1983–84).

Lin Yusheng. *The Crisis of Chinese Consciousness.* Madison, Wisc., 1979.

Lu Xun. *Selected Works.* 4 vols. Beijing, 1980.

Lunacharsky, Anatoly. *On Literature and Art.* Moscow, 1965.

Ma Hsu-lun. "Before I Was Sixty." *Chinese Education* 2:2–3 (Summer–Fall 1970).

McDonald, Joan. *Rousseau and the French Revolution, 1762–1791.* London, 1965.

Malia, Martin. "What is the Intelligentsia?" In *The Russian Intelligentsia*, ed. R. Pipes. New York, 1961.

Mannheim, Karl. *Essays in the Sociology of Knowledge.* New York, 1952.

Mao Dun. "From Guling to Tokyo." Translated by Chen Yu-shih. *Bulletin of Concerned Asian Scholars* (January–March 1976).

Mao Tse-tung. *Selected Works of Mao Tse-tung.* 4 vols. Beijing, 1967.

Marias, Julian. *Generations: A Historical Method.* Translated by H. C. Raley. University, Ala, 1970.

Meisner, Maurice. *Li Ta-chao and the Origins of Chinese Marxism.* Cambridge, Mass., 1967.

Metzger, Thomas. *Escape from Predicament and China's Evolving Political Culture.* New York, 1977.

Mills, Harriet C. "Lu Hsün and the Communist Party." *China Quarterly* 4 (October–December 1960).

Moller, Alan Gordon. "Bellicose Nationalist of Republican China: An Intellectual Biography of Fu Ssu-nien." Ph.D. diss., University of Melbourne, 1979.

Montale, Eugenio. "The Voice That Came in with the Coots." Translated by William Arrowsmith. *New York Review of Books* (16 April 1981).

Montesquieu, Baron de (Charles de Secondat). *The Spirit of Laws.* Translated by T. Nugent. Chicago, 1952.

Morin, Edgar. "L'événement Sphinx." *Communication* no. 18 (1972).

Mullin, Glenn, and Nicholas Ribush, eds. *Teachings at Tushita: Buddhist Discourses, Articles, and Translations.* New Delhi, 1981.

Nietzsche, Friedrich. *Thus Spake Zarathustra.* New York, 1924.

Nora, Pierre. "L'événement-monstre." *Communication* no. 18 (1972).

North China Herald (16 April 1927).

Okazaki Yoshie, ed. *Japanese Literature in the Meiji Era.* Tokyo, 1968.

Peyre, Henri. "The Influence of Eighteenth-Century Ideas on the French Revolution." *Journal of the History of Ideas* no. 10 (1949).

Pickowicz, Paul G. "Ch'u Ch'iu-pai and the Origins of Marxist Literary Criticism in China." Ph.D. diss., University of Wisconsin, 1973.

Plekhanov, G. V. *Art and the Social Life.* London, 1953.

Pollard, David. "Chou Tso-jen and Cultivating One's Own Garden." *Asia Major* 2 (1966–67).

———. *A Chinese Look at Literature.* Berkeley, 1973.

Pomper, Phillip. *The Russian Revolutionary Intelligentsia.* New York, 1970.

Price, Don C. *Russia and the Roots of the Chinese Revolution.* Cambridge, Mass., 1974.

Qu Qiubai. "The Question of Popular Literature and Art." Translated by Paul G. Pickowicz. *Bulletin of Concerned Asian Scholars* (January–March 1976).

———. "Who's 'We'?" Translated by Paul G. Pickowicz. *Bulletin of Concerned Asian Scholars* (January–March 1976).

Rawski, Evelyn Sakakida. *Education and Popular Literacy in Ch'ing China.* Ann Arbor, 1979.

Rieff, Philip, ed. *On Intellectuals*. New York, 1969.

Reiss, Hans, ed. *Kant's Political Writings*. London, 1970.

Rickett, Adele Austin, ed. *Chinese Approaches to Literature from Confucius to Liang Ch'i-ch'ao*. Princeton, 1978.

Roy, A. T. "Attacks upon Confucianism in the 1911–1927 Period: From a Daoist Lawyer, Wu Yu." *The Chung Chi Journal* 4:2 (July 1965).

Roy, David T. *Kuo Mo-jo: The Early Years*. Cambridge, Mass., 1971.

Russell, Bertrand. "Modern China—III: Chinese Amusements." *The Nation* (28 December 1921).

———. *The Problem of China*. London, 1922.

Sartre. Jean-Paul. "Plea for Intellectuals." In *Between Existentialism and Marxism*. London, 1974.

Scalapino, Robert A., and George T. Yu. *The Chinese Anarchist Movement*. Berkeley, 1961.

Schlereth, Thomas J. *The Cosmopolitan Ideal in Enlightenment Thought*. Notre Dame, Ind., 1977.

Schneider, Laurence A. *Ku Chieh-kang and China's New History*. Berkeley, 1971.

———. *A Madman of Ch'u: The Chinese Myth of Loyalty and Dissent*. Berkeley, 1980.

Schwarcz, Vera. "Ibsen's Nora: The Promise and the Trap." *Bulletin of Concerned Asian Scholars* (January-March 1975).

———. "A Curse on the Great Wall: The Problem of Enlightenment in Modern China." *Theory and Society* (May 1984).

Schwartz, Benjamin. "The Intelligentsia in Communist China: A Tentative Comparison." In *The Russian Intelligentsia*, ed. R. Pipes. New York, 1961.

———. *In Search of Wealth and Power: Yen Fu and the West*. New York, 1969.

———. "The Limits of 'Tradition' and 'Modernity' as Categories of Explanation." *Daedalus* (Spring 1972).

Schwartz, Benjamin, ed. *Reflections on the May Fourth Movement: A Symposium*. Cambridge, Mass., 1973.

Seymour, James D., ed. *The Fifth Modernization: China's Human Rights Movement, 1978–1979*. Stanfordville, N.Y., 1981.

Shaw, George Bernard. "On the Quintessence of Ibsenism." In *Ibsen: The Critical Heritage*, ed. M. Eagan. London, 1972.

Shils, Edward A. *Intellectuals and the Powers*. Chicago, 1972.

Snow, Edgar. *Red Star over China*. New York, 1944.

Spence, Jonathan. "On Chinese Revolutionary Literature." In *Literature and Revolution*. Yale French Studies, no. 39. New Haven, 1967.

———. *The Gate of Heavenly Peace*. New York, 1981.

Stacey, Judith. *Patriarchy and Socialist Revolution in China*. Berkeley, Ca. 1983.

Sullivan, Lawrence, and Richard Solomon. "The Formation of Chinese Communist Ideology in the May Fourth Movement: A Content Analysis of *Hsin ch'ing-nien*." In *Ideology and Politics in Contemporary China*, ed. C. Johnson. New York, 1972.

Tagore, Amitendranath. *Literary Debates in Modern China, 1918–1937*. Tokyo, 1967.

Tao Xingzhi. "The False Intellectual Class." *Chinese Education* (Winter 1974–75).

Teilhard de Chardin, Pierre. *Letters from a Traveller*. London, 1962.

Teng, Y. S., and J. K. Fairbank, eds. *China's Response to the West*. New York, 1966.

Ting, Lee-hsia Hsu. *Government Control of the Press in Modern China, 1900–1949.* Cambridge, Mass., 1974.

Voltaire. "Fanaticism." In *Dictionnaire philosophique.* Translated in Peter Gay, ed., *The Enlightenment: A Comprehensive Anthology.* New York, 1973.

Wakeman, Frederic. "The Price of Autonomy: Intellectuals in Ming and Ch'ing Politics." *Daedalus* (Spring 1972).

————. *History and Will: Philosophical Perspectives of Mao Tse-tung's Thought.* Berkeley, 1973.

Wales, Nym (Helen Snow). *Notes on the Chinese Student Movement, 1935–1936.* Stanford, 1959.

Wang Gungwu. "May Fourth and the GPCR: The Cultural Revolution Remedy." *Pacific Affairs* (Canada) 52:4 (1979–80).

Wang Jingxi. "The Relation between Spontaneous Activity and Oestrous Cycle in the White Rat." In *Comparative Psychology Monographs.* Baltimore, 1923.

Wang, Y. Chu. *Chinese Intellectuals and the West, 1872–1949.* Chapel Hill, N. C., 1966.

Willis, Janice D. *On Knowing Reality: The "Tattvartha" Chapter of Asanga's "Bodhisattvabhumi."* New York, 1979.

Witke, Roxane. "Mao Tse-tung, Women, and Suicide in the May Fourth Era." *China Quarterly* (September 1967).

Wohl, Robert. *The Generation of 1914.* Cambridge, Mass., 1979.

Wylie, Raymond. *The Emergence of Maoism: Mao Tse-tung, Ch'en Po-ta, and the Search for Chinese Theory, 1935–1945.* Stanford, 1980.

Wu Tien-wei. "Chiang Kai-shek's April 12 Coup of 1927." In *China in the 1920s: Nationalism and Revolution,* ed. F. G. Chan and T. H. Etzold. New York, 1976.

Yeh Sheng-t'ao. *Schoolmaster Ni Huan-chih.* Translated by A. C. Barnes. Beijing, 1958.

Yue Daiyun. "Some Characteristics of Chinese Intellectuals Found in Fiction." Unpublished paper, presented at the Berkeley Center for Chinese Studies, Colloquium series, February 1984.

Zen, Sophia H. Chen (Ch'en Heng-che). *Symposium on Chinese Culture.* Shanghai, 1931.

Index

Compositor:	Asco Trade Typesetting Ltd.
Text:	10/13 Baskerville
Display:	Baskerville
Printer:	Maple-Vail Book Mfg. Group
Binder:	Maple-Vail Book Mfg. Group